VERY
STRANGE
BEDFELLOWS

VERY STRANGE BEDFELLOWS

*The Short and Unhappy Marriage
of Richard Nixon and Spiro Agnew*

JULES WITCOVER

PublicAffairs
New York

Published in the United States by PublicAffairs™, a member of the Perseus Books Group.

Public Affairs books are available at special discounts for bulk purchases in the U.S. by corporations, institutions, and other organizations. For more information, please contact the Special markets Department at the Perseus Books Group, 11 Cambridge Center, Cambridge, MA 02142, call (617) 252-5298, or email special.markets@perseusbooks.com.

Library of Congress Cataloging-in-Publication Data
Witcover, Jules.
Very strange bedfellows : the short and unhappy marriage of
Richard Nixon and Spiro Agnew / Jules Witcover. —1st ed.
p. cm.
Includes bibliographical references and index.
ISBN–13: 978–1–58648–470–5 (hardcover)
ISBN–10: 1–58648–470–2 (hardcover)
1. Nixon, Richard M. (Richard Milhous), 1913–1994. 2. Agnew, Spiro T., 1918–1996. 3. Nixon, Richard M. (Richard Milhous), 1913–1994—Psychology. 4. Agnew, Spiro T., 1918–1996—Psychology. 5. Presidents—United States—Biography. 6. Vice-Presidents—United States—Biography. 7. United States—Politics and government—1969–1974. I. Title.
E856.W57 2007
973.924092'2—dc22
2007000950
First Edition

10 9 8 7 6 5 4 3 2 1

To John and Sara

CONTENTS

Contents

ACKNOWLEDGMENTS

Most of the best personal sources for the story of the contentious relationship between President Richard M. Nixon and Vice President Spiro T. Agnew, including the two principals, have passed to their eternal rewards. They have left behind, however, a rare and in some cases unprecedented record on which this account has been constructed. In addition to the memoirs of Nixon and Agnew, books by Nixon's chief lieutenants, H. R. "Bob" Haldeman and John Ehrlichman, and others revealingly chronicled that bizarre partnership.

Most enlightening of all, however, were the Nixon White House tapes, available at the National Archives in College Park, Maryland, prior to shipping to the Richard M. Nixon Presidential Library at the former president's birthplace in Yorba Linda, California, now administered by the archives staff. While the tapes have been principally scrutinized in documenting the Watergate scandal and cover-up that led to Nixon's resignation in August 1974, they also include a host of largely overlooked conversations dealing with the Nixon–Agnew political marriage and ultimate divorce.

The principal archivist of this collection at College Park, Sam Rashay, was indispensible in introducing me to the research task, and serving as a continuing guide to the most fruitful tapes and documents throughout the process. Because some of the tapes, particularly those recorded in Nixon's hideaway in the Executive Office Building, were of poor quality, I did my best to reconstruct the exact conversations with the diligent assistance of my wife, Marion Elizabeth Rodgers, whose acute sense of hearing eclipses my own. When the precise words could not be determined, I have paraphrased and so indicated, or edited out the garble and noted omissions, often irrelevant to this story, with ellipses. Unfortunately, the tapes cover only the period from February 1971, when the taping system was installed, through July 16, 1973, when its existence was disclosed by White House aide Alexander Butterfield at the Senate Watergate hearings and promptly discontinued.

In the Maryland Room of the Hornbake Library at the University of Maryland in College Park, the depository for Agnew's papers, archivist Lauren Brown was of notable additional assistance on matters touching on the Nixon–Agnew relationship. Also, Kenneth J. Hughes Jr., a Nixon White House scholar, pointed me to some specific tapes in the same regard.

As further guides to the tapes, and much additional information on the subject, *The Haldeman Diaries: Inside the Nixon White House*, by H. R. Haldeman, published by G. P. Putman's Sons, New York, 1994, and a CD-ROM of expanded diary material by the same publisher, were indispensible companions in the search. I thank the Haldeman Family Trust for permission to draw extensively on them.

Having covered Richard Nixon and Spiro Agnew as a reporter in Washington throughout their tenures, and having written books on each of them, I was able to call on my own research and interviews conducted with both principals during that time. Just as important was the thorough and invaluable reporting, especially in Maryland, done by Richard M. Cohen, my *Washington Post* colleague and friend, in the course of co-writing our 1974 book on the investigation of Agnew that led to his resignation in October 1973. Also, Nixon's own memoir and that of his second White House chief of staff, General Alexander Haig, provided inside accounts of Nixon's machinations to bring about Agnew's departure from the line of presidential succession, amid the Watergate scandal and Agnew's desperate efforts to save himself.

All these materials also document Nixon's relentless but ultimately failed attempt to replace Agnew with former Texas governor John Connally, object of his great admiration, first as vice president and then as a potential successor in the Oval Office.

Interviews with important members of the Nixon and Agnew staffs and leading Republican political figures added personal recollections and interpretations to the written and recorded history. Those who generously agreed to interviews included Lamar Alexander, Patrick Buchanan, Alexander Butterfield, John Dean, Alexander Haig, Melvin Laird, John Sears, and William Timmons of the Nixon staff, and John Damgard, Victor Gold, David Keene, and C. D. Ward of the Agnew staff. Also, the four principal Agnew prosecutors in Baltimore—George Beall, Barney Skolnik, Tim Baker, and Ronald Liebman—each granted me a telephone interview in 2006, as did Richard Darman, one of Attorney General Elliot Richardson's chief aides during the investigation. I drew as well on my interviews for previous books with then governor Nelson A. Rockefeller of New York and George Hinman, his chief political adviser, and many fellow reporters on the campaign trail of that period. In addition, several most helpful accounts of the Watergate affair are listed in the bibliography. Finally, my thanks go to Peter Osnos, Robert Kimzey, and Clive Priddle, of PublicAffairs; to my editor, William Whitworth; and to my longtime agent, David Black, for their encouragement and professionalism in guiding this project to completion.

Long after the resignations of Nixon and Agnew, the periodic release of the White House tapes was amusingly and accurately described by my friend Watergate sleuth Bob Woodward of *The Washington Post* as, in the Hallmark greeting card motto, "The gift that keeps on giving." That was certainly true of the Watergate story, but also of the Nixon–Agnew saga, as the reader will find in these pages. Reporters, historians, and other writers often say they wish they could have been a fly on the wall at a certain private event or during a certain period. The existence of these tapes enabled me to be just that, listening to first-person connivings and observations of the Nixon–Agnew administration, one of the most immoral and corrupt in the history of the United States. Its players endlessly carped and plotted not only against political foes but at times against each other as well.

When the White House tapes were first released during the Watergate scandal, Nixon's use of profanity was a shocking revelation, though merely of a good-ol' boy variety that never sank to the level of men's locker-room banter. More jolting to the ear listening now is the callousness, and the duplicity, of a president and his chief henchmen as they scheme to shape public opinion, dominate the political scene, and ultimately depose one of their own who has fallen from grace.

Because the tapes proved to be so self-destructive to the principals, future journalists and historians may never have a similar opportunity to examine and explore the hearts and souls of tomorrow's presidencies. So we can be grateful for these recordings, and not the least to Richard Nixon himself, for his eventually hapless decision to install the taping system that was his own undoing, and that informs us as well of new details of Agnew's torment and demise.

Jules Witcover

Washington, D.C.

September 4, 2006

INTRODUCTION

In the spring of 1971, in the third year of the political marriage of Richard M. Nixon and Spiro T. Agnew, a phone call came from the White House to John Damgard, a young aide to the vice president. David Parker, President Nixon's scheduler, informed Damgard that Nixon didn't want to attend that year's Gridiron dinner, the annual roast of Washington politicians by the White House press corps' elite, and wanted Agnew to fill in for him. Damgard dutifully conveyed the message.

"If the president wants me to substitute for him at the dinner," Damgard later recalled Agnew's telling him, "all he has to do is pick up the phone and ask me. I've never said no to him before, but I'm not going to do it on the basis of your asking me to do it. If the president wants me to do it, that's different."

Damgard called Parker back and relayed what the vice president had said. Word was passed to H. R. "Bob" Haldeman, Nixon's chief of staff, who informed the president. Exasperated but always avoiding personal confrontation at all costs, Nixon instructed Haldeman to send the same message again. The same reply came back from Agnew through Damgard. It went on like that, back and forth.

"For whatever reason," Damgard recounted later, "Nixon would not pick up the phone and ask Agnew to do it, and this stalemate existed for days and days. The dinner sponsors would call, saying they wanted to put Agnew's name down in the program 'because we understand from the White House that Agnew's going to substitute for the president.' And I told them, 'I can't tell you to put down Agnew's name because he has told me that, so far, he has no intention of doing it.'"

More days passed, and finally one afternoon, as Agnew was reviewing some policy paper or other in his office, a uniformed military attaché from the White House appeared with an envelope he had been instructed to deliver personally to the vice president only. Admitted to the presence, he handed over the envelope. Inside was a handwritten note from Nixon. It said, as Damgard best recalled later: "Dear Ted. I would very much appreciate your presence at this year's Gridiron dinner. Thanks, Dick." And so Agnew went.

Damgard said later: "I made the mistake of saying to Agnew, 'The president doesn't want to go and wants you to substitute for him.' After that, I worked very, very hard to find out in advance what Nixon would want Agnew to do and then, without telling Agnew, I would present the invitation in such a manner that Agnew would accept it on the basis of its merits. And I never again said, 'The president wants you to do this.'"[1]

As Agnew himself recounted the awkward episode later in his memoir, he finally relented only after Nixon had phoned him on a Sunday—a "very unusual" occurrence. "We chatted for about ten minutes on a variety of subjects," Agnew recalled. "He closed by mentioning what a great job one of the cabinet had done on *Meet the Press* that day. Then he paused a moment and continued about how important TV was. He paused again. I said it certainly was, and that ended our conversation." It was the next afternoon, the vice president remembered, "when I was given a handwritten letter *from the president*. With charming simplicity, he requested me to attend the Gridiron dinner, allowing that it would be a sacrifice but no more than Ike had demanded of him. He promised to go next year. Naturally, I went to the dinner. Unnaturally, I had a marvelous time."

Then Agnew wrote: "I really would have enjoyed serving in the vice presidency with Lyndon Johnson, because if anything had gone wrong, probably he himself would have picked up the phone and said, 'Agnew, what the hell are you doing?' Or he would have said, 'I've got a hell of a problem. Come over here. I want to talk to you about this.' Unfortunately, I could have no such man-to-man talk with President Nixon. Absolutely none. I was never allowed to come close enough to participate with him directly in any decision. Every time I went to see him and raised a subject for discussion, he would begin a rambling, time-consuming monologue. Then finally the phone would ring or Haldeman would come in, and there would be no time left for what I really had come to talk about. He successfully avoided any subject he didn't want to be pinned down on. He preferred keeping his decision-making within a very small group. I was not of the inner circle."[2]

The rather sophomoric waltz over attending the 1971 Gridiron dinner, between the leader of the free world and the man who would succeed him if destiny dictated, said volumes about the personal and professional relationship between them. And it hinted at why a partnership that had begun with high mutual admiration eventually crumbled in bitter resentment and mutual dislike, and the political demise of both men as well.

The separate paths Nixon and Agnew took to their relationship as political and personal strange bedfellows, and how it flourished at first but in time disintegrated, provides the framework of this book. It is a story of two men's common backgrounds and political outlooks but clashing styles, egos, and temperaments, which in the end produced the only case in American political history of back-to-back political suicides of a vice president and the president under whom he served.

Those Americans who did not live through the nearly five-year Nixon–Agnew partnership, or were too young to remember, are not likely to appreciate fully the contentious and divisive environment in which that partnership was born, and how together the partners effectively fostered and cultivated it. Their rise to national power came at a time of uncommon unrest in the country, only five years after the assassination of John F. Kennedy, which had shaken the American people and the Democratic Party. A year later, the Republican Party as well was shattered with the landslide defeat of presidential nominee Barry Goldwater. Thereafter, the Great Society of Lyndon Johnson, spurred at first by legislative triumphs, sputtered in the face of the mounting protests against the Vietnam War and Republican allegations of over-reaching at home. The civil rights movement was also splintering, as many whites recoiled from the militancy of new black leaders switching from the fruitful pursuit of legal and social justice to abrasive and inflammatory demands for equal economic opportunity.

The turmoil in America in the presidential election year of 1968, germinated by the war in Vietnam, the civil rights struggle at home, a cultural revolution, and a generational rebellion in the streets, provided an ideal atmosphere for the Nixon–Agnew mantra of law and order. And in a year marked by two more jolting tragedies, it proved decisive. The assassination of Dr. Martin Luther King Jr. during an economic boycott in Memphis ignited race riots across urban America. Six weeks later, the gunning down of Senator Robert F. Kennedy on the night he won the California Democratic presidential primary, left the nation in shocked disbelief, wondering what catastrophe would befall it next. The answer came at the Democratic Convention two months later in the streets of Chicago, when marching protesters were clubbed in a police riot that underscored the disarray of the Democratic Party and its hapless standard-bearer by default, Vice President Hubert H. Humphrey. All this was fodder for the Nixon–Agnew domestic war on the war in the streets.

With American campuses across the nation also in noisy revolt over the disruptions and inequities of the draft and the war, and with the demagogic rhetoric of Alabama's Governor George Wallace adding racist fuel to the flames, the stage was set for the political comeback of Richard Nixon and the emergence of Spiro Agnew as twin preachers of the politics of repression, under the guise of patriotism. Four decades later, echoes of the phenomenon reverberated in the tandem chorus of George W. Bush and Dick Cheney trumpeting another senseless war, and the expansion of executive power in its pursuit.

In the course of the Nixon–Agnew effort to play on the nation's fears and prejudices, the 1968 campaign launched a destructive demonization of liberalism and the American news media. Not long afterward, that effort nurtured in turn a resurrection of the conservatism that had seemed buried in the ashes of the 1964 Goldwater debacle. And by 1980, the revival flowered in the election of Ronald Reagan and the era of neoconservative Republicanism that followed.

Well before that happened, however, Nixon was able to position himself as a moderate, in part because of the very presence of Nelson Rockefeller on the Republican left and Reagan on the right. In any event, political ideology never had a firm hold on Nixon. He sought the presidency essentially to get power, and then to keep and extend it. It was Agnew who emerged as the ideologue, and that fact became an element in his trouble within the administration. But at the outset, as the reader will see, it was the newcomer's talent for pure political hatchetry that first endeared him to his superior, who saw him as a fitting stand-in on the firing line.

Years earlier, Nixon had set the pattern, as a slashing partisan who won election first to the House of Representatives and then to the Senate as a Red-baiting character assassin against his Democratic opponents. He had continued in the same vein as Dwight D. Eisenhower's running mate in 1952 and 1956. His description of Democratic presidential nominee Adlai Stevenson as "Adlai the appeaser . . . who got a PhD from Dean Acheson's College of Cowardly Containment" set a low bar that Agnew later easily and repeatedly lowered, in the 1968 campaign and beyond.

As president, Nixon sought to seize the Eisenhower high road, leaving his new companion to tread the low as Nixon's Nixon. As vice president, however, Agnew soon stole the spotlight with language and vitriol that were more than a match for the old master. And as the Vietnam War dragged on, Agnew's resentment grew over playing a back-row second fiddle in policy-making, and the partnership began to unravel. The cheerful helpmate was turning into a whining malcontent, with the relationship spiraling down to the ultimate crash.

In that outcome, both Nixon and Agnew assigned heavy blame to the nation's news media. Nixon's position came out of a long history of perceived press hostility that had been well earned. Agnew's on the other hand was more tactic, seen in the manner in which he used commentators as foils in his argument of news media run amok. Together, Nixon and Agnew exploited public cynicism and resentment toward what Agnew liked to call "a tiny and closed fraternity of privileged men elected by no one." The newsmen may not have been unnerved but the television executives were, and an air of intimidation wafted through many newsrooms. The relationship between the Republican Party and much of the working press (as opposed to the managerial arm) had never been particularly warm. But thanks to Nixon and Agnew it turned increasingly to an adversarial one, laden with suspicion on both sides.

Accordingly, the drama of the Nixon–Agnew partnership gone wrong played out in an ugly time of public anger and social and racial conflict. It seemed to magnify Americans' distrust in, and even contempt for, political leadership and politics itself. The daily chroniclers of the saga thus toiled in a poisoned atmosphere that only compounded the divisions in the land, and often bred a more sharply combative journalism that invited more attacks from Nixon and Agnew.

Notably, it was not the falling out between Nixon and Agnew that eventually ended their partnership; unrelated events were responsible. Even so, the mutual mistrust and dissatisfaction that developed between them underscored the imperative of compatibility, both political and personal, between running mates.

What follows is an account of what happened leading up to Nixon's decision to choose Agnew as his running mate and then to keep him on the ticket a second time—and the unexpected aftermath. As a result of Nixon's decision, two very strange bedfellows headed the country for nearly five tumultuous and ultimately regrettable years in a disgraced partnership. It is a cautionary tale, but also a revealing look, thanks to the Nixon White House taping system and the candor of the participants, into the raw business of political and policy decision-making with the window shades down—but, fortunately for us, with the tape running.

Chapter 1

SNARED ON
THE REBOUND

RICHARD M. NIXON WAS NOT THE REPUBLICAN LEADER WHOM Governor Spiro T. Agnew of Maryland originally wanted to see elected president in 1968. Rather, he hoped through a coalition of fellow governors to put Nelson A. Rockefeller of New York in the White House. Agnew knew of Rockefeller's promise in 1965, in seeking a third term in Albany, not to seek the presidency again after losing the GOP nomination to Barry Goldwater in 1964. But he set out in 1967 to change the New Yorker's mind.

As early as 1965, when Agnew was the elected Baltimore County executive, he had cast his eye on Rockefeller. In the wake of Nixon's defeat in his 1962 bid for the governorship of California, coming on the heels of his loss for the presidency in 1960, Agnew like many other Republicans had pretty much dismissed Nixon as a nominee again. Ormsby "Dutch" Moore, an Agnew political aide at the time, remembered that after the conservative Goldwater's 1964 debacle, "Ted wanted to be in there backing a liberal who had a chance of winning," and his clear preference was Rockefeller. Nevertheless, Moore recalled, Agnew also tried to sound out Nixon on his political plans, though he did not know the man at all. "He wrote him about November [of 1965] and didn't get an answer until maybe January or February," Moore said. "This was when Nixon was in his law firm [in New York]. I can remember Ted yet, saying, 'That damn Nixon, he won't even answer your letters. No wonder he can't get elected.'"[1]

My own personal connection with Nixon began around this time, with a similar experience after having observed him from a distance for more than a decade as a regional reporter covering Congress for a group of small newspapers. When private citizen Nixon, recovering from his defeats for the presidency in 1960 and for governor of California in 1962, led a Republican comeback in the 1966 congressional elections, I spent a full week with him as he campaigned in several states on behalf of GOP candidates. His press secretary at the time was a young fellow named Patrick Buchanan, whom I had known when he was an editorial writer for the *St. Louis Globe–Democrat* and with whom I later shared a microphone in Washington in a tame radio forerunner of the *Crossfire* show. When Buchanan introduced me to Nixon at our hotel in Detroit the night before the tour began, the great man was friendly but warily distant from the start.

Day after day, I rode with Buchanan and Nixon in the former vice president's car as a silent but watchful companion, observing the personal and political man at work in conversations with aides and local politicians, at private meetings and at rallies. He was a twice-beaten candidate himself but as a former vice president and presidential nominee he maintained a distinct luster within the party family that made him a welcome arrival wherever his schedule took him. He was relentlessly cordial to fellow Republicans as he dispensed wisdom to candidates and their managers, while methodically placing them in his political debt for what by this time was his strategy to resurrect his own electoral fortunes.

Nixon's dislike and suspicion of the press and his discomfort in the presence of its members was well known, but he treated me with uncommon courtesy through our week together. He regarded me with an uneasy eye as I observed him morning to night, trying to take a reading on his rare combination of outward confidence and painstakingly obvious awkwardness and self-doubt. He bent over backward to sound genial and approachable toward the press, but there always was that guarded sense that he saw us as the enemy. On one leg of that trip, when I was late for a takeoff, he held the plane and graciously brushed aside my apology. When I told Congressman Pat Hillings, another Nixon intimate on the trip, about it, he laughed. "The rest of us wanted to take off without you," he told me, "but he said, 'No, he's the only reporter we've got!'"

In that 1966 campaign, Nixon did indeed begin to restore his credibility within the Republican Party. Two-thirds of the sixty-six House candidates for whom he spoke won, as the GOP picked up forty-seven seats in the House and three in the Senate. Late in the campaign President Lyndon B. Johnson unwittingly helped Nixon by attacking him for criticizing the administration's war policy "in the hope he can pick up a precinct or two or a ward or two," thereby spotlighting him as the leader of the opposition. After the election, in an interview in his Park Avenue apartment, Nixon told me: "There was a big swing vote in the last days. Johnson's attack made it swing that way. . . . I couldn't believe it. It was too good to be true. . . . You never build up a major spokesman on the other side."

Other Republicans were impressed, but apparently not Spiro Agnew. He began talking up fellow-governor Rockefeller for president with colleagues like Governor James Rhodes of Ohio, who had little use for Nixon. At the Yale Republican Club in April 1967, Agnew announced he intended to cajole Rockefeller into running one more time as the darling of the GOP governors.

Even as Rockefeller still coveted the presidency, he had conspicuously thrown in with another GOP member of the governor's club, George Romney of Michigan, who had just won solid reelection to a second term. Furthermore, Rockefeller's commitment had financial heft behind it—as much as $400,000, according to some reports.[2] He had no illusions about Romney, a straight-arrow former head of American Motors who had forestalled the company's eventual death and moved into the governor's chair in Lansing with little political experience, and none in foreign policy. But Rockefeller despised Nixon, and he saw Romney as an acceptable moderate alternative to the shopworn but still opportunistic Californian.

At Yale, Agnew, himself then regarded as a moderate Republican, said he had nothing against Romney, "but it so happens that I'm tremendously impressed with Governor Rockefeller. I think that if he wants to run, he ought to get in now." Asked about the New Yorker's divorce and remarriage, which had hurt his chances for the nomination against Goldwater three years earlier, Agnew said it "will not have any affect," and he cited Rockefeller's strong reelection for a third term in Albany as proof.[3]

Agnew was not alone in pursuing Rockefeller. Tom McCall, the liberal governor of Oregon, where Rockefeller had won the Republican primary in 1964, shared Governor Rhodes's low opinion of Nixon, and he sent a letter to fellow governors urging them to delay endorsing anyone until they could act as a group. On the copy to Rockefeller he added a postscript calling on him to make himself available. But Rockefeller replied: "I'm out of it. If we moderates want to preserve any chance of nominating a candidate who can win, we'd better stay behind George Romney. . . . Any move to undercut him or proliferate the moderate support or even to consult with a view to looking to other candidates will, in my humble opinion, simply deliver the nomination to the other side." He didn't have to spell out that to him "the other side" was Nixon. So he told both Agnew and McCall: "I am not a candidate, and under no circumstances will I run."[4]

But Agnew was dazzled by the way the energetic Rockefeller dominated governors' conferences, with charts and papers on his latest ideas on getting things done at the state level. He was not deterred. "I have a feeling Governor Rockefeller could be persuaded if there is substantial evidence of a wave in his direction," Agnew said to reporters. But if Rockefeller would not budge, he added, "I would be rather foolish to continue." To find out once and for all, Agnew called on his quarry shortly afterward in his Manhattan office, and they talked for ninety minutes. Rockefeller turned him down flat. When Agnew came out, he told awaiting reporters: "I am disappointed. I feel a tremendous sense of need to have a candidate of the Rockefeller type."[5] Without naming Nixon, Agnew's comment was a clear slap at the former vice president.

During this time, though Rockefeller's support of Romney remained firm, the Michigan governor's candidacy was going nowhere. Once, in an interview, when I asked Rockefeller what he would do if Romney's campaign tanked, he replied with some irritation: "I'm just not going to knock myself out thinking about it." Asked why his name continued to surface as a candidate for the nomination, he said: "I'll be darned if I know. All I know is these people weren't speaking that way the last time [in 1964] when I was working like hell for it."[6]

Romney's lack of foreign policy experience was coming through in an inability to express a consistent position on the Vietnam War, whose conduct by Lyndon Johnson was emerging as a likely central issue in the approaching 1968 presidential campaign. In August of 1967, on a radio interview in Detroit, Romney was asked about his inconsistency on Vietnam. He blurted out that on a recent visit there "I just had the greatest brainwashing that anybody can get when you go over to Vietnam" by the American generals and diplomatic corps. "I no longer believe that it was necessary for us to get involved in South Vietnam to stop Communist aggression," he said.

The "brainwashing" remark put the final torpedo in an already sinking ship. As often happens in politics, the comment crystallized a public impression that the well-meaning Romney was not up to the job of president. Democratic senator Eugene J. McCarthy of Minnesota, soon to enter the 1968 race against Johnson, captured the prevailing ridicule by observing of the "brainwashing" confession: "I would have thought a light rinse would have done it." Speculation about a Rockefeller candidacy started up again as a result, and Agnew's hopes for it were rekindled, despite Rockefeller's continued dismissal of the possibility.

At a series of governors' conferences, Agnew still plugged away. At an Asheville, North Carolina, meeting, he proposed a unity ticket of Rockefeller for president and freshman governor of California Ronald Reagan for vice president. In the fall, as the governors of both parties engaged in the mother of all political junkets, a cruise to the Virgin Islands aboard the S.S. *Independence*, *Time* magazine put the two Republicans on its cover, generating talk of a "dream ticket." Agnew's own dream took on a new clarity, even as Rockefeller responded on deck by telling me and another reporter, Jack Germond of the Gannett Newspapers, not only that "I'm not a candidate" and "I'm not going to be a candidate," but also for the first time—twice—that "I don't want to be president."[7]

Elsewhere on the ship, when word of Rockefeller's latest, strongest disavowal reached Agnew, he responded: "That's pretty definite. But I still say if he's drafted it would take a pretty emphatic individual to turn down a genuine draft. Indeed, I can't conceive of it." To the ears of Nixon operatives aboard, however, the words were a signal to intensify their efforts to recruit other governors and stem any thought of a bloc forming a stop-Nixon effort. At yet another governors' conference, in Palm Beach a few weeks later, two Nixon political aides, Bob Ellsworth and John Sears, told Agnew they were aware he was still for Rockefeller, but were sure Nixon would be the nominee. They said the Nixon camp wanted to remain on friendly terms with him in the interest of a unified party. Agnew told them he had nothing against Nixon and would support him if he did get the nomination. But at the same Palm Beach conference, Ohio's Rhodes linked arms with Agnew and McCall and whispered: "Boys, let's put this one together for Rockefeller." So Agnew pressed on.

In January of the new election year, Agnew announced that he was forming a "Draft Rockefeller" organization in Maryland in the hope it would spread across the country. A few weeks later, he was buoyed by the surprise decision of Romney, confronted by humiliating polling numbers against Nixon in the impending New Hampshire primary, to quit the presidential race. Nixon, counting on a landslide victory on primary day, suspected a plot to bring Rockefeller into the campaign against him, but Rockefeller was just as surprised as the rest. A heartened Agnew met with his would-be candidate again in New York, who for the first time said he would run, according to Agnew, "if there is a broad base of support for him." But Rockefeller told him, he said, he didn't want to run simply as a stop-Nixon vehicle, though that certainly was in his mind.

Agnew had met Nixon for the first time only weeks before, at a Republican women's reception in New York, arranged by a mutual political associate, Maryland state senator Louise Gore. At a private gathering at her apartment afterward, they had an amiable chat and Agnew pointedly told Nixon that his pro-Rockefeller efforts were in no way meant to be seen as anti-Nixon. The hostess recalled later that "it was almost as if one picked up the other's thought from. . . the other; they were so engrossed in each other that they forgot we were in the room. When I walked Mr. Nixon to the elevator, he told me, 'Your governor—your governor—make him speak out more. He's got a lot to say.'"[8] It was just a comment, but it turned out to be a prophecy. After Romney dropped out, Agnew went to New York again to inform Nixon personally that while he was running a Draft Rockefeller effort, he admired the former vice president but thought the New York governor had a better chance of being elected. One Nixon operative observed later: "We had pretty well kissed Agnew off. . . . We had no reason not to. He was openly and strongly for Rockefeller."[9]

In March, after conversations with other governors, Rockefeller cited the imperative for the Republican nominee to attract Democrats and independents—an obvious assessment that Nixon was not the one to do so. Therefore, he said, "I am not going to create dissension within the Republican Party by contending for the nomination, but I am ready and willing to serve the American people if called."

It was a categorical invitation to be drafted, and an eager Agnew agreed to chair a national Rockefeller-for-President citizens' committee to achieve it. He didn't know it at the time, but he was not the first choice for the chairmanship. Former Pennsylvania Governor William Scranton had agreed to serve, and only when he backed out was Agnew asked to help open an office in Annapolis staffed by a Rockefeller man. At the first Rockefeller-for-President national meeting, which drew Republicans from seventeen states, Agnew delivered a pep talk, and a few days later he attended a meeting with Rockefeller at his Park Avenue apartment in New York with other party leaders. Most left with the expectation that Rockefeller's declaration of candidacy was now only a formality.

During all this time, Nixon was methodically tending to business in New Hampshire, collecting old political chits and rebuilding fences. He announced his candidacy with a personal letter to Republican voters and held a kickoff press party at the old New Hampshire Highway Hotel. He stood on a table and said he was turning over a new leaf with the press. Candor, he said, would be his byword, and he promised that he would provide regular interviews and briefings along the way, and that his press secretary Pat Buchanan, with whom I had made that 1966 southern swing, would keep the reporters informed of his whereabouts at all times.

So, it was a surprise the next morning to learn that while we were sleeping, Nixon at the crack of dawn had slipped out of the hotel and conducted a "town meeting" with some hand-picked college students, farmers, and other locals, filmed by his own crew to be excerpted for television ads. So much for a fresh start. We were all mortified, mostly for swallowing Nixon's promise of candor. The old press skepticism returned along with the old Nixon.

Meanwhile, Romney kept slogging along. The most memorable moment for me came at a bowling alley where the earnest and determined Michigan governor tried his hand at duckpins, the smaller version of the game, in which the player gets three smaller balls to knock down the ten, rather than two balls, as in regular bowling. After the three allotted balls, seven pins were still standing, so Romney kept trying. He finally knocked over the tenth pin—with his thirty-fourth ball. Romney's hapless performance was a metaphor for his campaign, and he dropped out before primary day, leaving Nixon with an empty victory.

On March 12, another political earthquake shook New Hampshire when the aforementioned and little-known Gene McCarthy scored a near-upset of President Johnson in the Democratic primary, winning 42.2 percent of the vote. Four days later, Senator Robert F. Kennedy of New York, a bitter LBJ foe, jumped into the race, threatening to split the Democratic Party wide open. The development did not go unnoticed by Rockefeller.

Five days after that, Rockefeller held a nationally televised press conference in a major New York hotel. That morning the *New York Times* had reported that Rockefeller would be announcing that at last his hat was in the ring. To share the happy moment with the Annapolis press corps, Agnew had a portable black-and-white television set brought into his office at the state house and invited all the reporters in to watch with him. Rockefeller approached the microphone and to the astonishment of the audience declared that he had decided after all "to reiterate unequivocally that I am not a candidate campaigning directly or indirectly for the presidency of the United States."[10]

Agnew was thoroughly shocked and humiliated in front of a press corps that had never been very favorably disposed toward him. Rockefeller in advance had telephoned some other governors and party leaders who had been encouraging him to run and told them of his negative decision, but he did not call Agnew, the man who had been leading the parade for him. Rockefeller said later he had tried to get through, but couldn't. Outwardly, Agnew indicated no malice toward him as a result of the snub, and he even repeated that "I still think Nelson Rockefeller is the best candidate the Republican Party could offer." But he obviously had cooled, observing that "I'm in the process of revising and watching. I don't have anyone who's running at the moment that I can support."[11]

That last remark seemed at first to rule out Nixon, but Agnew added that "I am not against Mr. Nixon. He may—may—even be my number-two choice." However, not only Agnew's substantial ego but also his political stature in Maryland had taken a blow. Later in the year, he told the editors of the *New York Times* he had gone out on a limb for Rockefeller with many Marylanders and they all had been left hanging out to dry along with him. "It's not personal rancor," he insisted, "It's like hitting you where you work. This was an incursion into my political acceptability, and after all, what does a politician have but his credibility?"[12]

Agnew's disappointment and humiliation were not lost on the Nixon camp. John Sears, the young lawyer in Nixon's law firm who was serving as a principal delegate-hunter, was in Alaska at the time, courting Governor Walter Hickel. As Sears recalled the situation later: "Nixon was going crazy thinking Rockefeller was getting into the race, so I told him I'd go up to Alaska and get Hickel to come out for him. Everybody figured if Rocky got in, Hickel would go for him. He'd been for Romney, and Nixon had been mad at him over that.

"So I called up Milhous and said, 'One thing you've got to do, is call up this guy Agnew.' He thought Agnew was a Rockefeller guy so he was fighting me over it, which made you feel pretty good, because if he was fighting over it, it meant he was probably going to do it. But he didn't like the idea. I told him, 'Look, if you're even seen with the guy in the next week, it'll do a lot.' You know what it was, really? He didn't want to call somebody he didn't know. He didn't even want to call people he did know most of the time. So that's what you were dealing with."[13]

Nixon finally agreed to send another supporter, former congressman Bob Ellsworth of Kansas, to Annapolis to field Agnew on the short hop. Ellsworth arranged for a meeting between Nixon and Agnew in New York, and when Sears got back from Alaska he found a note on his desk to go in to see Nixon, which he did. "Milhous has just been out to lunch with Agnew," Sears recalled later, "and he's telling me what a great guy this is. This is just a fantastic guy. How he's smart and tough, and I'm thinking, 'Wait a minute, he isn't such a bad guy, but——.' What happened is he went out to lunch with him and all Agnew did was tell him what an asshole Rockefeller was. That got rid of the ice in the conversation very quickly."[14]

As often occurred with Nixon, a man with a galloping inferiority complex, especially about his appearance and his awkwardness with "manly" men, he was taken with the tall, erect, and impeccably groomed Agnew. The Maryland governor, for his part, was impressed with Nixon if only by his reputation and achievements, but he did not crumble at once. In fact, after the lunch he had told reporters he still thought Rockefeller would be the party's best candidate, but he was taking a good look at Nixon. He said he wasn't ready to endorse him but "I have a high regard for him. He's the front-runner."

That was enough for the Nixon strategists to step up the courtship. They weren't convinced they had heard the last of Rockefeller as a challenger. "The effect of Nixon and Agnew in even being seen together was to cause some people who had been behind Rockefeller to think twice before they started back on that path," Sears said. "It bought us some time, and anybody we could be seen talking to, or pick off, or get out of that camp would do a lot to help us lick Rockefeller in the end. . . . It would take that much more conversation with them in the future to get them back in Rockefeller's bag."[15]

By this time, there was indeed a further incentive for the New York governor to reconsider his decision to stay out of the 1968 presidential race. On March 30, in the course of a report on the war in Vietnam in which he announced a halt in the bombing of North Vietnam, Lyndon Johnson shocked a Sunday night television audience by declaring that to devote his full attention to the war, "I shall not seek, and I will not accept, the nomination of my party for another term as your president."

As LBJ dropped his bombshell, Richard Nixon was returning to New York on his chartered jet from Milwaukee, where he had held a reception to enlarge his certain unopposed victory in the Wisconsin primary two days hence. On landing, he had a comment ready. "This is the year of the dropouts," he said. "First Romney, then Rockefeller, now Johnson." He said he hadn't expected the president to drop out; Kennedy would now be the frontrunner. Nixon accurately forecast that LBJ's vice president, Hubert Humphrey, would step in as the administration candidate, backed by Johnson. "I'd be very surprised if President Johnson lets Bobby Kennedy have it on a platter," he added. Then Nixon turned to his own situation. "The Democrats are a divided party but our game could change too," he said. "Rockefeller will have to determine whether, after withdrawing from the race, he will enter it again."[16] Indeed, only days after Johnson's surprise decision not to seek reelection, Rockefeller was entertaining second thoughts about his own candidacy.

Whether Nixon recognized it at once or not, his new friendship with Spiro Agnew, Rockefeller's recently jilted former champion, suddenly took on a new significance. The New York governor already had begun trying to woo back his old suitor, starting with a too-late phone call after his March 21 pullout that was received by an icy Agnew. In the next days, Rockefeller's banker brother David called on Agnew and so did the governor's political right-hand man, George Hinman. "He was friendly but obviously down deep he was hurt," Hinman recalled. "He didn't talk much about it, he just didn't come along, either."[17]

❧ ❧

MEANWHILE, the Maryland governor had his hands full at home, where he was embroiled in a racial situation that would soon enhance his political appeal to the Nixon campaign. As a former Baltimore County executive, he owed his election as governor in 1966 to the Democratic gubernatorial candidacy of an avowed ultraconservative segregationist named George P. Mahoney. Mahoney's platform, summed up in the campaign slogan "A Man's Home is His Castle—Protect It," had caused liberals and moderates in both parties to flock to Agnew's support, assuring his election. In the process, in comparison with Mahoney, Agnew was seen widely as a centrist or even a liberal on civil rights.

But eight months into his term as governor, Agnew was confronted by a severe challenge, in the outbreak of violence in the Eastern Shore town of Cambridge, the site of racial mayhem four summers earlier. Black Power leader H. Rap Brown had been invited to speak by the town's Black Action Federation, and he delivered a bitter, vitriolic, anti-white harangue to an audience of several hundred black teenagers and young adults. He called on them "to get your guns . . . if you gotta die, wherever you go, take some of them with you. I don't care if we have to burn him down or run him out." Pointing to a local black elementary school, he declared: "You all should have burned that school long ago, you should have burned it down to the ground, brother." And later: "If America don't come around, we're going to burn America down."[18]

When Brown led a march in the town, police fired on the crowd, and in the early morning a fire broke out in the black school. The all-white fire department refused to respond, until the state attorney general on the scene ordered a fire truck to bring the blaze under control. Agnew gave orders for Brown's arrest; he was later apprehended and charged with inciting a riot and inciting to burn. Agnew, who as a county executive had a reputation as a defender of civil rights, locked onto Brown as pure poison as a black leader. Thereafter he never passed a chance to attack him to more moderate blacks who called on him. "He had a tape of Brown's speech in his office," one longtime associate recalled, "and he would keep playing it to black ministers who came in. 'Listen to that,' he would say. 'Isn't that incitement? Isn't it?'"[19] In his 1968 state legislative program, Agnew pushed bills to give himself as governor more powers to deal with riots.

In March of 1968, the student president of Bowie State College wrote to Agnew telling him of student impatience with the dilapidated condition of the school. Later in the month, when a favorite history professor was denied tenure with no explanation given, more than 200 undergraduates conducted a peaceable boycott of classes and asked Agnew to come to the campus. He declined, instead sending a fast-talking, condescending aide who only made matters worse. But still Agnew would not go. The result was a complete campus takeover by the students and then a police presence that produced a temporary settlement.

Meanwhile, in an unrelated event in one of Baltimore's toughest black neighborhoods, local leaders met with Stokely Carmichael, former head of the Student Nonviolent Coordinating Committee (SNCC) and an emerging leader of the Black Power movement. An undercover state police officer filed a report of incendiary talk that was duly passed on to Agnew. In Baltimore's black community, a split had already developed between older, established moderate leaders and the new militants.

The white mayor, Thomas D'Alesandro III, had undertaken a campaign against street crime, and the head of the Baltimore office of SNCC had denounced it as "a war on the black community," calling the police its enemy. State Senator Clarence Mitchell, one of Baltimore's most prominent, moderate black leaders, took to the Senate floor in Annapolis and, to the approval of white leaders, labeled the remarks "bigotry." The result was a "black unity" meeting of both the old and the new leaders to calm things down, with conciliatory comments made. Agnew had learned of that meeting, too, and drew his own conclusions.[20]

A few nights later, with Agnew having refused to go to the Bowie State campus, students piled onto buses and stormed the state capitol in Annapolis. Agnew ducked the protest by staying in the governor's mansion across the street. By nightfall, 227 of the students had been arrested and Agnew ordered Bowie State closed down. On the same night, Dr. Martin Luther King Jr. was assassinated in Memphis, and two nights later Baltimore was in flames. Agnew, from a riot command post in Annapolis, ordered the Maryland National Guard into the city as local black leaders fruitlessly tried to maintain calm in the black sections. Agnew went to Baltimore early the next morning and finally called for federal troops. By now, six people had been killed, 700 injured and 5,000 arrested.

Two days after the burial of Dr. King in Atlanta, about a hundred of Baltimore's most prominent and moderate black leaders responded to an Agnew invitation to meet with him in the city's State Office Building. On arrival, they were surprised to see tight security and a large battery of television cameras for what they had expected to be a private meeting with the governor. Agnew strode in accompanied by the head of the Maryland National Guard, General George Gelston—who was in uniform and carrying a riding crop—and a host of other uniformed officers.

A stern and somber Agnew began reading a formal statement to the assembled black leaders in which he immediately insulted these pillars of the community. "I did not request your presence to bid for peace with the public dollar," he said, as if they were responsible for the riots. Then, in what he obviously intended to be a compliment, he called on them to look around and note that each of them "has worked his way to the top," and that "the circuit-riding, Hanoi-visiting type of leader is missing from this assembly. The caterwauling, riot-inciting, burn-America-down type of leader is conspicuous by his absence."[21]

It was the sort of harangue that Americans far beyond Maryland would in time come to expect from Spiro T. Agnew. In an obvious reference to the black unity meeting of days earlier, he accused the moderates before him of meeting with the very rabble-rousers he had not invited and agreeing not to "openly criticize any black spokesman, regardless of his remarks." He said sarcastically that he did not blame them "for breaking and running in the face of what appeared to be overwhelming opinion in the Negro community. But actually," he lectured them, "it was only the opinion of a few, distorted and magnified by the silence of most of you here today."[22]

Agnew's attack caused an uproar in the room, as many got up and walked out. One visibly shaken black minister, Marion C. Bascom, an early supporter of Agnew for governor, said of him later: "He is as sick as any bigot in America."[23] Those who stayed heard Agnew continue to drone on, charging that the fires were started "at the suggestion and with the instruction of the advocates of violence" from out of town, specifically mentioning Carmichael and Brown. Unless they were repudiated by the black moderates still sitting before him, he said, most of Maryland's blacks "will be unjustly victimized by a hardening of attitudes in the decent white community." In a remark that later would seem preposterous having come from him, he deplored "this polarization of attitudes as an aftermath of violence."[24]

The meeting ended amid cries of protest that were widely reported the next day, not only in the newspapers and on the television channels of Baltimore but also around the country. Among those who quickly picked up on the uproar in New York was Pat Buchanan, then in the Nixon law office. He had first met Nixon when the great man had come to play golf with his newspaper's publisher in St. Louis, Richard Amberg. Young Buchanan caddied for Nixon and then left the paper to work for him. Buchanan assembled clips on Agnew's stormy confrontation with the black leaders in Baltimore, knowing they would be of interest to his boss, himself a strong advocate of taking a tough law-and-order posture toward racial disturbances and violence. Nixon, as Buchanan knew he would be, was impressed.

After he'd met Agnew, Buchanan said later, "The boss thought this guy was a very tough guy. This all in Nixon's mind was another indication that his first impression. . . was a valid one; that here was a real strong fellow who exuded this strength even in a touchy situation like this, and was not beleaguered by what people viewed as the politics of his past." After they'd met and talked, Buchanan said, "As long as we did the right things, we thought we could get him [Agnew], and it wasn't an unpredictable course we had to follow to get him."

While all this was going on, Nelson Rockefeller continued to get pressure to reconsider from other political figures more persistent than Agnew. One of them, Senator Thruston Morton of Kentucky, on the very day Agnew was chewing out the black leaders in Baltimore, called the Rockefeller operative in Annapolis who was busy closing up the draft office and told him to relocate the effort in New York. A new approach was now afoot, wherein Rockefeller would not compete against Nixon in any state primary and instead would launch a massive communications campaign designed to drive his numbers up in the polls. If successful, his strategists figured, the New York governor could go into the Republican National Convention in Miami Beach with a strong argument that he, not Nixon, was the only Republican who could win in November.

On April 30, Rockefeller finally entered the race for the GOP nomination. "I do this," he explained, "because the dramatic and unprecedented events of the past weeks have revealed in most serious terms the gravity of the crisis that we face as a people. . . . In the new circumstances that confront the nation, I frankly find that to comment from the sidelines is not an effective way to present the alternatives."[25]

The news surprised Agnew but did not dissuade him from his interest in Nixon. Agnew told reporters, "I think it is very good for the Republican Party that we have two candidates. Certainly Governor Rockefeller, as I said on many occasions, is a highly qualified person and may very well provide a formidable candidacy for the election in November." But, he pointedly added, "I do think a lot of things have happened since his [first] withdrawal. . . and I think it's a new ball game. I think I've got to take another look at this situation." It was not that he was "less enthusiastic" about Rockefeller, he said in response to a question, "but I'm much more enthusiastic for Mr. Nixon's candidacy than I was before."[26] Agnew clearly appreciated the beneficial position in which he now found himself.

In the period heading toward the Republican National Convention, with Nixon steadily accumulating delegates and Rockefeller struggling to make the case for himself through favorable polls, the former vice president occasionally would confer with Agnew, in the manner in which he often "conferred" with other Republicans whose support he wanted. He would listen to them and schmooze with them to give them a sense of participation in the campaign. But he also took an interest in some of Agnew's ideas on such subjects as welfare reform and job training. One Nixon campaign aide, John Ehrlichman, who was taking on domestic issues for his candidate, visited Agnew in Annapolis to discuss them further.

For the time being, all it amounted to was that Richard Nixon had found a new ally among many in his second quest for the presidency—a campaign marked with greater discipline and attention to detail than the first, which had led to his narrow, heart-breaking defeat in 1960 at the hands of John F. Kennedy. As for Agnew, he had rebounded from the disappointment of Rockefeller's erratic, disorganized flirtation with national politics. In Nixon, the little-known governor of Maryland now was associated with a less glamorous but more sure-footed candidate whom he was finding more and more attractive as a prospective president of the United States.

Chapter 2

SPIRO WHO?

In early May of 1968, Governor Agnew was still officially undecided on supporting a candidate for the Republican presidential nomination. He had made clear to Maryland reporters, however, that after his disappointing courtship of Nelson Rockefeller he had taken a shine to Richard Nixon, in response to some aggressive wooing from Nixon's campaign aides.

Agnew's sudden engagement in Republican national politics had not gone unobserved by the Annapolis press corps. He reported at a news conference that because of the "very dramatic changes" that had occurred in the past month, he was taking a careful reading of the prospects before deciding "where I am going to throw whatever influence I can have in this election."[1]

Agnew had previously brushed aside any notions that as a one-term governor from a small state he might wind up on the national ticket. One suspicious reporter now asked: "Governor, do you still maintain that you have no ambitions at all on the national scene?" When he answered that he did not have such aspirations, the reporter persisted. "On reflection of the one-time Rockefeller situation, that he was available for a draft," he asked, "are you available for a draft for the second place?"

Agnew replied, quoting an earlier Rockefeller comment, that "I don't consider myself standby equipment." Then, in a serious vein, he said: "It would be the height of temerity for me to suggest that coming from a state that never had a vice-president possibility and being only a little over a year in office, that this is something serious enough for me to consider at this time."[2]

A couple of weeks later, however, David Broder of *The Washington Post* interviewed Nixon and came away reporting that among those being considered as his running mate was Agnew. The next day, another veteran Nixon-watcher, Don Irwin of the *Los Angeles Times*, wrote much the same. Agnew said he was "very flattered" and phoned Nixon to tell him so.

When reporters asked Agnew whether he would make the same disclaimer that Governor Mills Godwin of Virginia had made, that he'd rather keep the job he already had, Agnew dodged by saying he considered the vice presidency "a very high office and a great challenge in itself." He would be going to the party convention, he said, as Maryland's favorite-son presidential candidate.

At the same time, though, Agnew took some actions that could be interpreted as romancing Nixon. For example, he made a speech in favor of "black capitalism" as the "answer to the despair of the ghetto"—a favorite Nixon proposal, and a reminder of how Agnew himself stood on racial violence. The recent riots, he said, were caused "not just by evil conditions but by evil men." The Republican solution, he said, "is not black power but green power—the power of the purse: Negro enterprise and industry."[3]

When Rockefeller in mid-May came to Baltimore with a party platform task force and held a joint press conference with Agnew, both men seemed stiff and embarrassed. Suddenly Rockefeller blurted out an apology to his fellow governor for earlier "having gone the wrong way at a psychological moment." Agnew, startled, said: "No apology is necessary. I don't accept the apology, as I don't think it's necessary at all. I don't think many people realize what a candidate for president has to go through."[4]

At a later evening reception given in Rockefeller's honor by liberal Republican senator Charles "Mac" Mathias, obviously arranged in an effort to close the breach, Agnew avoided the honored guest. Rockefeller addressed the crowd on the back lawn of the host's house and again made an embarrassingly impassioned plea for Agnew's forgiveness. Agnew replied in diplomatic niceties. Shortly afterward, on a television Sunday interview show, Rockefeller said of the situation: "I was down there in

Maryland the last few days and I think we are beginning to reestablish ties again."[5] But that was wishful thinking.

With Rockefeller leaving the Republican primary field to Nixon, the former vice president moved from state to state collecting convention delegates. All the campaign attention was on the Democratic side, as Robert Kennedy posted primary victories over McCarthy in Indiana and Nebraska before stumbling in Oregon. But he recovered in California on the first Tuesday in June, only to have his candidacy and his life snuffed out at the hand of an assassin disturbed by Kennedy's support of Israel. The tragedy sealed the nomination of Humphrey, who like Rockefeller did not contest the primaries. Unlike Rockefeller, Humphrey had the party establishment in his corner. He easily rounded up a majority of convention delegates outside the primaries, which assured his selection. Rockefeller, meanwhile, had to rely on trying to jack up his polling numbers in a vain effort to persuade the GOP convention to turn away from Nixon. It wasn't happening.

At a Republican governors' conference in Tulsa, Rockefeller made another direct pitch to Agnew. But he wasn't buying, and went out of his way to be critical. He told reporters: "I read Nelson's statement on Vietnam, and I don't know what it says." He said he preferred Nixon's position on dealing with civil disorder and was impressed by "a tremendous surge to Nixon after the King assassination and the subsequent riots."[6]

Agnew by now was openly wearing his confrontation with the black leaders in Baltimore as a badge of honor, and a not-so-subtle advertisement of his political value to the law-and-order campaign that Nixon was already running on his own. In a late-night chat with a few reporters in his suite at Tulsa's Camelot Inn, Agnew held forth on his outlook toward the black protest. Referring to a current Poor People's March on Washington, he declared it "out of hand" and asked: "Did you see the Cadillacs parked around Resurrection City [near the Lincoln Memorial]? I tell you, things are changing in this country. When I told those black leaders in Baltimore that I felt they were responsible for not reading the riot act [to black extremists], you should have seen the mail I got, not only in Maryland but from all over the country. . . . People are fed up with the riots. I've tried to be liberal but at some point you have to stop leading the people and start following them."[7]

Six days later, Agnew called on Nixon in his New York apartment. Aides said they had talked about civil disorders and demonstrators. When Agnew held his next news conference in Annapolis he made no mention of his visit to Nixon, but sounded the Nixon law-and-order theme in response to questions on street protest. He said he thought Nixon would be tougher than Johnson in dealing with it, because "he's concerned, as are most people in this country right now, that there is a wave of permissiveness that has been allowed to prosper and flourish." What voters wanted, he said, were politicians who "actually have the courage to put their foot down and say no to some of these unreasonable requests."[8]

The Annapolis reporters had no difficulty recognizing Agnew's open playing up to Nixon. One asked, noting that he was speaking out more on national issues: "Are you pledged to serve the full four years as governor?" Agnew replied: "I was elected to serve four full years, and I would say this just to give you a hint: we don't have a lieutenant governor here, and under the [state] constitution, I suppose what happens if I were to move to the national scene is that we would have a Democratic governor very quickly. Now that doesn't sound very likely to you, does it?"[9]

Pressed on whether he would consider "any offer at the national level that you might get after the November election" [presumably a cabinet appointment in a Nixon administration], Agnew said he would have to consider it, but it was unlikely to happen.

Two days later the Maryland state party picked its convention delegates, most of whom were already supporting Nixon. But the delegation as a whole committed itself, in a formality, to Agnew as its favorite son. At his next news conference, he said, "I intend to serve out the four years" as governor "no matter what—as long as I'm alive, that is."[10]

Meanwhile, Nixon, though having methodically signed on enough delegate support to put him close to the nomination, kept a wary eye not only on Rockefeller but also on freshman governor Ronald Reagan. The Californian, also heading his state's huge delegation as its favorite son, downplayed any talk of a serious bid for the presidential nomination while quietly touring western and southern states to confer with fence-straddling delegates. So Nixon in his disciplined way made pilgrimages to the most conservative of Republican leaders—Barry Goldwater, John Tower, Strom Thurmond—to secure his base on the party's right wing against any possible defection to Reagan. Then he settled in at his Key

Biscayne retreat to plan for the convention, which was to be held in Miami Beach in August. A key element in the strategy was to have a string of favorite sons break his way if either Rockefeller or Reagan posed a serious threat at the convention. Included in that calculation, obviously, was Ted Agnew of Maryland.

❧ ☙

AMONG THE MAJOR DECISIONS Nixon would consider at Key Biscayne was his choice of a running mate. As a man who incessantly reviewed, even agonized over, past political mistakes, he was determined not to repeat them. Nixon dissected his failed 1960 presidential campaign for weaknesses and errors, vowing to correct them. One mistake, obviously, had been his pledge to campaign in all fifty states. It had locked him into a late trek to Alaska that had consumed valuable time and left him exhausted for the campaign's homestretch. He wasn't going to do that again in 1968. Another was his 1960 dawn-to-midnight schedule, which also left him a physical basket case. This time around, as he had already demonstrated in the primaries, he was undertaking a much less taxing regimen, relying more heavily on well-spaced set speeches covered by television.

Finally, Nixon reflected on his 1960 selection of United Nations ambassador Henry Cabot Lodge as his running mate, which he had lived to regret. Lodge not only was too casual a campaigner for Nixon's taste; he also was given to major gaffes. At one point he promised that Nixon if elected would appoint a black to his cabinet, which was not for him to say, as well as politically inept for a Republican appealing to a conservative, southern base. And beyond that, the insecure Nixon thought the tall and aristocratic Boston Brahmin had upstaged him.

The relationship between Nixon and Lodge was so cool that they did not see each other for two years after the failed campaign. They finally met in Lodge's office in Saigon when Lodge was John Kennedy's ambassador to South Vietnam, whereupon he told Nixon: "You know, Dick, all those stories about how I took a nap every afternoon in the 1960 campaign? They weren't true."[11] According to an eyewitness, Nixon just stared at him. In the approaching campaign, he wanted an energetic running-mate, and a politically sensitive one, yet one who clearly was willing to play second fiddle.

As Nixon in Key Biscayne began hearing the thoughts of his young aides, the name of Ronald Reagan quickly emerged. John Sears recalled later: "I was for Nixon picking Reagan, frankly, because I thought our real problem was [Alabama governor George] Wallace. We had him winning more states [as a third-party candidate] than he eventually did. I thought that was good politics. But I also thought Nixon would never take a guy like Reagan, because he thought Lodge had outshined him [in 1960] and he wasn't going to do that again."[12]

Once when Sears was alone with Nixon, he mentioned Reagan. "Most of the time if I gave him any advice," Sears recalled, "you sort of had to make him think it was his own idea, or say it was. And you had to be alone with him, because if there was anybody there and you were telling him what to do, that was too embarrassing for him." Nixon responded to the suggestion by asking: "But what kind of president would he make, Reagan?" Sears replied: "Oh, I've got this all wrong. I thought *you* were going to be the president. I thought we were talking about vice president, and being slavishly loyal to the president." Sears recalled: "He laughed. That was the only time [in the campaign] I heard him laugh. Then he changed the subject."[13]

But the notion of choosing a counter to Wallace remained. Nixon himself was often perceived as a centrist, and aides to his right and left proposed running mates who would help him on one side of the spectrum or the other. Pat Buchanan also was strong on Reagan, feeling that the charismatic California governor could be an effective candidate in the South and could free Nixon up to concentrate on the North. Another young and moderate speechwriter, Ray Price, pushed Mayor John Lindsay of New York or Senator Charles Percy of Illinois as attractive to the urban, industrial states of the North and Midwest, adding enough strength to make up for Wallace's Dixie support.

In all these early staff discussions, Agnew was never seriously injected, and Nixon never mentioned him either. But by mid-June, Sears remembered, "He got very afraid, after everybody on the staff had had his say about the vice presidency, that by picking either on the conservative side or on the liberal side he might provoke another split in the party. Nobody ever suggested Agnew, and Nixon wouldn't mention anybody when we talked about it. He'd just listen. But it was sometime around there that he got down to trying to figure out who could stand in the middle with him, and avoid the problem of bringing the convention to blows about its factions. . . . It just became more and more apparent that he wasn't seriously considering anybody readily identifiable on either side."[14]

Agnew by this time, with his new law-and-order rhetoric, had begun to shed his early reputation as a moderate or even a liberal compared to George Mahoney, the Democratic segregationist he had defeated for governor of Maryland. But to those Republicans who hadn't closely followed his transformation in his small and low-profile state, Agnew remained a moderate or, in many cases, a nondescript cipher. Once Nixon got beyond Reagan on one side and Lindsay and Percy on the other, Sears said, "I don't think he had anybody else in mind. So by the process of elimination you just had to figure it had to be someone in the middle there someplace."[15]

It was also clear that inasmuch as foreign policy was Nixon's strong suit, he would want somebody who had credentials on the domestic side and would not be likely to kibitz his own decisions on foreign affairs. Above all, after eight years as the docile and uninfluential vice president to Dwight D. Eisenhower, Nixon might talk about the importance of the vice presidency, but he didn't have any plans to build it up in an administration of his own. He wanted somebody, simply, to do as he was told, and smile as he did.

What Nixon wanted, Sears said at the time, was "strictly a second-liner," and not only for reasons of his own shaky ego. Polls were taken that showed none of the prospective running mates would help the ticket; indeed, they suggested that Nixon would run best alone. But that wasn't possible, so the next best thing would be to choose somebody who in a sense was a nobody on the national scene.

In late July, Nixon went to Montauk Point, on Long Island, with only a few aides, ostensibly to prepare his nomination acceptance speech and to examine the hundreds of letters he had solicited from party leaders on the choice of his running mate. "Any time you see R. N. polling people," Sears said later, "you can be sure he's not seeking their opinion. He just wants to substantiate his own views. He's not the kind of man who comes to a situation without an opinion. In spite of all this searching and consultation, the fact we got who we did proves he wasn't coming to it with an open mind."[16] Another intimate said: "Of course he had no intention of taking that advice when he asked for it. That's just Dick's way of making

people feel they're involved in important decisions. It doesn't cost anything, and some people eat it up."[17]

During this period, Nixon journeyed to Annapolis for a dinner at the
governor's mansion for a group of wealthy Maryland contributors to a
fund to pay Agnew's political expenses. Agnew, like Nixon, was an ama-
teur pianist, and as Nixon left that night, he told some of the other guests:
"If I'm elected, I assure you there will be two piano players in the White
House." The remark drew little attention.[18] During this time, Nixon
wrote later in his memoir, John Mitchell, his law partner and campaign
manager, asked Agnew to place the candidate's name in nomination, and
told him "if he did a good job, he would be considered for the second spot
on the ticket. To that extent, at least, Agnew's speech was an audition."[19]
[19] The offer to nominate Nixon assured the first-term Maryland governor a moment in the national spotlight, but little was made of it at the
time. After all, Agnew was just another of the favorite-son candidates
Nixon's campaign was courting to put him over the top on the convention's first presidential roll call.

At the convention, Nixon made the usual round of state delegations.
He indicated he was leaning toward a middle-road running mate by assuring them he would not select someone who would be divisive. That
was another way of saying he wasn't going to choose anybody perceived
to be in either extreme wing of the GOP—not Reagan on the right and
certainly not Rockefeller, Lindsay, or Percy on the left. A tape recording
of one of Nixon's sessions with a southern state delegation, obtained by
the *Miami Herald*, had him denying "some cockeyed stories that Nixon
has made a deal" and telling the delegates, "I am not going to take, I can
assure you, anybody that is going to divide this party."[20]

It was easier to divine whom Nixon was not considering than whom
he was. But those who knew him best insisted later there were certain
clues that should have tipped them off. They knew he liked "strong"
men, physically and temperamentally, and especially if he perceived them
as self-made, as he liked to see himself. And he liked to "discover" comers
in the party. As Sears put it later: "Here all of a sudden was a guy out of
nowhere who he had never thought of. The timing of their personal contact was such that in Nixon's mind he was able to form his impression of
Agnew against this background of personalities that he had some feeling
about in the past, with a pretty fresh outlook. His personal contact with

him started fairly early to enforce this idea that he was a good, strong, tough guy that maybe nobody had thought of."[21]

Before the convention opened and party platform hearings were to be held, a development occurred that made it pretty clear that Nixon would not have to shop around the vice-presidential nomination in order to nail down his own nomination for president. Rockefeller's advance men, counting on their candidate's expensive efforts to boost himself in the polls, orchestrated the flashing of huge spotlight messages on the sides of the major convention hotels that said: ROCKY CAN WIN. But at the same time, the last pre-convention Gallup Poll came out in the *Miami Herald* showing Rockefeller, the self-proclaimed candidate of the people, running only even with Democrat Hubert Humphrey, and Nixon, derided by the Rockefeller strategists as the candidate of the politicians, two points ahead of Humphrey. The air went out of the Rockefeller strategy, even as the spotlights continued to flash their message.

Agnew arrived at the convention in the first days of August still uncommitted in public to any candidate, and holding the Maryland delegation as its favorite son. But the offer to him to nominate Nixon made certain he would deliver most of the delegation. Rockefeller had another private meeting with Agnew but got nothing from him. Other favorite sons such as Romney and Rhodes talked of holding out their delegates to bar a first-ballot Nixon nomination, but the day after Agnew's arrival in Miami Beach he announced he was bowing out as Maryland's favorite son and endorsing Nixon. That was the end of any glimmerings for a stop-Nixon effort.

On endorsing Nixon, Agnew had said it was "not in the cards" for him to be his running mate. But in his speech nominating Nixon, he said all the right things for someone who had his eye on the second spot. "We are a nation in crisis, victimized by crime and conflict, frustrated by fear and failure," he said to a convention hall curious but certainly not mesmerized. "A nation torn by war wants a restoration of peace. A nation plagued by disorder wants a renewal of order. A nation haunted by crime wants a respect for the law. A nation wrenched by division wants a rebirth of unity."[22] He sounded as if he had taken the words right out of Nixon's mouth.

The next night, Nixon watched his first-ballot nomination on television from his luxurious suite at the Hilton Plaza. The roll call dragged on until about 2 A.M., after which he settled in for long deliberations on his choice of a ticketmate. In 1960, he had performed the same routine, calling in party leaders to "consult" while having decided all along to pick Lodge, as a fellow centrist. But in 1960 Lodge was a well-known, highly regarded and prestigious figure in the party, and little vocal opposition was heard. This time around, Nixon wanted to test his surprise choice. So he held three separate meetings, the first with staff and chief supporters, the other two with various party leaders. In each he floated a name that did not come up from any of them until he casually threw it in. Other governors who were in the Nixon camp, like Walter Hickel of Alaska and Tim Babcock of Montana, were invited to the first session, but not Agnew, whose absence apparently caused no stir.

According to participants, many of the twenty-five attendees at the first meeting had been privy to Nixon's earlier musings about looking for a fellow centrist, so much of the talk was about middle-road prospects. Only when Nixon himself offered, "How about Agnew? That was a hell of a nominating speech he made," was the possibility broached, and it got no reaction. Nixon let the discussion go on for a while longer, until he summarized what he had heard, which was what he had wanted to hear. "So your general advice is that I pick a centrist," he said, leaving it at that.[23]

The second meeting was somewhat smaller and was more of a general schmoozing of members of Congress and state party stalwarts, plus a few outsiders like the evangelist Billy Graham, to make them feel they were part of the process. Nixon threw out nine or ten of the names mentioned in the first meeting, including the again-absent Agnew's, with no particular emphasis or reaction.

Barry Goldwater was among the attendees, and he reported later that on the way out of the room Nixon walked him to the door. It was now around five-thirty. "He put his arm around me," Goldwater said. "'Could you live with Agnew?' he asked. 'Hell, yes,' I told him, 'he's the best man you could have. He's been firm, and so what if he's not known? No vice president ever is.'"[24] (Goldwater certainly could vouch for that. Four years earlier, as the party's presidential nominee, he had chosen sharp-tongued Representative William E. Miller of New York, a near-invisible face in the crowd picked, he explained, because "he drives Lyndon Johnson nuts!")[25]

By this time Nixon had clearly convinced himself that his inclination for a centrist of low profile was the right solution. But because there had been a lack of enthusiasm for Agnew, one insider said later, Nixon decided to pause in the process and rest for an hour before holding a third meeting, the smallest. It was confined to the Senate and House minority leaders, Everett Dirksen and Gerald Ford, Republican National Chairman Ray Bliss, and a few other legislators and state leaders. One of Nixon's closest friends, Lieutenant Governor Bob Finch of California, was a repeater from the second session, and again no Agnew.

The talk once more was of middle-road prospects, and this time Nixon mentioned Governor John Volpe of Massachusetts, Senator Howard Baker of Tennessee and—Agnew. The mentions again drew little enthusiasm. So Nixon decided on one more, unannounced, meeting with only six insiders: Mitchell; Bob Haldeman, the campaign chief of staff; Congressman Rogers Morton, the convention floor manager; Bob Ellsworth, the chief delegate hunter; Senator John Tower, his chief southern ally; and Finch again.

In addition to Volpe, Baker, and Agnew, Morton and Finch were thrown into the pot by Nixon. Baker was considered too inexperienced, Morton only a congressman, and Finch only a lieutenant governor and also a Nixon crony. Volpe as an Italian Catholic drew some comment, but he had lost his own state's primary against a Rockefeller write-in, and chances of a Republican's carrying Massachusetts in any event were slim. Finally, Nixon asked, according to a participant, "Who should I take?"

One of the group suddenly spoke up. "I think it should be Finch," he said. "You know him, you know you can trust him, you know he can handle himself. And he doesn't have to be built up nationally." But Mitchell wouldn't hear of it. "You can't do it, it's nepotism," he told Nixon. Finch, highly agitated, jumped up. "No, I won't do it!" he said. "I won't put myself through it." He cited personal family stresses and said he was not going to go through a national campaign. Nixon called him into an anteroom alone. After a few minutes of private talk, they returned, with Finch calmed down and Nixon behind him.[26] [26] The nominee turned to Morton, a Marylander, and according to Nixon himself later, asked him for a frank appraisal of Agnew, his former governor. Morton thought a moment and said Agnew had a tendency to be "lazy." To which Nixon replied: "Rog, maybe you would be the better choice for me," but Morton told him: "If it's between me and Ted Agnew, Ted would be the better choice."[27] So after checking once more with Mitchell, Nixon turned to Morton and said: "Call Agnew."[28]

The news was not a total surprise to Agnew, who was waiting in his suite at the Eden Roc, down Collins Avenue. Two nights earlier, he had informed an old friend, Walter Jones, that he had been told he was one of about ten being considered, and later one of four. By the time Morton got around to calling him after the marathon meetings, it was a little past noon. He took the phone from his closest aide, Stanley Blair, and heard Morton say: "Ted, are you sitting down?" "Yes," Agnew replied. "Good, because you'd better," Morton said. "I've got a man who wants to talk to you." Nixon got on and broke the news. The conversation was short. Agnew accepted, saying he was greatly honored, then turned to his wife Judy and told her: "I'm it."[29]

When Nelson Rockefeller learned of Nixon's choice, he told me: "I talked to Strom Thurmond that night, and he was describing how they had picked. He said the basis of the selection of Mr. Agnew was that he was the least worst of the candidates that were proposed by Mr. Nixon. That was his description."[30]

But Nixon had his own view. In revealing the surprise choice to the campaign press corps, he said: "All of you know, from having covered me since the early days in New Hampshire, the emphasis I put on the vice presidency and the need for selecting a man who was, first, qualified to be president; second, one who could campaign effectively, and, third, one who could assume the new responsibilities that I will give the new vice president, particularly in the area of the problems of the states and cities."[31] Actually, few could recall his having said much about it. At the mention of Agnew, the crowd's gasp was audible. Nixon, obviously pleased that he had sprung a surprise, strode out, smiling, as the phrase "Spiro who?" entered the political lexicon.

For all of Nixon's emphasis on Agnew's experience in local affairs, he later wrote in his memoirs why he really picked him. "From a strictly political standpoint," Nixon said, "Agnew fit perfectly with the strategy we had devised for the November election. With George Wallace in the race, I could not hope to sweep the South. It was absolutely necessary, therefore, to win the entire rimland of the South—the border states—as well as the major states of the Midwest and West. Agnew fit the bill geographically, and as a political moderate he fit it philosophically." Nixon added that "in my two meetings with him before the convention I never raised the possibility that he might be considered for the vice presidential spot" (this after writing in the same memoir that Mitchell had held out that very prospect).[32]

Agnew, after watching Nixon's announcement on television, paid a call on him in his suite and then went downstairs for a press conference of his own. After acknowledging that he was "stunned" at the selection, he fielded a series of questions about his positions on civil rights. He vowed his support, but noted that "I expect fully that no civil rights can be realistically achieved without the restoration of order, without the abandonment of the condoning of civil disobedience." The remark was a pretty good encapsulation of what he would be preaching through the fall campaign. He concluded by acknowledging that "the name of Spiro Agnew is not a household name. I certainly hope that it will become one within the next couple of months." It was a hope that would be realized beyond his imagination.[33]

In selecting Agnew, Nixon had expected that the choice would be seen as centrist. But both conservatives and liberals in the party, especially those who knew of Agnew's recent racial complaints, saw it otherwise. The conservatives were elated. Reagan praised the selection, saying Agnew "stands very strong on what I think is going to be the number-one issue in the campaign—law and order."[34]

The liberals viewed the Marylander as a defector who had been paid off for switching from Rockefeller to Nixon, and some of them urged John Lindsay to challenge Agnew for the vice-presidential nomination on the convention floor. The Nixon strategists quickly snuffed out that notion by recruiting Lindsay, and also Percy, to second Agnew's nomination, to be put before the hall by Morton. Some die-hard liberals persisted, however, and persuaded the hapless George Romney to run in Lindsay's place. On the first ballot, he was snowed under: Agnew 1,120 votes, Romney 186.

In his brief acceptance speech after Nixon had spoken, Agnew was appropriately humble. He sought to put the best face on what had been a rare rebuke—a floor challenge to the traditional right of the presidential nominee to choose his running mate. Agnew elected to cast it as no more than a tribute to Romney.

"As a political animal and a relatively sensitive individual who hopes he will never lose his sensitivity," he said, "I am not unaware of what took place in this convention hall tonight. I am aware that the reasons that motivated it were not directed at me in any personal sense and were merely responsive of the opinions of those that took part in the nomination of that great governor of Michigan."

Agnew then proceeded with fawning gratitude to put himself completely in the service of Richard Nixon. He said he recognized "that a vice-presidential nominee does not come to the successful fruition of his nomination by virtue of his personality or his attractiveness or his ability to generate a wave of enthusiasm on his own. He comes here because he is the selection of the man who does all those things on his own, the presidential nominee. I am privileged that that great future president of the United States, Richard M. Nixon, has seen fit to invest in me his confidence to do the job. But I will not be satisfied, ladies and gentlemen, until I prove to you that I am capable of doing a job for the Republican Party and the American people in November."[35]

In the next two months of the presidential campaign, Spiro T. Agnew would prove in unanticipated ways his capability in the first regard, if not the second. He would succeed in making himself a household name, though not always in the way he had intended. On the last night of the convention, Nixon's only expressed reservation about his choice was, ironically as matters turned out, about his speech-making ability. He told William Safire, one of his speechwriters: "Agnew's a tough, shrewd Greek. We've got to figure a way to sell him. He can't give a speech worth a damn, but he's not going to fall apart.... He wears well. Get him on press conferences, panel shows, talking about the cities, answering questions, but no set speeches. He's no speechmaker."[36]

The next day, Nixon told reporters he had no doubt that he had made the right decision on his running mate. At a press party at his Key Biscayne retreat, the talk got around to that surprise selection. "There is a mysticism about men," the presidential nominee fulsomely pontificated about Agnew. "There is a quiet confidence. You look a man in the eye and you know he's got it—brains. This guy has got it. If he doesn't, Nixon has made a bum choice."[37]

Between then and election day in November and beyond, Richard Nixon would have cause to ponder that comment. But for now he basked in his own political astuteness in plucking a relative unknown to be his campaign sidekick and, if they succeeded, his presidential stand-in. In Agnew's winning campaign for governor in 1966, his campaign song, based on the Frank Sinatra hit "Chicago," proclaimed: "My kind of man, Ted Agnew is." That, indeed, seemed to be Dick Nixon's confident reading as the team of Nixon and Agnew sallied forth after Labor Day against the Democratic lineup of Vice President Hubert H. Humphrey and Senator Edmund S. Muskie of Maine.

The Republican team brought together two men of similar beginnings and backgrounds but strikingly different temperaments, yet at the outset they seemed to develop a personal rapport. Each came from a relatively humble start. Born and raised at opposite sides of the continent, Nixon was the son of a small-town grocer in the town of Yorba Linda, not far from Los Angeles, Agnew the son of the proprietor of a small restaurant in Baltimore. As boys, both were avid readers and grew up in serious, disciplined homes of hardship but not deprivation, with hard-working fathers and strong-willed mothers. Reserved by nature, both were encouraged to learn the piano, which in time provided them with what limited entry they had into local and school social circles.

Neither was very athletic, though Nixon did become a scrub on the Whittier College football team, and Agnew played tennis on a neighborhood court and took chemistry courses at Johns Hopkins University but dropped out. Neither was much of a ladies' man; an Agnew classmate said he doubted that young Ted, as he was called, ever had a date in high school.[38] As for Nixon, his shy romance with fellow would-be thespian Thelma "Pat" Ryan became part of his personal lore.

Both young men served as junior officers in World War II—Nixon in the navy, Agnew in the army. Nixon, known in the service as "Nick," was a transportation officer in the South Pacific only on the fringes of combat, winning a reputation as a shrewd poker player. Agnew was an infantry officer in a close-in support unit in the Battle of the Bulge that later moved deep into southeastern Germany. Both attended law school, Nixon at Duke, Agnew taking night courses at the University of Baltimore, and both started in active politics as Republicans, though Nixon at a relatively higher level than his new running mate.

Nixon's political beginning was the well-known stuff of Hollywood movie-making; just out of the navy, he was recruited by a search committee for a candidate for Congress. When General George Patton, the World War II hero, said he wasn't interested, and when the remaining frontrunner suddenly died, Nixon was selected, and elected to the House of Representatives in a tough Red-baiting campaign against liberal Democrat Jerry Voorhis.[39] He then went on to the United States Senate and the vice presidency, and his party's presidential nomination in 1960.

By contrast, Agnew had a rougher climb. After seeing combat in the Battle of the Bulge, he resumed night law school in Baltimore, then started his own small law firm. When it failed, he took a job as an insurance claims investigator and adjuster. He answered a newspaper advertisement and became an assistant personnel manager for a local supermarket chain.

Recalled into the army in the Korean War, he served at camps in Maryland and Georgia and escaped another overseas assignment when the army acknowledged it had mistakenly called up an overseas combat veteran, and released him. Back at the supermarket chain, he handled petty tasks that included dealing with shoplifters. Restless, he briefly joined a local law firm and then started another of his own in which he represented the meat-cutters and butchers' union in its negotiations with Baltimore area stores, winning strong contracts for 500 black fishermen. In the mid-1950s, he went back to night school to study accounting at Johns Hopkins, took a new law partner, and moved out to Towson, the Baltimore County seat.

The move marked his immersion in suburban life, complete with PTA and Kiwanis attendance, bowling nights, Baltimore Colts worship, and neighborhood parties with Ted often at the piano. Soon he got involved in a successful charter reform effort for the county and switched his registration from Democratic to Republican on the advice of a local judge. After the local GOP won control of the county council, he was appointed in 1957 to the county board of appeals, which reviewed zoning decisions, at a salary of $3,600, and became chairman the next year.[40]

In 1960, as Richard Nixon was running unsuccessfully for the presidency, Agnew ran for a county circuit court judgeship; also like Nixon, who subsequently ran for governor in California and lost again, Agnew was down but not out. Though he also suffered another loss, in a bid for a county council seat, Agnew was picked by the Republican Party as a proven good-government candidate and was elected Baltimore County executive, backing among other things a public-accommodations bill. A split in Democratic ranks benefited him in that race, as did another one in 1966, when Agnew chose to run for governor. Campaigning as a moderate with a record (disputed by liberal Democrats) as an effective conciliator in the field of civil rights, he supported a housing-discrimination ban. The Maryland Democrats self-immolated in a three-man primary fight in which Mahoney, the ultraconservative perennial candidate, emerged with the nomination. Democratic-majority Maryland was appalled, and Agnew as the anybody-but-Mahoney Republican nominee was swept into the governor's chair.[41]

As similar as the new Republican running mates were in their unpretentious beginnings, they were strikingly different in style and temperament. Nixon from his earliest years was a bundle of insecurities and self-doubts that were manifested in a transparent inferiority complex, which he endured through a lifelong struggle belying his impressive accomplishments in public life. While he was outwardly cordial in public, he was suspicious of everyone, friend and foe alike, and shunned personal confrontation. He preferred the comfort of addressing large crowds from a distance, and there was little brilliance or poetry in his oratory. He abhorred one-on-one meetings except with his most trusted aides, and he almost always delegated the delivery of unpleasant or difficult messages. He was afflicted with a debilitating sense of inferiority that he often tried to masquerade with tough talk in private. He was self-conscious about his appearance, awkwardness, and ill-at-ease nature. He seemed to question his own manliness and was overly impressed by big, handsome, and commanding males, almost to the point of envy for their presence, their confidence, and their easy assertiveness. He was largely a man without genuine humor, or much of an ability to appreciate that of others. His jokes were often self-deprecatory but delivered self-consciously, and in attempts to put others at ease, he usually failed.

Agnew, by contrast, brimmed with a self-confidence and self-esteem that enabled him to accept with alacrity his steady climb up the ladder of public success. Even as Nixon's own successes never seemed to convince him adequately of his own worth, Agnew's merely confirmed to him his personal assurance that he could handle whatever came his way. Nixon, for all his efforts, was physically uncoordinated and a nondescript dresser; Agnew was smooth, elegant, and supremely sure of himself. He carried himself erectly and was a clothes horse, immaculate in dress and fastidious in his grooming, with his thinning hair always plastered in place. He was often aloof even to the point of exuding a sense of superiority, and not only did not shirk confrontation but invited it. He loved the sound of his own voice, and the extravagant vocabulary it commanded. He was head-strong and unwavering in his convictions and at the same time intolerant toward those who disagreed with him, and often oblivious of their feelings.

If there was one thing about which these very strange bedfellows saw eye to eye, it was in their loathing of the press and television commentators. It was a shared repulsion that in a short time would be a centerpiece of their political message, voiced most aggressively by Agnew and lauded by Nixon the harsher and more pointedly his running mate delivered it. But regarding many other matters and circumstances, their differences bore seeds of conflict that would be obvious to insiders as their political marriage ran its course. For now, however, they approached the fall campaign with great optimism, against a Democratic team already burdened by internal dissension over a stalemated war in Vietnam and the discredited president forced to the sidelines in large part by his failure to end it.

Chapter 3

NIXON'S NIXON

Aₗₘₒₛₜ from the start in the fall campaign of 1968, Republican vice-presidential nominee Spiro Agnew gave the man at the top of the ticket reasons to second-guess himself on his choice. For openers, the press reaction to his nomination was not at all what Nixon expected. The press often cast him as right-wing extremist, not the centrist Nixon and Agnew himself perceived him to be.

In an interview in his Eden Roc suite the day after his nomination and speech, Agnew complained that "it's being made to appear that I'm a little to the right of King Lear," who, he said, "reserved to himself the right to behead people." The thought set him off on a long defense of his civil rights record in Maryland as Baltimore County executive and governor. "This is hard to take for a guy who passed the first local public-accommodation legislation south of the Mason-Dixon line," he said. "For the son of an immigrant who felt the sting of discrimination, it's hard to be referred to as a bigot. I think it should be perfectly obvious that if my civil rights position were what has been depicted, John Lindsay would never have seconded my nomination and neither would Chuck Percy. And since Mr. Nixon sees my role in the cities as vital during the campaign, I would never be effective in those areas. But that doesn't mean that I condone violence."[1]

These remarks revealed not only Agnew's thin skin politically but also his determination not to be a drag on Richard Nixon's presidential bid. As a political figure who had come from nowhere, and as he had made clear in his acceptance speech, Agnew's gratitude to Nixon was deep, and a psychological weight on him as the fall campaign began.

The first order of business after the convention, and a courtesy call by Nixon and Agnew on President Lyndon Johnson at his Texas ranch, was an intensive planning meeting of two weeks in San Diego, at a nearby resort called Mission Bay. In keeping with Nixon's microscopic review of his failed 1960 presidential effort, with an eye to correct its mistakes and misjudgments, Nixon and his strategists had already decided that tighter communication between the presidential and vice-presidential campaigns would be imperative. The notion had nothing to do with Agnew, who at that time had not yet been selected, and everything to do with Lodge, whose 1960 performance was rated as wanting. Nixon himself had said in an interview in Oregon before the convention: "Haunting this campaign is the specter of 1960."[2] Around that time, it was settled that John Sears would travel with the vice-presidential nominee to make sure any gaffes could quickly be assessed and dealt with by "the mother plane" flying Nixon around the country.

At the same time, Nixon was mindful of the difficulties he had experienced as Eisenhower's running mate in 1952, when the so-called Checkers scandal broke and Ike's strategists plotted to knock him off the ticket. Although Eisenhower finally embraced him, he remembered that it had taken a long time to smooth things over. Nixon was determined that he would not treat his running mate in the same shabby fashion. According to Sears, whenever Agnew made a mistake Nixon would call him "from time to time and tell him, 'Don't sweat it, you're doing a fine job.'"[3]

Nevertheless, there were signs of trouble soon after Agnew joined the team at Mission Bay. According to Pat Buchanan, his high opinion of the new running mate was not shared by two of the most important figures in the campaign and later in the Nixon administration—chief of staff Bob Haldeman and especially domestic affairs adviser John Ehrlichman. They grilled Agnew intensively on a range of issues and were not impressed. The Mission Bay sessions "did not seem to go very well," Buchanan recalled later. Agnew, he said, was not seen then as "a firebrand," rather as merely "a tough law-and-order guy, though a progressive Republican on the environment and things like that."[4] But from the start, Ehrlichman and Agnew appeared to be on a collision course, because Ehrlichman considered domestic affairs to be his bailiwick and

Nixon had pointedly said publicly that he intended to take advantage of Agnew's experience as a governor.

There never was any intention that Nixon and Agnew would campaign together, and they didn't. So the opportunity for any real bonding for the two men on the road (such as conspicuously occurred years later between Democratic presidential nominee Bill Clinton and running mate Al Gore) never presented itself or was purposely arranged. Nixon was a notorious loner, and besides there never was any notion that Nixon and Agnew would be real partners in the campaign, or later. As Eisenhower's running mate in 1952 and 1956, Nixon had learned his "place," and he saw Agnew as his number two in the same light, regardless of what he said to the contrary.

A major factor that conditioned the use of Agnew in the campaign was the thought that he could be an effective counter to Wallace in the South. That was especially so as his views on racial violence had emerged from his experience in Baltimore with the black leaders in the wake of riots after the King assassination. "We always knew," Sears said later, "that it would depend on whether the number two man was a little to the left or a fellow who was to the right, as to how we'd use him." Agnew, he said, "by that time anyway, was beginning to appear to be more and more a fellow to the right, even though he had this background of how he had come to office [against segregationist Mahoney]. So things like schedule were reevaluated, and he started right out of the box viewed as a fellow who could be used to hold the party together in its conservative wing, and helpful against Wallace."[5]

At the same time, the Nixon strategists decided it was also imperative to shore up Agnew's centrist credentials in the eyes of the rest of the electorate. For this reason, on his first campaign swing he was sent to the Midwest, where he spoke to the annual Veterans of Foreign Wars Convention in Detroit and addressed not the Vietnam War but social justice at home.

"You know how strongly I feel about the absolute necessity for respect of law," he told the predominantly white audience, "but that's not the whole answer. With law and order must come justice and equal opportunity. Law and order must mean to all of our people the protection of the innocent—not, to some people, the cracking of black skulls." In words that almost sounded as if he were lecturing himself for his outburst against the Baltimore black leaders, Agnew said: "In our frailty and human selfishness, we have too often shut our minds and our consciences to our black countrymen. We need to respond to conscience rather than react to violence. We must aggressively move for progress—not out of fear of reprisal, but out of certain faith that it is right."[6]

Agnew did a good job with set speeches and texts, but from the outset some of his extemporaneous remarks revealed a lack of political sensitivity that caused concern in the Nixon camp. At a farm in Cedar Rapids, Iowa, he was taken to look at the pigs. Apparently they brought to his mind the "nomination" of a porker at the Democratic presidential convention during a Yippies anti-war demonstration. Trying to be funny, he wondered aloud whether "they came from Chicago" and, addressing one of the pigs, said, "Hello, Alice." Then, apparently thinking he might be offending human Alices, he explained it was the first name that came to him, and said "it could just as well have been Mabel," thus doubling the crop of potential offended ladies.[7]

Neither humor nor striking a defensive pose, however, came naturally to Agnew, and before long he was back on the offensive, with young protesters his favorite target. He blamed an "overly permissive society" for tolerating an "unconscious anarchy" in the country. "I wanted to do a lot of silly things when I was that age, too, but my parents wouldn't let me," he said. "It was that simple. If you tell me the hippies and the Yippies are going to be able to do the job of helping America, I'll tell you this: They can't run a bus, they can't serve in a government office, they can't run a lathe in a factory. All they can do is lay [sic] down in the park and sleep, or kick policemen." In one speech in New York, he said he saw a "definite link" between rebellious students on campuses and the communists. On NBC News's *Meet the Press*, he charged that they were "under control of the Communist Party U.S.A. or of Moscow."[8]

When Hubert Humphrey at one point called Nixon "a cold warrior," a rather mild reference for the time, Agnew went after him. "If you've been soft on inflation, soft on communism, and soft on law and order over the years," he said, "I guess other people look hard." The words "soft on communism," a carryover from the Red-baiting of Senator Joe McCarthy a decade earlier, hit a particularly jarring note among Democrats. Agnew made it more jarring to them by saying: "When you see the similarities between now and before the war, Humphrey is beginning to look a lot like Neville Chamberlain. Maybe that makes Mr. Nixon look more like Winston Churchill."[9]

Comparing Humphrey to the architect of the Munich pact of appeasement of Hitler, and Nixon to Britain's savior from Nazism, made the Democrats apoplectic, to the consternation of Nixon strategists who were working hard to bury their own man's reputation for character assassination. But Agnew went blissfully on. He accused reporters of attempting to "build these catch phrases into something they don't mean," and insisted he had "no desire to go back to the Joe McCarthy witch-hunting days." The reaction to those days, he said, "has been an overreaction. When you see communist involvement all over the world, it is pretty unrealistic to say it can't happen here. A certain measure of it is happening here."[10]

The more Agnew talked, the more it was like striking a match to gasoline, but he wouldn't back down. In a Washington news conference, he said Humphrey seemed to be for "peace at any price," not that different from Chamberlain's infamous reference to "peace in our time" in giving Czechoslovakia over to Hitler. He and Nixon, he said, were "not going to be squishy soft as this administration has been" on crime and "knowing your enemies," adding: "I guess by nature I'm a counterpuncher. You can't hit my team in the groin and expect me to stand here and smile about it."[11] Calling Nixon a "cold warrior" didn't seem a particularly low blow, but Agnew in defending himself characterized it as such.

The Nixon strategists saw nothing wrong with Agnew's backing up the head of the Republican ticket, but the way he had chosen to do so made them nervous. After all, one of their own prime challenges was to counter Nixon's clinging reputation as a political hatchet man who had alleged Democratic associations with communism in his climb to the political stratosphere. Pinning communism on his opponents had won his seat first in the House of Representatives and then in the Senate, and as Dwight Eisenhower's campaign hit man he had used the same general theme to run down the whole Democratic Party. He was the hard-hitting campaigner who accused Harry Truman's secretary of state, Dean Acheson, of "color-blindness—a form of pink eye toward the communist threat," and who called Truman, Acheson, and the 1952 and 1956 Democratic presidential nominee, Adlai Stevenson, "traitors to the high principles" of their party.[12]

As the old Nixon was busy selling a new Nixon to the voters, the last thing he needed was his running mate reminding voters of the old. Mary McGrory of the *Washington Star* wrote that "the governor of Maryland has been attempting to prove that the old Richard Nixon is alive and well in Spiro T. Agnew."[13] The "Tricky Dick" label was one skeleton his campaign needed to keep in the closet, and here was his ticketmate dragging his own replica into the open when the campaign had barely started.

Agnew, however, seemed oblivious that in raising the communism issue he was behaving like a Nixon clone. "Don't get left with the impression that my campaign is going to be a communist hunt," he told reporters.[14] But two Republican leaders, Senate Majority Leader Everett Dirksen and House Majority Leader Gerald Ford, immediately distanced themselves from the remarks on Humphrey, saying they saw "no evidence" of the charge that he was "soft on communism."

Surprisingly, nothing was heard from Nixon or his strategists on "the mother plane" about Agnew's remarks. The presidential nominee was holding to his personal assurance to his running mate that he wouldn't be held on a short leash the way Eisenhower's managers had gripped him. But as traveling reporters continued to pepper Agnew about his references to Humphrey, the candidate himself began to get worried, and so did Sears. His Nixon-assigned watcher finally told Agnew in his motel room that it might be best if he issued some kind of apology to Humphrey and put the matter behind him. So Agnew called a news conference and did exactly that—in his fashion.

"The remarks I made that have been widely quoted concerning Vice President Humphrey must be examined in the context they were offered," he began. After reviewing the exchange between himself and Humphrey prompted by Humphrey's labeling of Nixon as a "cold warrior," Agnew said: "If I left the impression that I think the vice president was not a loyal American, I want to rectify that. I think he is a man of great integrity and I have a high respect for him." But not satisfied with that, he continued: "I don't agree with him on every issue, and the use of the comparison to Mr. Chamberlain and Mr. Churchill I think is a completely valid comparison. I think Mr. Chamberlain considered himself to be a very loyal Englishman. There were many people in England at the time he made his cry for peace at any price that believed this was a proper cry to make. He made it in good conscience and I think the comparison stands."[15]

When a reporter asked him whether he was cognizant of the derogatory connotation of "soft on communism" in American politics, Agnew said no. "Had I ever realized the effect that this expression would have," he said, "I would have shunned it like the plague. My record is not one of sympathy to inquisitorial procedures." Had he known his remark would have been interpreted "in some way to cast me as the Joe McCarthy of 1968," he said, "I would have turned five somersaults to avoid saying it."[16]

Nixon's running mate insisted that his comments on Humphrey were not part of any "grand strategy" in the Republican campaign. He said he had heard nothing from Nixon or any of his aides to indicate "there is any desire for me to retract or soft-pedal anything I have said." Nixon had chosen him, he said, "because he thought I had sufficient inherent good judgment and tact and decency to avoid these things. Now, I have never been one to go the low road in politics. I want to get off the low road. . . . I said 'squishy soft' and I am not proud of it. The vice president said 'wiggly and wobbly' [about Nixon] and I doubt if he is proud of that."[17]

The reporters were not satisfied, particularly about the Chamberlain comparison. Asked what evidence he had that Humphrey sought "peace at any price," Agnew said that an expression of hope by Humphrey that American forces could start leaving Vietnam in early 1969 amounted to that if he "fully expected to achieve those ends without a move by North Vietnam to protect the integrity of our forces."[18] In fact, in 1969 such forces did start leaving Vietnam without such a move by Hanoi, as part of the Nixon administration's Vietnamization policy.

A call finally came to Sears from Nixon's chief of staff, Haldeman. Before he could raise questions about Agnew's comments, Sears told him the matter had already been discussed with the vice-presidential nominee and had been handled. Haldeman said no more about it. Nixon personally not only was holding to his commitment to Agnew not to look over his shoulder; there was evidence he liked what his running mate was saying. When one of his speechwriters, William Safire, told Nixon at one point that columnists were sharply criticizing his running mate, he shot back: "You know why they're screaming at Agnew? Because he's hitting where it hurts."[19]

Soon, however, his running mate demonstrated again that such independence was politically foolhardy. At another news conference in Chicago, a reporter observed that there weren't many blacks in the crowds greeting Agnew and asked him whether he was at all concerned. "That hasn't occurred to me," he answered. "Very frankly, when I am moving in a crowd, I don't look and say, 'Well, there's a Negro, there's an Italian, and there's a Greek and there's a Polack.' I'm just trying to meet the people and I'm just glad that they're there and that they're friendly."[20]

At once, Agnew recognized that he had used an ethnic slur and told his entourage privately he knew he had screwed up. At first the remark went unreported. One of the traveling reporters, Robert Shogan, then of *Newsweek*, wasn't sure he had heard Agnew right and asked colleagues. "It was so unbelievable some weren't sure he'd said it," Shogan recalled later. "And if he did, was he kidding? How do you handle a thing like that? Nobody knew how to handle it. But here it came right on the heels of 'squishy soft.' It started to ooze out. It was a thrill a minute. This was a guy, we suddenly realized, who was saying anything that came into his head. . . . It said something about him."[21]

More examples of why Agnew deserved a short leash began cropping up in clusters. On a television panel interview in Chicago, he condemned all kinds of civil disobedience, prompting a question whether it wasn't so that "Jesus, Mahatma Gandhi, Henry Thoreau, and Dr. Martin Luther King" had practiced it. "Let me distinguish between those cases," he answered. "The people you have mentioned did not operate in a free society"—which certainly would have been a surprise to Thoreau and King.[22]

AFTER MORE OF THE SAME, "the mother plane" finally decided that Ted Agnew needed more help in finding the high road he had said he would make sure to travel after the fuss over his Humphrey remarks. An old Nixon speechwriter, Stephen Hess, was assigned, an Eisenhower administration veteran who had gone on to work for Nixon's 1960 and 1962 campaigns. Although the decision to dispatch Hess had pre-dated the recent Agnew flaps, his arrival at this period had all the appearances of a rescue operation. Indeed, columnists Rowland Evans and Robert Novak wrote that Hess was embarked on just such an effort, which did not sit well with the proud Agnew. After delivering one Hess speech, prompting

New York Times reporter Homer Bigart to write that Agnew had indeed used a text, the candidate refused to read any further Hess efforts. The new arrival was reduced to writing erudite position papers that Agnew routinely approved but, Hess speculated, never bothered to read.

Agnew's staff was peopled with old Maryland associates with whom he spent most of his time on the plane. Only occasionally would he venture out of the front cabin to the back, where the reporters, many of them veterans of his gubernatorial stint in Annapolis, sat and worked, and with whom he had cool relations. Attempts at levity usually fell flat. On a trip that eventually would reach Hawaii, a reporter asked him whether he would be going swimming there. Agnew, pinching a roll of flat on each side of his waist, said no, he didn't want to reveal his "love handles." The remark seemed out of character for the proper and distant candidate, doing nothing to dispel the climate of discomfort between him and the traveling press.

That atmosphere only deepened a few days later when the Agnew party, after an overnight stay in Las Vegas, headed west on the campaign plane. The night before, several of the traveling reporters had stayed up late gambling in one of the casino hotels and were sleeping off their folly when Agnew strolled back drinking a cup of coffee. One of the snoozers was Gene Oishi, a stocky native-born Japanese-American who covered him in Baltimore and Annapolis for the *Baltimore Sun*. Agnew glanced at the sleeping reporter and said to another reporter, Dick Homan of *The Washington Post*: "What's the matter with the fat Jap?" Homan, surprised, answered: "He was up all night in the casino." With that, Oishi awoke and said to the candidate: "That was a wicked city you took us to, Mr. Agnew."[23] In a moment, Agnew walked off.

Other reporters were startled by Agnew's remark. They asked Oishi whether he had such a nickname in Annapolis, and he said he did not. At first the incident generated some light banter among the reporters and between them and the Agnew staff. At one point a reporter sent a note up to the candidate's compartment that said: "Agnew is a thin-skinned, squishy-soft Greek with love handles."[24] Some of Oishi's colleagues wanted to write about the episode, but he discouraged them, considering the remark merely a bumbling attempt to be funny or friendly. But when the entourage reached Los Angeles, Oishi phoned his wife and mentioned Agnew's crack, and she was furious. So he agreed to have other reporters write about it and Homan did so, burying Agnew's question to Oishi in the very last paragraph of his story, inside the paper. But it was picked up by a Honolulu paper and splashed across its front page. While some of the reporters dismissed the remark as casual banter and said writing about it was sophomoric, others felt that competitive pressure—being beaten on a story—dictated joining in.

Some of the Agnew staff, going into damage-control mode, suggested that Oishi had really looked ill and Agnew had merely expressed concern, but the eyewitness reporters were not buying. The more some of them thought about the incident, the more they believed it was another example of Agnew's insensitivity, part of a pattern that warranted mention and analysis in print. Agnew in turn felt the accompanying press was going out of its way to "get" him by making a mountain out of a molehill. If he never felt particularly kindly to the press, his attitude was hardening into hostility, even as Nixon continued to reassure him. In reference to Agnew's explanation that he had called Oishi "the fat Jap" in a friendly way, Nixon sent him a revealing note: "Dear Ted: When news is concerned, nobody in the press is a friend—they are all enemies."[25]

It was unfortunate for Agnew that his traveling party was now in Hawaii, heavily populated by Japanese-Americans. One of them, Democratic representative Spark Matsunaga, lectured him on the House floor that "one does not win friends by insulting people of other racial backgrounds, particularly through the mouthings of racial prejudice."[26]

There was some discussion within the Agnew party on whether he should continue the Hawaii visit. Sears recommended that he do so and so advised the Nixon plane, and there was no disagreement or lecture from Nixon. Incredibly, the next morning aboard a smaller plane for some island-hopping, Agnew walked back again, spotted Oishi, and said: "How's the fat Jap this morning?" When other reporters told him it wasn't funny, Agnew was moved at a lavish luau on one of the islands to deliver another long defense, citing his own sensitivity as a boy to being called a Greek. He ended by apologizing "to any who might have read in my words an insult to their Japanese ancestry, or [referring to the previous ethnic slur] to any who might have read into my words an insult to their Polish ancestry. . . . Those who have misread my words, I only say you've misread my heart."[27]

Later, however, at a fence-mending party for the traveling press, the sparring began again over an attack Agnew had made in San Francisco against the appointment of Black Panther leader Eldridge Cleaver, once convicted of attempted murder, as a part-time lecturer at the University of California. The conversation spread to the homosexuality of Oscar Wilde and another flippant Agnew remark. It seemed that every time Agnew or his staff attempted to smooth things over, more controversy resulted. On return to the mainland, Agnew spoke at the National Press Club in Washington and said in yet another attempt at levity that since there had been so much speculation "on the Nixon–Agnew strategy, I have Dick's permission to reveal my secret role in our battle plans. I'm assigned the task of insulting all groups equally."[28]

Through all of Agnew's early campaign tribulations, it had to be remembered that Richard Nixon not only had selected him as his running mate but also had gone out on a limb in boasting about his own ability to size up a winner, and what a great choice he had made in the Maryland governor. He was not at this stage inclined to tear him down, even as his principal strategists were concerned about Agnew's bloopers and demonstrated insensitivity. Nixon wrote later: "No one felt worse than Agnew about such embarrassing misjudgments, and I admired him for the way he stood up to the vicious onslaught of national political exposure—the cruel cartoons, the slashing attacks, the stinging commentaries. I tried to reassure him, telling him that these efforts were mainly a way of using him to get at me."[29]

At one point, Buchanan, who liked Agnew, volunteered to switch from the Nixon plane to the Agnew plane to help him out, and Nixon and Haldeman agreed. "Nixon was just giving the same speech day in and day out," Buchanan remembered. "He kept up with the same game plan and sort of froze the ball and coasted." So Buchanan felt he wasn't needed there. When he got to the Agnew plane, he said, "the hostility of the press corps you could cut with a knife." Buchanan found Agnew in a depressed mood. "The idea that he was a drag on the ticket very much bothered him," Buchanan recalled, "but we got some of that behind him, and Nixon asked me to come back."[30]

❧ ☙

THE MONTH OF SEPTEMBER had been a testing ground for Agnew as a national campaigner, and he had not weathered it well. But one of the main reasons Nixon had chosen him for the ticket, as already noted, was his conviction that Agnew could be an effective counter against the strength of independent candidate George Wallace in the South. Wallace, however, was also demonstrating unexpected political appeal in areas of the North, and the time had come to make use of Agnew's hard-hitting law-and-order rhetoric there as well, to counter the feisty former Alabama governor.

In the campaign's efforts to undercut Wallace's strength, Agnew toured northern and border blue-collar enclaves, focusing now on targets likely to generate support for the Republican ticket. He went to the south side of Milwaukee and castigated student protesters as "spoiled brats who never have had a good spanking" and "take their tactics from Gandhi and money from Daddy." Wallace himself might have admired such phrases, which were not unlike his own.

In Cape Girardeau, Missouri, Raleigh, North Carolina, and Jacksonville, Florida, all in potential Wallace country, Agnew urged voters not to waste their ballots on Wallace as a candidate who couldn't be elected president. In all these places, he sold himself not as a centrist but unabashedly as a right-of-center candidate with a hard-line message. He criticized Muskie, his Democratic counterpart in the race, for once having watched idly while young men burned their draft cards. Such behavior, he said, was "inherent in the total permissive atmosphere that is sweeping the country, the atmosphere that allows irresponsible conduct." Addressing the poor and youthful dissenters in Indianapolis, he let them know who would be in charge: "We will listen to your complaints. You may give us your symptoms [but] we will make the diagnosis and we, the establishment, for which I make no apologies for being part of, will implement the cure."[31]

As a diagnostician of urban problems, however, Agnew was a doctor who didn't make house calls. At a press brunch in Pittsburgh, he was asked why, in light of his claim to be an urban specialist, he didn't venture into big-city ghettos. He responded that he didn't think "there's any particular gain to be made by debating on street corners. . . . You don't learn from people suffering from poverty, but from experts who have studied the problem."

A couple of days later, the same question came up in Detroit, with its share of low-income and racial ghettos. "I've been into many of them," he said, "and to some extent, I'd have to say this: If you've seen one city slum, you've seen them all. . . . I don't think it is imperative that I conduct showboat appearances through ghetto areas to prove I know something about the problems of the cities."[32] The response was a far cry from what he had said on the day Nixon chose him as his running mate, when he declared that he would "welcome the chance" to run in Northern ghettos.

Such remarks sent off more rockets among Nixon's strategists, but not for Nixon himself, who saw Agnew as a lightning rod drawing the flashes away from him. "The manure wasn't sticking to him," an aide said later, "and Agnew was becoming pretty popular in the South."[33] Agnew himself was upset because in press comparisons with Muskie, he was coming off as a bumbler and buffoon. On Sundays, when the campaigning tapered off or came to a complete halt, Nixon would phone Agnew and tell him not to sweat it, that he was still Nixon's man.

By this time in the campaign—late October—there was another reason for Agnew not to visit the slums, or for that matter anywhere else of political importance. It was the same reason that was keeping Nixon himself on a very confined travel schedule: the public-opinion polls showing the Nixon–Agnew ticket, for all of Agnew's gaffes, had settled into a modest but seemingly safe plurality lead at about 43 percent, with Humphrey rising somewhat but Wallace slipping. The assumption in the Nixon camp was that the Republican ticket would be the beneficiary of the Wallace falloff and therefore the smart strategy was, as one aide put it later, "pulling in the sails and riding it out."

Agnew's verbal miscues certainly encouraged that approach, but they did not dictate it. The driving force behind it was Nixon's vivid recollections of his failed 1960 campaign, in which in his own considered view he had been over-exposed and over-worked, with dawn-to-late-night speaking and hand-shaking that exhausted him. Furthermore, undertaking so many events each day did not accentuate the positive; that is, like Humphrey's eighteen-hour days in this campaign, Nixon's long 1960 daily schedule had shown him in a mix of effective and ineffective appearances, giving the press and television a wide choice to feature.

Too often, Nixon and his strategists concluded in retrospect, and in their negative appraisal of the news media as the enemy, that the candidate's weakest performances had received the coverage. This time around, they decided, it was better to limit Nixon's exposure to only a few daily events and a single carefully crafted speech, reducing the raw material for news coverage to what the campaign wanted. And if this approach also kept the unpredictable Agnew under wraps, that was all to the good.

Not much was said or written at the time about the Nixon strategy of a leaner, more disciplined campaign. Over on the Agnew campaign the traveling reporters suspected that "the mother plane" had heard enough of the would-be vice president's scatter-shots. Agnew aides were accused by reporters of playing "Hide the Greek," though Nixon did not order it. Sears recalled later: "We sort of got locked in at this point, to just try to ride it out; not do anything flashy, appear under very controlled circumstances, and let the Democrats do what they pleased."[34]

Typical was a trip that had started in Pittsburgh. The Agnew party spent the night at the Pittsburgh Hilton, then canceled the next day's events and stayed indoors. The accompanying reporters were told the candidate was busy with "staff work." As Sears later recalled it, "We sat all day in the hotel until night, then got into a motorcade and motored way out of town for a rally. Then we came back, we went to bed and the next morning left and arrived in the early part of the afternoon at the Detroit airport, where we made a fast move in the cars, a distance of about five hundred yards over to the airport motel, where we sat until night; then went to Cobo Hall for a rally, gave a speech, got out and came back. We spent the night and then flew home for the weekend on Thursday— to take some rest."[35]

The Pittsburgh visit was described in the local paper as a "non-day," and the traveling reporters griped incessantly about the isolation of Agnew in his compartment on the plane. On one trip to Corpus Christi, Texas, devoid of scheduled campaign events over the weekend, Agnew's press secretary, Herb Thompson, was besieged with demands for a news conference there. He went to Sears with the plea and was told, only half in jest: "Herb, you go tell those bastards that if they want to come along with us, there's good food and drink on the plane, and we'll drop down once in a while and get a night's sleep at a good hotel. Tell them we've got a nice weekend planned for them in Corpus Christi. They'll have a nice fishing trip planned for them in the morning, and a picnic in the afternoon, and on Monday we may make a speech. Tell them that after the next stop we're going to get up in that plane and just fly around. If they want to come along with the next vice president of the United States, okay. Tell them we'll land after a while and then we'll all go into town and take a nap."[36]

This late October reverie in both the Nixon and Agnew campaigns was abruptly interrupted, however, when Humphrey, after much agonizing, rekindled his own campaign with a speech in Salt Lake City in which he made a partial break with President Lyndon Johnson on the war in Vietnam. Humphrey cautiously called for a halt in the bombing of North Vietnam to encourage peace negotiations, and his campaign began to stir. LBJ, though unhappy with Humphrey's speech, pushed at campaign's end for a breakthrough in the peace talks that might rescue Humphrey at the eleventh hour. Both Nixon and Agnew uttered hopeful words of peace while continuing to hunker down.

The last thing Nixon needed now was a controversy over Agnew that went beyond his running mate's fiery rhetoric, which for all the bad publicity was winning votes for the ticket in Dixie and some blue-collar northern precincts. But the controversy did come, in a *New York Times* story and accompanying editorial raising questions about certain Agnew financial dealings as Baltimore County executive and governor of Maryland. They included purchase of land in connection with construction of a parallel span of the Chesapeake Bay Bridge and bank stock ownership.

Much of the factual information was old, and both Nixon and Agnew responded in high dudgeon, hoping by going on the offensive to turn the development into a campaign positive, or at least recast Agnew at this late juncture as a wronged party. Nixon went on CBS News's *Face the Nation* and accused the *Times* of "the lowest kind of gutter politics that a great newspaper could possibly engage in" and asked why the paper had waited until the closing days of the campaign to engage in below-the-belt politicking.[37] It made political sense for Nixon to come to the defense of his running mate, and also seemed to underscore the degree of confidence he continued to have in the beleaguered Agnew. In the end, Agnew demanded a retraction and the *Times* refused, while acknowledging some inaccuracies.

In a rare joint appearance on the night of October 31, Agnew shared the stage with Nixon at a massive rally in New York's Madison Square Garden. It was the night Johnson finally announced a breakthrough in

Vietnam peace talks, which the Republican ticket feared could snatch the election away. Nixon told the crowd he hoped the bombing halt would "bring some progress" in the peace talks and, pointing to Agnew, proclaimed that "neither he nor I will destroy the chance of peace" by injecting the development into the campaign.[38] Including Agnew in his remarks, and including him at the rally at all, was a notable departure from the modus operandi of the whole Nixon–Agnew campaign, of keeping them apart.

On the same day, in Texas, Humphrey had a huge rally in the Houston Astrodome, with President Johnson, who had cooled to his party's nominee, finally yielding and urging his election. Also present was Democratic governor John B. Connally, to the disappointment of the Nixon strategists. At the Democratic Convention in August, Connally had been defeated in efforts to preserve the unit rule enabling state delegations to vote as a bloc, and had sulked off. Nixon agents descended on him in the same way they had courted Agnew after Rockefeller had jilted him earlier in the year.

On the promise, made or implied, of a high cabinet post in a Nixon Administration, Connally had secretly helped them enlist leading Texas oil executives and other money men in the state. It was Connally Nixon had in mind—if Nixon carried Texas—when he talked later of having a bipartisan cabinet if elected. "He was supposed to raise money from the Democratic side and he was never supposed to appear with Humphrey when he came to Texas, but down toward the end he did," Sears recalled. When LBJ finally threw in with Humphrey and Connally showed up at the Humphrey rally, that was the end of Connally's cabinet prospects—for then. "And then Connally was supposed to 'help' with the vote count [in Texas] but didn't," Sears said. "Nixon didn't carry Texas and he got all upset with that." Later, after the election, Sears said: "If the fellow [Connally] had had more guts he'd be secretary of defense today."[39] But Nixon, a sucker for big, strapping, assertive men, always admired Connally, a sentiment that would have later ramifications for the Nixon–Agnew relationship.

On the day before the election, as Muskie joined Humphrey in a wild motorcade through downtown Los Angeles, and later that night on a nationwide marathon telecast, Nixon held a telethon of his own without

Agnew, in nearby Burbank. Agnew campaigned alone clear across the country, in safely Republican Virginia.

Nixon did, however, make use of a pre-planned question from the hand-picked moderator on whether, if he could choose his running mate all over again, he would still pick Agnew. "I certainly would," Nixon said. "I'm not unaware of the fact that Agnew has been the subject of some pretty vicious attacks by the opposition, but he's a man of great courage. He doesn't wilt under fire. . . . If he had to hold the highest position in the country, he'd be cool under pressure." Referring to those attacks, Nixon told his television audience that "to show you how really low they [the Democrats] got, Humphrey three weeks ago said that we have to remember that there is one chance in three that the next man we elect won't live out his term in office. If anything should happen to me, Agnew will be a strong, compassionate, good, firm man."[40]

Nixon's unequivocal affirmative response was an obviously intentional rebuttal to a flurry of commercials run by the Democrats that cast Agnew as a clown whose election and possible elevation to the presidency would be a grim joke on the country. One mentioned a President Agnew followed by canned laughter; another showed his face with the sound of a beating heart in the background. But Nixon's praise of Agnew also reflected internal Republican polls indicating that in Middle America he was becoming a hero, not a joke, and that he had succeeded in bolstering the GOP ticket in border and southern states against the feared Wallace incursion. In answering the question about Agnew, Sears said later, "Nixon wanted to be darned sure that all those people who might be viewing from all those places would understand that right off the bat, before they got to any other questions, he thought Agnew was one hell of a good guy."[41]

As Nixon's lead in the polls continued to narrow, fate—or the intervention of Nixon and/or Nixon agents sending word to Saigon that the South Vietnamese regime would get a better deal from a President Nixon than a President Humphrey—intruded. On the eve of the election, the Saigon regime reversed itself and pulled out of the peace talks, undercutting Humphrey's late surge, and his optimism.

Johnson strongly suspected that there had been such intervention through a strong Nixon supporter, Anna Chennault, the Chinese-born widow of General Claire Chennault, famed in World War II as commander of the Flying Tigers. He had Mrs. Chennault's phone tapped and she was put under surveillance by the FBI when she visited the South Vietnamese Embassy in Washington only days before the election. Agnew came under suspicion as the link to Mrs. Chennault as a result of an embassy tap in which she was heard to say, when asked whether Nixon knew of her role, "No, but our friend in New Mexico does." It so happened that Agnew's campaign plane was in Albuquerque at the time, but a check of telephone records indicated no calls to her from it. After the election, according to Nixon, J. Edgar Hoover told him Johnson had ordered surveillance on Nixon and Agnew, and thereafter Nixon insiders often talked of how the Democrats had bugged Agnew's plane.[42]

The election was close—a margin of victory for Nixon and Agnew of only half a million votes of 73 million cast. Nixon strategists later credited Agnew with helping to push the ticket over the top in Kentucky, Tennessee, and North and South Carolina, whose 41 electoral votes combined provided the electoral majority: 302 to 191 for Humphrey–Muskie and 45 for Wallace and running mate Curtis LeMay.

Some may have regretted the presence of Agnew on the ticket, but Nixon was not one of them. His running mate had indeed become somewhat of a laughingstock in many eyes in the process of becoming a household name in America. But he had done what had been expected of him. "Nixon had in mind that Agnew would go out there and support him, and he did that," Sears said later. "He was loyal, never raised any criticism, and acted as a kind of lightning rod for him."[43]

At the same time, as the president-elect and most of his campaign party celebrated the victory at the Waldorf-Astoria in New York, Ted Agnew watched the election returns back in Annapolis. To the end, each member of the Nixon–Agnew team went his own way. The important thing, though, was that the man from Maryland had become vice president of the United States, and he was determined to meet Nixon's expectations in his service in the new administration, in whatever capacity his political benefactor chose.

Chapter 4

GREAT EXPECTATIONS

WHEN THE TEAM OF RICHARD NIXON AND SPIRO AGNEW TOOK the oath of office on January 20, 1969, the spotlight appropriately was on the new president, not on his running mate, brought in on his coattails. The fifty-year-old Agnew led off the proceedings by reciting the prescribed words, and then he sat down, protocol allowing him no opportunity to say more. Thereafter, he remained sitting quietly as Nixon delivered his inaugural address, in which he counseled the nation that "greatness comes in simple trappings" and that "to lower our voices would be a simple thing."

Nixon went on to warn of "bombastic rhetoric that postures instead of persuading" and lecturing that "we cannot learn from one another until we stop shouting at one another—until we speak quietly enough so that our words can be heard as well as our voices."[1] The message could have been construed as a caution to Agnew, whose campaign oratory had fit Nixon's description of what needed to be avoided now. In much of Agnew's first year as vice president, he seemed to take his leader's words to heart, grateful to him for the opportunity to serve that he had never imagined only months earlier would ever come his way.

Agnew had ample reason to know the limitations of his new office, expressed down the years of the American Republic in phrases ranging from the philosophical and humorous to the dismissive and derogatory. John Adams, the first occupant, had observed of the vice presidency that "in this I am nothing, but I may be everything." He wrote to his wife

Abigail that "my country in its wisdom has contrived for me the most insignificant office that ever the invention of man contrived or his imagination conceived." Peter Finley Dunne's Mr. Dooley later observed that "th' Prisidincy is th' highest office in the gift iv th' people. Th' Vice-Prisidincy is th' next highest an' th' lowest. It isn't a crime exactly. Ye can't be sint to jail f'r it, but it's a kind iv disgrace. It's like writin' anonymous letters." And Woodrow Wilson called it a position "of anomalous insignificance and curious uncertainty. . . . The chief embarrassment in discussing [the] office is that in explaining how little there is to be said about it, one has evidently said all there is to say."[2]

Such remarks, however, no longer quite did justice to the vice presidency. When Harry Truman in 1945 suddenly became president with World War II still raging and with no knowledge of the development of the atomic bomb, the imperative of vice presidents being kept informed of vital presidential secrets became shockingly obvious. Even so, when Dwight D. Eisenhower succeeded Truman in the Oval Office with Richard Nixon as his vice president, he kept Nixon at arm's length, both functionally and socially. While the president used him as a good-will ambassador on many foreign trips, he never brought him into his decision-making inner circle. Asked at a news conference as Nixon prepared for his own run for the presidency in 1960 for "a major idea of his you had adopted" during Nixon's nearly eight years as his vice president, Eisenhower famously replied: "If you give me a week, I might think of one. I don't remember."[3]

Nixon never forgot that answer, nor the fact that in all the eight years he had never been invited to the Eisenhowers' residential quarters in the White House. As in the successful election campaign just completed, Nixon vowed to treat his vice president with more consideration and responsibility.

Two days after their victory, the president-elect had cordially invited his running mate to his Key Biscayne retreat to discuss Agnew's role in the new administration. After their meeting, Nixon told reporters he intended to take advantage of the vice president–elect's experience as a governor and county executive to involve him deeply in urban affairs and federal–state relations. He said Agnew would be the most active and utilized vice president in history. Nixon gave Agnew an office in the West Wing of the White House, only six doors down from the Oval Office, rather than confining him to the usual vice-presidential space in the Executive Office Building across a closed street in the executive compound on Pennsylvania Avenue.[4]

As a result, however, Agnew was largely separated from his staff. "He had room for maybe one staffer," his press secretary, Victor Gold, remembered. "He sat there in the office like a dummy. Finally, he gave it back and kept his EOB office." Gold said Agnew told him: "When I talked to Nixon [about the job], because of my status as a governor, I felt I could play a key role as a link to the governors. I wasn't here twenty-four hours when I knew I wasn't going to do a thing."

John Ehrlichman was the administration man who dealt with Agnew, Gold recalled, "and the only time Haldeman came over was to deliver messages directly from the president. Agnew felt he was looked down on as a provincial, and Nixon didn't talk to Agnew very much. He didn't like to talk to people. They had a number–two guy who they could cajole, they could sometimes order directly, but [in time] they just couldn't count on him to do what he was told. The way of the Nixon people was that you did what you were told. They didn't like to have his independence out there."[5] In what was taken as a particular slight, Gold said, the Agnew staff was never authorized to use the White House mess, and his staffers did not even have passes that would admit them to the White House proper, only to the Executive Office Building next door.

Agnew himself wrote later: "As far as my cooperating with the White House to better serve the president was concerned, I soon learned that everything was run as a closed corporation. Haldeman and Ehrlichman didn't tell me what they were doing. There was a lot of secrecy and jealousy and vying for the president's attention among the senior people. I finally got disgusted and started spending more time with my own staff across the street in the Old Executive Office Building. Bob Haldeman came to me and said they needed more space in the West Wing; would I give up my office there, since I rarely used it anyway? I said I would. The press made a great deal out of the symbolism of my losing the White House office, but I had no objections. If the president had picked up the phone and asked me to come in and work with him, I would gladly have stayed. But he never did. Our only interchanges came at the staff level."[6] There was the same gripe again.

According to Alexander Butterfield, Haldeman's deputy at the time, what actually happened was that Nixon decided Haldeman needed space more distanced from the Oval Office to give him more freedom from routine demands, so he took Agnew's office, and Butterfield, handling most daily chores for Nixon, moved into Haldeman's old office.

Despite Agnew's campaign gaffes, Nixon during this time displayed no diminution in his high regard for him, and Agnew set about his limited responsibilities with diligence and determination. His considerable store of personal pride had undergone a heavy assault in the campaign, particularly from the Democrats, and he seized upon the work at hand to combat the ridicule that still clung to him. A California entrepreneur came out with a Spiro Agnew watch that became a big seller and inspired the gag that Mickey Mouse was seen wearing one. Soon Spiro Agnew sweatshirts and dolls also appeared. To a man of his dignity and stature, such mocking was hard to take. His response was to do the best job he could in a no-nonsense fashion.

Almost from the first, however, he ran into what soon would be known in the White House as "the Berlin Wall"—the two-man buffer of Haldeman and Ehrlichman between Nixon and the rest of the staff, including the vice president. Only sixteen days after the inauguration, Haldeman wrote in his diary: "Strange problem with Agnew, who's hired LBJ's top advance man as an administrative assistant. No one seems to be able to dissuade him, the guy has turned out to be a total spy, has all the inside poop, etc."[7] Gold, Agnew's press secretary, when told years later of Haldeman's fears, could not identify such a person, nor could other Agnew aides who were questioned about it.[8]

The next day, Haldeman wrote of the same and other gripes about Agnew: "E [Ehrlichman] and I [Haldeman] had knock-down with VP [vice president], about his staff and office facilities. Hard to get anywhere. Afraid we made things worse, and that it will have to go to P [president]. VP has no concept of P's view of how he should handle the role, and I don't think he ever will. Real problem about him hiring LBJ advance man. He sees no reason not to, and apparently intends to buck us all the way. P also upset because VP got into act at Legislative Leaders Meeting and sided with Congressmen vs. Postmaster Red Blount and the P."[9] Winton Blount, an important Alabama Republican, was a Nixon favorite pushing a plan to make the Post Office a nonpartisan corporation, and not a man for Agnew to take on.

In Haldeman's handwritten notes for the same day, he jotted down advice Nixon told him to pass on to the vice president: "Talk to Agnew re how to handle self in leg[islative] mtgs. Should always take line from Pres, not to develop programs, just sell our programs. Defend cab[inet] members and Pres always. Point out how much better off he is than N[ixon] in Eise[nhower] Admin."[10] And when Agnew was quoted in the press the next day about an aspect of how intergovernmental relations would be handled, Haldeman noted: "Where did Agnew story come from? P should have said it."[11]

Two days later came still another early indication that Agnew needed to be reined in. The Nixon entourage was down at Key Biscayne and the new president was on the beach sunning himself and snoozing when, Haldeman wrote, "an aide had awakened him to say the VP was calling. Didn't take the call, wanted me to instruct the aide no calls down here except family. Agnew then called me [Haldeman] to see whether he should fly to Palm Springs and back tomorrow to present Bob Hope Golf Award. Said I'd ask P."[12] Nixon's terse reply: "Yes, go." Just as notable as Agnew calling the president on such a trivial matter was the fact that Nixon told Haldeman to tell the offending aide he would take calls only from family members, even if the caller was his vice president.

Agnew's troubles with the "Berlin Wall" surfaced early. Herbert Klein, the veteran San Diego editor who came on as the Nixon White House director of communications, wrote later in his book, *Making It Perfectly Clear*, that Agnew made a mistake at the start by letting himself be dominated by Nixon's inner circle on a matter regarding his own staff. In not standing up for a campaign press secretary whom Haldeman and John Mitchell made a scapegoat for Agnew's campaign gaffes, Klein wrote, "he lost ground. . . which he never would regain in a power-prone administration." On top of that, Klein said, Nixon's "inconsistent" relationship with his vice president "left Agnew insecure and easy prey for administration power brokers." Agnew, he wrote, " was under heavy early pressure from the Nixon political staff to cleanse himself of errors with the press" by ditching the "scapegoat.". . . Members of Agnew's "Maryland Mafia" staff "were attuned to things on a less than national basis," Klein noted, and as Haldeman and Ehrlichman moved "to absorb the power around the presidency in close quarters. . . Agnew did not fit their picture of governmental power, and he easily allowed himself to be muscled out. . . "[13]

The only constitutional task assigned the vice president was to preside over the Senate and, in the event of a tie vote, to cast the deciding ballot. Thus he had a rare legislative function for an officeholder in the executive branch, and he took his title of president of the Senate seriously. In his first two months, Agnew opened the daily Senate session himself, and from the presiding officer's chair recognized members seeking to speak, handing down rulings on the advice of the Senate parliamentarian. In his first year, he spent more time in the chair than Nixon had as vice president, or Humphrey. And as the first non-senator in the job in twenty-four years, he conscientiously accepted briefings from the parliamentarian and held lunches for small groups of senators of both parties. He carefully respected senatorial prerogatives and at first conferred with a light hand with members on certain Nixon legislative initiatives, to the point that Senate Majority Leader Mike Mansfield one morning rose and commended him for "a job well and assiduously done."[14]

In short order, however, as Agnew began to embrace the role of legislative lobbyist for the administration, he became more heavy handed, pressing senators on how they were going to vote on specific measures. They deeply resented the intrusion, and when the vice president asked conservative Republican Senator Len B. Jordan of Utah whether the administration had his vote on a certain bill, Jordan told him: "You did have, until now." Whereupon he announced that he would be guided by "the Jordan Rule"—if the vice president as a member of the executive branch tried to lobby him on any legislation, he would automatically vote the other way.[15] The incident was duly reported in the press and did not go unnoticed by Nixon.

Nevertheless, the president followed through on his pledge to make Agnew a working vice president. He appointed him a member and, in the president's absence, acting chairman of the cabinet, the National Security Council, the Urban Affairs Council, and the Cabinet Committee on Economic Policy. Nixon also established a new Office of Intergovernmental Relations and put Agnew in charge, with a mandate to be the administration's point man in dealing with governors, mayors, and other county and local officials. He also made him chairman, then or later, of the National Aeronautics and Space Council, the Marine Resources and Engineering Development Council, the Council on Recreation and Natural Beauty, the Rural Affairs Council, the Cabinet Committee on Desegregation, the Indian Opportunity Council, the Council on Youth Opportunity, and the Council on Physical Fitness and Sports. Obviously, Agnew would have enough to do, though many of these assignments were formalities with little more than oversight functions.

The new vice president was delighted. On creation of the intergovernmental office, he said he felt "right now as volatile as gas does. I am constantly expanding. The only problem I have is time."[16] On top of all this, he attended White House staff meetings and did not hesitate to speak out, especially on urban matters, about which he considered himself a resident expert. In meetings attended by Nixon, Agnew often expressed the viewpoint of the governors. The president treated him respectfully and he in turn was deferential to his boss. Once, early in the administration when a special meeting of the Domestic Council was called and Nixon did not attend, Agnew presided but not from the president's chair, a gesture that did not go unnoticed or unappreciated by others present. In so behaving, Agnew took a page from Nixon's vice-presidential book, when at meetings during Eisenhower's hospitalizations he always left the presidential chair unoccupied.[17]

The vice president at first accepted the traditional second-banana role of his office in good humor. As a speaker at his first Gridiron dinner in office, he drew laughs by poking fun at it. "I can say that the president has spared no effort to keep me fully abreast of foreign policy," he proclaimed with a straight face. "He has specifically requested Secretary [of State William P.] Rogers and Dr. [Henry] Kissinger to remind me whenever his press conferences are televised. And next week General [Earle B.] Wheeler [the chairman of the Joint Chiefs of Staff] has promised to brief me on the atomic bomb." He said it wasn't true that the Nixon–Agnew ticket was the result of "Strom Thurmond's intervention. . . . I wanted Mr. Nixon on my ticket before Strom even mentioned him to me." When Nixon phoned him in Miami with his decision and he told his wife, Agnew said, "Judy's eyes fill with tears and she said: 'Can you get out of it?'"

He went on to describe the vice presidency as "that rare opportunity in politics for a man to move from a potential unknown to an actual unknown," and he even had a new deprecating line about the job: "Adding the vice presidency to our government is a little like adding maternity benefits to Social Security. You're there, but nobody needs you."[18] Several of the gags came from comedian Bob Hope, who phoned them to Agnew's office a couple of days before the dinner.[19]

But Nixon's multiple assignments to Agnew apparently gave him an inflated interpretation of his role as approaching a partnership with the president, which clearly was not Nixon's intention. Haldeman's diary for April 23, 1969, three months into the new administration, reported cabinet members' demands for face time with Nixon, adding: "Agnew wants regular weekly appointment. P says we have to have a Sherman Adams [Eisenhower's chief of staff] to handle this and keep them away from him, so E and I are it, divided. I take big four [apparently secretaries of state, defense, treasury, attorney general], he takes rest. . . . Decided [special presidential adviser Arthur] Burns should explain to Agnew how the vice presidency works."[20] Haldeman, apparently after talking with Nixon, observed in his handwritten notes that Agnew "must not be involved in decisions, should never part[icipate] in discussions (Nixon never ever did that). . . . N[ixon] was most successful VP—saw DDE[isenhower] alone about 6 times in whole deal. . . . Only go to P when absolutely necessary. . . . (N always worked through [Sherman] Adams and [Gen. Wilton B.] Persons. . . . Must get away from apparent need (obsession) to establish an independent position. Must stop worrying about personal status."[21]

Two days later, Agnew apparently had not gotten the message. At Camp David, Haldeman wrote: "VP called just before dinner and said had to talk to P. He took the call. Later called me into bedroom to report, furious, that all he [Agnew] wanted was some guy to be director of Space Council. May turn out to be the straw that breaks the camel's back. He has just *no* sensitivity, or judgment about his relationship with P. After movie we were walking home and P called me back, again to ponder the Agnew problem, and that of general area of cabinet relationships. He's not really sure how to handle. His instinct is to be very distant and unavailable, but people tell him he needs more contact and this bothers him, because he thinks he may be handling wrong. Real problem is that none of them except Mitchell really knows how to relate to him."[22] Haldeman's entry conveyed not only Agnew's pushiness but also Nixon's extreme discomfort with personal contacts, especially with people he did not know well. Haldeman and Ehrlichman clearly were exceptions, and that explained their influence.

The vice president also seemed to have a basic misapprehension about the auxiliary role he was intended to play in the new administration, and particularly in the realm of foreign affairs. In a letter to the president's national security adviser, Henry Kissinger, on April 24, Agnew wrote: "Dear Henry: Would you please arrange to provide me with a regular briefing on national security affairs. I have in mind about half an hour each week, and want Stanley Blair [his chief of staff], Kent Crane and Mike Dunn [his military aide] of my staff to attend the briefings, with the proviso that we may take five minutes or so alone when the need arises."[23]

It was not until two weeks later, on May 7, that Kissinger replied: "Dear Mr. Vice President: I would be pleased to brief you—and whatever members of your staff you select—weekly on national security affairs. I suggest we begin next week, and have asked that an appointment be arranged for either Wednesday or Thursday (May 14 or 15). Since it would probably be more convenient for you if we did not set a permanent time, I will have my secretary arrange a time each week which will most easily fit into your schedule."[24]

More evidence that Agnew did not yet get the picture on how he was to fit into the operation of the Nixon administration, not to mention his apparent insensitivity to the Nixon old-boy network, came in an "eyes only" letter Agnew sent to the president on May 16. It reported "a great feeling of disaffection among the Republican members of the Senate concerning the apparent direction of HEW policy" under Nixon's old California buddy, Bob Finch. Agnew expressed concern about "the continual surfacing of radical left ideas through the framework of HEW," in the prospective award of a grant of a hundred thousand dollars to the National Welfare Rights Organization, with which Agnew said he "had some personal experience," presumably as governor of Maryland. "I regret that I must raise these unpleasant matters," Agnew wrote, "but I feel that you should be informed that Secretary Finch's public posture is upsetting a broad segment of our natural political support, notwithstanding his disclaimers of being out of step with campaign policies."

Nixon dismissed the matter with a scribbled note on the letter to Finch: "Please talk to VP."[25] That must have been quite a tone-setter for Finch–Agnew relations.

The vice president also took his concerns about what he saw as the infiltration of "radical left" influence in the adminstration's foreign affairs directly to Nixon in a July 18 memo labeled "Top Secret–Eyes Only." It warned: "I am deeply disturbed by the current involvement of so-called 'peace activists' in negotiating the release of certain POWs by North Vietnam. The composition of the 'delegation' to Hanoi apparently includes one Rennard [Rennie] C. Davis—indicted for actions during last summer's disturbances at the Democratic National Convention and only permitted to make the trip as a result of an appeal to Judge Kerner; a James Johnson who refused to comply with orders to Vietnam while serving as an Army private; and at least one national officer of SDS [Students for a Democratic Society]."

The memo continued: "Our obvious concern for the earliest possible release of any and all of the prisoners perhaps outweighs the obvious propaganda advantage conceded to the enemy by our use of such intermediaries. There is, however, another important consideration. By allowing only our own far left wing to participate in what is in effect a selective release program, do we not strike most directly at the morale of the remaining prisoners?

"Surely, the criteria for release under such circumstances must [underlined] include tacit 'cooperation' with their captors. It would be unrealistic to assume otherwise. It seems clear that while there should be a premium for steadfast opposition to the enemy, exactly the reverse may well seem to be true to the many who remain in captivity. It would be difficult to put together a group of Americans less well suited to conduct negotiations, and I strongly question whether hope for results [justified] the risks and probably costs."[26] Nixon, apparently ignoring the "eyes only" caveat, had a copy sent to Kissinger.

Five days later, Agnew sent essentially the same memo to Secretary of State William Rogers and Secretary of Defense Melvin Laird, specifying that "the president shares my concern." He added: "If release comes to be viewed by the prisoners themselves as a 'reward' for tractability or docility, they may become demoralized. Further, if the enemy perceives clear and important advantages in such a program of limited and selective release, the confinement of the great majority may be lengthened."[27]

The vice president's other relations with cabinet members were fractious on occasion. When he approached Laird, a former Republican leader in the House, and pushed for some Pentagon appointments for Agnew associates, Laird balked. As a condition for taking the huge department, Laird said later, he had extracted a promise from Nixon that he would choose his own subordinates. "Agnew did not like that very well," Laird recalled. "He resented it that I had that authority. He felt it should not have been given to me because it wasn't given to any other cabinet officer. He complained to Nixon about it, that he didn't think that was proper. And he complained that I was having a few too many Democrats that I was appointing. I felt I had to have a bipartisan group over at Defense. He did object to that," but to no avail, Laird remembered.

The new vice president also was unhappy, Laird recalled, when he learned that Nixon had decided, in the event he were to become incapacitated, "that I would have the football"—meaning access to the secret procedures for control of U.S. nuclear weapons. Agnew, Laird said, "had a little bit of resentment that Nixon didn't fully trust him." The transfer never took place, Laird said, though it came close once in a brief communications breakdown. Agnew also opposed him on creating the all-volunteer army, the former defense secretary said, but it was eventually part of the Nixon program, so the vice president had to swallow it.[28]

Agnew's unhappiness about his minimal direct access to Nixon surfaced early in a briefing for cabinet members by Roy Ash, chairman of a new Commission on Executive Office Reorganization. The new secretary of the Department of Housing and Urban Development, George Romney, voiced opposition to another White House staff apparatus making it harder for himself and others in the cabinet to meet directly with Nixon. Agnew joined in, saying he shared the concern.

Immediately one of the commission members, John Connally of Texas, objected. Ehrlichman wrote later: "Had Big John not stood quickly to say that the commission's recommendations were the president's desire, and that it was really not an open question, Agnew might have put the issue to the cabinet and confronted Nixon with a difficult vote of no confidence."[29] The way Connally slapped down Agnew was remembered by Nixon long afterward, and he cited it to others as an impressive demonstration of Connally's strength and decisiveness. It wasn't likely that Agnew forgot it either, especially later when Connally would cross his path in a more significant regard.

Butterfield, recalling the same incident later, said: "I remember the day Nixon became aware of Connally and became enamored of him. As Ash droned on, Connally in his genial way, not wanting to take anything away from Ash, said something like, 'What Roy's getting at,' and he nailed it all down in ten minutes." From then on, Butterfield remembered, Connally was Nixon's man, and told him he could stay at Aspen Lodge, Nixon's own getaway at Camp David, anytime he wanted.[30]

Meanwhile, Agnew could not completely shake his old campaign image as a clod. On a Nixon return from Europe, his vice president greeted him, as befitted protocol, prompting a *Chicago's American* cartoonist to depict Agnew inquiring of the president: "How are things with the Limeys, Krauts, Dagoes and Frogs?"[31]

The public perception of Agnew as a harsh critic of campus and street disorders also lingered, though as vice president he sought at first to express his concerns in milder terms in speeches to governors and other governmental officials, and always in harmony with Nixon's own words. When the president in a speech to the U.S. Chamber of Commerce said there could be "no compromise with lawlessness" on American campuses and that school officials should show some "backbone" in dealing with campus violence, Agnew echoed him. He told an audience in Honolulu that conciliatory college officials "dismiss too lightly the grave implications of campus disorders and the reaction to them that is reverberating across the country."[32]

But even as Nixon, interested in erasing negative memories of his own hard rhetoric, sought to hew to the high road, Agnew's language began to become more combative. At a graduation at Ohio State in June, he lashed out at permissiveness in his own generation in words as harsh as those that later on would be written for him by White House wordsmiths. "A society which comes to fear its children is effete," he declared. "A sniveling, hand-wringing power structure deserves the violent rebellion it encourages. If my generation doesn't stop cringing, yours will inherit a lawless society where emotion and muscle displace reason."[33]

Up to this point, there was still no public indication from Nixon that he was anything but pleased by his vice president's performance on the stump, or that Agnew himself had any concerns with his role in the administration. Privately, however, as the Haldeman diaries showed, the new vice president was already complaining. In those first months, he actually was getting a very large slice of the action. But the fact was that Nixon, and Haldeman and Ehrlichman, were just whipping the administration into shape. As it assumed greater discipline and structure, many domestic tasks that had been given to Agnew were now being assumed by others, especially cabinet members, who were getting firmer control of their departments. He began to be structured out, and other domestic experts began moving in. According to one insider at the time, "He got the vice-presidential blues. . . . He felt he could honcho the domestic side of it and have a larger hand in it,"[34] but others, like Daniel Patrick Moynihan, Arthur Burns, George Shultz, and particularly Ehrlichman, were crowding him. "Agnew kept in touch with the mayors and governors," Damgard recalled, "and if from time to time they weren't getting what they wanted from Ehrlichman, they appealed to Agnew. And when Ehrlichman saw Agnew as a competing force on what he wanted to do, he worked very hard to undermine him."[35]

C. D. Ward, who became Agnew's assistant on intergovernmental relations, recalled later one occasion on which Nixon told Agnew he wanted him to lead the administration's efforts to deal with busing to achieve school desegregation in the South. Agnew told Ward to call the involved agency for a briefing, and when he did so, he was told "that won't be necessary." Agnew did not take such rebuffs easily, but at first he mostly kept his mouth shut.[36]

As far as the public knew, Agnew until now had remained the loyal subordinate to Nixon. But as he sensed a loss of his influence, he began to go public with views that were at variance with the administration line—a cardinal sin for a number-two man. When the administration proposed allowable limits on federal tax deductions on municipal-bond interest, Agnew as a former county official urged the Advisory Commission on Intergovernmental Relations to lobby against it as an inhibition to state and local bond sales.

Again, just before of the launch of the Apollo 11 spacecraft that put men on the moon for the first time, in July 1969, Agnew at a news conference at Cape Kennedy went public with an argument he had been making within the administration to put men on Mars by the end of the century. After the successful launch, he went into the firing room and told the ecstatic ground team: "I want to tell you I bit the bullet for you today as far as Mars is concerned. But on the other hand, I want to let you know that I may be a voice in the wilderness."[37]

He was correct about that assessment. Some weeks later, back at the White House, Ehlrichman came across a briefing paper that said a Space Advisory Committee headed by Agnew, Ehrlichman wrote later, "was about to make some recommendations to the president that. . . Nixon could not live with." Ehrlichman continued: "It seemed obvious to me that Agnew. . . owed it to the president not to include a proposal our budget couldn't pay for. A Mars space shot would be very popular with many people. If the committee proposed it and Nixon had to say no, he would be criticized as the president who kept us from finding life on Mars. On the other hand, if the committee didn't recommend it, we avoided the problem altogether."

The president's science adviser, Lee DuBridge, had agreed with the recommendation. "DuBridge was perhaps to be forgiven for failing to understand such a political argument," Ehrlichman wrote, "but I saw no excuse for Agnew's insistence that the Mars shot be recommended. At our meeting, I was surprised at his obtuseness. . . . I had been wooed by NASA, the Space Administration, but not to the degree to which they had made love to Agnew. He had been their guest of honor at space launchings, tours and dinners, and it seemed to me they had done a superb job of recruiting him to lead this fight to vastly expand their space empire and budget."

So Ehrlichman confronted him directly. "I finally took off the kid gloves," he wrote. 'Look, Mr. Vice President, we have to be practical. There is to be no money for a Mars trip. The president has already decided that. So the president does not want such a trip in the Space Advisory Committee's recommendations. It is your job, with Lee DuBridge's help, to make absolutely certain that the Mars trip is not in there.'"

The vice president seethed. As Ehrlichman reported, "Mr. Agnew was not happy to be told what to do by me. He demanded a personal meeting with the president. This was a matter for constititutional officers to discuss. I overlooked the obvious innuendo that I was lying to Agnew about what the president had decided. 'Fine,' I said. 'I'll arrange it at once, and someone will call you.'" About an hour later, Erhlichman wrote, "the vice president called me. He had decided to move the Mars shot from the list of recommendations to another category headed 'Technically Feasible.'"

When Ehrlichman reported to Nixon what had happened, the president told his lieutenant: "That's just the way to handle him. Use that technique on him anytime." Then, Ehrlichman wrote, "Nixon looked at me vaguely. 'Is Agnew insubordinate, do you think?'"[38]

Arguments like the one over the Mars shot came to be commonplace with Agnew. "Nixon found early that personal meetings with Agnew were invariably unpleasant," Ehrlichman wrote. "The president came out of them amazed at Agnew's constant self-aggrandizement. Nixon recalled that as vice president he had seldom made a request of any kind of Dwight Eisenhower. But Agnew's visits always included demands for more staff, better facilities, more prerogatives and perquisites. It was predictable that as Agnew complained and requested more and more, Nixon would agree to see him less frequently."[39]

Ehrlichman was not the only ranking Nixon man who couldn't get along with the vice president. "At first, in 1969," he wrote, "I was sent to see Agnew when Haldeman realized that he and the vice president didn't get along well. The president's idea was that a high-level staff person should listen to Agnew [when an appointment with the president had been requested] and try to deflect his imprudent demands; I was expected to arrange for the ministerial tasks to be done by our staff, and I was supposed to show Agnew why his other demands ought not to be pressed in talks with the president. None of that worked, of course."[40]

Nixon's decision to give Agnew responsibility for dealing with the governors, mayors, and county officials was a natural one, given Agnew's prior governmental experience. "But it turned out," Ehrlichman wrote, "that he was only an excellent conduit for their complaints—especially the gripes of [Governors] Ronald Reagan, John Bell Williams [of Mississippi] and a few other conservatives. Notwithstanding Agnew's 1968 love affair with Rockefeller, Rocky soon gave up on Agnew's liaison and began calling me directly. I tried to wean Rockefeller back to Agnew until the governor went to the president and insisted that I be his avenue to the president instead of Agnew. 'Agnew doesn't play them well,' Nixon explained to me."[41] In light of the Agnew–Rockefeller history, that was no surprise in this instance.

In handling the assignment of liaison with the governors [which Ehrlichman himself wanted and later got], Ehrlichman said, "more than once I was called into Agnew's office to hear his complaints. If he were going to be able to do the intergovernmental relations job for the president, he'd say, he had to have more help from the White House staff, not the sort of resistance he was getting. The budget people, the congressional-liaison staff and my domestic-policy experts were to be told that a vice-presidential 'request' was to be given heed. I tried to explain that such staff people usually were following established presidential policy, which probably didn't please the mayor or governor the vice president had on the phone. That was why they were calling him." But, Ehrlichman wrote, Agnew let himself become the servant of the governors and mayors. "His job was to sell our policy to them, not theirs to us," but more often than not, that was what happened. So it was not surprising that before long, Agnew segued into taking the stump as the administration's blunt instrument against its critics. "Speechmaking and traveling were less taxing and more interesting," Ehrlichman suggested with evident contempt.[42]

In the summer of 1969, Agnew also bucked the administration on welfare reform. He endorsed a resolution at a National Governors' Conference in Colorado Springs calling for a full federal takeover, at a time the administration had just come up with a new plan within a state-based structure. Shortly afterward, however, he became a prime salesman for the administration's plan for an anti-ballistic-missile system. On the day the Senate was voting on it, Agnew and Nixon were at a meeting at Camp David, and Agnew had to leave because he might have to break a tie vote on the measure. As he got up to depart for Washington, Nixon said in jest: "You know how to vote on that, don't you?" Agnew shot back: "If it's a tie on ABM, Mr. President, I'll be on the phone about the welfare program."[43] Ted Agnew was not above needling Nixon in return.

When, in October 1969, the Executive Office reorganization that was clipping Agnew's wings was well along, he aligned himself against it with cabinet members who also felt undercut. Nixon summoned Haldeman, Ehrlichman, and veteran strategist Bryce Harlow to consider what to do about the vice president. Harlow, a soft-spoken and genial older man with diplomatic as well as political skills, was chosen as the messenger from Nixon.

"Say that the president pointed out to you," said Nixon, "that it is traditional in this town to try to divide the president from his vice president. I'm an expert. For eight years the press tried to divide me from Eisenhower. Without success. They are playing the same game now. He can't let it happen. And," Nixon added, looking at his two top lieutenants, "the staff is never to criticize the vice president."[44]

Two weeks later, Ehrlichman wrote, Nixon was informed that Agnew was fighting with the State Department over his desire to go to Vietnam, Formosa, and seven other Asian countries, "and State was afraid to let him go." Deadpan, Nixon said: "I'm sort of afraid to have him go too. If they kill Nixon, they get Agnew. I'd hate to have anything happen to him."[45] Nixon said it in jest, but it was clear that less than a year after he had selected the governor of Maryland as a great choice to be a heartbeat away from the presidency if anything happened to him, he already was revising the judgment.

The vice president, however, was not without allies in the White House. One was Harry Dent, Nixon's specialist on southern politics. In a memo on September 29, after a political meeting of White House staff and party congressional leaders at Camp David that the traveling Agnew had missed, Dent wrote to him: "In concluding the meeting, the president paid special tribute to you for your great capacity, your good work to date, and your courage. He told them all to make good use of you, and I explained to him that everybody was already making good use of a very cooperative vice president. He understood you were out on a series of speaking engagements. Of course, he wants you at all future meetings whenever possible. . . . You were also highly praised by Senator [Robert] Griffin [of Michigan] for the good job you are doing in the Senate. Everyone also joined in the praise. This was Spiro Agnew Day."[46]

But others did not always treat him to his satisfaction. Despite his earlier "instruction" to Kissinger to "provide me with a regular briefing on national security affairs" and Kissinger's written agreement, the vice president eventually became dissatisfied with the help he was getting from the national security adviser. Kissinger's deputy, General Alexander Haig, felt obliged on October 2 to send a memo to his boss reporting that an Agnew aide "tells me the vice president will undoubtedly be quite up-set that you were unable to brief him this morning"on an approaching Agnew trip to the Far East. "I recommend that you call the vice president this morning and explain your predicament, informing him that you will see him next week at his convenience."[47] The vice president was learning where he stood in the White House pecking order.

He was also learning that his growing penchant for left-wing bashing was not universally embraced therein. At one point, an aide to Kissinger named William Watts, a former employee at the Ford Foundation, sent a confidential memo to his boss informing him that Agnew had questioned him about what Agnew believed, erroneously, was the foundation's financing of that summer's National Conference on the New Politics, conducted by the well-known radical activist Marcus Raskin. Watts told Kissinger that Agnew had asked him to get him more information, including the names of the board of the Ford Foundation. Kissinger scribbled on the memo: "Let us stay out of it. You are not working for the vice president. If he wants facts let him write to [MacGeorge] Bundy," then the head of the foundation.[48]

For most of the first year of the Nixon–Agnew administration, the vice president had in his fashion generally observed Nixon's inauguration plea "to lower our voices" and "stop shouting at one another," with the exception of an occasional outburst against campus violence. But as negotiations aimed at ending the Vietnam War dragged on, anti-war protests became louder and more frequent. A huge nationwide demonstration called Vietnam Moratorium Day was scheduled for Wednesday, October 15. As it approached, Nixon pointedly declared that it would not have any influence on his war policy. "Under no circumstance will I be affected whatever by it," he declared.[49]

In Dallas six days before Moratorium Day, the vice president told Republican fund-raising dinner guests that the approaching war protest was "ironic and absurd," and was planned to scar the one political figure really working to end the war. "Only the president has the power to negotiate peace," he said. "Congress cannot dictate it, the Vietnam Moratorium Committee cannot coerce it, and all the students in America cannot create it. By attacking the president, the protesters attack our hope for peace. They weaken the hand that can save."[50] Two days later in Montpelier, Vermont, he said, "The time has come to call a halt to this spiritual Theater of the Absurd, to examine the motivation of the authors of the absurdity and challenge the star players in the cast."[51]

On the eve of Moratorium Day, Nixon met Agnew at the White House and told him he was going to stay out of the whole business, but wanted Agnew to take a shot at the organizers. Haldeman wrote in his diary: "P decided he would not get into it, but wanted VP to take it on, to get maximum possible coverage. So we set him up, had Buchanan do a statement, frantically got him [Agnew] into a review with P and barely got before the cameras in time for the evening news. . . . Result was we got the coverage, question now is whether it helps or hurts."[52] Agnew condemned the Moratorium organizers for not repudiating a telegram from the North Vietnamese regime wishing them success in their day-long protest. Despite fears of violence, the event went off in a restrained and responsible fashion, with a bizarre coda. In the early morning hours, Nixon appeared unannounced at the Lincoln Memorial and had a long talk—about football!—with camping students who were of a more serious mien in making the pilgrimage.[53] Agnew's carefully planned harangue at the organizers got lost in the highly publicized Nixon change-of-heart about giving Moratorium Day a wide berth.

Agnew, meanwhile, had in mind nothing as frivolous as football talk. His original expectation to be occupied as the Nixon administration's overseer on domestic affairs was adrift in the reorganization of responsibilities. So, spurred by his success as a new social critic, especially regarding the behavior of the nation's young, he would embark on another mission perhaps even more suited to his talents. He would take the message against the various destructive forces in the country to the grass roots—or at least to the conservative Republican faithful. There was no evidence that Richard Nixon had any objections. Ted Agnew was still his boy, and what came next would in one regard at least boost his standing with his constituency of one.

Chapter 5

AROUSING THE
SILENT MAJORITY

Richard Nixon's tactic of addressing rebellious American youth with friendly discussions on the fortunes of gridiron heroes was not part of his vice president's political playbook. On the next Sunday night he went to New Orleans for another Republican fund-raiser, carrying with him a text that mildly defended the president's dealing with the main issues raised by Vietnam Moratorium Day. Agnew, after glancing through the dull nine-page text, jotted down a one-page introduction in his own words that opened a new chapter in his already controversial political career.

As was his custom, Agnew delivered his remarks in a deceptive calm, in the nature of a stern professor advising a group of parents about their wayward offspring. "Sometimes it appears that we are reaching a period when our sense and our minds will no longer respond to moderate stimulation," he said. "We seem to be approaching an age of the gross. Persuasion through speeches and books is too often discarded for disruptive demonstrations aimed at bludgeoning the unconvinced into action.

"The young—and by this I don't mean by any stretch of the imagination all the young, but I'm talking about those who claim to speak for the young—at the zenith of physical power and sensitivity overwhelm themselves with drugs and artificial stimulants. Subtlety is lost, and fine distinctions based on acute reasoning are carelessly ignored in a headlong

jump to a predetermined conclusion. Life is visceral rather than intellectual, and the most visceral practitioners of life are those who characterize
themselves as intellectuals. Truth to them is 'revealed' rather than logi-
cally proved, and the principal infatuations of today revolve around the
social sciences, those subjects which can accommodate any opinion and
about which the most reckless conjecture cannot be discredited."

He went on: "Education is being redefined at the demand of the uneducated to suit the ideas of the uneducated. The student now goes to college to proclaim rather than to learn. The lessons of the past are ignored
and obliterated in a contemporary antagonism known as the generation
gap. A spirit of national masochism prevails, encouraged by an effete
corps of impudent snobs who characterize themselves as intellectuals. It is
in this setting of dangerous oversimplification that the war in Vietnam
achieves its greatest distortion."

Agnew's phrase, "an effete corps of impudent snobs," would soon be
cited as a prime "Agnewism," as such catchy denunciations would come
to be known. Though other, more colorful phrases would, in a short time,
be uttered by him at the suggestion of Nixon speechwriters, this one was
his own, demonstrating that he didn't need outside help to come up with
language designed to arouse many and antagonize many others.

"The recent Vietnam Moratorium," he continued, "is a reflection of
the confusion that exists in America today. Thousands of well-motivated
young people, conditioned since childhood to respond to great emotional
appeals, saw fit to demonstrate for peace. Most did not stop to consider
that the leaders of the Moratorium had billed it as a massive public out-
pouring against the foreign policy of the president of the United States.
Most did not care to be reminded that the leaders of the Moratorium refused to disassociate themselves from the objectives enunciated by the enemy in Hanoi. If the Moratorium had any use whatever, it served as an
emotional purgative for those who felt the need to cleanse themselves of
their lack of ability to offer a constructive solution to the problem. Unfortunately, we have not seen the end. The hard-core dissidents and the professional anarchists within the so-called 'peace movement' will continue
to exacerbate the situation. November 15 is already planned—wilder,
more violent, and equally barren of constructive result."[1]

The speech, and especially the phrase "effete corps of impudent snobs,"
made page one in newspapers across the country the next day, a rare pub-

licity coup for the occupant of an office traditionally ignored. It alerted reporters and editors to await Agnew's succeeding bombastic utterances and slanders for prominent display in print and on television evening news shows. They were news but they also were entertainment. Among the readers was the man in the Oval Office, who digested with relish Agnew's hot copy appearing on the president's daily news summary.

For his own part, Agnew needed no encouragement to continue in that combustible rhetoric. The next night in Jackson, Mississippi, he revamped his anti-intellectual speech to appeal to a Dixie audience. "For too long," he said at another Republican fund-raiser, "the South has been the punching bag for those who characterize themselves as intellectuals. Actually, they are consistently demonstrating the antithesis of intelligence. Their reactions are visceral, not intellectual; and they seem to believe that truth is revealed rather than systematically proved." Agnew's words, as intended, generated a visceral response from the emotional crowd, which loved the intellectual-bashing. Shoveling more red meat on their plates, he declared that "their course is one of applause for our enemies and condemnation for our leaders. Their course is a course that will ultimately weaken and erode the very fiber of America. They have a masochistic compulsion to destroy their country's strength whether or not that strength is exercised constructively. And they rouse themselves into a continual emotional crescendo—substituting disruptive demonstration for reason. And precipitate action for persuasion. This group may consider itself liberal, but it is undeniable that it is more comfortable with radicals."[2]

The crowd itself responded with an emotional crescendo to Agnew's linkage of liberals and radicals. But by now some in the White House were getting concerned about possible overkill as the vice president increasingly free-lanced on the stump. Party leaders from major cities, some of whom themselves had participated in some aspect of the generally restrained Vietnam Moratorium Day, or had young members of their families involved, let it be known they didn't appreciate the sweeping nature of the vice president's harangue. Agnew himself said later that his fourteen-year-old daughter Kim had wanted to join the day but he "wouldn't let her" because "parental-type power must be exercised."[3]

At a White House meeting over Agnew's inflammatory remarks, Rogers Morton, the party chairman, and congressional leaders Gerald

Ford and Hugh Scott, all moderates, reported that nervousness was mounting among Republicans on Capitol Hill. But Harry Dent, a Nixon political aide from South Carolina, spoke in support of Agnew's going after the protesters. Meanwhile, the vice president continued in his attack mode, two days later charging Democratic Senator Edmund Muskie with playing "Russian roulette with United States security" by proposing a unilateral moratorium on testing multiple nuclear warheads—an unusual Agnew venture into this field.[4]

The harsh tone of the vice president's remarks generated repeated questions from White House reporters as to whether he was speaking for himself or for the toned-down Nixon, himself now conspicuously if uncharacteristically striding on the high road. Each time the presidential press secretary, the officious Ronald Ziegler, was asked whether Agnew's speeches were being cleared by the White House, he said the vice president never had to clear his remarks because he was speaking for himself.

A week after Agnew's shot at Muskie, he appeared with Nixon at a White House reception for the Ethnic Groups Division of the Republican National Committee. "The vice president," the president said, "from time to time feels he's very much in touch because of his Greek background. . . . Now, I'm not Greek but I'm very proud to have the vice president with his Greek background in our administration, and he has done a great job for this administration."[5] It wasn't clear whether Nixon was praising the man or his Greekness, but the president usually said so little about Agnew that it was taken as a compliment. Actually, later that day the president told Haldeman, as the chief of staff wrote later, that he was determined not to let [the Agnew critics] "drive a wedge" between him and his stand-in, "in spite of flack about VP speeches."[6]

The same night in Harrisburg, Agnew, thus encouraged, turned the heat up several notches. By way of countering criticism of his remarks in the South, he noted that he had criticized "those who encouraged government by street carnival and suggested it was time to stop the carousel. It appears that by slaughtering a sacred cow I triggered a holy war. I have no regrets. I do not intend to repudiate my beliefs, recant my words, or run and hide."

Going after the war critics again, Agnew said: "Small cadres of professional protesters are allowed to jeopardize the peace efforts of the president of the United States. It is time to question the credentials of their leaders. And if, in questioning, we disturb a few people, I say it is time for them to be disturbed. If, in challenging, we polarize the American people, I say it is time for a positive polarization. It is time for a healthy in-depth examination of policies and a constructive realignment in this country. It is time to rip away the rhetoric and divide on authentic lines."[7]

Not even Nixon in his most combative days had so pointedly invited dividing the American people between those who were for him and those who were against.

Agnew, repeating his assault on that effete corps of impudent snobs, made crystal clear what he thought should happen to them: "America cannot afford to write off a whole generation for the decadent thinking of a few. America cannot afford to divide over their demagoguery, or to be deceived by their duplicity or to let their license destroy liberty. We can, however, afford to separate them from our society—with no more regret than we should feel over discarding rotten apples from a barrel."

Now Agnew was really on a roll. He blasted "avowed anarchists and communists who detest everything about this country and want to destroy it." He called them "vultures who sit in trees and watch lions battle, knowing that win, lose or draw, they will be fed." He excoriated "merchants of hate" and "parasites of passion" who were "ideological eunuchs whose most comfortable position is straddling the philosophical fence, soliciting votes from both sides." As a wind-up, he laid down a challenge: "Right now we must decide whether we will take the trouble to stave off a totalitarian state. Will we stop the wildness now before it is too late, before the witch-hunting and repression that are all too inevitable begin?"[8]

The remarks were astonishing, even coming from this new sensation of the political stage. In one breath he had called for polarization of the American people and "discarding rotten apples from a barrel" and in the next warned of witch hunts and repression. Not since Barry Goldwater's famous defense of "extremism in defense of liberty" at the 1964 Republican convention that nominated him had a major political figure expressed such venom. Goldwater himself loved it. "If Ted Agnew keeps on expressing the sentiment of the vast, overwhelming majority of the American people," he said, "he may find himself being boomed for president before it's even his turn."[9] It seemed by now that the same thought may have occurred to the vice president.

What, one might have asked at this point, had ever happened to Nixon's inaugural call on the American people to lower their voices and bring the country together after the divisive campaign of 1968 that had elected the Nixon–Agnew team? Was Nixon just minding his own more lofty business in the Oval Office, or had he quietly unleashed his vice president to be an even more venomous version of the slasher he himself had been as Eisenhower's hatchet man?

In Philadelphia a few weeks later, Agnew gave his own answer to Nixon's inaugural plea. Repeating his condemnation of "a carnival in the streets" by a "student minority" that was raising "intolerant clamor and cacophony," he declared: "I, for one, will not lower my voice until the restoration of sanity and civil order will allow a quiet voice to be heard once again."[10] Agnew's favorite device of alliteration peppered his remarks, but not as conspicuously as it soon would.

❧ ❧

AROUND THIS TIME, Pat Buchanan got the idea of capitalizing on Agnew's growing popularity and media attention by turning to a favorite Nixon complaint—the instant analyses of network television commentators. In early November, the president had gone on nationwide television to discuss his Vietnam policy. He hoped to diffuse the next major antiwar demonstration, scheduled for November 15, by more radical organizers than those who had put together Moratorium Day. Among the guest analysts commenting on the speech had been President Johnson's chief negotiator in the Paris peace talks, W. Averell Harriman. He and other network and guest commentators essentially dismissed the speech as an old-hat exercise in accentuating the positive.

In a revealing diary entry indicating that Agnew was far from freelancing in his fiery speeches, Haldeman wrote: "Considerable discussion of Buchanan's idea of VP doing a major speech blasting network commentators. P feels it's a good idea. I discussed it yesterday with VP and he too is interested, but felt it was a bit abrasive. (Kind of humorous with all the attention he's getting for his recent 'hatchet man' tactics). Needs to be said and he's the one to do it."

On the eve of the speech in Des Moines, which had been scheduled as a routine talk to a meeting of Midwest Republicans, there was also this entry: "P really pleased and highly amused by Agnew speech for tomorrow night. . . . Worked over some changes with Buchanan and couldn't contain his mirth as he thought about it. Will be a bombshell and the repercussions may be enormous, but it says what people think."[11] Indeed, Nixon also wrote later that he had taken a personal hand in the speech. "I toned down some of Buchanan's rhetoric and gave it to Agnew," he said. "We further moderated some sections that Agnew thought sounded strident, and then he edited it himself so that the final version would be in his words."[12] (One can only wonder what had been too "strident" for Agnew's taste.)

To make certain of the reaction, the White House the next day released the full text of the speech several hours in advance, sending the networks scurrying frantically to air it live. Pool coverage was hastily arranged for all the networks, and Agnew did not disappoint them, launching into an assault on the "instant analysis and querulous criticism" of the famous men in the studio booths.

"The audience of seventy million Americans—gathered to hear the president of the United States—was inherited by a small band of network commentators and self-appointed analysts," he intoned, "the majority of whom expressed in one way or another their hostility to what he had to say." It was, he went on, "obvious that their minds were made up in advance." Although "every American has a right to disagree with the president of the United States and to express publicly that disagreement," he said, the public ought to have had the right to listen "without the president's words and thought characterized through the prejudices of hostile critics before they can even be digested."[13]

Agnew took particular aim at Harriman's tour as peace negotiator, saying: "Like Coleridge's Ancient Mariner, Mr. Harriman seems to be under some heavy compulsion to justify his failures to anyone who will listen." ABC News, the vice president charged, had "trotted out Averell Harriman for the occasion" and he had "recited perfectly" the critical line sought. He went on to allege that Harriman had "swapped some of the greatest military concessions in the history of warfare for an enemy agreement on the shape of the table." The charge alluded to the bombing halt over North Vietnam in November 1968 that had broadened the peace talks—talks that Nixon supported at the time and continued later as president.[14]

Harriman actually had prefaced his remarks by saying, "I wouldn't be presumptuous to give a complete analysis of a very carefully thought out speech" by Nixon. He added that "I'm sure he wants to end this war and no one wishes him well any more than I do." Harriman benignly observed, however, that "he approaches the subject quite differently from the manner in which I approach it." He concluded: "I wish the president well. I hope he can lead us to peace. But this is not the whole story that we've heard tonight." That was hardly "querulous criticism."[15]

Agnew saved his best, or worst, for the paid commentators. He called them "this little group of men who not only enjoy the right of instant rebuttal to every presidential address, but more importantly wield a free hand in selecting, presenting and interpreting the great issues of our nation." He characterized the network reporter as "the presiding judge in a national trial by jury," and said of the commentators: "A raised eyebrow, an inflection of the voice, a caustic remark dropped in the middle of a broadcast can raise doubts in a million minds about the veracity of a public official or the wisdom of a government policy. . . . What do Americans know of the men who wield this power?" Nothing, he said, "other than they reflect an urbane and assured presence, seemingly well-informed on every important matter."

But the public did know, he went on, that they all lived and worked in Washington or New York, read the same newspapers, and talked "constantly to one another, thereby providing artificial reinforcement to their shared viewpoints." Agnew said nothing of the fact that most of the network commentators had traveled widely before they attained their prominent jobs, and that many continued to do so.

"Is it not fair and relevant," he asked, "to question [the] concentration [of power] in the hands of a tiny and closed fraternity of privileged men, elected by no one, and enjoying a monopoly sanctioned and licensed by government?" Agnew said he wasn't suggesting censorship, merely asking "whether a form of censorship already exists when the news that forty million Americans receive each night is determined by a handful of men responsible only to their corporate employers, and filtered through a handful of commentators who admit their own set of biases."

He called on the public to complain to their local television stations, and thousands who heard him responded in agreement. The top network executives squealed like stuck pigs. Frank Stanton, president of CBS, called the speech "an unprecedented attempt by the vice president of the United States to intimidate a news medium which depends for its exis-

tence upon government license." The fear was soon reinforced by the revelation that Dean Burch, appointed by Nixon as chairman of the licensing
Federal Communications Commission, had called the networks for tran-
scripts of their commentators' remarks after Nixon's Vietnam speech.
Burch responded by calling Agnew's speech "thoughtful, provocative and
[deserving of] careful consideration by the industry and the public."[16]

At the White House, according to Haldeman's diary entry the next
day, Nixon "was really pleased with VP talk last night. . . and feels he's
now become a really good property, and we should keep building and
using him."

Four days later, Haldeman wrote: "The debate on Agnew rages on,
with P fully convinced he's right and that majority will agree. I talked to
Stan Blair and told him to tell VP to keep up the offensive, and to keep
speaking, now is major figure in his own right. P wants him to get maximum exposure right away."[17]

Agnew by now needed no urging, from Nixon or anyone else. Not
only did the president not object to the spotlight shining on his stand-in,
he relished it, and seemed happy to have Agnew function as a lightning
rod drawing criticism to himself. Nixon press secretary Ron Ziegler continued to say Agnew was speaking his own mind and his speeches were
not cleared by the White House. The most Ziegler would allow was that
Buchanan "may have, and I think did have, some thoughts" on the Des
Moines speech, but Haldeman's diaries proved that Nixon's speechwriter
had more than "some thoughts" about it.[18]

Indeed, Buchanan was becoming a close confidant and cheerleader for
Agnew, and in short order they turned their attention to another blast at
the news media, this time the newspapers. The draft of Agnew's speech
was so hot that some cool heads in the White House ran up a caution flag
on the day before it was to be delivered in Montgomery, Alabama, with
the *New York Times* and *The Washington Post*, two old Nixon nemeses,
targeted. Haldeman's entry for the day warned: "*Huge* problem late today as Ziegler tells me of the VP's speech for tomorrow night, a real blast,
not just at TV, now he takes on newspapers, a lot of individuals and the
kids again. Pretty rough, and really does go too far. Problem is Agnew is
determined to give it and and won't listen to Ziegler, or [White House
communications director Herb] Klein. Blair said, 'Only I could turn it
off,' so I said he should. Now we'll see what happens."[19]

It was clear now that the Spiro T. Agnew, who less than a year earlier was a compliant second banana whose main gripes were staffing limitations, had already become secure enough to make more serious demands on the administration. At least in his role as the voice of what the president had called the Silent Majority, which Nixon vigorously applauded and wanted extended, Agnew was throwing his weight around, to the distress of some other insiders, including the second-most powerful man in the administration—Bob Haldeman.

Haldeman's diary entry on the day of the speech reflected the concern: "Day starts deep in the Agnew problem, as we try to decide what position to take. Finally E [Ehrlichman], Harlow and I agreed the original speech would be harmful, to a substantial degree. So we told P about it (since Blair had made it clear to me that nothing short of P would cause VP to make any change). P agreed, after I skimmed through the objectionable area, then said only way to handle was through whoever had written it. I didn't know. P looked at first page and said obviously it was Buchanan. He was right. I spent a long time with Pat, but as the final version came out it didn't do much good. It still hits very hard, especially at the *New York Times*. I did get out the highly personal and defensive segments. P made point that Agnew must be cool and calm and never defend against attacks from a lower level."[20]

The Montgomery speech as delivered focused on concentration of ownership among the nation's major press organizations, with particular focus on the *Times* and the *Post*. Agnew carped at the *Times*, suggesting that lack of competition made it soft and charging, erroneously, that it had ignored a strong letter of congressional support for Nixon's Vietnam policy. As for the *Post*, he alleged that in its ownership also of *Newsweek* magazine and a Washington television station, "all grinding out the same editorial line," it had a stranglehold on public opinion. The allegations were far off the mark, ignoring the fact that the *Times* and the *Post* were probably the two most committed and innovative newspapers in the country in serving their readers—as well as among the harshest critics of the Nixon administration.

The vice president insisted he was "opposed to censorship of television or the press in any form." Defensively, he observed that "for the purpose of clarity, before my thoughts are obliterated in the smoking typewriters of my friends in Washington and New York, let me emphasize I am not recommending the dismemberment of The Washington Post Company. I am merely pointing out that the public should be aware that these four powerful voices [the *Times*, the *Post*, *Newsweek*, and the *Post*'s television station] harken to the same master." Each, as Agnew must have known, had its independent editorial policy, but the vice president did not let that distinction interfere with his assault.

He warned that "the day when the network commentators and even the gentlemen of the *New York Times* enjoyed a form of diplomatic immunity from comment and criticism of what they said—that day is over. . . . When their criticism becomes excessive or unjust, we shall invite them down from their ivory towers to enjoy the rough and tumble of the public debate. I do not seek to intimidate the press, the networks or anyone else from speaking out. But the time for blind acceptance of their opinions is past. And the time for naïve belief in their neutrality is gone."[21]

Nixon not only indicated approval but also urged Haldeman to drum up even more attention to his stand-in. When a new internal public-opinion poll was taken in late November showing the vice president's popularity continuing on the upswing, the president sent Haldeman a memo: "It occurred to me that one way you could see that the Agnew poll got a good ride would be for Buchanan or [press aide Lyn] Nofziger to get in fifteen of the more conservative columnists and give them a little preview of it. The main point I wish to emphasize, however, is that it must not be treated as a poll which we took but simply one that came to our attention."

Nixon, though, was not anxious to be associated personally with the divisive views about the prominent television analysts expressed by Agnew. The memo continued: "I am inclined to go harder on his own popularity rating and not quite so hard on the agreement with him about the television commentators, although the second point can be made as second lead."[22]

In early December, Nixon told reporters during a televised news conference that Agnew had "rendered a public service in talking in a very dignified and courageous way" about the press coverage. He had no complaints himself, he said, "just so long as the news media allows, as it does tonight, an opportunity for me to be heard directly by the people and then television commentators will follow."[23] They did indeed, offering only the briefest of recapping and summing up—ABC for one minute, CBS for four and NBC for eight. Agnew had reason to believe that his message had gotten through where it counted.

Within the White House, differences continued regarding the vice president's effectiveness and how he fit in as a member of the team. Some other staff aides who had been against Agnew ever since the Mission Bay post-convention meetings of the year before felt that Nixon, as one of them put it, "had created a Frankenstein monster." Moving toward the new year, this aide said, "the doubts on the one hand and the feeling that the vice president was a valuable ally on the other endured."[24]

But as long as Nixon himself continued to encourage the smoking rhetoric and expressed pleasure at the public response to it among Republicans, Agnew was unassailable. On another of his speeches, Haldeman recorded in his diary that "P really pleased afterwards with the VP's attitude and approach. He really relishes taking on a fight, and he does it very well. P is concerned though about letting Buchanan run loose with VP because he's almost too willing to take up the cudgel."[25] At the same time, Nixon told Haldeman to handle him with kid gloves. "Got into VP setup," his chief of staff wrote. "P wants us to persuade him to cut back on extraneous activities, but said 'whatever he asks for I have to give him,' so you have to get him to cut back voluntarily."[26]

The man who barely a year earlier had acknowledged that Spiro Agnew was not a household name was now indisputably that, and largely by his own making. He was big news, almost as big as the president himself, and certainly louder, and deference had to be paid.

Chapter 6

HOT-AND-COLD
HONEYMOON

At the start of 1970, Nixon sent Agnew on a twenty-three-day, eleven-nation tour of Asia, giving rise to much press speculation that the purpose was to get him out of the domestic limelight for a while.

Before Agnew left, Nixon in a rare departure called him in for a talk about the trip, and Haldeman in his diary later wrote this account: "P wants him to go on around the world since he'll be halfway at Afghanistan. VP already has itinerary set and very reluctant to change. P told him he should now stop talking about the media except for some light quips, and said the VP could now talk about all those things he had been talking about before but no one was listening, and now they'll listen because he's become a national figure. Sort of a back-handed compliment, not intended that way. Main point was to get the VP back on to constructive ground and stop him from riding the media issue to death. He got the point."[1]

In advance of the trip, Agnew demonstrated another of his efforts to deal himself a hand in foreign policy. He wrote a memo to Secretary of State Rogers, John Hannah, head of the Agency for International Development [AID], and Peace Corps director Joseph Blatchford telling them he wanted AID and the Peace Corps "to examine the feasibility of developing some pilot projects wherein the resources of the respective agencies could be coordinated. This would appear to be extremely desirable with respect to the Peace Corps' plans to increase its activities in the area of technically trained Corps members." The vice president asked for a report from the recipients. One of them wrote on the memo in an unidentifable hand: "On the basis of what is Agnew doing this?"[2]

The White House was flooded with applications from newspapers to send reporters on the trip, but only ten press seats were available. One of the vice president's prime targets, the *New York Times*, got one of them, but the other, *The Washington Post*, did not. Anticipation of a string of Agnew gaffes that would ruffle international feathers went unrealized as the vice president, with foreign-policy experts from the State Department aboard, essentially stuck to his script. The only bump was a demonstration against Agnew by Peace Corps volunteers in Afghanistan.

An "eyes-only" memo to Nixon upon his return suggested his pre-trip interest in the Peace Corps was not idle. The vice president alerted him that "among our Peace Corps volunteers are a hard core of anti-war people who make a very bad impression by demonstrating against the Administration position in Vietnam. These people seek press exposure and in two places I visited were rather embarrassing. In Bangkok, Peace Corps volunteers made public statements against the Vietnam war and wore black armbands during my stay. The Thai government was quite incensed and provided me with detailed information on the situation." Nixon jotted in the margin: "Disgraceful."

Agnew further wrote that the American ambassador in Afghanistan had reported "difficulty in stopping a Peace Corps demonstration" and was able to do so only when an aide had met with them and promised a later meeting with the ambassador. "I feel very strongly that our ambassadors should be directed to avoid conferring with dissatisfied Peace Corps volunteers," Agnew wrote, adding that it was "inappropriate in my judgment for our high-level diplomats to be pressured into meetings with these malcontents." To that, Nixon scribbled to Kissinger: "I completely agree—put out an order." Agnew went on, writing that the ambassador's response to their demands "was too conciliatory, and I let him know personally," to which Nixon wrote: "Right."[3]

From this and other evidence, the vice president was continuing to operate as a responsible if a bit intrusive member of the Nixon team. That evidence apparently did not, however, earn him and his wife, Judy, the warm embrace of other insiders. In a memo from Haldeman to one of the White House social staff after the Nixons' first "Evening at the White

House'" event in early February, the chief of staff asked: "How did the Agnews happen to end up in the receiving line and upstairs afterwards?"[4]

Haldeman also was concerned about Agnew's growing penchant for talking about himself. He told speechwriter Buchanan that they had to change Agnew's style, that in his speeches he needed to lard them "heavily with praise" for Nixon and the administration and not "toot his own horn." On issues, Haldeman said, Agnew should not take a position unless Nixon had already spoken or if he gave a specific order for Agnew to do so, and that the vice president should "do more kicking the other side."[5]

Ehrlichman, too, continued to have severe reservations about the vice president, at least about his ability to take on important policy tasks. When Nixon decided in early 1970 to put planning for a new health progam in Agnew's hands, Ehrlichman wrote later, "health experts were to be added to the vice president's staff, along with a speechwriter and TV specialists. Agnew then chaired a series of interdepartmental meetings on health issues, but he seemed incapable of organizing the work and guiding the staff to the result. I watched the vice president closely during this health project, trying to discover the cause of his mental constipation. I concluded that the man was exceedingly narrow; new thoughts were unwelcome to him. As a result, his health project did not gather for the president all the practical alternatives for a final choice. Instead it became a narrow reflection of Spiro Agnew's preferences. One by one the resource people dropped away from the effort (as did I), and it languished. . . . Spiro Agnew had struck out on health."[6]

When Agnew, as chairman of the cabinet committee on school desegregation, got heavily involved that spring in an effort to peacefully dissolve the dual school system in the South, his enthusiasm for making a splash had to be reined in. Haldeman wrote in his diary: "Agnew made a big pitch for his using a new Buchanan speech about the end of the desegregation movement." But Nixon, he went on, "doesn't want VP to get out beyond his own position and thus become oversold as the southern strategy man. Afraid to dilute or waste the great asset he has become."[7]

According to Ehrlichman, "Harlow, Haldeman and I were called in [by Nixon] and Bryce Harlow was sent off with orders for Agnew. To mollify the vice president, Haldeman and I were to stay out of the new arrangement: 'You, Bryce, are to clear any of his statements on school integration or civil rights,' Nixon said. 'Tell him I'm very pleased with the

way he's handled himself, so far. But he's not to have any press conferences. Anything he wants to say that's not [in accord with policy] must be
okayed by me in advance. Tell him I don't want any new ground broken.
Say: I'd hate to have to repudiate something he said."[8]

That particular report from Ehrlichman revealed not only the bad
blood between Nixon's two top advisers and Agnew, but also Nixon's
own pointed disinclination to deal directly with his vice president. As
with others, the president preferred to convey his wishes through third
parties. This withdrawn manner in his private dealings was a sharp contrast from the way he often presented himself in large public events,
when he gave in to much glad-handing and back-slapping among old
political associates. But in this as in so many other ways, he did so awk-
wardly, with gestures that often seemed out of sync, and with what came
off as feigned enthusiasm. Agnew was the opposite: frequently aloof,
even withdrawn in crowds, well-groomed almost to an antiseptic degree.
When Nixon traveled, he played the hale party man, inviting old politicians to his suite to discuss their mutual business and having a drink or
two. Agnew on the other hand abhorred such familiarity except with his
small traveling circle, often skipping pre-dinner receptions and staying
in his hotel suite until his appearance was required, and retreating to it
afterward.

Nevertheless, the president and his vice president did seem to be on
good, if distant, terms. When, early in March, Nixon had decided not to
attend the college graduation of his daughter Julie for fear of being a dis-
tracting presence, Agnew talked him out of it. "VP told him he was
wrong in not going," Haldeman recorded, "and this caused him to reconsider; thinks now he should just go and sit in audience and take the heat if
there's a demonstration or a bad speaker."[9]

The president and his vice president did make a rare joint appearance
at the 1970 Gridiron dinner of Washington newspaper correspondents
and editors. Two nights before the affair, Nixon called Agnew to the
White House for a secret meeting, which turned out to be a rehearsal for
a gag Nixon had worked up on his own, with only Haldeman in on it. At
the dinner, the president strolled onto the stage and called the vice president to join him, asking him whether there really was a southern strategy
in which he played a key role. On cue, Agnew replied emphatically: "No,
suh!" Then they sat down at separate pianos. Each time Nixon began to

play a favorite of a former president—"Home on the Range" for FDR, "The Missouri Waltz" for Harry Truman, "The Eyes of Texas" for LBJ, Agnew on the other piano loudly interrupted with "Dixie." They wound up playing a duet of "God Bless America" and "Auld Lang Syne," the traditional Gridiron closer, in a public display of frivolity uncommon for both of them. As Haldeman described it in his diary: "P's idea was an absolute smash hit. . . . Great idea and beautifully executed. P called me after we got home, was really pleased with how it had come off, as he should have been. Feels he'll never be able to top it, and won't even go next year.'"[10]

If this kind of jovial joint appearance suggested that Agnew was growing into something approaching a partnership with Nixon, however, that interpretation was well off the mark. Nixon's words and actions within the White House clearly indicated otherwise. In an "eyes-only" memo around this time to Haldeman, Ehrlichman, and Henry Kissinger, the president wrote that he didn't want to be bothered with what he called "low-priority items" beyond "a semiannual report indicating what has happened." He instructed Haldeman: "In the arranging of my schedule, have in mind these priorities. Great pressures will build up to see this and that minor or major official from the low-priority countries. All of this is to be farmed out to Agnew. For example, the minister of mines from Venezuela is a case in point; he should not have been included on the schedule, and I do not want this to happen again."[11]

Agnew, however, was not reluctant to inject himself into an executive role when he could. About one occasion in late March of 1970 on which Ehrlichman three years later had cause to reflect, Nixon's number-two aide wrote: "The vice president told Nixon that he was concerned about the way GSA [the General Services Administration] awarded its contracts in the Eastern states. Agnew asserted that 'our friends' were being discriminated against. Someone [presumably Agnew] should monitor this important form of patronage." Ehrlichman wrote that soon afterward, he got a phone call from Robert Kunzig, the GSA administrator, saying an Agnew assistant had called him and ordered that such matters be cleared through the vice president. Ehrlichman informed Haldeman, who checked and found "there had been no decision to give Agnew such sweeping control of the GSA." Ehrlichman wrote then: "To me this was simply another case of Agnew trying to grab some of the White House levers. It didn't occur to me that Agnew might be seeking to profit finan-cially from such control; I ignored the signals. Obviously, Spiro Agnew was a problem that required constant vigilance; more attention than I, for one, was able to give."[12]

Nixon himself had no intention of overseeing Agnew's actions. Indeed, he avoided his vice president whenever he could, in part because Agnew insisted on kibitizing on how the president needed to counsel more with him and with cabinet members. Ehrlichman wrote later of Nixon: "In the spring of 1970, after one of his rare meetings with Agnew, Nixon com-plained that his vice president had become an advocate of the 'crybabies' in the cabinet. Agnew had lectured him on the need for the president to have his department secretaries in more often for consultation. 'The damned crybabies just want therapy, of course,' Nixon said. 'They'll say, 'Oh, help us' and 'protect us.' Imagine that damned Agnew!'"[13]

THE ONE IMPORTANT ARENA in which Nixon definitely did want Ag-new involved was on the Lincoln Day fund-raising circuit, where he served up generous portions of alliterative ridicule against his targets, from Democrats in general to liberals in particular. In Lincoln, Nebraska, he drew peals of laughter by saying the public was "ready to run for the Rolaids" at Democratic complaints about him, and in Chicago he at-tacked "supercilious sophisticates" who pushed for open-admission poli-cies in the country's universities. In Atlanta, he responded to anti-war pickets outside his hotel and specifically laid claim to being the voice of the Silent Majority, with this harangue:

> The liberal media have been calling on me to lower my voice and to seek accord and unity among all Americans. Nothing would please me more than to see all voices lowered; to see us return to dialogue and discuss and debate within our institutions and within our gov-ernmental system; to see dissatisfied citizens turn to the elective process to change the course of government; to see an end to the vil-lification, the obscenities, the vandalism and the violence that have become the standard tactics of the dissidents who claim to act in the interests of peace and freedom.

But I want you to know that I will not make a unilateral with-drawal and thereby abridge the confidence of the Silent Majority, the everyday law-abiding American who believes his country needs a strong voice to articulate his dissatisfaction with those who seek to destroy our heritage of liberty and our system of justice. To pene-trate the cacophony of seditious drivel emanating from the best-publicized clowns in our society and their fans in the fourth estate, yes, my friends, to penetrate that drivel, we need a cry of alarm, not a whisper. . . . Let the few, the very few, who would desecrate their own house be made fully aware of our utter contempt."[14]

Such declarations began to arouse the concern of the president, who saw in them now a bit more of personal self-aggrandizement than he liked. After one conversation with Nixon around this time, Haldeman recorded in his diary that Nixon "made point again that we need to change the Agnew approach. He is a very effective salesman for himself but not for the administration. Has become too much of an issue and a personality."[15]

More concern surfaced about a week later when Agnew's speaking tour had taken him to Des Moines and he was about to leave for Hous-ton. At the White House, Nixon was meeting with the Danish prime minister when word came that the third space mission to the moon, Apollo 13, had suffered an explosion in one of its oxygen tanks en route and was ordered to abort the moon landing and return home. After an initial notion of having Nixon fly to Houston, the Apollo 13 base, it was decided otherwise, Nixon not wanting to be seen as grandstanding. Haldeman quickly got on the phone to Agnew and told him not to pro-ceed to Houston either.

"I got into a bind with VP," Haldeman wrote in his diary, "by ordering him to halt on runway at Des Moines as he was leaving for Houston. Made him sit and wait for over an hour while P was with prime minister, then raised question with P, and he fully agreed VP should not go to Houston for same reasons P shouldn't, *plus* upstaging P. VP mad as hell, but agreed to follow orders and go to Florida and wait."[16] Agnew as a high elected official champed at getting orders from the unelected Halde-man, even if told they came from the president. It was an irritant that only grew as time went on and Haldeman's role as the second-most powerful man in the Nixon administration was cemented.

Through this period, Agnew continued to oversee the Office of Intergovernmental Relations, but not to his own satisfaction. In mid-April, Nixon sent out a memorandum creating a new subcommittee of his proposed Domestic Affairs Council incorporating Rural and Urban Affairs Councils. Agnew countered with a memo to Nixon urging that he reconsider and instead work through his intergovernmental relations office while "integrating it into the decision-making process of the Domestic Affairs Council." The memo reflected Agnew's general concern that his voice was not being adequately heard in a timely way, and by inference that he was being reduced to a role of implementer of decisions already made. It was a fear that increasingly plagued the vice president, and was confirmed by a reply from Ehrlichman, deftly positioning himself to be the administration's domestic czar. He wrote Agnew that his proposal was, among others, "currently under study" as part of a sweeping executive office reorganization.[17]

According to party officials, Agnew's assaults on administration critics before partisan audiences around the country were bringing millions of dollars into state GOP treasuries, and the vice president was valued particularly in that light. One who was displeased with him, however, was Governor Tom McCall of Oregon. When the vice president turned down his invitation to speak to a meeting of the Education Commission of the States, which the governor chaired, McCall loudly complained. According to a staff memo in the Agnew files, McCall deplored "the vice president being able to run around all over the country addressing what he called 'right-wing groups' and harming relationships with students and youth, but here he was turning down a very positive opportunity to speak to a meaningful audience that could help him and all of us in regard to the troubles before the nation today."[18]

At this time, it seemed, the vice president had more pressing political work to do. Nixon had suffered defeat in the Senate of two conservative Dixie nominees to the Supreme Court, Clement F. Haynsworth Jr. of South Carolina and G. Harold Carswell of Florida. Agnew brought a message to southerners that by gaining Republican control of the Senate in the coming fall elections, Nixon would yet put one of their ilk on the highest court. In Columbia, Senator Strom Thurmond in his introduction of the vice president predicted to wild applause that "South Carolina will favor Spiro Agnew," and Agnew obliged, in his customary non-threatening tone of voice, with some vicious gags using Nixon as his straight man.

His only disagreement with the president came, he said, when Nixon "decided to convert the White House swimming pool into a sumptuous new press room. It wasn't that I objected to using the swimming pool for this purpose. It was just that I resented his insistence that the water be drained out."[19] The crowd loved the notion of drowning the whole White House press corps, and other similar thinly veiled hatemongering in the guise of humor.

As part of Agnew's general attack on liberals, he began focusing on academics in some of the nation's most prominent eastern universities. A particular target was the president of Yale, Kingman Brewster Jr. Agnew called for his ouster for having sympathized with students who went on strike in support of Black Panther leader Bobby Seale, on trial for murder. Brewster had also criticized Nixon's election as "a hucksterized process," which led Agnew to declare "it is time for the alumni of that fine old college to demand that it be headed by a more mature and responsible person."[20]

This and other criticisms of academic leaders came in the context of increasing unrest on American campuses over the war in Vietnam and rising racial conflict. A study of campus tensions by the American Council on Education assigned some of the blame to "political exploitation of campus problems by some public figures" like Agnew and Ronald Reagan.[21]

Regarding the Vietnam War, Agnew offered more than his oratory in aggressive support of Nixon's policy. In April of 1970, as the president pondered military action to wipe out enemy sanctuaries in Cambodia from which attacks against South Vietnam were being made with impunity, his vice president urged the strongest possible response. According to Henry Kissinger, Agnew took on the more cautious Secretary of State William Rogers and Secretary of Defense Melvin Laird, who advocated minimum force. He egged Nixon on to attack two sanctuaries, known as Parrot's Beak and Fishhook, when only one of them was under consideration as a target.

Kissinger wrote later that at this point "Agnew spoke up. He thought the whole debate irrelevant. Either the sanctuaries were a danger or they were not. If it was worth cleaning them out, he did not understand all the pussyfooting about the American role or what we accomplished by attacking only one. Our task was to make Vietnamization [the assumption of all military operations by the Saigon regime] succeed. He favored an attack on *both* Fishhook and Parrot's Beak, including American forces. Agnew was right."

This interjection into Nixon's realm of foreign policy expertise reflected the growing confidence of Agnew the domestic-policy man, but also a certain disregard of his own limits and of Nixon's sensitivities. Kissinger went on: "If Nixon hated anything more than being presented with a plan he had not considered, it was being shown up in a group as being less tough than his advisers. Though chafing at the bit, he adroitly placed himself between the vice president and the cabinet. He authorized American air support for the Parrot's Beak operation but only 'on the basis of demonstrated necessity.' He avoided committing himself to Fishhook. . . . After the meeting, Nixon complained bitterly to me that I had not forewarned him of Agnew's views, of which I had been unaware. I have no doubt that Agnew's intervention accelerated Nixon's ultimate decision to order an attack on all the sanctuaries and use of American forces."[22]

In the end, Nixon decided to go after Fishhook as well. But in his critical meeting with NSC members on the planning, Kissinger noted, "Agnew was not invited. Even though he was now taking his vice president's advice, Nixon was still smarting from Agnew's unexpected sally and was determined to be the strong man of *this* meeting."[23] The vice president, who had been taken on the team for his background in domestic political and policy matters, suddenly was finding and expressing his voice in military and foreign affairs. It was clear by now that he was of a mind not to take a back seat anywhere in the administration, if he could manage it.

Chapter 7

BIG MAN ON CAMPUS

W<small>HAT THE ADMINISTRATION CALLED THE</small> "<small>INCURSION</small>" <small>INTO</small> Cambodia, in April of 1970, inflamed American campuses as a reckless expansion of the war, and Agnew was thrown into the breach with an appearance on CBS News's *Face the Nation*. He defended the action as necessary to protect U.S. forces in South Vietnam, and he lashed out at "the dissident and destructive elements in our society" that were "simply utilizing this as a vehicle to continue their antisocial, outrageous conduct." Reminded near the close of the interview of Nixon's inaugural plea for lowered voices and asked whether he had "increased divisiveness in this country, and if so to what end," he demurred: "When a fire takes place, a man doesn't run into the room and whisper, 'Would somebody please get the water?' He yells, 'Fire! and I am yelling 'Fire!' because I think 'Fire!' needs to be called here."[1]

On the very next day, a protest at Kent State University in Ohio, ignited by the Cambodia action—and fanned by Agnew's rhetoric—spread to campuses across the land. National Guardsmen, rushed to the Kent State campus by Republican Governor James Rhodes, fired on student protesters and killed four of them. In Washington, Agnew responded to the moment with a prepared and blistering attack on the demonstrators. If some in the audience thought his words "show a certain insensitivity" at that precise hour, he said, he was responding to "a general malaise that argues for violent confrontation instead of debate." He targeted "tomentose [hairy] exhibitionists who provoke more derision than fear" and "who in their feverish search for group acceptance are ready to endorse tumultuous confrontation as a substitute for debate."

In the course of this tirade, Agnew singled out patrician Mayor John Lindsay of New York, who a month earlier had been critical of officials who were "ready to support repression as long as it is done in a quiet voice and a business suit." The vice president responded against other officials "ready to support revolution as long as it is with a cultured voice and a handsome profile."[2]

At the White House, meanwhile, news of the Kent State shootings rattled Nixon. "He's very disturbed," Haldeman wrote in his diary that night. "Afraid his decision set it off, and that is the ostensible cause of the demonstrations there. Issued condolence statement, then kept after me all the rest of the day. Hoping rioters had provoked the shooting, but no real evidence they did, except throwing rocks at National Guard. Talked about how we can get through to the students, turn this stuff off. . . . Main need now is to maintain calm and hope this serves to dampen other demonstrations rather than firing them up. Hard to tell yet which will result. . . . P is troubled by all this, although it was predicted as a result of the Cambodian move."[3]

Agnew's smoking rhetoric continued to delight many Republicans, but now it was turning off others of a more moderate bent. One was Nixon's secretary of interior, Walter J. Hickel, the former governor of Alaska who had flirted with the Nelson Rockefeller candidacy before being brought into the Nixon fold. He wrote a letter to Nixon urging him to rein in the vice president as a first step in rebuilding shattered lines of communication with the nation's youth. "I believe the vice president initially has answered a deep-seated mood of America in his public statements," Hickel said. "However, a continued attack on the young—not in their attitudes so much as their motives—serves little purpose other than to further cement those attitudes to a solidity impossible to penetrate with reason."[4] Later, Hickel on the CBS News show *Sixty Minutes* repeated the observation without specifically mentioning Agnew.

There was talk at the White House about appointing a special commission to investigate the Kent State shootings, but Nixon wanted to hold off. Meanwhile, Hickel's letter of protest was leaked to the *Washington Star*. The story, Haldeman wrote in his diary, was "designed to enhance the 'collapse of the presidency' theory. P pretty calm about it last night, pretty cold-blooded today. Feels Hickel's got to go as soon as we're past this crisis.'" [Seven months later, Hickel was fired.] Haldeman continued: "This led to a rising 'anti-cabinet' feeling as he [Nixon] thought more about it. Went back to deep resentment that none called him after speech [on Cambodia] and none rose to his defense on this deal. So he struck back by ordering the tennis court removed immediately. Feels cabinet should work on own intiative to support P, and they haven't."[5] Ironically, one of the heavy users of the White House tennis court was Agnew, who was defending Nixon on Cambodia more forcefully than anyone else.

Nevertheless, Haldeman referred in the diary to "an Agnew problem, result of the Hickel letter, and stories that P is muzzling him. Wants VP to avoid any remarks about students, etc.; VP strongly disagrees. I passed the word. VP said he would act only on order of P."[6] Once again, Agnew was smarting over directions from an unelected presidential subordinate.

Shortly after the Kent State shootings, Nixon went to the Pentagon to discuss the Cambodian situation and afterward referred to college demonstrators as "these bums, blowing up campuses."A group of university presidents met with Nixon, protested strongly about both his and Agnew's comments, and urged the president to refrain from further hostile remarks about students. Nixon assured them he would do so. After the university presidents had left, Haldeman wrote, Nixon "took me on a tour of south grounds to discuss tennis court removal and life in general. Feels very concerned about campus revolt and basically helpless to deal with it." The visiting academics, Haldeman wrote, "all blame Agnew primarily, then P's 'bums' crack. General feeling is that without Kent State it would not have been so bad, but that even without Cambodia there were a lot of campuses ready to blow."[7]

The next night, Nixon held a news conference on Cambodia, preceded by much advice from Haldeman and others. "The hard line," Haldeman wrote later, "was mainly from K [Kissinger] who feels we should just let the students tear it for a couple of weeks with no effort at pacification, then hit them hard. Most of the others leaned the other way and wanted a full apology for the 'bums' and a tight muzzle on to Agnew's rhetoric. Fortunately P was shrewd enough to accomplish both objectives without giving in on either."[8]

Several days later, Agnew in a taped interview with television personality David Frost said he thought the president's reference to "bums" was "a little mild." But he conceded that if the National Guardsmen at Kent State had fired first, they could be charged with murder and their actions couldn't be condoned. On the other hand, he said, had the students not thrown rocks at the Guardsmen, there would not have been any shooting. Frost countered that had Cambodia not been invaded, there would not have been demonstrations. Maybe so, Agnew replied; certain elements were ready to riot over anything. As for Hickel, he said, he probably hadn't read the Agnew speeches in their entirety. The students were being heard, he added, "but the fact that they are heard does not necessarily mean they must be heeded."[9]

There was Agnew's father-knows-best assertion again. As for his heated rhetoric, he explained to the British audience: "In a desire to be heard, I have to throw what people in America call a little red meat once in a while, and hope that in spite of the damaging context in which those remarks are repeated, that other things which I think are very important will also appear."[10]

One thing that was getting through to the American people was that Spiro T. Agnew was not your garden variety vice president, about whom so many jokes on the obscurity of that officeholder were part of the nation's political lore. The man's determination to become a household name was not only already achieved; in the Gallup Poll he ranked third behind Nixon and evangelist Billy Graham among the most admired men in America, and five of every eight men asked about him had a favorable opinion.[11] If Agnew thought he had a right to speak out, he certainly had reason to think so.

Reports, however, began circulating that the president had told Agnew to cool his rhetoric. In early May, in Boise, Idaho, the vice president insisted otherwise to reporters. He told them that a White House aide had called him with a message from Nixon. "The president wanted me to understand thoroughly he was not attempting to put any kind of muzzle on me," Agnew said, "and that he was not opposed to the kind of things I have been saying." While he would continue to criticize "criminal conduct" by war protesters, "we never meant to imply that a great majority of the students were involved in this kind of conduct." That night, Nixon said at a rare news conference he would never try to tell Agnew what to say, but that he did advise all his cabinet members to remember that "when the action is hot, keep the rhetoric cool."[12]

Relatively speaking, Agnew held his acid tongue during a visit to Atlanta, where he substituted for the president at the dedication of a Confederate memorial to Robert E. Lee, Jefferson Davis, and Stonewall Jackson carved on the side of Stone Mountain. But an *Atlanta Constitution* editorial called Agnew's participation "a shame and a disgrace" and, comparing him with Lee, said the vice president "has the grace of a drill sergeant and the understanding of a [nineteenth-century] prison camp warden." Agnew fired back. He agreed, he said, that rhetoric should be cooled, and "I think the best place it should begin is on the editorial pages of some of the eastern newspapers."[13]

A week later, at another Republican fund-raising dinner, in Houston, Agnew elaborated: "Lately, you have been exposed to a great deal of public comment about vice-presidential rhetoric and how I should 'cool it.' Nowhere is the complaint louder than in the columns and editorials of the liberal news media of this country, those really illiberal, self-appointed guardians of our destiny who would like to run the country without ever submitting to the elective process as we in public office must do." If they would lower their voices, he said, so would he, but "this I am sure they are unwilling to do, and there is too much at stake in the nation for us to leave the entire field of public commentary to them."

Then Agnew launched a fusillade of criticisms at not only the *Atlanta Constitution* but also the *New York Times* and *The Washington Post*. He singled out the *Post*'s Pulitzer Prize–winning cartoonist, Herblock, "that master of sick invective," for a sketch showing a National Guardsman with a box of bullets, each labeled with an Agnew bit of invective and one marked with Nixon's "bums" characterization of student protesters.

Agnew said he didn't mean to attack all members of the press, but he was bothered "that the press as a group regards the First Amendment as its own private preserve. . . . That happens to be my amendment too. It guarantees my free speech as much as it does their freedom of the press. So I hope that will be remembered the next time a 'muzzle Agnew' campaign is launched."[14]

Nixon, meanwhile, far from any desire to shut Agnew up, simply wanted him to pivot away from bashing students to three other specific targets he wanted assailed—key Democrats of the Johnson administration he believed could be painted as responsible for the mess in Vietnam. In a memo to Haldeman dated May 13, Nixon wrote: "I believe that the next Agnew attack—one that would come with great responsibility and could have enormous effect—would be one on the three turncoats, [Clark] Clifford, [W. Averell] Harriman and [Cyrus] Vance, or call them the three Monday-morning quarterbacks or what have you. . . . These three men were all architects of the policy that got us into Vietnam and that escalated the fighting so that our casualties were the highest in five years. . . I think this would make an excellent speech by Agnew. It should be built up in advance and it would bring a howl of outrage from the other side, but it needs to be said and it will have repercussions in a few other quarters as well. While he is talking along this line Agnew might drop in, and this would be the time to do it, the fact that the likes of [Senator J. William] Fulbright who voted for the Tonkin Gulf Resolution and many Democratic senators were completely silent when Johnson was escalating American participation in the war and now are jumping to criticism. You should pick them name by name in this instance."[15]

The task was assigned to speechwriter Buchanan, who apparently threw himself into it with a bit more enthusiasm than Nixon intended. A dozen days later, Haldeman noted in his diary: "Buchanan has a hot new Agnew speech blasting Harriman, Vance, and Clifford, for Thursday night. P a little leery, wants to be sure it's not too rough." Two days later, Haldeman wrote that Nixon had called "to have me turn off VP on his very tough speech for tomorrow about Harriman, Vance, Clifford. P feels this is not the time for it."[16]

Others in the White House also were concerned about the tough law-and-order rhetoric. Later in May, after a riot in Augusta, Georgia, sparked by rumors of police brutality in the killing of a jailed prisoner, presidential adviser Pat Moynihan, a prominent Democrat, sent Nixon a memo urging him to condemn violence and call for a federal investigation. A copy went to Agnew, inspiring him to send a memo of his own to Ehrlichman for Nixon's attention. He wrote that he found Moynihan's comments "disturbing and even somewhat frightening. We must not fall into the usual trap of separating and dissecting a fragment of a disorder. It has become fashionable in the liberal community to totally disregard the unlawful and outrageous acts which may have led to isolated instances of police overreaction and to focus on a single result which serves their thesis.

"It is obvious from these reports that none of the incidents arose out of improper police conduct. They all began with the usual civil rights propaganda techniques. We have had enough maudlin sympathy for lawbreakers emanating from other areas of government. The only thing that keeps the country together is the steadfast resolve of the White House not to be trapped into such attitudes. In my judgment, nothing makes the average American any angrier than to see the pained, self-righteous expressions of a Muskie or a Percy as they attach like leeches to the nearest Negro funeral procession.

"Please be certain that these opinions reach the president. This is a time when he must not crack under the steady onslaught of pressures in this direction. The polls show that the people are with him and not with the whiners in the Senate and in the liberal community." When the memo came back from Nixon, Ehrlichman noted that he had underlined the reference to Senators Muskie and Percy and jotted down next to the paragraph: "E—I agree."[17] Nixon appeared to have gotten vicarious pleasure reading words of the sort he often had uttered himself in earlier incarnations.

Nixon, however, was more concerned about law and order on the campuses right now in the uproar over the Cambodia "incursion." To learn how it was playing at various colleges, a group of young White House aides was sent around the country to sample student sentiment on the president's handling of the war. One of the aides, Lee Huebner, returned reporting that "the most frequently quoted comment on the campuses was that the vice president's rhetoric was a thorn in their flesh, and we had to go back and tell him to cool down. So we did. . . . There was a sense that he really wanted to get at the bottom of it, to talk it out. . . . When he finished, he did say he didn't think it was time to go after the college students any more and he was going to cool it on that front; he was going to lay off the students. And he did."[18]

If so, the cooling off didn't last long. Soon after, Nixon appointed a new presidential commission on campus unrest that included a twenty-two-year-old Harvard junior named Joseph Rhodes Jr., an African-American and an acquaintance of Ehrlichman's. Rhodes had been student president at the California Institute of Technology when Nixon's number-two man first met him, and became sort of Ehrlichman's eyes and ears on campus unrest then and when he went to Harvard on a fellowship. Ehrlichman wrote later: "There was no secret about his views on the war, Spiro Agnew and Richard Nixon. But our differences were put rationally, and all our talks were completely honest on both sides." Upon his appointment, Rhodes told the *New York Times* he would "try to figure out. . . who gave what orders to send police on campus [at Kent State and Jackson State, a black college, also the site of shootings]" and whether the police "were thinking about campus bums when they pulled the trigger," clearly a reference to Nixon's earlier putdown.[19]

Agnew, again at odds with Ehrlichman, immediately responded. Seeing a wire-service report in Detroit of what Rhodes had said, he held a news conference. If the report was correct, he said, "Mr. Rhodes should resign immediately. He clearly does not possess the maturity, the objectivity and the judgment to serve on a fact-finding body of national importance. "At the same time," Agnew said, "my remarks should in no way be interpreted as an implied criticism of a presidential appointment. Having used a relationship of mutual trust with presidential adviser John Ehrlichman for his own political gain, Rhodes is no longer entitled to the cloak of dignity that a presidential appointment would throw around him."[20]

Despite the disavowal of taking issue with Nixon, the attack on a presidential appointee who was a friend of Nixon's number-two aide demonstrated once more Agnew's political insensitivity. Ehrlichman, at Camp David for a domestic staff planning meeting, immediately called Rhodes at Harvard and, Rhodes reported later, told him: "That son of a bitch! Don't worry about it. The president wants you to know he's not happy about it." In short order, Ron Zeigler reported there would be no changes on the commission.[21]

Ehrlichman in his later memoir of his White House years wrote what happened: "Agnew belatedly realized he had given the president a narrow choice between Joe Rhodes and Spiro Agnew, and he scrambled to shore up his demand that Rhodes must go. Agnew's constant ally Governor Ronald Reagan had also been hit by Rhodes in the same press conference [on reports of campus killings in California] . . . Agnew called me as soon as he returned from Detroit to report that 'Ronald Reagan is furious at Rhodes.' Agnew called John Mitchell too. Agnew called me back to ask if I intended to remove Rhodes from the commission. I said I could not. Then I called Joe Rhodes to tell him what was going on."

Ehrlichman continued: "Near the end of the day, the president called, too. I said it was unfortunate that Agnew had created such a difficult choice. But it seemed to me there were only two options: the president could toss off the only student on the commission because he'd misconstrued the 'bums' remark and opposed the war and Spiro Agnew was against him, or he could repudiate his vice president. Nixon said he'd sleep on it. The next day, William Scranton [the commission chairman] called to urge that Rhodes be retained. A few minutes later Spiro Agnew's aide called to say the vice president was 'too busy' to come to make his scheduled talk to our domestic policy meeting. A headline in the [Washington] *Evening Star* that day was 'PRESIDENT REBUFFS AGNEW ON STUDENT.' Nixon had sent Ron Ziegler to tell the press he would not remove Rhodes. In my view that was the only possible way Nixon could have gone. Agnew was exceedingly foolish to have issued an ultimatum which would have required the president to repudiate a bright, black student at the very time we were trying to quiet the colleges."[22]

When Nixon met with Scranton on the commission's goals, he urged the chairman to meet with Agnew. According to Ehrlichman, Nixon told Scranton: "He [Agnew] does have some ideas about this, and he doesn't have horns. At all costs you don't want him in an adversary position. And you know, Rhodes was wrong about Reagan. No one in California has been killed on a campus by any officer." Scranton replied: "I've told Rhodes to say nothing more to the press, but I'm sorry the vice president said what he did about Rhodes." Nixon said: "I am too. Reagan called me and he was very mad. John Mitchell called twice. I don't rebuff my vice president—I don't do that—but before he had a press conference he should have called Ehrlichman or someone. He didn't, did he?" Ehrlichman answered: "No, sir. He didn't."[23]

The night of the Rhodes incident, Haldeman wrote in his diary: "Flap about Agnew as he blasted our appointee to Kent State Commission. Creates awkward situation as Ziegler has to repudiate VP in effect. P concerned that VP would cut loose like this without checking first. Actually hurts him [Agnew] more than anyone. And builds up the guy he attacked, a militant black from Harvard [Joe Rhodes]. E in the middle as it's his boy, and he staunchly defends the appointment."[24]

Haldeman's diary notes for the next day demonstrated once again how Nixon abhorred confrontation: "[Nixon] wanted me to meet with VP to explain the whole incident and assure him it was *not* a rebuff, his judgment was correct, but we can't remove Rhodes now because of the fuss. VP really blew it by blasting publicly instead of working it out internally."[25] If Nixon had mixed feelings about Agnew at this point, it was clear from the observations of Ehrlichman and Haldeman that they believed the vice president had to be held on a much shorter leash from then on.

⬱ ⬳

THE FOLLOWING DAY, Nixon summoned to the presidential yacht *Sequoia* the group of insiders known as FRESH—Bob Finch, Rumsfeld, Ehrlichman, George Shultz, and Haldeman—to talk about Agnew's latest gambit. Over dinner, the president voiced his own growing reservations about his vice president, recorded by Haldeman later that night: "Quite a bit about Agnew, as P revealed he has a lot more doubts than he has expressed before. Ended up that we should discuss the problem and come up with basic recommendation for P as to exact role of Agnew and how to implement it, which P will then cover with him."[26]

Ehrlichman wrote later of the same *Sequoia* conversation: "The vice president proposed to deliver a speech the following Saturday which harshly blasted the Congress. Those on the staff who had seen drafts of the speech warned the president that it was a very bad idea." Nixon, after reviewing current vice presidential troubles, told the group, "I want you people to program Agnew." As Ehrlichman recalled, "I looked around the table; he had the wrong group. I reminded Nixon that Haldeman and I had both struck out with Agnew before, and by now Agnew must be furious with me over his Rhodes embarrassment. We couldn't program Agnew to leave a burning building.

"The other three were liberals, in Agnew's way of looking at people. I doubted that they could do what the president wanted done. Shultz wasn't willing to agree, but Finch and Rumsfeld were. As we talked about who might do some good, the president eliminated Pat Buchanan and John Mitchell. Pat couldn't and John wouldn't. In thinking then about what *motivated* Spiro Agnew, I realized I didn't have a clue. I didn't take his presidential aspirations seriously. He wasn't a Nixon team player. Maybe he was just a dedicated public servant who wasn't too bright."[27]

In any event, Nixon's doubts about Agnew continued to rise, and after the president had gotten an earful of complaints from a group of college presidents, Haldeman recorded his concern: "The Agnew question again. The college men raised it as they always do. An easy scapegoat. P wondering if we are all wrong, is he really polarizing the youth? Really hard to figure whether he does more harm or good. He's certainly not neutral."[28]

Other Republicans were reacting negatively against the vice president as well. On the day before he was to speak at a large party fundraiser in Cleveland, Haldeman reported in the diary: "Flap about [Ohio Senator] Bob Taft's refusal to attend Agnew dinner in Cleveland tomorrow. Built through the day, as Harlow maneuvered to get pressure put on Taft. Ended with Taft calling Harlow and refusing to go, really stupid. P really furious about his attitude, and says won't help him in campaign [for reelection]."[29] Ehrlichman in his book said that Taft had said publicly that "Agnew would offend his black and Jewish constituents . . . . Nixon ordered Bryce Harlow to call Taft and protest; that was no way for a Republican candidate to talk about the vice president. The Harlow protest, although mild, was truncated. Taft hung up on Bryce."[30]

Agnew's Cleveland speech included what Haldeman had called the "hot new" Buchanan attacks on Harriman, Clifford, and Vance that Nixon had earlier postponed, as well as his own suggested raps at Fulbright. The vice president called these and other Democrats "Hanoi's most effective, even if unintentional, apologists," and threw in fellow-Republican Lindsay as one of his own party's "summertime soldiers and sunshine patriots" who had split with Nixon on the war. Fulbright, he said, had supported the American troop buildup in 1964 "but when the seas became choppy, the storm clouds arose and the enemy stubbornly resisted, one could soon glance down from the bridge and see Senator Fulbright on the deck demanding that the ship be abandoned and staking out a claim to the nearest lifeboat."

He called Harriman, Clifford, and Vance men "whom history has branded as failures," singling out Harriman as having "succeeded in booting away our greatest military trump—the bombing of North Vietnam for a mess of porridge. . . . As one looks back over the diplomatic disasters that have befallen the West and the friends of the West over three decades at Tehran, Yalta, Cairo—in every great diplomatic conference that turned out to be a loss for the West and freedom—one can find the unmistakable footprints of W. Averell Harriman." Agnew charged Harriman with accepting the 1962 Geneva Agreement on Laos when it ignored the likely use of the Ho Chi Minh Trail by the enemy. "Down Harriman's Highway have come half a million North Vietnamese troops," he said, "to bring death to thousands of Americans and hundreds of thousands of South Vietnamese."[31]

According to Ehrlichman later, "Nixon decided that if Taft and the others wouldn't have Agnew, our new Native American brothers might. Maybe the Native American vote could be won if pursued. 'Let's put Agnew on at least six Indian reseervations between now and November,' Nixon ordered. 'Let's tie him to Indians. And,' he said, 'Pat [Nixon] should also do Indians.'"[32] Ehrlichman's report in his memoir gave no indication that Nixon was jesting.

Over the Fourth of July holiday, Nixon, at his summer retreat in San Clemente, held long talks with his key advisory group of Finch, Rumsfeld, Ehrlichman, Shultz, and Haldeman, including discussion of the forthcoming midterm election campaign. It underscored Nixon's desire to have Agnew downshifted to a supportive, less combative role amid a growing feeling that he was becoming too divisive. Haldeman wrote in his diary: "Most of FRESH meeting was about VP, how to define and then implement his role. P feels his [own] role must be above the battle, maybe no candidate speaking, just push on foreign policy and overall administration posture. Thinks VP can supplement. Use him primarily on fund-raising, get him to use a stump speech instead of always a new one, not try to make national news, build candidate. Agreed VP can't continue to appear to be an unreasonable figure, and against everything. Must go over to positive and especially avoid personal attacks. Okay to attack Congress. Problem is he has no close advisors or friends and P has not given him adequate guidance. Agreed to my idea of having Harlow travel with him."[33]

Around the same time, Ehrlichman wrote in his book later, Nixon asked him one day: "Do you think Agnew's too rough? Could we just use him in fund-raising until November? His style isn't the problem, it's the content of what he says. He's got to be more positive. He must avoid all personal attacks on people; he can take on Congress as a unit, not as individuals."[34]

From Haldeman's notes and Erhlichman's recollections, it was clear that Nixon was getting concerned about Agnew's growing popularity, prominence, and independence. His cautions on going positive and eschewing personal assaults suggested that he thought his vice president might be overplaying the role of Nixon's Nixon.

Back in Washington a few days later, Haldeman wrote: "Had meeting in afternoon at EOB [Executive Office Building], about plan for VP. P made pitch to Harlow to take on responsibility (to travel with VP and offer him guidance) and he's basically agreed, didn't have much choice. All agreed that he (VP) is the big gun for campaign, but must not use overblown rhetoric, personal attacks, racism, anti-youth. P fears he will be destroyed by forces he may underestimate. Feels, too, that he must not just be limp guy praising Family Assistance Plan. Should be strong, vigorous, kick Congress, praise P, lay off kids, blacks and ne'er-do wells, and from time to time, kick the bejesus out of the networks, to keep them honest. Imperative that he shift thinking to terms of local play, no national headlines, Must build for the candidate."[35] In Haldeman's private notes, he added that Nixon emphasized that Agnew had to be reminded that "what counts is how many states you win."[36]

As part of the discussion about the fall campaign, Nixon made clear that he wanted to do or say as little as possible about school desegregation in the South. Agnew, who earlier had advocated a stronger courtship of white southerners to remind them that the Nixon administration was the first in more than a century "to welcome the South back into the Union,"[37] did not hesitate to disagree. In an early August meeting with Nixon, Mitchell, Attorney General Elliot Richardson, and others, Haldeman wrote: "P made it absolutely clear no one is to do more than law requires. No political gain for us. Do what is necessary, low profile, don't kick South around. All appeared to agree and seemed optimistic, except VP, who felt they were glossing over the problem, especially about bureaucracy not on our side being overzealous. VP argued pessimism."[38]

Agnew, clearly, was not a figure reluctant to say his piece, inside or outside the administration. For all of Nixon's desires to have his vice president show more restraint, over the rest of the summer leading up to the campaign he did not lower his voice. He called Democrats who backed an amendment against future use of American troops in Cambodia "Cassandras of the Senate... trying to forge new chains upon the president's freedom of action, "and charged the "Fulbright claque in the Senate" with providing "great comfort" to the enemy. He called a McGovern–Hatfield bipartisan amendment on ending the war "a blueprint for the first defeat in the history of the United States."[39] It was all part of advance volleys in his party's effort to purge the Senate of Vietnam doves and possibly gain Senate control in November.

Not everyone in the White House wanted a cooled-down Agnew. A young, ultraconservative Haldeman aide, Tom Charles Huston, soon to be made director of a new White House unit on internal snooping, wrote a memo to Haldeman around this time urging that the vice president be set loose on tax-exempt foundations critical of the administration: "Pat Buchanan has been researching the activities of Ford, Brookings and other tax-exempt organizations for some time in anticipation of preparing a series of broadsides for the Veep to launch. These attacks would be on higher and less vulnerable ground than an attack based merely on their anti-Adminisration foreign policy briefings, and thus would be more effective. In short, the material is available to blast the hell out of these outfits and to scare the living hell out of them, assuming [IRS Commissioner Randolph] Thrower is willing to cooperate even passively. I suggest that Pat be asked to crank these speeches out and that the Veep unload at the earliest possible time.

"There is also the low road which should not be passed by. We can gather a great deal of material about the pro-Hanoi and anti-American activities of some of these outfits which would arouse the wrath of the unenlightened folks west of the Appalachians. I think John Lehman [another White House aide] and I could pull this material together and put together a hefty package which could be turned over to some people on the Hill and some friendly columnists to soften up the enemy in anticipation of the Veep's more gentlemanly attacks."[40]

Before undertaking his fall campaign assignment, Agnew made a second Asian trip, a nine-day visit to five countries that was a further demonstration of Nixon's confidence in his stand-in, in spite of his reservations as dutifully recorded by Haldeman. Agnew's main challenge on the trip was to assuage the South Korean government about American plans to withdraw twenty thousand men and replace them with more weapons. He largely succeeded, and his only near-gaffe was in telling reporters en route to Korea that the administration would "do everything we can to help" the new regime of Lon Nol in Cambodia, setting off speculation on the dispatch of U.S. troops there.[41] Agnew clarified his remarks in Phnom Penh, saying he had not meant to imply any American military involvement, and on his return home, administration aides praised him for clearing all diplomatic thickets.

It was a supremely confident Spiro Agnew who now turned again to the domestic role that had in fact made him a household name in his own country. As the self-appointed spokesman of the Silent Majority, he set out to mobilize its voters in November to drive from Congress, and especially from the Senate, those Democrats and a few Republicans up for reelection who stood in the way of the Nixon agenda in foreign and domestic policy. The man who had started out as Nixon's secret political weapon was a secret no more, and he approached the challenge with greater zeal than ever.

Chapter 8

PURGE OF
THE RADIC-LIBS

Richard Nixon knew well the importance of the congressional midterm elections. In 1954 and 1958, as Eisenhower's vice president, he had labored hard in behalf of Republican candidates to maximize support in the House and Senate for his administration's legislative agenda. And in 1966, as a private citizen, he had used the so-called off-year elections to resurrect his own political fortunes, campaigning for GOP candidates across the country and taking major credit for his party's gain of a whopping forty-seven seats in the House of Representatives.

So as the country approached the midterm elections of 1970, Nixon was primed to send his own vice president onto the hustings with a particular eye on the U.S. Senate, where a pickup of seven seats and strong party allegiance would create a 50–50 tie that could be broken by the president of the Senate, Spiro T. Agnew. Six years earlier, a host of Democrats had been elected to the Senate in the wake of the crushing presidential defeat of Republican nominee Barry Goldwater, and Nixon calculated that a number of them would be vulnerable running for reelection without the advantage of having an incumbent Democratic president, Lyndon Johnson, at the head of their ticket.

With that general game plan in mind, Nixon, in early August of 1970, called Agnew in and delivered his marching orders for the campaign, along with a bit of political wisdom he had learned from his own personal experience as a seasoned stumper. In every contest in which he was engaged, from his first race for a U.S. House seat in California in 1946 to his successful election as president in 1968, Nixon had won when he had run as a candidate of the "out" party. He had done so in his election to the Senate in 1950, for vice president in 1952, and for president in 1968, each time attacking the incumbent party. On the other hand, when he had campaigned in defense of the "in" party with a Republican in the White House, in 1954, 1958, and 1960, he was on the losing side. It did not take political genius to conclude that going on the attack, and the harder the better, was the surest ticket to electoral success.

But Nixon also knew that a candidate did not have to come from the "out" party to be a winner if he could manage to campaign as if he were the "out" candidate. Democratic President Harry Truman in 1948 had proved the point by running for reelection against what he called "the do-nothing Congress" controlled by the Republicans. He accused them of blocking his program at every turn, and won. This time around, in 1970, Nixon would have Agnew, despite the fact that they were part of the "in" party, go hammer and tongs after the Democratic-controlled Congress, and especially the Senate, which was making his life difficult, particularly over the Vietnam War.

With Agnew, Nixon had only to preach to the choir; he already had a convinced student, indeed a prize student, in attack politics against select members of the Senate. His vice president was ready, willing, and able to rally the Silent Majority in the fight against liberal foes he identified as downright radicals. Nixon had by now warmed to the Agnew style if not the Agnew personality. He fully supported and enjoyed his slashing stump manner and rhetoric, and he opened the spigot of his party's fund-raising arm to bankroll whatever his vice president required to slay the opposition candidates.

In subsequent high-level planning meetings for the off-year election campaign, Nixon brought in Bryce Harlow, the trusted and level-headed veteran of the Eisenhower years. He in turn recruited Pat Buchanan and Bill Safire, the two Nixon administration speechwriters already working closely and enthusiastically with Agnew in his now famous, or infamous, assaults on the liberal establishment, including the press, television, and academia. A fourth aide, Martin Anderson, a young and amiable issues specialist, also joined Nixon and Agnew in crafting the fall campaign.

Finally, another old Nixon California hand in the art of attack politics, Murray Chotiner, was added to the brew.

The vice president would be a two-pronged weapon, firing up the faithful with his smoking rhetoric while raising large amounts of campaign money for Republican Senate candidates lured into running against vulnerable Democratic incumbents. One Republican senator particularly critical of the president on the Vietnam War, Charles Goodell of New York, was also fingered as a target under circumstances whereby his seat, but not Goodell himself, could still be salvaged for the Nixon camp. Nixon told his attack team at one meeting "We are not out for a Republican Senate. We are out to get rid of the radicals," and that included the errant New Yorker, a Nelson Rockefeller ally. "We are dropping Goodell over the side," he said, explaining that there was an acceptable alternative for Goodell's seat in Conservative Party candidate James Buckley, who eventually was elected in a three-man race.[1]

In shaping the Nixon–Agnew message for the fall campaign, two new political books were major contributors. The first was *The Emerging Republican Majority* by Kevin Phillips, then a young campaign aide to John Mitchell and later the influential political theorist. It charted the growth of a basically white, conservative, middle-class society running through the new South and across the southwest Sun Belt to California that bore a sharp resemblance to Agnew's Silent Majority. Among this society's greatest concerns was adherence to law and civility, translated by Goldwater in 1964 and by Nixon in 1968 as "law and order." The second book was *The Real Majority*, by Richard M. Scammon, former chief of the Bureau of the Census, and former Lyndon Johnson speechwriter Ben Wattenberg. It argued that the decisive voting bloc was not on the right, as Phillips contended, but in the center, which was where Democratic candidates had to identify themselves to be successful. And in the center, they said, was the similar concern about law and order, called by Scammon and Wattenberg "the Social Issue," meaning legitimate community worries about crime, race, and youth behavior. Democrats, they argued, could not afford to dismiss such concerns as expressions of bigotry and thus leave them to be politically exploited by the Republicans.[2]

Nixon, for all his image among Democrats as a conservative, had long before recognized the importance of being positioned as a centrist, and indeed he often referred to himself that way. He had won the 1968

Republican presidential nomination by occupying a middle ground between Nelson Rockefeller on the left and Ronald Reagan on the right. And in the general election that followed, he did the same between Hubert Humphrey on the left and George Wallace on the right, holding the Scammon–Wattenberg "real majority" in the center. In the approaching congressional elections of 1970, Nixon understood that to cast his right-of-center administration as centrist or moderate, the surest way was to paint the Democrats not simply as liberal and left-of-center but as extremist, or even radical.

In the pre-campaign deliberations, Agnew along with Buchanan and Safire began to play around with the most effective means of nailing the Democrats as way outside the American political mainstream. In this context, the regular party labels would not do; the more inflammatory division was conservatives against liberals or, better yet, against radicals. "Radical" conjured up far-out hippies, anti-war student demonstrators, and free-wheeling intellectuals on and off campuses. Agnew, Buchanan, and Safire considered the possibilities of a new label. One was a combination, such as "radillectuals," but it didn't sound right. The Republicans had already done a good job of demonizing the word "liberal." What about "radical liberals"? Agnew liked it and started using it to describe the political opposition. According to one of the conspiring speechwriters later, Agnew "shortened it to 'radic-libs' himself. . . . I think we have to say he was the author. There were a number of ideas and thoughts, but that was the one he opted for, and the genesis of it doesn't make that much difference."[3]

Shortly after Labor Day, Nixon had a final meeting with the Agnew traveling team (interestingly, sans Agnew) to go over the attack plans on the eve of its departure around the country, and he was well pleased. According to Haldeman's diary notes: "Long morning meeting with political operations and VP's crew for the campaign. P really in his element as he held forth, for Safire and Buchanan, on speech content, campaign strategy, etc. Came up with some darn good lines and ideas, all the stuff he'd like to say but can't. P was delighted with Pat's kickoff speech for VP, which really hits hard. Really wants to play the conservative trend and hang the opponents as left-wing radical liberals. Said to say, 'Our opponents are not bad men, they are sincere, dedicated, radicals. They honestly believe in the liberal left.' And force them on the defensive, to deny it, as they did to us about Birchers [members of the ultra-right-wing John Birch Society] in '62."[4]

Safire, recalling the same meeting in his book on the pre-Watergate White House, painted Nixon as a hands-on overseer of Agnew on the campaign trail. He told Harlow, in charge of the Agnew plane: "Will you have TV along? Don't let Agnew spend time with the network specials. Play the wires and local TV. When he was abroad—and I watched this pretty carefully—the only time he got adequate coverage was when he concentrated on the wires and TV. Forget the columnists."

According to Safire's account, Nixon continued to deal with Agnew the way he wished Eisenhower had treated him as vice president: "Don't work him too hard. Give him a chance to look good and feel good. . . . If you get a good line for Agnew, get him to repeat it. Use it again. Every good line must become part of the American memory. There's a realignment taking place. Agnew can be a realigner. If he can appeal to one-third of the Democrats, we'll win two-thirds of the races."[5]

The next day, the vice president was off on the campaign trail, but more as the maligner he already was than as a realigner. In Springfield, Illinois, speaking from the steps of the state capitol, Agnew said Republican Senator Ralph Smith, under challenge from Adlai E. Stevenson III, son of the two-time Democratic presidential nominee, had to be returned to his seat "because your country just cannot afford any more ultraliberals in the United States Senate. There was a time when the liberalism of the old elite was a venturesome and fighting philosophy—the vanguard political dogma of a Franklin Roosevelt, a Harry Truman, a John Kennedy. But the old firehorses are long gone. Today's breed of radical-liberal posturing about the Senate is about as closely related to Harry Truman as a Chihihuahua is to a timberwolf. . . . Ultraliberalism today translates into a whimpering isolationism in foreign policy, a mulish obstructionism in domestic policy, and a pusillanimous pussyfooting on the critical issue of law and order."[6]

With alliteration flowing and Buchanan and Safire at their airborne typewriters, Agnew was on his way. Buchanan was the author of the above example and in Agnew's speech the next night in San Diego Safire contributed "nattering nabobs of negativism" and "hopeless hysterical hypochondriacs of history." Safire later insisted that the use of such outrageous alliteration was done in jest and as an attention-getter, and it certainly was that. There was nothing especially funny, however, about the term "radic-libs." Agnew himself later identified "radic-libs" as members of Congress who "applaud our enemies and castigate our friends and run down the capacity of the American government. . . who seek to overthrow tradition, whether or not it is effective, and whether their solutions are workable or not." He said he did not "impugn their patriotism. . . . What I impugn is their judgment, which I think is perfectly horrible. . . and so I call on the majority of the people to turn them out of office."[7]

Through the fall campaign, Agnew zeroed in on the Democrats he labeled "radic-libs"—after Stevenson, Senators Philip Hart of Michigan, Albert Gore Sr. of Tennessee, Vance Hartke of Indiana, William Proxmire of Wisconsin—and on the one Republican, Goodell of New York, all with the approval and the delight of Richard Nixon, who was only too happy to hand off his bludgeon, like a distance runner passing on a baton. When Gore, a fierce opponent of the Vietnam War who also had voted against Nixon's two southern nominees for the Supreme Court, showed up at an Agnew rally in Memphis, Agnew said his appearance was "in the tradition of civility in politics." But afterward, he went downtown and called Gore "for all intents and purposes southern regional chairman of the eastern liberal establishment," who "found the temptation to be loved by his Washington and Manhattan friends irresistible" and "his obligations to the citizens of Tennessee secondary to his liberal community credentials." Agnew said he wasn't questioning the "patriotism or sincerity" of Gore. Indeed, he said, "he is most sincere in his mistaken belief that Tennessee is located somewhere between the *New York Times* and the Greenwich *Village Voice*."[8]

In another campaign team meeting with Nixon, this time with Agnew present, the president gave his vice president advice directly, but not about the substance of what he was to say; rather, about how to court the public—this from a man who abhorred meeting the average voter and was transparently awkward at it. Rather than meeting with union leaders, he said at one point, according to Safire: "Rank and file is always more important than fat cats. Walk into a plant one day. Be late for a meeting. And just for the ducks [sic] of it, you might pop onto a campus—completely unplanned. Be unpredictable. Go for the color in the next two weeks and then the hard substance the last three weeks to Election Day. Remember, the airport fence is no longer a new picture—go to a department store, the salesgirls will go right up the wall."⁹ Safire did not record Agnew's reaction to these instructions from the expert.

In any event, Agnew did not need Nixon's advice on how to meet the common people. He had his own formula for success on the stump, and his toughest challenge in the midterm campaign was getting rid of the one rebellious Republican on Nixon's hit list, Charlie Goodell of New York. Before being appointed by Rockefeller to the Senate seat left vacant by the death of Senator Robert Kennedy, Goodell had been a reliably conservative member of the House from an upstate Republican district. As a senator with a statewide constituency, however, he had to take into consideration the new circumstance as he ran for the seat on his own. Furthermore, the war in Vietnam grated on him and he had become a vocal critic, advocating early U.S. troop withdrawal in opposition of Nixon's policy of slower disengagement through a buildup of South Vietnamese forces. In the eyes of both Nixon and Agnew, Goodell now fit the definition of a radic-lib.

For Nixon, however, advocating or working for the defeat of a fellow Republican was contrary to his political instincts. A major element in his success was his staunch adherence to party loyalty and the dividends it always brought him in his own campaigns. At first, he was inclined to hold his nose and support Goodell as preferable to his liberal Democratic challenger and equally vociferous opponent of the war, Representative Richard Ottinger. Nixon had hoped to find a conservative Republican to run against Goodell but gave up on the idea when Goodell got an early and strong commitment of support from Rockefeller. With the Democrats holding a clear registration edge in the Empire State, it appeared that there was little Nixon could do to save Goodell even had he wanted to.

But a serendipitous development surfaced that gave the conniving Nixon an option to hold the Goodell seat for a supportive candidate anyway. The state's Conservative Party, which during the Rockefeller governorship gave right-wing Republicans a place to go, decided to force a three-way race for the Senate seat and nominated James Buckley, brother of columnist William F. Buckley. If the new entry could be bolstered while the national Republican Party merely paid lip service to Goodell, Nixon's reputation for party loyalty could be preserved while at the same time Goodell was being quietly cast aside. The trick was to throw up a smoke screen behind which the dirty deed could be carried out.[10]

Rockefeller, who was also up for reelection and had no love for either Nixon or Agnew, sent word that he did not want either of them campaigning in New York that fall. At first, that was all right with Nixon, who saw Goodell going down anyway, and it was decided that Agnew would be kept out of the state. But as Buckley began to show unexpected strength, Nixon hatched a new scheme.

Before embarking on a convenient European trip, he saw to it that Republican National Chairman Rogers Morton, as a sop to Rockefeller, would go to New York, make a pro forma appearance with Goodell, thus preserving a semblance of Nixon's party loyalty, and then disappear. Next, Agnew would go in, ostensibly on his own initiative as a known loose cannon, and do a job on Goodell. Nixon in Europe could claim deniability in it all, and was convinced as well that Agnew's attacks on Goodell might bring him just enough, but not too much, support from liberals seeing Ottinger fading, enabling Buckley to sneak in.

To pull off the coup, it was essential that Agnew appear to be freelancing against Goodell, but not before Morton had completed his role as the friendly national party chairman. Goodell himself helped the process along by taking on the vice president and giving him a convenient opening. Agnew had attacked the recently released report of the Scranton Commission on campus unrest, calling it in his trademark fashion "pablum for permissiveness."

Goodell responded: "Mr. Agnew has long been saying that it is the duty of men in public office to speak out against violence in our universities. That is precisely what this report does—only the report, unlike the vice president, speaks in balanced and moderate language." At the same time, Goodell was careful not to separate himself from the leader of his party. "In no conceivable sense is it [the report] scapegoating the president for a problem which, as we all know, has long antedated his accession to office," he said, and Nixon was "far ahead of Vice President Agnew in exercising constructive leadership on the issue."[11]

Ted Agnew was not one to let a volley go unanswered. Asked in a television interview in faraway Minot, North Dakota, to identify any Republicans on his radic-lib list, he disregarded the go-slow timetable and blasted Goodell: "I'm not going to weasel on that question. I'm going to forthrightly say that I would have to put one Republican who seeks re-election this year in that group. That is Senator Goodell. . . . He has certainly proposed and stimulated the kind of leadership that encourages the dissident elements of our society. . . . Senator Goodell has left his party."[12]

The condemnation came even as Rogers Morton was in Rochester, New York, giving Goodell the party's official, if insincere, blessing. In a joint press conference with him, Morton stammered that Agnew "spoke on his own." As far as he was concerned, Morton said of Goodell, "if he's a Republican in New York, he's a Republican with me. . . . I'm trying to develop a team. I'm trying to build a party. I'm looking at it from an entirely different point of view." As for Goodell, he was only too happy to have the vice president hammer him; it might be throwing him a lifeline by persuading liberals to rally to him. He was certain, he said, that "the people of New York will not allow Spiro Agnew to pull the lever for them in November."[13]

In Salt Lake City, Agnew let Goodell have it again: "When a man consistently opposes a president of his own party on the greatest issues of the day; when a man makes public opposition to all his party stands for a major article of his political faith; when a man also goes out of his way publicly to reject support of his president that has not been offered; when a man attempts to curry favor with his party's leading adversaries by gratuitous attack on many of his fellow party members—then I think that man has strayed beyond the point of no return."

As for the seeming contradiction posed by Morton's mission in New York, Agnew told a news conference that the party chairman "has a little different job than I do—he's strictly a party functionary. . . to elect Republican candidates, and as such he has to be a party loyalist. . . . But I think there's a time when the vice president has to leave his party if he feels in good conscience he can't support its candidates. And that's what I'm doing." In fact, he said, he was going to New York the next day for a private fund-raising lunch for New York candidates for national office supporting Nixon—meaning Buckley.[14]

So much for the careful timetable. Though Agnew supposedly was to be operating on his own hook, at the White House Murray Chotiner let the cat out of the bag, telling a reporter Agnew was representing Nixon's views. But Goodell refused to believe that the president was throwing him over the side. Nixon, he said, "was for me. . . . I still think he supports me."

The naïve Republican leader in the Senate, Hugh Scott of Pennsylvania, said in a tone of desperation: "I'll be glad when the president gets back [from Europe]. When the president is away, those who are not president are disposed to play."[15] And Agnew's reputation as marching to his own drummer validated the observation with many. At the lunch in New York, Agnew didn't endorse Buckley by name, but the message was clear.

In Pittsburgh, the vice president further gave the game away, calling Nixon "the prime mover of our concerted effort to root out of positions of power those radical liberals who frustrate progress at home and undercut our efforts for an honorable peace abroad." When Rockefeller disclosed that he had called the White House asking Nixon to keep Agnew out of his state, the vice president shot back: "I have no intention of, simply because of cries to quiet me, of being quieted. And I don't think the president has any intention of indicating any displeasure with what I've said so far. . . . I think the president is aware of the thrust of my remarks. He certainly hasn't condemned me for them or tried to modify them in any way. He leaves it up to me what I want to say." Asked further about Nixon's support, he replied: "That's something the president will have to answer. Let me put it this way—you notice I'm still talking."[16]

Agnew was now in full flight, and began to wing his words recklessly, even for him. In New Orleans, meeting with newspaper editors, he outdid himself. Still going after his favorite target, in remarks he later said he believed were off the record: "If you look at the statements Mr. Goodell made during his time in the House and compare them with some of the statements I have been referring to, you will find that he is truly the Christine Jorgensen of the Republican Party."[17] The reference was to the first person known to have undergone sex-change surgery in Denmark. Earlier, when a laughing Agnew had tried out the line on Bryce Harlow, his Nixon-appointed handler, Harlow had pointedly told him: "That's one we can't use."[18] But the vice president went ahead with it anyway.

George Hinman, Rockefeller's chief political adviser, a normally mild-mannered man and a strong Goodell supporter, shot off a telegram to Agnew in care of the White House: "It is a matter of the deepest regret to one who is bound to our party and to our national administration by deep ties of friendship and loyalty, to have our proud banner so lightly dipped in filth against another Republican whose only offense is an independent view of the issues of life and death in our time. Reasonable men can and do differ on Senator Goodell, but no fair-minded person can do anything but deplore your references to him today in New Orleans."[19]

Christine Jorgensen wasn't happy either. She sent Agnew a telegram of her own: "Blatant use of my name in connection with your political feud with Senator Charles Goodell is not only unfair but totally unjustified. I am proud that I was born a U.S. citizen and I resent the implication that I am in any way lending aid to radicals or any subversive groups. It is contrary to my personal conviction. I request that some effort be made to correct these wrongful impressions." In a separate interview in Hollywood, she said of her tormentor: "Mr. Agnew in the past couple of months has been rather too much a bull in a china shop, striking out at anyone and using a form of comedy which I don't think is appropriate to his office. I've felt at various times after reading his remarks, 'My goodness, we have a clown in the White House, and this man is one breath from the presidency.'"[20]

Goodell, calling for "a politics of reconciliation, not vituperation," sought to capitalize on the situation by challenging Agnew to a debate, but the vice president brushed him off. "I'm challenged to debates every day," he said. "I guess I'd be debating all the time if I listened to those requests." He likewise dismissed Jorgensen, calling her demand for an apology "a calculated additional attempt at publicity," as if she had started the whole thing.[21]

Through all this, some White House aides continued to insist that Agnew was out there on his own. Presidential counselor Bob Finch repeated in mid-October that the White House was staying out of the New York election, to which Agnew responded: "I suppose he was expressing a personal hope, or a conviction, or possibly a straddle. Let me just make one thing clear. As the vice president in the Nixon administration, I'm not on a frolic. I'm out here doing a job for the administration. And while everything I say has not received the express clearance of the president, I have a sense of purpose and definition in what I'm attempting to accomplish." A few days later, Finch, in a Washington backgrounder, acknowledged the scheme to get Goodell in a coordinated White House strategy. Nixon originally had "a gentleman's agreement" with Rockefeller to stay out of New York, he said, "but then a poll showed Goodell running third, and we figured if it was going to be a throwaway vote, we might as well go for Buckley, because he would be a vote to organize the Senate for the Republicans."[22]

At this point, Nixon was back from Europe, greeted with disappointing news about how the election was going generally. It didn't appear that there was much chance for the Republicans to pick up the seven seats needed to gain control of the Senate. For all of Agnew's flamboyant efforts, the attacks on radical liberals were not winning out over Democratic pocketbook criticisms of a stagnant economy. Despite Nixon's observations of how he intended to stay above the political in-fighting in the mode of Eisenhower, he decided he had to join the fray, using the trappings and power of the presidency to turn the tide. But that didn't stop him from employing some of his old campaign tricks, such as finding targets in his audiences who would serve as foils for his favorite law-and-order theme. The team of Nixon and Agnew was going all out on the offense as the "outs" against the "ins" of the congressional Democrats, soft on campus and street violence.

Nixon wrote later of his decision to become a political combatant himself after all. Earlier, he said, "I felt confident that I would not be needed because in Ted Agnew we had the perfect spokesman to reach the Silent Majority on the Social Issue. Our strategy worked brilliantly at first. The Social Issue had liberals on the run everywhere, with Agnew in hot rhetorical pursuit. He stirred up predictable emotions—Hubert Humphrey called him 'the brass knuckles of the administration'—but in fact his salvos were remarkably restrained for campaign rhetoric and hit right on target."[23]

At the outset of Nixon's first campaign swing, using the impressive Air Force One with "United States of America" emblazoned on its long fuselage to impress the common citizenry, Nixon found his whipping boys as he spoke at the airport in sedate Burlington, Vermont. A couple of very small rocks about the size of a golf ball were tossed his way but fell far short of him. He and his aides quickly made the most of it, telling reporters who hadn't seen the errant throws or the perpetrators. Nixon immediately labeled them as troublemakers representative of the worst elements in the society, who constantly sought to "tear America down"— a smooth segue from his successful 1968 campaign pitch, and Agnew's own message as well.

"You hear them night after night on television," Nixon said, "people shouting obscenities about America and what we stand for. You hear those, and see them, who, without reason, kill policemen and injure them, and the rest. And you wonder: Is that the voice of America? I say to you it is not. It is a loud voice, but, my friends, there is a way to answer. Don't answer with violence. Don't answer by shouting the same senseless words that they use. Answer in the powerful way that Americans have always answered. Let the majority of Americans speak up, speak up on November third, speak up with your votes. That is the way to answer."[24]

All this from a couple of little rocks the size of a golf ball. Aboard Air Force One, presidential political aide Charles Colson said: "Those rocks will mean ten thousand votes for [Senator Winston] Prouty," the Vermont Republican seeking reelection.[25] At the airport rally in Teterboro, New Jersey, not far from New York City, admission was by ticket issued by the local party organization, and undesirables with long hair or hippie garb were turned away. Once all the Nixon partisans were in position up front, the ragtag rejects were allowed in, and when hecklers started chanting their anti-war, anti-Nixon slogans, Nixon responded with a broad grin and his overhead V-for-victory signal. He then launched into his speech, playing off the demonstrators. In Green Bay later, he told the crowd: "One vote is worth a hundred obscene slogans."[26] His strategy, however, was just the opposite; every obscene slogan might bring him a hundred votes from the offended in the crowd.

Agnew meanwhile accused the press of not providing adequate coverage of the Burlington two-rock toss that missed Nixon, referring to the president as "the target of a shower of rocks by young radical thugs" who had never been identified by reporters as such.[27]

As Nixon complained about obscenities shouted about him, Agnew continued his hammering of radic-libs, even in places where no one running fit the description, and he trotted out all the buzz words guaranteed to fire indignation in Dixie hearts. In Raleigh, he attacked "smug elitists back in Georgetown" and pledged that if enough radic-libs were ousted from Congress "we'll have a strict constructionist from the South on that Supreme Court whether Birch Bayh and Ted Kennedy like it or not." And in Greenville, South Carolina, where Strom Thurmond called Agnew "the greatest man this country has produced since John C. Calhoun and Robert E. Lee," the vice president accused the radic-libs of "aping other apologists—those who indulged in the Nazi excesses in the late twenties and early thirties." He topped it all off by mildly and defensively telling a screaming crowd that "those red-hots who complain about vigorous rhetoric are the world's worst in scurrility and libel and intemperance of expression. I wouldn't," he solemnly intoned, "stoop to such invective."[28]

With this Nixon–Agnew one-two punch flailing away only a week before election day, it was time to deliver the final blow to Charlie Goodell's political career. He was already tottering, as seen when he attended an annual dinner-dance of Queens County Republican Clubs with Rockefeller. The popular governor generated lusty cheers until he tried to put in a good word for Goodell; the cheers turned to boos and catcalls, causing Goodell to shout a few words and then hastily depart.

With Rockefeller's unwelcome sign to Agnew still up, the vice president came into the state for a supposedly nonpolitical speech to the Navy League of the United States. He assured the audience that "constrained by your nonpartisan, or should I say bipartisan, environment, I checked my political hat at the door. So I will not dwell this evening on the Senate contest in this state. After all, it seems to be going rather well [he meant for Buckley] but, so no one can possibly be offended, I will chastely observe that there are three candidates in New York. I oppose two, and don't oppose one—but to keep things nonpolitical I will not give the names. I trust you will construe that in the spirit intended."

Agnew then launched into his standard attack on radical liberals, justifying the partisanship he had just disavowed by saying their views on national security were relevant to the concerns of the Navy League. "I am not—very definitely not—attempting directly or indirectly or slyly attempting to intrude this 1970 campaign into your deliberations," he insisted while doing just that. "I submit that the nature of my involvement in the Senate race in New York manifests my determination to reach beyond the ordinary practices of American politics in order that larger national needs may be served." Yes, such as getting Charlie Goodell and his opposition to the Vietnam War out of the U.S. Senate. Without mentioning Goodell, the only Republican in the pack, by name, he concluded: "I believe that these people, so sincere in their beliefs, must be replaced, regardless of which party they belong to, before they irretrievably damage the security of the United States."[29]

Agnew also took the occasion of the Navy League dinner to reply to a report by David Broder in *The Washington Post* that Nixon was closely following then Congressman George Bush's bid for a Senate seat in Texas as a possible replacement for Agnew on the 1972 ticket. The vice president told the audience, "I'm not an uncertain man. . . . Some of my friends in the liberal media are already plotting my demise. . . . To my friends in the media who would like me replaced, gentlemen, I'm not an insecure man, either." And following up in remarks to reporters the next day, Agnew said: "I have a close relationship with my president. Just because someone makes a comment that I'm about to be dumped down the drain, I don't subscribe to it." Nixon, in Longview, Texas, at the time trying to help Bush's Senate bid (on Election Day he lost to Democrat Lloyd Bentsen), came to Agnew's defense, saying he was "doing a wonderful job. I must say he's one of the great campaigners in history."[30]

This wasn't the first time a question had been raised about the security of Agnew's political fortunes. Earlier, when a reporter in Memphis had asked about the possibility that he might be dropped from the Republican ticket in 1972, he insisted, "It wouldn't disturb me in the slightest. . . . All I'm trying to do is do the best job of being vice president that I can do, and that means supporting the president. We intend to re-elect President Nixon. Now, whether I'm part of that or not is virtually unimportant because the president is the important office."[31]

But with all the attention Agnew was getting, and the latest approval of his campaign performance from Nixon, he had no reason at all to wonder if his place on the 1972 ticket might be in jeopardy, and indeed it was not—not then. Late in the midterm campaign, however, when Nixon met with Agnew again to give him his marching orders for the conclusion, Agnew surprisingly broached the subject. According to Ehrlichman later, he "artlessly" opened the meeting by saying: "Mr. President, as I travel around, I get a great many questions about our 1972 ticket." Nixon nodded, Ehrlichman wrote, and finessed the matter, saying: "Of course, this far ahead the president can't say anything. Just say," he told Agnew, "we're only thinking about November of 1970. You can say, 'The president has shown great confidence in me so far, and I hope it will continue.'"

Nixon then turned to Ron Ziegler [his press secretary], Ehrlichman reported, and told him: "Ron, I want you to get out immediately that the president is delighted with the vice president's campaigning. He's had a big impact, good crowds, and from reports we've had from all over I'm impressed with the intensity of the vice president's campaign." Nixon said to the others present: "Then I want you others to do some back-grounding," spreading the word that "the president is grateful to the vice president. The president knows how hard this kind of campaigning is. He's having a big impact. He's partisan, but we're not doing a high-road, low-road operation [which was precisely what it was]. I'm not so partisan, because I'm the president of all the people. I work with both parties in the Congress even when some of them are sincerely wrong."[32] If Nixon had any reservations about keeping Agnew on the ticket with him in 1972, he was doing a great job of hiding them.

FIVE NIGHTS BEFORE THE ELECTION, as Nixon was making his basic speech in the municipal auditorium in San Jose, a large and raucous young crowd gathered outside to protest him. When he came out, he spontaneously climbed on the hood of his car and defiantly flashed his V sign at the demonstrators with both hands. Thus incited, they started shouting obscenities at him and throwing rocks and bottles. Nothing hit him and he was whisked away, as aides circulated reports that he had narrowly missed injury. The San Jose scene became an updated version of the earlier Burlington two-rocks saga.

Haldeman described it, and the intentional Nixon strategy to invite vi-olence, in his diary: "San Jose turned into a real blockbuster. Very tough demonstrators shouting '1–2–3–4 etc.' on the way into auditorium. Tried to storm the doors after we were in, and then really hit the motorcade on the way out. We wanted some confrontation and there were no hecklers in the hall, so we stalled departure a little so they could zero in outside, and they sure did. Before getting in car, P stood up and gave the V sign, which made them mad. They threw rocks, flags, candles, etc. as we drove out, after a terrifying flying wedge of cops opened up the road. Rock hit my car, driver hit brakes, car stalled, car behind hit us, rather scary as rocks were flying, etc. but we caught up and all got out. Bus windows smashed, etc. Made a huge incident and we worked hard to crank it up, should make really major story and might be effective. . . . All through the day [Nixon] delighted in giving the 'V' to the peaceniks."[33]

Nixon himself described the scene in historic terms, as he was often wont to do, as if to embellish his own importance and peril. "As far as I knew this was the first time in our history that a mob had physically attacked the president of the United States," he wrote in his later memoirs. "I did not care what these demonstrators or their leaders thought about me personally, but if they did not respect the office of the presidency, I thought that people should be made to recognize that fact and take sides on it."[34]

Agnew, in a well-coordinated plan, immediately picked up on the incident, telling a crowd in Belleville, Illinois: "When the president of the United States. . . is subject to rock and missile-throwing it is time to sweep that kind of garbage out of our society. Yes, I say separate them from the society in the same humane way that we separate other misfits who interfere with social progress and interfere with the conduct of the business of one of the greatest nations in the world." He didn't specify what "humane way" he had in mind. Nixon, meanwhile, was telling a huge Republican rally in Phoenix: "The time has come for the great Silent Majority of Americans, of all ages and of every political persuasion, to stand up and be counted against appeasement of the rock throwers and the obscenity shouters."[35]

On the final Sunday, the synchronized team of Nixon and Agnew met in San Clemente to compare notes and take stock of how they had done. After two hours, Agnew came out and by his comments indicated concern that after all their assaults on radic-libs, permissiveness, campus violence, and rock-throwing, the strategy may have been trumped by the Democrats' repeated charges of a failed economy. Agnew accused them of using "scare tactics" and "the big lie," countering them by citing growth in the gross national product, new housing starts, and lower interest rates. But after weeks of selling law and order, radic-libs, and Goodell as the Christine Jorgensen of the Republican Party, it was a little late to be hyping prosperity.[36]

On election eve, the Democrats did their best to draw the stylistic contrast. The Republican Party bought television time to air Nixon's speech in Phoenix; the Democrats countered with a sober, controlled talk from Senator Muskie sitting in the kitchen of an old house in Maine expressing disappointment with the tone of the Nixon–Agnew harangues. "There are those who seek to turn our common distress to partisan advantage," he said, "by not offering better solutions but by empty threat and malicious slander. They imply that Democratic candidates for high office. . . men who have courageously pursued their convictions in the service of the Republic in war and peace, that these men actually favor violence and champion the wrongdoer. That is a lie, and the American people know it is a lie. . . . How dare they tell us that this party is less devoted or less courageous in maintaining American principles and values than are they themselves. What contempt they must have for the decency and sense of the American people to talk to them that way, and to think they can make them believe."[37]

Afterward, the White House strategists knew they had been outsmarted. Haldeman wrote in his diary of election eve: "TV night, and a real disaster! There was terrible audio problem on the tape of Phoenix and we didn't know how bad it was until the first network, NBC, went on the air. We had bought all three. Complaints poured in, including to the P. After all kinds of checking we could only conclude we had laid a bomb. Also our purchase gave Muskie three quarter-hour shots (for the Democratic reply on all three networks). His production was very good, but the content and delivery pretty bad. I think we came off with a net plus, but not what it should have been." That judgment was distinctly not shared by press analysts, who later credited Muskie's performance with catapulting him into early frontrunner status for the 1972 Democratic presidential nomination.

Haldeman's diary continued: "When the real facts were apparent, P was very calm and understanding, although he had been cranking pretty hard at first. Considerable division of opinion within staff about net effect, I think most feel it was bad, some think a disaster. The hard-liners still feel it was good. But the whole mess points up the necessity of checking and rechecking on all these things. We certainly would have been better off to have nothing, and then Muskie, too, would have done nothing."[38]

Nixon agreed. He subsequently wrote in his memoirs: "In contrast with the harsh tone of my Phoenix speech, Muskie sounded calm and measured as he spoke from the homey setting of his summer house in Cape Elizabeth, Maine. What should have been a comparison based on substance thus became a comparison based on tone, and there was no doubt that Muskie emerged the winner. As John Mitchell put it, the Phoenix speech made me sound as if I were running for district attorney of Phoenix, rather than president of the United States addressing the American people at the end of an important national campaign."[39]

Back in Washington on election night, the White House took a suite at the Washington Hilton to watch the returns, and various cabinet members moved in and out. Agnew held a party on a lower floor for his staff and White House aides who had accompanied him on the campaign, and later joined the White House party and Nixon. The news was very disappointing—a net gain of only two Senate seats of the seven needed for control, eventually nine House seats lost, and a disaster in the gubernatorial races, with the Democrats picking up eleven states, including Pennsylvania and Ohio.

All Agnew got out of 32,000 miles of travel and an estimated $3.4 million raised was reinforcement of his reputation as a rabble-rousing divider. He was depressed with the loss of former fellow governors but somewhat buoyed by the defeats of three Democrats he had tagged as radic-libs—Gore in Tennessee, Joseph Tydings in Maryland, and Joseph Duffey in Connecticut—and Goodell in New York, and the election there of Buckley. Walter Hickel, the secretary of interior, who had written to Nixon complaining about Agnew, later wrote in his book *Who Owns America?* that when Gooddell's loss came on the television screen, "Agnew strode over to the TV set and said: 'We got that son of a bitch!' He was far more elated about having helped defeat Goodell than in winning in some other area of the country."[40]

An immediate post-election analysis memo from Colson to Nixon spread the blame around for the weak Republican showing, with Agnew coming in for a share only in terms of the timing and staleness of his assault. "In general, we probably peaked too early," Colson wrote his boss. "The vice president peaked in late September, his line became very predictable and with many voters 'old hat.' Once committed to it, there was, of course, no way to turn around; perhaps the tempo and approach could have been varied. Clearly, the vice president had a very healthy impact in arousing our troops, raising money and generating campaign activity. (His Goodell strategy was a key to New York.) Once he had peaked, however, his line became increasingly ineffective in winning either Democrats or Independents."[41]

In an interview late in the campaign with Walter Mears of the Associated Press, Agnew had foreseen possible damage to his reputation. "I'm tremendously vulnerable," he said, in light of his strong personal effort to strengthen the Republican hand. "No matter what happens," he said, "you can be pretty well assured that the adverse results will be laid to my doorstep, the good results will be attributed to something else."[42]

It turned out he did not have to bother himself about the latter outcome. The Colson memo was mild and, more important to Agnew, the only words of dissatisfaction from Nixon were mild. Later, he wrote to Haldeman that Agnew should "de-escalate the rhetoric without de-escalating the substance of his message. He should be shown fighting for something rather than just railing against everything."[43] After two years of their political marriage, all was still well between them, at least as far as public signs were concerned.

Chapter 9

MARRIAGE OF
CONVENIENCE

AFTER SLEEPING ON THE DISAPPOINTING RESULTS OF THE 1970 midterm elections, the White House strategists awoke the next morning and, apparently with clearer partisan heads, found that the results had not been so bad. They discovered that the election in fact had produced what they convinced themselves they had been seeking after all. It was not numerical control of the Senate or anything like that, but an "ideological majority" of like-thinking members who shared the Nixon outlook regardless of party. They included not only Conservative Party winner Jim Buckley in New York but also certain Democrats like Lloyd Bentsen of Texas, against whom Nixon had campaigned vigorously in a failed attempt to put George H. W. Bush in the Senate.

Bentsen and other newly elected Democrats, however, would not cooperate with this Republican fantasy, saying they intended to remain Democrats in organizing the Senate and adhering to their ideological anchors in their party. These declarations did not stop Nixon from telling reporters he had won "a working majority of four" in the Senate—counting Bentsen. Nixon handyman Bob Finch circulated to Washington reporters and editors around the country a memo described as "expanded notes from a cabinet and White House staff meeting," which argued that Nixon's intervention late in the campaign had been decisive in saving the day.[1]

At the first post-election staff meeting at Key Biscayne on the following Saturday, among the major business items were a cabinet shakeup in which Hickel and Romney were to be given their walking papers, and new responsibilities for the vice president now that his heavy campaign duties had been fulfilled. Haldeman wrote in his diary that night: "Discussed need for new roles for VP, positive and constructive. Environment, health, congressional relations, labor union relations, South, take on all [Democratic] presidential candidates."[2] The notation suggested that Agnew was going to be rewarded for his labors on the stump with the larger role he craved in matters of substance.

But a meeting Nixon held around this time with select columnists, to put his positive spin on the negative results of the election, generated speculation that all was not well concerning the vice president's standing in the official Nixon family. One of the columnists, Richard Wilson, the pro-Nixon Washington Bureau chief of the Cowles Publications, wrote without specific attribution but enough footprints to make clear his source: "It turns out that Vice President Agnew is expendable. It also turns out that the Democrats successfully defused the law-and-order issue. In discussing the outlook with his associates, Nixon is becoming increasingly circumspect about Agnew. Nixon is the first to recognize Agnew's great effort in 1970 and the last to criticize him for how he performed and what he said. Far be it for Nixon to criticize Agnew for doing the same thing Nixon did as vice president in 1954 and 1958. Still, don't take any bets on Agnew being on or off the ticket in 1972. A prospective bettor really won't have enough information until he sees all the horses in the race. . . . So it appears that Vice President Agnew is a hostage to President Nixon's political prospects. If Agnew is needed in 1972, he will be kept; if not, so long, Spiro."[3]

The columnist's musings and others like it were enough to keep speculation going about the political future of the controversial vice president. By now, with his slashing attacks, Agnew was rivaling Nixon himself as the man Democrats most loved to hate. At the same time, he was becoming the new darling of Republican conservatives, and many independents and conservative Democrats as well. His own star was rising in prognostications about his possible candidacy not for vice president again in 1972, but as the GOP presidential standard-bearer in 1976, when Nixon could not run again.

For the time being, at least, Nixon was limiting himself to reassurances about Agnew's vice-presidential future. Herb Klein, the White House communications director, pointedly told reporters that in his personal opinion (which rarely was not in lockstep with Nixon's own) "presuming that President Nixon runs [in 1972], Agnew will be on the ticket." As for the criticism of his campaign performance, Klein said, "President Nixon remembers he had a lot of criticism in 1954 and 1958" in the same vice-presidential role.[4] In other words, Eisenhower's Nixon had no complaints about Nixon's Nixon.

Others might have seen the 1970 midterm elections in which Agnew had played such a large role as a Republican defeat. But that didn't include a host of party faithful who shortly afterward paid $150 apiece for what the clever sponsors called "an intermingling of interested individuals aimed at animated acclamation and appreciation for guess whom? Household word Spiro." Agnew accepted the appropriately alliterative plaudits by claiming that he and Nixon had actually bucked the historical off-year trends by cutting customary losses and making "political water run straight uphill." He declared the campaign a success in forcing the Democrats to buy into the Republican law-and-order pitch. They had "spent the last three years cozying up to radical dissenters," and then they "turned tail and ran. . . . As they fled, they stripped off their leather jackets, pinned on sheriff's badges, then turned to their constituents transformed—now all Wyatt Earpy and swearing evermore to stand foursquare for law and order."[5]

Nixon, returning from Paris, where he had attended the funeral of Charles de Gaulle, wired his appreciation of Agnew, calling him "one of the most able and devoted Republican leaders I have known," and insisting that as "the great campaigner of 1970" he had been unjustly attacked.[6] Agnew now was regarded as a strategic asset, Buchanan recalled later.

As a reward to himself and his family members, the vice president took them off for a brief vacation in Hawaii. There he gave a long interview to James Naughton of the *New York Times* in which he responded to all the speculation about his future with seeming indifference. "I've always treated my political life as a sort of furlough from the practice of law," he said. "So I suppose your public life has to come to an end sometime or another. . . that you're not always going to be a public man. . . . And it doesn't distress me to think that that may happen—any time." He said he wasn't interested in being rich but desired, "in my later years, at least, [to] be comfortable," and would like to write a column or do "something in the electronic medium—commentary or some sort of interview program." In other words, join the fraternity he had so lately and vitriolicly attacked.[7]

Agnew followed this ironic confession with a notably conciliatory speech to the Associated Press Managing Editors Convention. He astonished his listeners by saying that "time and time again I have found surprisingly complimentary coverage of my viewpoints by journalists I happen to know do not suffer from ardor for Agnew. I have seen Niagaras of words and interpretations erupt almost overnight from your fraternity over public events, inundating the American people with astonishingly detailed information about important people and issues—and I have marveled how well you have made this the best-informed nation on earth. The entire process, as well as most of its people, I admire immensely. I regard America's press as the best and strongest in the world."[8]

Could this be a contrite press-basher engaging in a bit of fence-mending because of higher political or professional ambitions? The assemblage clearly was baffled. Or was it a recognition that now that Nixon was assigning more substantive responsibilities him, as chief liaison to state and local officials whose backing he would be seeking for a more venturesome domestic agenda, he had to cool his smoky rhetoric?

In mid-December, Agnew had his first significant task in this regard in representing the president at a meeting of the Republican state governors at Sun Valley, Idaho, and he had his work cut out for him. Their ranks had been depleted in the midterm elections and some of the losers, attending one final governors' conference, were in a blame-placing mood against Agnew himself. One of the defeated governors, Winthrop Rockefeller of Arkansas, had wired Nixon criticizing Agnew for going too hard after Dale Bumpers, the Democrat who beat him. Others tempered their remarks in hope of getting a federal appointment, as often happened with gubernatorial losers of the party controlling the White House.

As Agnew was flying to Sun Valley, he read a *New York Times* account of all the grumbling among the Republican governors. He scribbled out remarks designed to set them straight. It so happened that at the same time, Republican National Chairman Rogers Morton, on a mission of commiseration to the governors, about half of them now lame ducks, had also been tasked at the last minute to break some big news to them. He told them that Nixon was indeed going to put a former governor in his cabinet, but not one of them. He announced the surprise appointment as secretary of the Treasury, considered the third highest cabinet post, of John Connally of Texas—a Democrat! The bombshell jolted the Republican governors, especially the job-seekers among them. Governor Frank Sargent of Massachusetts, one of those whose job was not on the line, was perhaps the only one present who saw some humor in it. He asked of Connally as the new chief administration money man: "Can he add?"[9]

Nixon, already thinking of reelection in 1972, recognized, Sears said later, that "his real vulnerability was keeping the states he had won in the South and picking up another big state—Texas. In Nixon's mind, it [Connally's appointment] had a lot to do with making damn sure that this time he carried Texas. He had lost it now twice in national elections [in 1960 and 1968] and he knew how pivotal it would be if he got a real good Democratic opponent in 1972. Plus the fact that Connally fit this mold that for some reason Nixon swooned over—all this stuff maybe Nixon would have liked to have done himself, except he didn't think he was up to it."[10]

☙ ❧

NIXON'S POLITICAL ROMANCE with Connally was fast-developing, with eventual serious complications for Agnew. As early as March of 1970, the Texan had impressed the president by telling him he had to be tough and rule his cabinet with an iron hand. According to Haldeman, Nixon then "was strongly of the view that he [Connally] would be ideal head" of his new budget office, but it didn't happen. However, Haldeman wrote at the time, "Connally tracks well with P and would be an excellent addition if we could get him on."[11] After the elections in November, Haldeman noted, "P was really impressed with John Connally at [Roy] Ash dinner last night. Wants to get hooks into him. Is convinced he can be brought over [to Republican ranks] for '72."[12]

A couple of weeks later, Connally spent an hour with Nixon at the White House, during which the president pressed him to take the Treasury cabinet post. That night, Nixon flew to New York for a speech, and on the plane back to Washington, he eagerly briefed Haldeman at length about getting Connally aboard. Haldeman wrote that night: "He now wants me to call Connally and give him a further push on it. He originally had thought of having Billy Graham call, but decided that wouldn't be too good an idea. In reviewing this, P wanted me to make the points that he had only discussed this thing with me, and had asked me to call John. That the P wanted him to know that he feels urgently that Connally is desperately needed in this position now, and for another more important position in the future."

Haldeman then recorded the fervent pitch Nixon wanted him to make to Connally: "That he needs you as an advisor and counselor, that we've got to change the Treasury's system and that's important, but really he wants you here as a counselor, advisor and friend. He wanted me to say that I hope and pray you won't turn him down. He's fought a long, lonely fight, has no one in the cabinet to talk to. If you come in, you and Mitchell will be his closest confidantes. P does not want to use you politically, he doesn't want you to give up your Democratic registration; he wants you because he thinks you're the best man in the country that he could have as his advisor in national and international affairs. He feels you're the only man in the Democratic Party that could be president, and that we have to have someone in the cabinet who is capable of being president."[13]

It was a high-powered courtship worthy of Lyndon Johnson, without LBJ's personal nose-to-nose, bear-hug intimidation, of which Nixon was neither temperamentally nor physically capable. Haldeman went on in a latter-day imitation of John Alden wooing Priscilla Mullens in behalf of Miles Standish: "In some way, the P has a simpatico feeling for you. Please don't turn him down on this. The P, as you know, is a man to keep his own counsel; nobody except me knows that you're under consideration, and I want to tell you how strongly I feel that this will change the future of the country. The P doesn't have a man in the whole shop that he respects in this way, and he's very concerned about the whole question of determining whether the United States or Russia is going to be number one. He's not interested in the idea of political purposes, either in Texas or to get a Democrat in the cabinet, and you'd be free to do what you want. He wants you because of what you are."[14]

The next morning, Nixon pressed Haldeman again to be sure he reached Connally, and with the president's explicit instructions in hand, late that night his chief of staff finally got the Texan on the phone and laid it on heavy, reading from prepared talking papers and clearly playing on Connally's presidential ambitions. Haldeman afterward wrote in his diary: "Interestingly enough, he seems to be favorably inclined towards taking the job. He was obviously pleased that I had called, and that I felt as strongly as I did about his taking it. He made the point that he wasn't just interested in just being secretary of Treasury or any other department, but he was very much impressed with what the P said about wanting his help on a broad basis and wanting to put him on the NSC."[15]

It was the kind of offer Ted Agnew had thought and hoped had been extended to him when Nixon chose him to be his running mate, and when he had met the president-elect at Key Biscayne after the election. The extravagance of Nixon's appeal to Connally demonstrated how mesmerized the president had already become by the Texan. And it was an indication of the large shadow he was certain to cast over Agnew's ambitions for a greater policy role in what already was in name only the Nixon–Agnew administration.

Connally, Haldeman went on, made it clear he would be making a great sacrifice to succumb to his suitor's pleadings: "He has the problem of personal finances, and will have to make extensive adjustments. He's apparently paying about $80,000 or $90,000 a year in interest now, so he'll have to divest himself to reduce the interest load. He said he'd try like hell to do this, because he recognized the importance of taking on the assignment. One of his concerns, although he felt it probably would not be a problem, was the flak we'd get from within the Republican Party, and the concern that they might waylay him at every corner. . . . Wants to be sure in his own mind that he can make the contribution that the P wants. He recognizes the problem of no leadership in either of the parties. He was highly pleased and delighted with the P's remarks to him, said he would do anything to help him, but wants to be sure he really can help by doing this. If he does it, he'll do anything in his power to do it right."[16] Unsaid by Connally, apparently—but obvious—was that he wanted to be sure he really could help his own political future by agreeing.

Two days after Nixon's fawning pitch to Connally via Haldeman, the two met for breakfast at the White House and the deal was struck. Haldeman jotted in his notes that day: "I've never seen P so pleased from a personal standpoint. He thinks this can really make the difference."[17] When it was announced to the cabinet and the press corps a week later,

the cabinet members swallowed it in surface good grace and the reporters, in Haldeman's words, were "absolutely flabbergasted," which
was what Nixon hoped. As a further indication of Nixon's determination
to keep Connally happy, he told Haldeman to "be sure Connally feels free
to fire anyone at Treasury. Don't be obligated." Finally, he also had
Haldeman tell Ziegler to "get names of Connally's family and partners"
and to send the new secretary's children a note from Nixon saying "how
pleased I am re your father's acceptance."[18]

CONSIDERABLY LESS PLEASED with the Connally appointment, however, were the Republican governors assembled in Sun Valley, and into
this hostile environment strode Agnew. If he sought to console them
about their own plight, the first words he chose fell far short. "Some of
our most talented associates have fallen in political combat," he said,
brushing aside his own role in the fight, the defeat for which many of
them blamed him. "But I would remind you that they are not dead, they
are only temporarily disabled. They need our rehabilitative political care
so that those who wish to can return again to active duty. And we hope
it's soon."[19] To the lame ducks in whose ears the news of Connally's appointment still buzzed, the comment must have sounded particularly
insensitive.

But that was not all, far from it. Agnew went on: "What they do not
need, those who have fallen in the political wars, are excuses and rational-
izations for their defeats. What is not needed is assessment of blame—
they don't need it, and neither do those whose shoulders occasionally
become repositories of the fault [obviously meaning himself]. They don't
even need it when it masquerades as constructive criticism."

Agnew indicated a moment later that he meant to be talking about the
press, but many of the governors not surprisingly thought he was referring to the losers among them. "I for one am not ready to accept the
analysis of columnists and commentators who are ideological antagonists" for why the Republican governors lost, he said. The party should
make its own assessment, not accept that of the "opinion makers of acad-
eme and the media," he went on. "I mean, after all, where were they
when we needed them?" This from the man who so recently had stood
on his head commending the American press in his Hawaii speech. He

told them he had come "in this time of trial and tribulation to consult with my brothers, and if necessary to debate with them, and if convinced by logic to make changes and to be their advocate for change."[20]

But Agnew's cutting remarks generated little brotherly love among his old gubernatorial colleagues. Oregon Governor Tom McCall, already one of Agnew's most outspoken critics, stormed from the hall, calling his remarks a "rotten, bigoted little speech" that was off the mark. He said it was the most divisive speech ever given by such a high official. Governor Robert Ray of Iowa, like McCall a moderate, said he was "amazed" at Agnew's speech. Only Governor Ronald Reagan of California said it was "fine, right, and proper."[21]

In a private meeting with the governors the next morning, Agnew did not back off. Afterward, one governor quoted him as saying "all of the press was here to crucify the Republican Party and the vice president" and that "some of the problem with a lot of Republicans is that they go out of their way to pat Sandy Vanocur [then of NBC News] on the ass and get on his boob tube." And when Agnew confronted McCall for his remark that the vice president had delivered a "rotten, bigoted little speech," McCall shot back: "I'm not sure I said 'rotten.'" He also denied that he had ever called on Nixon to drop Agnew from the ticket in 1972, saying he had simply raised the question of whether Nixon would want to run again with someone who had campaigned "with a knife in his shawl."

Another governor said Agnew had defended his slashing campaign style by saying: "You've got to chop their nuts off before they chop off yours." And after two years of insisting that he spoke as his own man, he told the critical governors: "Any schoolchild would *know* the vice president is just an extension of the president."[22]

Actually, Agnew had come to see himself as considerably more than that, and he had become increasingly irritable at having ceremonial matters sloughed off on him. He did, however, miss one such event that normally might have fallen to him that could have brought him some positive publicity in these trying days. A few days before Christmas, presidential aide Dwight Chapin sent Haldeman the following memo: "Attached you will find a letter to the president from Elvis Presley. As you are aware, Presley showed up here this morning and has requested an appointment with the president. He states that he knows the president is very busy, but he would just like to say hello and present the president with a gift."

Chapin said Presley wrote that he wanted to help Nixon with the drug problem among the young. Chapin recommended that another White House aide, Bud Krogh, meet with the singer and then shuttle him into the presence for a few minutes. Chapin wrote that he and Krogh "both think it would be wrong to push Presley off on the vice president." In a bottom checkoff box, Haldeman first wrote: "You must be kidding." But he later approved and the much-publicized photo opportunity of the president and the King followed. Agnew was left out in the cold.[23]

Meanwhile, John Connally was wasting no time ingratiating himself with Nixon, who after another long talk with his new Treasury secretary gushed to Haldeman about the Texan's ideas about how to boost Nixon's public image. Haldeman told his diary a few nights after Christmas: "[President was] very cranked up and enthusiastic. . . . Connally brought up the whole PR subject, and made the point that it's much more important than we seemed to have realized to get across a more accurate picture of what the P is really like. He apparently emphasized the points of discipline, austerity, spartan-like appoach to things, hard work, boldness, delgating duties. He said that regardless of what the characteristics are, the main thing is to emphasize them and get them out. He thinks it's very important that this kind of image get out soon as to what Nixon's really like, and that it's up to the cabinet and his staff to do it. He said the cabinet was a fine group, but there's not a strong man in it, and feels they should be out talking. . . . He feels there's a very good story to tell here, that people would like to hear about the way the P works, which would create enormous confidence. Also, we need to get across the boldness, courage, and strong man."[24]

Connally, according to Haldeman, capped off the schmooze by comparing Nixon with three of the greatest men in history, telling him: "Lincoln was the great figure of the [nineteenth] century and Churchill and de Gaulle were the two great figures of the [twentieth] century; the big thing about all of them is their comeback from defeat, not their conduct of wars, etc. Connally feels we should very much build the comeback story."[25]

That one was right up Nixon's alley; he often mused about how great men picked themselves up from defeat and kept fighting—as he did after his presidential loss in 1960 and his humiliating defeat for governor of

California in 1962. Connally's observations were patently self-serving, not only in massaging the self-confidence-deprived president but also in deftly declaring himself at the outset the strongman of a cabinet heretofore lacking one.

In the new year, Connally continued inflating Nixon's confidence. He told him, and Haldeman, "that he had met last week with a small group of the top bankers in New York, and had taken the opportunity to devote fifteen minutes. . . to just talking about the P, and what kind of a man he is. . . that the P has the best concept of his problems than any man Connally knows; that he is isolated to a certain extent, as any president has to be; that he has allocated his time better than any man he has ever seen; that he has an extremely competent staff and delegates more than any other president, and it's the only way a president can operate effectively; he is highly disciplined mentally and physically; knows his people, their strengths and weaknesses, and his adversaries and their strengths and weaknesses, both foreign and domestic; that he's ruthless enough to be a great president."[26]

All this was a particular mouthful from a man who intimately knew the domineering Lyndon Johnson, and Nixon and Haldeman seemed to swallow it whole. A short time later, Connally at Camp David gave Haldeman and Ehrlichman a dose of the same medicine, as Haldeman recorded later: "Connally thinks we should portray the P as a student of the presidency. . . that he understands the uses of power. That [his incursions into] Laos and Cambodia, are demonstrations of his perceptive use of power. . . that he recognizes that the Marshall Plan is a thing of the past, that what he's doing is far-reaching in concept. . . ."[27]

Connally knew the two Nixon insiders' high regard for their boss and their great influence on him. And he knew that telling them something was the same as telling Nixon. He obviously decided it wasn't a bad idea to lay it on thick with them as well. When it came to flattery, John Connally had learned the art from a master—his old friend Lyndon Johnson. And what Connally had just said about Nixon also could be said of himself—that he was ruthless enough to be president. It sounded as if the same thought had occurred to the former governor of the great state of Texas.

Chapter 10

THINKING
THE UNTHINKABLE

Tʜᴇ ʜᴇᴀᴠʏ ᴍᴀssᴀɢɪɴɢ ꜰʀᴏᴍ Cᴏɴɴᴀʟʟʏ, sᴏ ᴀᴘᴘʀᴇᴄɪᴀᴛᴇᴅ ɪɴ ᴛʜᴇ Oval Office, only reinforced Nixon's growing disenchantment with Vice President Agnew, who continued to be disturbed about being on the outside looking in. Despite the assurances that he was going to have more significant involvement in decision-making, he had been pretty much cut out of the administration's health care initiatives by now, and didn't like it. In mid-February of the new year, while he was out in California on other business, he took his gripe directly to Nixon, to the president's chagrin.

As Haldeman described the incident in his diary: "The principal problem arising this morning was in relation to the VP, who apparently called the P from California to object to the health message as it's presently contemplated. The VP feels there's some serious mistakes being made in this, and that adequate consideration hasn't been given to them, and also that he was misrepresented in the option paper going to the P. This of course created quite a flap, resulting in a session on the plane with [Caspar] Weinberger [the deputy budget director] and Shultz to discuss the whole thing. The P felt the paper probably hadn't been adequately staffed, but his principal concern was that the VP would come to him with it, rather than working it out with the staff.

"He feels we've got to keep the VP out of substantive policy development, that we cannot have him fighting the White House staff or the cabinet, that he must not get involved in policy because he tends to zero in on one feature and jump on it rather than looking at the whole picture. He feels we need someone on the staff who has the confidence of the VP who can hold his hand, and he's decided Weinberger is the one who should do this. He also has concluded that the real problem is that the VP's staff is not strong enough, and we have a need to build it up. . . . Weinberger agreed to take this on, and also to try to untangle the current problem by talking with the VP and trying to get it all straightened out."[1] In Haldeman's personal notes on this particular situation he asked himself: "How did VP call get to P today?"[2] Obviously somebody at the gates had fallen down on the job.

Several days later, in the Oval Office, Nixon leveled with Haldeman on his own concerns about Agnew. Up to now, such confidences had been safe from prying ears, or revealed later only in the retelling by the recipient. But on this occasion, Nixon's easily recognizable voice activated a new secret White House taping system just installed that before long would have momentous consequences for his presidency. "We've got to get another man in there, Bob," the deep Nixon baritone is heard insisting, in a commentary on the vice president's weak staff. "I don't know what to do, but you've got to get somebody. . . . We can't spare Safire, Buchanan, or Harlow." Reflecting his disenchantment with Agnew himself, Nixon says: "What's really involved here is the vice president's survival. He either starts to shape up or I can't use him."[3]

Around this time, the Nixon White House launched new revenue-sharing proposals with the governors, as part of a government reorganization. Agnew had been led to believe he would be importantly involved. However, under the label "the New American Revolution," the vice president found himself relegated to the job of salesman on the stump while Shultz, as head of the newly reorganized Office of Management and Budget, and Ehrlichman, as overseer of all domestic affairs, became the policy heavies. Agnew felt that as a former county executive and governor, he was well-qualified to be in the middle of things rather than simply a huckster for this new "revolution." He seldom had a chance to discuss policy with Nixon and he was forever being informed by aides that "the president wants you" to do or say this or that—an old technique by subordinates to get things done that they wanted. An Agnew confidante said of the device at the time, "He's learned about it. He doesn't go for it. He wants to be told by the president, not some underling. He doesn't forget that he's vice president of the United States."[4]

It was in this contentious climate that Nixon's request to his vice president to substitute for him at the annual Gridiron dinner, issued verbally through an aide, got Agnew's back up. Nixon himself, as vice president, had never thought of balking at any such bidding from Eisenhower, and Agnew's attitude rankled him in return.

The whole silly fiasco started in early February, when Nixon told his personal aide, Dwight Chapin, he wanted Agnew to be his stand-in at the dinner of the male Washington press corps' self-styled elite, which featured skits by members ribbing the president and other members of his administration. The club's motto, often honored in the breach, was "the Gridiron singes but it never burns." Nixon was sick of being a foil for what he considered his enemy, and having to smile and laugh in a good-natured manner he seldom felt.

Chapin turned to old Nixon California hand Herb Klein, the on-again, off-again editor of the conservative *San Diego Union*, who was always on call for political duty and at the time was the White House director of communications. On February 2, Klein sent Nixon a memo observing that, "should you still be of the mind not to attend, the vice president would most appropriately be the person who would speak at the conclusion [of the dinner]. This would give us another opportunity to have the Republican speaker [the Gridiron always had one from each party] another one of our own people." Apparently allowing for the possibility that Agnew would balk, Klein went on: "I know you have looked at this as an opportunity to build someone and my suggestion would be to consider Bob Dole first, or alternately [sic], Bill Rogers."[5] Eight days later, Chapin sent a memo to Klein and press secretary Ron Ziegler, with a copy to Nixon scheduler David Parker, saying again Nixon wanted Agnew to go, but that Dole or Rogers as substitutes would be okay.[6]

The vice president continued to balk at being Nixon's back-up for news-media affairs. On February 24, Klein sent Haldeman a memo: "As you may know, the vice president has turned down the Radio-TV Correspondents Association dinner. I am pushing hard on him to accept the Gridiron dinner on March 13. I think it's an absolute essential. Would you jog him again because as of this morning he is still undecided." Haldeman scribbled on the bottom of the memo: "Raised Q with P—said it is essential," and then he scrawled across the page: "He *has* to do it—per P."[7] On February 27, Haldeman in his diary wrote that Nixon "had asked Harlow to get into the VP problem the other day, and Harlow called me today to say that he did talk to [Agnew Chief of Staff Arthur] Sohmer about the Gridiron, and he thinks maybe he's made some progress there."[8]

Around the same time, Nixon political aide Charles Colson felt it necessary to send a memo to Chapin noting that the president had told him to ask Agnew to attend an American Legion dinner in his place but "the vice president has turned us down." Colson added: "I am not sure I can characterize the president's remarks as an order, but it came reasonably close."[9]

Connally, meanwhile, never had any problem connecting with Nixon, about business or pleasure. Also on Febuary 27, when Haldeman got the call from Harlow reporting "progress" on the Gridiron flap, Nixon had the Connallys up to Camp David for the weekend. He celebrated the Texan's birthday with dinner and a special cake in his honor. Haldeman and Ehrlichman also were invited, and Haldeman wrote in his diary: "The P selected *Around the World in 80 Days* as the movie because the Connallys hadn't seen it and he was sure they would be delighted with it, which they basically were. He was hysterical through it; as each scene was coming up, he'd say, 'You're going to love this part,' or 'the scenery is just great, now watch this closely,' and so on. He obviously has seen it time after time and knows the whole thing practically by heart. He also got a kick, as did Connally, out of identifying the old stars as they appear in their bit parts."[10] The Agnews were never entertained thus by the Nixons; their treatment duplicated the cold shoulder Dick and Pat got from Ike and Mamie in the 1950s.

Nevertheless, Agnew, seeing his population ratings soar, especially within the party, and with the fulsome praise from Nixon for his campaign efforts, still had reason to think he was headed for bigger things within the administration. But, according to Agnew press secretary Vic Gold, such aspirations by the vice president began to chafe on Nixon and Haldeman. "They liked what he had done in the 1970 campaign," Gold said later, "because he did pretty much what Buchanan and Safire wrote for him. But then he got too big and began being seen as a loose cannon."[11] And as he became more visible, John Damgard said, "I think Nixon in some ways got a little jealous of him."[12] Another Agnew aide, David Keene, said the Nixon inner circle "treated him like some hired guy they could tell to do whatever they wanted. They didn't think he had the discipline or the depth to handle things. They didn't know what he would do from one minute to the next."[13]

Nixon, for his part, was aware of Agnew's petulance and didn't want to be bothered with it. Nor did he care for his stand-in's constantly trying to elbow in on the comfortable inner circle of himself, Haldeman, Ehrlichman, Finch, Weinberger, and Shultz. If there was going to be any outsider admitted it was not going to be Agnew, but John Connally.

Nixon saw the Texan as the kind of real man he wished he was himself—strong and tough to the point of overpowering and self-assured, as the uncertain Nixon never could be. Prior to bringing Connally into the administration as secretary of Treasury, Nixon had said to Ehrlichman: "Every cabinet should have at least one potential president in it. Mine doesn't." The Connally appointment in Nixon's mind filled the vacuum. It wasn't too long before he began to think more about what to do to position the man Nixon wanted to succeed him when the second term he anticipated was over.

It wasn't so much that Nixon was down on Agnew, John Sears said later, as that he was up on Connally. At the same time, he said, Nixon's lack of self-confidence, and his consequent self-loathing, led him to tear down others. "If you were out of his presence and there was any way to pick you apart, he'd do it," Sears said. "That way he didn't feel so badly about himself. Of all the people who hated Nixon, Nixon had the lowest opinion of himself [of] anybody. It was always, 'Everybody's against me.'"

The more Nixon looked at Agnew compared with Connally, the more he began to regret the choice of vice president he had made, and the more he thought about a basic change. In Nixon's mind, Sears said, "here's another guy, Connally, who seems to be well-off financially, a self-made man who acts like a big deal. Who could get easily fooled by that? Nixon."[14] He would have put him in the cabinet at the end of the 1968 campaign, had Connally not let him down in Texas, Sears said, but Nixon's high evaluation of him had not waned.

The automatic recording system that had just been installed in the Oval Office and in Nixon's hideaway in the Executive Office Building adjacent to the White House captured the president's conversations for his private use. Except for Haldeman, his chief aide Alexander Butterfield—who supervised the installation—and perhaps one or two other insiders, visitors were not aware that conversations were being recorded. On March 25, the president, in a long talk with Haldeman in the Oval Office captured by the recording system, made abundantly clear Nixon's growing admiration for Connally and his corresponding lessening ardor for Agnew. As heard on the tape, he begins with another complaint that neither Agnew nor anyone in the cabinet has the ability to sell his administration's agenda and message.

NIXON: "At the present time, I'm afraid they're not going to pay any attention to anybody else. I mean we can talk about cabinet officers involved, we can talk about Agnew and all the rest. God-damn it, they're all—it's just not getting across. They can't do it. If Connally were vice president, I'd have somebody who could get it across now and then. Strangely enough, it's raw, but God-damn it, he's good. But I'll tell you his [Agnew's] problem. And this is the great advantage that John Connally brings. He [Agnew] has a very serious lack of judgment, and he's stubborn as hell. . . ."

HALDEMAN: "Yes, Evans and Novak have done a column on Agnew today, which is, I believe, perceptive. They make the point that Agnew, there's several events involved here. First of all, that Agnew is, has become, a complete 100 percent ideologue. He is obsessive against the media, and that everything he does, and this is confirmed, Rumsfeld was saying last night, he was involved with him in a cabinet meeting with Connally . . . .Agnew started on media, and someone else would start on [something else] and [Agnew] would go back on the media. And it was obvious that's all he's concerned with. The other thing is that he is totally concerned with his own image. And Shultz makes this point, that . . . he's not interested to be anywhere you'd be, because he thinks it would hurt his image to be with you."

NIXON: "His image. . . Oh, shit, he ought to go out and speak to universities. I'm going to make that suggestion right now."

HALDEMAN: "He wouldn't have anything to do with Shultz's desegregating the south committee of which he was the head of, you know. He's in over his head. See, what he sees is, that he is our bulwark to the right, and that he must preserve, absolutely lily-white and pure, his rights and credentials, so as to be, and I think he believes this honestly, I don't think this is any—"

NIXON: "To hold Reagan off."

HALDEMAN: "Well, to hold Reagan off and maintain your tie to your basic constituency over there. . . . They point out that he [Agnew] will listen to no one except the president. That he will not take any White House staff or—"

NIXON: "Or go to the Gridiron."

HALDEMAN: "You can't turn him off. . . You can't tell the vice president what to do."[15]

The matter of Agnew subbing for Nixon at the Gridiron dinner, meanwhile, dragged on. Nixon, instead of simply picking up a phone and asking Agnew to go, finally did write him the personal note that the vice president accepted as a request fitting to his own status, and spoke in Nixon's place.

In his speech, Agnew didn't hesitate to needle the man who imposed the command performance on him. "The president asked me to express his regrets that he was unable to be here tonight," he began. "As you know, he had to leave for a working vacation in Key Biscayne—because Martha Mitchell is using the Oval Office. Don't laugh, gentlemen. I happened to overhear her talking on one of the president's phones. And I can say this: I hope to God that Kosygin has a sense of humor."

Prior to the speech, Gridiron members had performed a skit in which one of them impersonating John Connally sang a song whose lyric ended with "Maybe I will end up V.P." Agnew cracked: "I wouldn't worry about John Connally replacing me in 1972. Have you ever heard a Texan trying to pronounce 'pusillanimous'?" And endorsing Nixon's declaration of a New American Revolution, Agnew added: "But I'll be damned if I'll take the White House staff's advice and move my winter headquarters to Valley Forge."[16]

❧ ❧

YET FOR ALL THE JESTING, and Nixon's continuing praise and propping up of his vice president as an effective campaigner, his early love affair with Agnew clearly had soured. And so, on Wednesday, April 7, 1971, a day on which Nixon made a major speech on Vietnam, he had a long talk with Haldeman in the Oval Office that broached the matter in a very direct way. He began, heard on the White House tape for that day, by lamenting the weakness of his cabinet, identifying only three men— Mitchell, Connally, and Richardson—as "big men." When Haldeman mentions the vice president, Nixon says sourly: "Oh, Agnew," reflecting his concern about having him in the line of presidential succession.

As Haldeman later wrote, Nixon "got to talking about Connally and the VP, and revealed his thought that the way out of the whole deal is have the VP resign later this year, which then gives the P the opportunity to appoint a new VP under the new law of succession." Nixon is heard to say on the tape for that day: "We've got to do something, but I don't know what the Christ to do. What's he [Agnew] going to resign for? He resigns, what? Because he's sick or tired of the job or decides to do something else? Decides to own a television network and so forth? That would be great. Get somebody to buy CBS and have Agnew run it."

HALDEMAN says: "If you wanted Agnew to resign, first of all he would be perfectly apt to do it. Secondly, he's got the opportunity. He's tied up for instance with Bob Hope and [could] go into the television area. Hope's playing in that cable TV business and all that. He could go into that area."

NIXON: Hope is in cable TV?"

HALDEMAN: "Yeah. . . [but]. . . Hope may not help."

NIXON: "You see, here's the way, the only way really that I can get [Connally] on as vice president, in an effective way, is to appoint him as vice president. By the law, Agnew resigns as vice president. I as President under the law appoint the vice president. Check the new, uh, law." (He's referring here to the Twenty-fifth Amendment, ratified in 1967 after the vacancy four years earlier when President Kennedy died and Vice President Lyndon Johnson succeeded him.)

Nixon tells the White House phone operator to connect him with John Dean, his young legal counsel, and while he's waiting to be connected, he tells Haldeman: "You see, that's the way the law was written. You have to find some way to find a new vice president. The president appoints him. How the hell else you gonna get him? And then the Congress approves him. If he's on there, if he's appointed as vice president. . . the whole Congress approves him. That's the way it has to be done. . . . You see, if you don't, and you have to try to get the convention to nominate him, a Democrat, it's a harder problem. But if I appointed Connally, then after I appointed—"

The phone rings, interrupting Nixon's explanation. It is Dean, calling back.

NIXON [making a weak stab at camouflaging the purpose of his inquiry]: "John, is that constitutional amendment on presidential succession that's passed, I mean it's now in the law, is it not? What is the situation, because I have to [hesitating], because I have to, one of my daughters is doing a paper and, or I wanted to find out, the, uh, in the case of the—I know what happens in the case of the president, but in the case if the vice president dies, does the president appoint and then [get] approval of Congress? Why don't you go check and call me back? I want to know what happens in the event the vice president either is incapacitated or resigns. It's a good, good question. I'd be interested to know whether it does. My recollection was that the, er, president appoints, because I recall when they asked me what ought to be done, I said I couldn't see any [other] way to do it, because the vice president had to be the president's man. The president's got to appoint him. . . . Fine. Call me back."

When Nixon hangs up, he comments derisively to Haldeman, without having told Dean the real reason he wants the answer: "That's his big thrill for the month."[17] (Dean, interviewed years later, was asked whether he was aware of the real purpose of Nixon's inquiry. He said the president's reference to one of his daughter's school papers was a transparent dodge, but that he didn't know at the time the extent of Nixon's thinking about getting rid of Agnew.)[18]

While Nixon is waiting, Haldeman immediately starts laying out a timetable for the Connally-for-Agnew coup. "That's interesting," he says. "The latter part of this year, when things are on the upswing, and he [Agnew] has a reason."

NIXON: "What is his reason?"

HALDEMAN: "Well, once he knows [he's on the way out].. . . I mean he has reasons of his own on that. I think he would play a very willing co-conspirator."

Nixon suddenly has a brainstorm: "Hey, Bob. Let me ask you about the [Supreme] Court. I have a problem in the court. . . ."

HALDEMAN: "He wouldn't be able to be confirmed."

NIXON: "That's my problem. I'm very much afraid if you put Agnew on it would raise holy hell in the country, of course."

HALDEMAN: "He'd recognize that, and wouldn't want to go through—"

NIXON: "—wouldn't want to go through the torture of being vice president [again]."

HALDEMAN: "I'll tell you, he has come to Bryce and said, I'm sure this is true, Bryce has said, he likes hobnobbing with Frank Sinatra, Bob Hope, the big money. . . "

NIXON: "He likes it?"

HALDEMAN: "The fast crowd, and the golf course, the pretty houses. He'd have no problem moving into that. He could move out, if he wanted to call it a law practice, or if he wanted to go into a corporate thing of some kind, make himself a damn good bundle. He could stay public in attacking the media, which he'd like to do. It wouldn't be bad at all for us. There would be no question at all [that] he'd clear his speeches with you or anything at all."

NIXON: "The only problem would be, the only problem is, would he get an audience if he wasn't vice president?"

HALDEMAN: "They say he wouldn't, but I just wonder, I just wonder. . . "

NIXON: "Let me tell you what I think is the problem. You gotta get Hoover out before he's forced out. With Agnew, it'd be too God-damned bloody a battle. Well, some people say, have the bloody battle about him and not about yourself. But it'll reflect on us, and then one hell of a bloody battle about Agnew, the vice president, all that sort of thing. . . " (Nixon was referring here to concern that unless FBI Director J. Edgar Hoover, another darling of the right wing, could be persuaded to retire first, which Nixon devoutly desired, the conservative firestorm of Agnew's departure on top of it would be politically devastating.)

HALDEMAN: "He [Agnew] still has 50 percent approval or something."

NIXON: "I know he does. I know he does. But his opposition, the hatred of me is strong; the hatred of him is violent. Now, that's just the difference. See my point?"

HALDEMAN: "Sure."

NIXON: "And the hatred of me is not, I mean, I'm quite aware of it. If I got the war over with, the hatred, everybody's gonna love me, and I don't give a damn, but people aren't gonna hate me. But with Agnew, if we get the war over with, they're still gonna hate his guts. . . "

HALDEMAN: "Well, the dislike of you is by people we can't get over no matter what. The hatred of Agnew is partially winnable."

NIXON: "Winnable by me."

HALDEMAN: "Right. A lot of people who will not vote for [you], will not vote for you if Agnew is your vice president."

NIXON: "I think so too. . . . The poll may not show that up, either. But I think by the time they make the record [against Agnew]—? "

HALDEMAN: "Just like Stevenson tried to do to Eisenhower [against Nixon], they'd go all out on the—"

NIXON: "But you see, they didn't work it with me, because basically I was too God-damn clever for 'em. And also. . . I was not that much of a lightning rod. Frankly, most of the stuff on me was made up. Let's face it. With Agnew, he's asked for some of it. I don't mean a lot of it, I agree with him 80 percent of the time, but God-damn, the other 20 percent of the time, I don't. And also, if you're in a second-term situation, people do think of the possible death of the president. A hell of a lot of presidents have died, at sixty-one, sixty-two, sixty-three. . . "

HALDEMAN: "That's why you'd be at at the age where people are going to think about it."

NIXON: "Quite vulnerable. Eisenhower had his heart attack when he was sixty-four. They're gonna think about it. . . . No matter what your health record is, and they know what a bitchy job this is, and they know what a man's been through, and they're gonna say it, the actuarials and the rest, well, they all know what the cholesterol is and the rest, and there's always that possibility."

HALDEMAN: "The issue with Connally, of course, is he'd be able to hold on to most of the people who'd be concerned about dumping Agnew. . . . A hell of a lot of 'em."

NIXON: "He'd hold all of the South except a few Republicans in the South. But Connally's gaining a lot. Every time Connally goes out— Incidentally, did you get him on *Meet the Press* or not?"

As Nixon rambles on about showcasing Connally, the phone rings. It is Dean. Nixon takes the call: "Hello. Yes, John. I get it, John. Thank you, thank you." He hangs up and tells Haldeman: "I was exactly right. It only takes a majority of both houses of Congress. A simple majority. Agnew's got to [go], see what I mean? That's the only way to handle the thing. It'll be a hell of a bombshell. But as I look at the situation, Bob, it can only be done if we're [Congress is] out."

On the tape, Nixon and Haldeman can be heard calculating the time frame for the move in the late fall or as late as inaugural day of the second term. Haldeman suggests to Nixon that Agnew could say he was resigning "because he is moving into another field that he wants to get into now, and because he wants to serve you in your reelection as a private citizen. . . ."

Nixon muses: "The way it would have to be done is, I would ask Bryce to sit down. . . and [rather than] go through the battle, [have] Agnew give a little thought to it. What makes me think he might do it is, his attitude about going to the ball game. He's a little queasy about being booed at the ball game."[19]

THUS DID THE PRESIDENT OF THE UNITED STATES and his chief lieutenant, apparently seriously, plot about getting the man first in destiny's line to become leader of the free world to step aside voluntarily, maybe for a job in television. Haldeman wrote afterward that Nixon "was up late tonight and on the phone to me even after I got home, three or four times, in the usual follow-up kind of activity."[20]

(Nixon was right about Agnew's reluctance to be put on display at a baseball game, where particularly in Washington politicians risk a negative crowd reaction. In 1971, the last season of the old Washington Senators, Agnew aide John Damgard, knowing Agnew's attitude and fearing Nixon might ask the vice president to substitute for him in throwing the traditional first ball at the opening game at Robert F. Kennedy Stadium, invented an insurance policy for his boss. He asked Agnew's scheduler, Ernie Minor, a native of Cincinnati, to arrange for the vice president to be invited to throw out the ball at opening day of the Cincinnati Reds of the National League, who, like the Senators, known as "first in war, first in peace, and last in the American League," traditionally started the season a day early. Cincinnati, Damgard pointed out to Agnew, was a hotbed of Republicanism and hence was probably a safer venue. Damgard submitted a check list with three choices: "A) Throw out the first ball in Washington. B) Throw out the first ball in Cincinnati. C) No balls at all." Agnew checked the third.)[21]

That same night, Nixon made a major speech on Vietnam, and Agnew, in California, phoned him to laud his delivery. On the White House tapes, Nixon is in an expansive mood, bantering with Agnew and encouraging him, giving no sign that earlier in the day he had been plotting with Haldeman about how to depose his vice president who was gushing all over him.

NIXON: "How are ya? In California, eh? That's great."

Agnew: "Yeah, California. I had a good interview with the Copley [Newspapers] people this afternoon."

NIXON: "Oh, they're great people. My God, if we only had more papers like that, we'd be in clover."

AGNEW: "That's true. Well, Mr. President, I think you pulled all the keys again tonight. . . . I'm trying to be completely objective. I thought it was the most effective of all the Vietnam speeches by far, particularly the part where you put the paper down and just went off the cuff on that very personalized impression."

NIXON: "Well actually I was really speaking from the heart, because [when] that little Kevin, the four-year-old, saluted me, my God, what do you do? You almost come apart."

AGNEW: "Well, it came through extremely well, and not just that part. I thought the whole speech was extremely well-organized and effective. It just did a great amount of good as far as defusing all of this incipient demonstration and what-not."

NIXON: "Basically, the problem is that the country is in sort of a neurotic state, but we've got to fight it, because we've got to do the right thing, that's all. So history will look back and say, did we crumble or did we measure up? That's why I said at the last, that generations in the future will look back and say we had the courage to do the right thing. I'm not sure we have, but by God, you and I are going to be damn sure we do everything we can."

AGNEW: "That came through strong and clear tonight. I think you'll find, even the analysis on CBS was fairly—"

NIXON [breaking in, laughing]: "I hope you didn't look at it. You did, I bet you did. Don't do it! Don't look at those God-damned television buggers."

AGNEW: "I want to see whether they're getting any religion, Mr. President."

NIXON: "Nah, they won't get any religion. [Agnew laughs uproariously.] But anyway I appreciate the fact you kicked those bastards in the gut."

Agnew goes on to tell Nixon that the CBS analysis was fair and "a departure" for them "that came across as a very positive analysis and the first I've ever seen." Nixon shoots back: "God, don't get your hopes up. The next one will be negative."

AGNEW [soberly]: "I'm as cynical as you are about that, maybe more so."

NIXON [the batttered veteran]: "No, no, no, no, not more so. I've been through it more than you have."

The president, warming up now and switching his Vietnam targets, says: "The real problem, Ted, is the fact these God-damned senators and congressmen, they're all crawling and straining and whining around. Damn it, they ought to stand up and be men. The real question is, if they want us to get out after a certain date, why the hell won't they say so? Then, by God, all right, we'll get out by a certain date and let them be responsible for Vietnam going communist. All right, but they won't do that."

AGNEW: "Well, they see they have a different perspective than you have, Mr. President. They're not looking at a short term of service and doing a job. They're looking at a lifetime in the Senate, and that's why—"

Nixon: "I know. Well, we're gonna do the right thing, and we're doing the right thing, we're gonna stick to it. Tell old Bob Hope that I hope he noticed what I said about the Vietnam servicemen, because I did that for him. After my call with him on the telephone, that I wrote that whole section. Remember, I said by God somebody's got to stand up and speak up for the men that serve in Vietnam. Wasn't that good?"

AGNEW: "Well, the whole speech was outstanding."

NIXON: "But tell Bob that that section was a result of my conversation with him. Will you do that?"

His loyal vice president said he would so advise the president's secret speech writer.[22]

꙰ ꙰

A FEW DAYS LATER, Nixon had a long talk with Connally that demonstrated how and why the big and confident Texan was making the president look past the obedient, fawning Spiro Agnew toward him as his adviser of choice—and would-be vice president. In the course of a discussion of foreign policy, supposedly Nixon's strong suit, Connally unabashedly takes it upon himself to tell Nixon he needs to stop being so soft and get tougher.

CONNALLY: "Mr. President. . . I would hope that, somewhere, some instance would occur where it's likely to be a major [dispute] or something, where you just say [you're] withholding [your approval], you're denying this or you're denying that because you're getting tired of getting kicked around, this nation getting kicked around. I'd use those words. . . .'The country's fed up and so am I.' I'd use those words. If I have one suggestion to make, it's that you're, in your defense, and I contribute to some of this, you're always too controlled; that you're always too studious, too precise, always right . . . . You say, 'I'm sick and tired of it,' or 'I'm fed up with this nation being kicked around' or some similar expression, whatever comes natural to you. Because you're not a stranger now. People view you now as a very studious, very cautious, always good. But carry it too far, it leaves you a very cold and aloof man. If you have to be one or the other, it's better to be that than an irrational man. But every now and then, and I've basically said this to you before, that you display some emotion, something that reflects a real interest on your part; some reaction that is a very genuine reaction; a spur-of-the- moment reaction, whatever it might be."

In other words, Connally was telling the president of the United States to stop being such a stiff, and Nixon was taking it all in without the slightest disagreement or offense.

Connally tells him about a major conference in Texas of "top hunters and fishermen from around the world" where he could talk about conservation of the ecology and the environment. "You should visit the forum you want and the subject you want," he lectures the president, "but somebody ought to be watching for things like this. . . . It gets you a little out of the ordinary."

Connally goes on to tell Nixon that his cabinet is composed of a bunch of stiffs too, who ought to be out on the firing line regularly defending him and his policies.

NIXON: "You're right, but you know, the cabinet does make a hell of a lot of speeches."

CONNALLY: "But they don't take on anybody. We got to be prepared to take on some of these people."

NIXON (agreeing): "Gotta fight!"

After some more of this critical talk from Connally, Nixon says, "Interestingly enough, you know, Agnew's not that kind of a guy. Is this the horrible guy you're reading about?" In fact, he says, Agnew recently "took the bull by the horns" to answer criticism of Nixon's handling of the war by Democratic Senator J. William Fulbright. "As a matter of fact when you go through the line, who the hell else you got there? . . . I think the country doesn't want us to sit back and take that stuff, [but] I can't be the one to kick the hell out of these people," Nixon says. "Or do you think so?"

Connally says, "No, you cannot." Nixon listens to some more of this counsel and finally asks him if he'd like to see some more presidential "outrage." Connally seizes the opportunity to butter up the president good and proper. "You have a marvelous voice and you know how to use it," he tells Nixon, "and you do use it in private conversation. . . . But every now and then I'd just take the bridle off a little, that's all I'm saying. . . enough to reach the average fella."

Finally, Nixon gets down to business: "Let me ask you about Agnew."

CONNALLY: "He speaks their language, and the great value of the vice president is, whether they like him or whether they don't, whether they always agree with him or whether they don't, I think he says what he believes. I think he's candid enough to say what he believes, and they think that of very few men in political life. A lot of politicians are at a very low ebb."

Connally's comments on Agnew, however, begin to sound a warning signal: "Now, I think the vice president has made some mistakes. He's almost reached the point, and I said almost reached the point, where if he's not careful he's going to convince people he's doing this for effect, not because he says what he thinks. If he goes beyond that thin line. . . then he can't survive, because he will be completely discredited then. He hasn't reached it yet. . . . And there's one other point, that he has to be careful not to use too much alliteration, because then people begin to think, 'Well, he's just trying to be clever."

NIXON: "I don't think you can be too cute."

CONNALLY: "No, you can't."

NIXON: "You can be funny now and then."

CONNALLY: "Funny, humor, great. He does that well."

NIXON: "Very well."

CONNALLY: "Extremely well. But when he's attacking a Muskie or a Humphrey. . . he has to be careful of the language he uses. It can be mean, it can be tough, but he can't just have a string of adjectives, a string of words of alliteration. It's a delicate thing to handle. . . . And God knows, he's been a tremendous drawing card now. And he's been a whale of a soldier."

NIXON: "He's been the one to take 'em on when others have not."

CONNALLY: "That's correct. He's been the one what nobody else would do."

NIXON: "God-damn right."

CONNALLY: "And he came at a time when you really needed somebody to take 'em on."[23]

At the same time, however, Connally was continuing to speak and act in ways that provided in Nixon's receptive mind a sharp contrast with the vice president about whom he was having increasing doubts. In another taped conversation with Nixon about a severe drought in Texas, Connally demonstrates the kind of forcefulness—and manliness—that the president so admired. Discussing the plight of Texas cattle farmers, Connally warns Nixon concerning his relief officials: "Don't let 'em just put you on the grain program, because all that does is run up the price of grain and doesn't help. What they really need, in addition to some grain I suppose, I'm no authority. . . is hay."

Connally proceeds to tell Nixon that hay can be imported from Colorado, New Mexico, and Arizona, and under Harry Truman "the most effective program they ever had was, the government picked up the [cost]. But if there weren't sufficient—"

Nixon breaks in, quick to agree if only because of his fixation on winning Texas's electoral votes in his approaching reelection. "Oh hell," he says, "whatever it is, it's Texas, God-damn it, they've got to be helped!"

As Connally discusses the shortage of rainfall and how his own cattle and farmland have been affected, Nixon's phone rings. It's retired General George A. Lincoln, head of the Office of Emergency Preparedness, the disaster relief agency. Nixon tells him: "I'm sitting here talking to John Connally about the Texas situation. He's just back. I wonder if he could talk to you a bit, and you fill him in with what you're doing and he could sort of give you his view. . . particularly with regard to the rain and the hay."

Connally takes the phone, and after brief pleasantries launches a tour de force: "I don't know a thing, I don't pose as an expert, I merely want to give you this much information. Number one, it is damn bad. That much I know, over a very, very wide range of space. It's just as bad as they say it is. Secondly, don't just let it go with just a grain program, because all you do is run up the price of grain. . . . All right, but [throw in] some hay." Connally tells Lincoln that "the most effective thing, and this is what the farmers say," is the Truman approach in which "the farmers bought the hay but the government transported it for them for free. . . . What they're trying to do is save their cow herds."

Connally the rancher tells him "there's no hay in Texas" and what's he's doing himself to save his own cattle. Then, in authoritative presidential tones with the president sitting by taking it all in, Connally the politician adds: "Don't wait too damn long where everybody else gets the credit for it. I just have a few observations to make. Secondly, don't be too niggardly. Remember that the average person, and [this] is what I heard at the corner cafes down there. They all sit around, they don't have a damn thing to do, they can't work. . . so they all sit down and talk. And they just say, 'By God, if there's a famine over in India, they God-damn sure get the food over there, and they don't mind givin' it away. They have all the wheat in Russia, the communists, but they don't give 'em food or anything else they want. But when it comes to us, we got to go through all the God-damn rigaramole, this and that, and we can't ever be helped.' This is an unfair advantage, but nevertheless that's their attitude."

Nixon is heard clearing his throat. Connally concludes: "So all I'm sayin' is, if you gonna do somethin,' hell, don't be niggardly about it, go on and do it. It costs a little bit more money, [but] you're gonna get credit only to the extent that you do it voluntarily. Don't wait so long that they think they made you do it. . . . I'd just follow that up as quickly as I could. I don't want to run your business. . . ."

When Connally hands over the phone, Nixon offers: "You can't screw around. You're absolutely right. You've got to also show that they care about it right now! Right now! Right now!"

Connally, having just shown Nixon how a president should take charge, tells him: "That's right. The main thing you need again is, you need leadership, you need to display leadership. And to just let it drag, let it drag, and take one halting step and another halting step, it requires a decent step." He tells Nixon that Lincoln had said that in an earlier drought there had been a hay program and "a big hassle" over the cost and larger ranches getting all the hay.

"Oh, Christ," Nixon replies. "We don't care about that. Just do something. Do it again. Better to get in a hassle doing something than to get in a hassle for doing nothing."

CONNALLY: "That's right."[24]

The Texan's display of forcefulness apparently struck home with Nixon, because in a separate White House tape the president is heard citing Connally's defense of the Texas farmers, and the failure of his own secretary of agriculture, Clifford Hardin, to respond similarly. He tells Haldeman he should have heard Connally "raise hell about that God-damn thing in Texas. He says, 'God-damn,' he says, 'Hardin should be out there charging, saying I worry about that hay, is that farmer going to get that hay?' You know, it's talking about that hay. He's not farting around about [what] it ought to cost the country. See what I mean? We talk in terms of statistics and all the rest. Everything we get out there, there isn't a God-damn word of warmth." Then, suddenly, Nixon segues to his vice president: "Agnew has no warmth. He's a cold fish. But his words sometimes have warmth. That's why Agnew is a personality."[25]

From all this, Connally seemed to be sympathetic to Agnew and to be conveying the idea that Nixon ought to keep him on the ticket as long as the vice president continued to defend him so steadfastly and didn't go overboard with his steamy rhetoric. And Nixon in his forceful agreement appeared to be going along.

The president called Haldeman in and told him that he and Connally had discussed Agnew, "and he thinks Agnew can survive. I do not agree. . . . I don't know what the hell we're gonna do."[26] Haldeman wrote in his diary that Nixon "told me to have a private talk with Connally regarding the vice presidency, and start getting him built up and ready for it."[27]

Chapter 11

BULL IN A CHINA SHOP

Around this time, Agnew committed a pair of political faux pas of unusual dimension, even for him, that could only heighten Nixon's desire to get rid of him. For two years, the president and his national security adviser, Henry Kissinger, had been diligently pursuing a move that would mark Nixon as an innovative force in foreign policy— an opening to China. In the spring of 1971, as a statutory member of the National Security Council, Agnew was present during a discussion of Nixon's attempts to thaw out relations with the Far East giant, still referred to, especially in Republican circles, as Communist China. As a staunch defender of Taiwan and opposed to its replacement by mainland China on the United Nations Security Council, Agnew spoke out.

According to William Timmons, Nixon's top liaison with Congress, UN Ambassador George H. W. Bush had just reported that the United States did not have the votes in the UN to save Taiwan's seat. "Mr. President," Timmons recalled Agnew saying, "I think it's very simple. The Security Council has every right to do whatever they want, and we have every right to kick their asses out." The next day, according to Timmons, Haldeman informed Agnew: "Your presence won't be required at NSC meetings henceforth."[1]

For Nixon, a confirmed anti-communist, to break the long diplomatic freeze between Beijing and Washington would be a huge coup for him. An opportunity presented itself in April, when an American table tennis team competing in the world championship in Japan was invited to play exhibition matches in China, where the sport was fanatically pursued. The invitation was accepted and the Nixon administration built on the breakthrough by announcing the end of its trade embargo against China, to coincide with the new "ping-pong diplomacy." Nixon started referring to the regime as "the People's Republic of China" rather than the old "Communist China" or "mainland China." The American players were no match for the Chinese, who sympathetically used second-stringers in order not to humiliate their visitors, and stories of the new friendly competition filled American newspapers.[2]

It so happened that at precisely this time, Agnew went to another Republican governors' conference at Colonial Williamsburg, Virginia, in his role as administration liaison with his old colleagues, somewhat tarnished by his earlier meeting with them at Sun Valley. There, he took it upon himself in a post-midnight meeting with a select group of reporters to air his differences with the new developments toward China. On two previous trips to Asia, Agnew had stopped in Taiwan to reaffirm the U.S. commitment to Chiang Kai-shek, which he personally supported. And in White House discussions about China, he had repeatedly cautioned about trusting the regime in what was then known as Peking and reaching out to it.

In a most uncommon gesture for Agnew, he unexpectedly suggested to his press secretary, Vic Gold, that he'd like to have a drink or two with some of the reporters covering the conference. Gold ran out into the hotel lobby and rounded up nine of them. Because of the lateness of the hour, he phoned some of them in their rooms, rousing them for what Gold explicitly said would be an off-the-record chat. Agnew in his suite cordially greeted them, and they sat down with him and two other aides, Roy Goodearle and Peter Malatesta. Agnew at first seemed not to have anything particular in mind to talk about, though he did make his usual points about the need for the press to be more self-critical. He complimented some of the reporters he knew, while criticizing their editors and management.

Eventually the subject turned to the ping-pong diplomacy development, with one reporter asking Agnew whether he played the game and whether he was any good at it. He said he was a pretty fair player, probably good enough to beat the Chinese leaders, Mao Tse-tung and Chou En-lai. Getting more serious, Agnew said he was disturbed by how the

American press had handled the story, particularly one account by the *Associated Press* reporter in Tokyo. The AP man credited Peking with a diplomatic coup by using second-level players in "an exquisite display of Chinese tact and politeness to guests" who were no match for them. Agnew said he feared the glowing accounts of the young Americans about their reception would give their countrymen a severely distorted impression of the hard and repressive life in China, and create false hope about the chances of peaceful co-existence with the communist regime.

In his view, Agnew said, the United States had taken a propaganda beating in the China visit, and he told the reporters that, at a National Security Council meeting just prior to it, he had argued in vain against the administration's course of seeking to ease relations with Peking. He said he feared an adverse reaction on Taiwan and among Americans toward that regime. While he endorsed lifting the recent travel and trade restrictions, he expressed worry that the United States might appear too eager to reach an accommodation with China.[3]

After nearly three hours of talk, the reporters left, still under the off-the-record ground rules. Reporters like myself, who were not present and were not bound by it asked for an opportunity to talk to Agnew about the same subject. The press secretary went to Agnew, but he declined and refused to lift the ground rules. "Absolutely not," he told Gold. "They'll go with it but I'm not going to release it." Gold said later that Agnew "knew exactly what was going to happen"—that there would be hell to pay—as a result of his meeting with the reporters. "He understood the ramifications. That was calculated. It was deliberate. I think he really felt deeply about the [China] policy. I do think if he had had better relations with the president, and the president had let him in on something, it would not have happened. . . . All they had to say was, 'Mr. Vice President, we're going to do this;' fine, he never would have done it [held the press meeting]. He was surprised about it [the overture to Peking] as much as anybody, and this was his way of saying, 'Screw you.'"[4]

David Keene, one of Agnew's political aides, agreed. "Agnew believed he was being undermined. He was a very strong supporter of Taiwan and it was a way he could say things he believed, and show he was one who was not going to do just as he was told. And he was very proud of it." (When Nixon went to China in the following February, Keene recalled, "It was a complete surprise to Agnew. It was humiliating. It pissed him off mightily." Upon Nixon's return, Agnew went out to Andrews Air Force Base in suburban Maryland to greet him. When he got back, he phoned Keene and asked him: "Do you know what I thought as they rolled up the stairs to the plane? I wondered if he'd be carrying an umbrella."[5] (Like-minded Keene, a rock-ribbed anti-communist, needed no explanation of the reference to Neville Chamberlain's acquiesence to the surrender of Czechoslovakia to Hitler at Munich in 1938.)

In any event, before long another reporter, Tom Ottenad of the *St. Louis Post-Dispatch*, and I, working then for the *Los Angeles Times*, learned of the midnight press meeting and gleefully wrote the story from details provided by some of our professionally frustrated colleagues. Our accounts were sort of "absentee" scoops, resulting from Agnew's adherence to the off-the-record mandate imposed on the reporters present. The stories were soon picked up by the wire services, and they hit Washington and the Nixon administration hard. For the first time on a truly major issue, the vice president was second-guessing the president. To make matters worse, the next day at lunch Agnew told the Republican governors essentially what he had told the Williamsburg Nine the night before, but softened; he said he had reservations about the administration policy but supported it.

At the White House, Nixon was furious. Haldeman recounted in his diary "a monumental flap arising from a rather weird, off-the-record press deal that the VP had Sunday night in Williamsburg. Apparently, after midnight he called nine press people to his suite and spent three hours in an off-the-record backgrounder with them, during which he expressed his disagreement with the idea of letting down the barriers with China and his extreme dissatisfaction with the press reporting of the Chinese ping-pong tour. This, of course, has created exactly the kind of flap that should have been expected."[6]

The Nixon White House tapes recorded the president's reaction in a conversation with his national security adviser, Henry Kissinger. "I suppose you saw what our Peck's Bad Boy did yesterday," Nixon says. "My guess is that this was a ten-minute, probably, little dialogue where he popped off, as he does, on this subject, not knowing his ass from his face. And it can only be harmful, it can only be harmful because, Henry, you and I know that he's exactly right in what he says, but God-damn it, why does he have to [sound off] on the thing? Now the question is, how do we get it knocked down? I really think Agnew's got to knock it down."

Kissinger offers: "Well, I can get him under control." Nixon orders him to do so, and to "even make the point to him that he has created, he has created, by this, enormous harm and he's got to correct it." Kissinger then asks: "Why couldn't Ziegler say the vice president was speaking for himself?"

Nixon rejects that idea. "The difficulty with this, Henry, is that it makes me look—you see, you cannot say the vice president is speaking for himself. The vice president cannot speak for himself in foreign policy. He can speak for [himself] in the press, but not in foreign policy. He has got to speak for the administration. He's in the NSC, Henry, and the moment he goes off on a tangent, it is not understood. You see, that would be the easy way out of it, but you know what's going to happen, it destroys him too. It's going to destroy him, but it can also hurt us. I think what you have to do is you've got to get off that wicket. He's got to eat crow, and say, 'Now look, I was completely misunderstood.' I don't know. What do you think? It was a dumb damn thing for him to do."

Nixon can be heard on the White House tape pounding his desk as he assails his vice president for, among other things, speaking out of school at an NSC meeting. "He shouldn't have said that about the NSC, for example," he says. "That's just dumb, that's just dumb. God-damn, what he's trying, to sit up there and say that, you know, hell, I argued against this, and I—I mean, it sounds like [cabinet members George] Romney and [John] Volpe and those other people saying they argued [over] wage and price controls. God-damn them, they're not supposed to say it, not once the decision is made. I mean, what the hell, the vice president, his job is to support the president."

Kissinger repeats that "my frank opinion is that we are better off having Ziegler say that there are always free discussions in the NSC and the vice president was expressing his personal view, that he thought it was an off-the-record meeting at which he expressed his personal view. And then let the vice president say of course he supported the policy. If he says he was misunderstood, there'll be nine guys swearing that he said it."

Nixon takes the occasion to make some choice observations about dealing with the press. He says Agnew erred in "editing an individual story" and then he unloads: "I think the stories are lousy, all of them. I think all of the reporters are a bunch of bastards. That's why I've never had them in for a drink. That's his mistake number one. Never—have—a—drink—with—reporters. Believe: I have never had a drink with a reporter in twenty years—never. Not one. One of the reasons they don't trust me, because I never relax with them. That's true." Kissinger, laughing, injects: "That's right."

NIXON goes on: "All the bastards—they never did [trust him, or have a drink with him]. I'll bet you what happened there. He and [aide Peter] Malatesta were sitting there having a couple of drinks, trying to talk about the God-damned press, [when Agnew said] 'Call them up. Get 'em in here and let's talk about this, let's level with them . . . off the record and try to get it settled. Get [press secretary] Vic [Gold] out of bed and tell him to get his ass up here, and get the press."

KISSINGER tells Nixon: "Actually, I sent Haig over on Friday to brief him on China policy, so he had—" Nixon breaks in: "Did he? Really?" He tells Kissinger that Agnew doesn't see "the big picture."

NIXON: "Well, let's just be sure that he supports the president's policies, not that I support his policies."

KISSINGER: "Actually, it won't hurt us with the Chinese. . . . It's useful for them to remember that there are significant elements on the right [in the United States]."

NIXON: "That's right, I agree, [but] it does hurt us in American public opinion."

KISSINGER: "It might even help you get the liberals. . . ."

NIXON, in briefing Ziegler on what to tell the press, instructs him: "Remember, though, Henry's point is well taken. Be sure they don't get the impression I support the vice president's views. The vice president has his own views [but] he has no views on that unless they're mine."

After Ziegler has left the room, Nixon tells Kissinger about Agnew: "Let me say this, though. I just don't think he's got good judgment. . . . He just pops right off there now, that's just so God-damned—that's the thing, that he didn't realize, that he didn't know, he didn't know, that he shouldn't get into something like this. What do you think? Huh? Or you think he did?"

KISSINGER: "He just feels very strongly that what we're doing is wrong."

NIXON: "But because he doesn't see the big game, Henry. He doesn't see the Russian game, does he?"

KISSINGER: "Not at all. He looks at it entirely from his point of view... of Chiang Kai-shek."

NIXON: "... And we can't tell him about it [because of his close allegiance to Taiwan]. You see, that's what he does. He can't run with the Russian game because he's for that policy and would ruin the Chinese game. God-damn it, he is—I don't think we better put him on any more foreign trips. What do you think?"

Later, however, Nixon relented in what some insiders surmised was a way to get his bumbling vice president out of his hair for a time.

When Kissinger offers that "he's behaved well on the—" Nixon interrupts: "I know, I know, but he gets to be that he's an expert. That's the thing. He went to China, he's been to Korea, you know, he's been to all these places.... Well, that's the danger. A little bit of knowledge and you become an expert. You go to Taiwan once, and 'I know about the China thing. I know Chiang Kai-shek, I know more than they even think they know.' But Agnew doesn't see the point there. On the business of recognition, he wouldn't see that it's not only separating recognition and admission to the UN and trade.... You know, Henry, the thing about the Agnew thing that irritates me is, God-damn it, we handled this Chinese thing with extreme subtlety and skill and got good credit for it, and [referring to the press] now these sons of bitches will jump on the Agnew thing. I think they'll jump on him, rather than on me."

KISSINGER: "They'll jump on him, Mr. President. Everyone knows that he doesn't know anything."

NIXON: "It may destroy him, though."[7]

Haldeman, by way of clarification, wrote in his diary that Nixon "says it's clear that he [Agnew] doesn't understand the big picture in this whole Chinese operation, which is, of course, the Russian game. We're using the Chinese thaw to get the Russians shook. Dobrynin will be back later this week, and Henry will get a reading on how it's working."[8]

Nixon later wrote of the incident that "a bull in the form of Ted Agnew inadvertently careened into this diplomatic China shop.... Agnew had expressed his reservations about our trade and visa overtures to the Chinese Communists at a recent NSC meeting, but I had never imagined that he would discuss his doubts with reporters. I told Haldeman to get word to Agnew to stay off this topic."[9] Haldeman pointedly added: "The P got again to the point that Agnew shows qualities here that are very damaging. He wants me to talk privately with Connally, and to move very, very slowly; but to start getting him with it, in this area of possible vice presidential candidate."[10]

In his final word on the ping-pong fiasco, according to Haldeman, Nixon "agreed with Ron's recommendation that the VP's authorized him to say that there is no difference on the part of the VP with the P's policy on China; the VP completely agrees with the initiatives the P has taken."[11]

Ziegler carried out the order, dutifully telling reporters that he had talked with Agnew by phone that morning and had been authorized to say "there is absolutely no disagreement over policy." The press secretary went on to do what he could to throttle the story of a Nixon–Agnew split. "You should not pursue the story that there is a difference of opinion within the administration," he urged, "particularly a difference of opinion between the vice president and the president regarding the recent initiatives that the United States government took toward the Republic of China. There is no difference of opinion."[12]

Through all this, however, not a public word came from Nixon, who often on previous occasions of criticism directed toward Agnew had himself or through aides expressed his support. But with Kissinger working diligently on a secret plan for a direct, dramatic presidential opening to China, Agnew's outburst of policy independence particularly dismayed Nixon, and fueled an unhappiness toward his vice president that had already approached a breaking point. Kissinger wrote later of Nixon's reaction: "The relationship between the president and any vice president is never easy; it is, after all, disconcerting to have at one's side a man whose life's ambition will be achieved by one's death. Nixon's sense of being surrounded by potentional antagonists needed no such encouragement. He wrote off this gaffe as another example of Agnew's unsuitability to succeed him—a view he held about most potential candidates—and ordered Haldeman to ask Agnew to desist from further comments about China."[13]

Agnew's ventures away from his customary domestic battleground to foreign affairs particularly irritated this foreign-policy-oriented president. For example, during negotiations with Moscow over the first Strategic Arms Limitation Agreement, known as SALT I, Agnew did not hesitate at National Security Council meetings to inject views that contradicted administration policy. But after a while, he wrote later, "I usually kept my mouth shut because Bob Haldeman once told me, after I had participated perhaps too enthusiastically, 'The president does not like you to take an opposite view at a cabinet meeting, or say anything that can be construed to be mildly not in accord with his thinking.'"

Agnew continued: "In brief, I was told to keep quiet. But at this session, after waiting in vain for someone to object, I said: 'It doesn't make sense to me to negotiate an agreement which leaves the Russians with a great superiority in throw-weight. . . . When they have improved their technology to the point that it is close to parity with ours, we are left with a crippling inferiority." Agnew said he went on to express the need for a guarantee of on-site inspections of missile sites, but "the president just gave me a poker-player glance. . . . Looking back, I now believe that Mr. Nixon's disaffection with me had its roots in my outspoken criticism at NSC and cabinet meetings. I felt that a vice president should contribute, not just observe. Since I was given no chance to contribute in private, I had to do it in front of the family. The president did not have the inner confidence to take even implied criticism of his predetermined decisions. . . ."

"Gradually, I learned it was better to keep my objections to myself when I disagreed with Mr. Nixon's policies. When Bob Haldeman told me the president would appreciate my not speaking up, I presumed that he was conveying a message from the top. But I would have appreciated it much more if the president himself had called me over and said, 'Look, if you have something to say, let's talk about it privately. Don't say it at meetings because there are leaks, and I don't want the administration to look divided.' But he never did that."[14]

❧ ☙

One position about which there was no need for lengthy discussion between Nixon and Agnew was their attitudes about the press; they both thoroughly despised and distrusted it. Each year, Nixon reluctantly attended the annual White House Correspondents' Dinner, a larger version of the Gridiron dinner, at which his piano duet with his vice president the year before had scored such a hit with the assembled reporters and editors. At the 1971 dinner, however, there was no encore, and Nixon returned to the White House seething at all the anti-administration jokes and carping, and wondering whether Agnew's open contempt for the press wasn't the right approach.

In a long memo to Haldeman the next day, Nixon complained that "the reporters receiving the awards were way out left-wingers" honored for stories on "Carswell, wire-tapping, Army surveillance, etc. I had to sit there for twenty minutes while the drunken audience laughed in derision as the award citations were read." While he professed to be "not a bit thin-skinned," he dismissed the notion of some of his staffers that "as a result of my going there and sitting through three hours of pure boredom and insults that I thereby proved I was the 'good sport' and therefore may have softened some of the press attitude toward the president. On the contrary," he wrote, "the type of people who are in the press corps have nothing but contempt for those who get down on their level and who accept such treatment without striking back. That's one of the reasons they have some respect for Agnew. Incidentally, I think Agnew is right in not going to such events in the future."

Nixon went on to cite an aide's telling him "there will never be anything to surpass the piano duet act that Agnew and I put on at the Gridiron last year, and yet, he said, 'Within twenty-four hours after you did that, the press was more vicious than ever.' Also, Agnew's excellent performance at the Gridiron this year did him no good whatever." Therefore, Nixon instructed Haldeman, "under absolutely no circumstances will I attend any more dinners of this type in the future. . . . I want you to inform Ziegler of this now because I know they make their plans well in advance. We need no excuses for my not going. I simply do not care to go and also I do not want any pressure whatever put on Agnew to go. He is to go only if he wants to go."[15] That was a switch from his view when he earlier had pressed the vice president to sub for him at that year's Gridiron dinner.

As for Agnew, he blithely went on with his tasks of selling revenue-sharing to the governors, assailing war protesters as "the same scruffy individuals" who caused the disruptions in Chicago in 1968, and questioning the patriotism of Senate doves against the war. When the latter remarks brought a demand for an apology from Democratic Senator J.William Fulbright of Arkansas, one of the most outspoken critics of the Vietnam War, Agnew shot back: "He lies in his teeth. I challenge him to prove I ever made such a statement."[16]

Such blunt exchanges disturbed Nixon. In mid-May, on a flight from New York to Washington, he called Haldeman to his cabin and complained about Agnew's latest belligerent behavior. Haldeman in his diary that night wrote: "The P feeling that he shouldn't be doing this kind of thing, and he got back into the discussion of whether we could work out a resignation, and that led to the question of who could replace him, and it boils down to the only possibility being Connally. . . . He discussed the possibility of leaving Agnew in and then making the change at the time of the election, going with Connally as a national unity ticket, leaving him as a Democrat. It seems to me, we'd be better off to go the route of an Agnew resignation if we could work it out. We'd get over the trauma and get people used to Connally in the role ahead of time."[17]

The problem with that scenario was that Agnew had been elected in 1968 and hence Nixon could not simply fire him. He could have put sufficient heat on Agnew to step aside, possibly offering him another position, but it would be hard to talk so ambitious a politician into surrendering the job that had him next in the line of succession for the presidency. And if he were reelected in 1972, the vice presidency would be an obvious and strong stepping stone to his party's presidential nomination in 1976.

A couple of weeks later, Nixon broached the subject again with Haldeman, who recorded in his diary that night: "He says he thinks it's time for me to sit down and have a frank, confidential talk with Connally about the problem. See if he thinks it can be pulled off. He feels Agnew doesn't really have it, he's not broad-gauged enough. And he (the P) doesn't want to raise this in the terms of he's (the VP) broken his pick, but rather the question of whether he has the grasp to handle the job, and the question of whether we can avoid his being the issue and that being very negative. Also that we just can't keep working him in the South, because whatever he says down there will play all over the country. Also he's not upbeat, he doesn't give anyone a lift. . . . It all adds up to the P's convinced that he can't do the job, and that will affect his ability to campaign. Also, he has a lousy staff, even with the huge budget. So I'm supposed to get into all this with Connally."[18]

Soon after, Haldeman met Connally at Camp David and, Haldeman wrote, Connally "basically agrees that there's a problem and that either we have to change the VP's posture and attitudes, and the P must give him something to do in a very clear-cut way. If he's going to keep him he has to use him; otherwise, he's got to let him go. He is inclined to agree that he's more likely to be a liability than an asset, and that replacement would probably be a good idea, if it could be done without creating a stir. He wasn't aware of the possibility of appointing a replacement, but seemed very much intrigued about it when I raised it. He didn't express any thoughts as to who the replacement should be. He felt that it should not be either an all-out conservative or an all-out liberal, but rather a man in the P's basic image, who will articulate the P's position well, principally one who will be an asset in the campaign. He said he'll give it some thought as to specific suggestions as to who it ought to be, but he didn't have any ideas offhand. Obviously, he was very interested in the whole concept of the change being made."[19]

The notion that John Connally, a politician down to his toes, was not "aware of the possibility" of replacing a vice president under the Twenty-fifth Amendment, and that he "didn't have any ideas offhand" of who might be that replacement, challenged the credibility of both politically seasoned men in the conversation. Considering Connally's political ambitions and his perception of his own abilities, it probably didn't take him very long to think of the best man.

But for all this atmosphere of internal conflict and indecision, Ted Agnew remained vice president of the United States, with that impressive political army known as the Silent Majority, largely recruited by him, marching in lockstep behind him. With a reelection campaign now only half a year away, he wasn't finished yet; not by a long shot.

Chapter 12

ANYWHERE BUT PEKING

Despite Nixon's sinking confidence in Agnew, or perhaps because of it, he had decided in June to send the vice president to South Korea for the inauguration of President Chung Hee Park and then on to Singapore, Kuwait, Saudi Arabia, Africa, and western Europe, amid speculation that the president wanted to get him off the front pages at home.

At the time, Kissinger, without Agnew's knowledge, was continuing sensative negotiations with China that the White House hoped would lead to an unprecedented visit of an American president to Peking [now Beijing]. Nixon therefore was startled and appalled when Agnew asked for a direct meeting with him and proposed that on his South Korean trip—he pop over to China!

The very notion of the vice president suggesting that he precede him reinforced Nixon's concern about this bull loose in his China scheme. He immediately informed Haldeman, who wrote in his diary that night: "The P had a pretty busy schedule. He met with the VP at his request, and it turned out he wanted to make a pitch for his going to Red China while he's on his trip to the inauguration in Korea. It was almost unbelievable, because he raised it in a way that made it awkward for the P to have to tell him that he couldn't go, and then once told, he didn't give up. He kept coming back to how nice it would be if he could do that, that he, of course, should [also] go to Taiwan because he always has on his other trips, and if he went to Taiwan, it wouldn't be a good idea to just do that and not go to Peking. The P could hardly believe that he was really putting it that way, but he did."[1]

The White House taping system captures the remarkable exchange, in which the vice president half-apologetically introduces his proposal.

AGNEW: "I just wanted to see you because I had an idea. I don't know if it's worth anything or whether it's not, but I thought I'd ask you about it. You know, I'm going to go to this [clears throat] Korea trip, and there's some feeling, although I haven't discussed any itinerary with Henry, there's some feeling that we ought to stay away from Taiwan, because of the situation. I don't know what the decision is on that, but the thought came to me that it might be, I don't know how the mainland Chinese would think of this, but. . . looking back and recollecting your visit to the Soviet Union, it might not be a bad thing if we could do it, if I could go to the PRC [People's Republic of China]—and Taiwan."

There is a long pause before Nixon replies, stammering: "Well, the problem, the problem is the time. Er, the, er, I don't think they will be, I'm afraid I have to go through a [check] on that. I'm afraid we will not be, we will not move far enough to see in our own, uh, talks with them. I have in mind, I have very much in mind, the possibility of [meeting] with the Chinese. We don't want to be in the position of going too fast, because of the fact that if we do, if we pushed that way, and also that we're not scaring a hell of a lot of other people, get a lot of people disturbed, angry at us. I'm inclined to think, I'm inclined to think, some other spots would be useful, I think on the Taiwan—"

AGNEW: "This may be a bad thing then."

NIXON: "You can't go to Taiwan at this point. . . . And you don't want to say anything right now. Something, something may come, I can tell you that something could come of the Chinese thing in terms of movement within two or three months. It will not be within two or three weeks, though. You see, we're gonna to make a statement on trade on June the tenth. We're trying to work grain in the damn thing so we can get some of our farmers a little happy. All soft goods, all soft goods, nothing, nothing heavy, nothing strategic. But in terms of the travel thing, they haven't accepted any of the Democratic candidates [who were seeking entry]. They've turned them all down, so far."

AGNEW: "Well, that's what, that occurred to me, Mr. President."

NIXON: "As far as we're concerned, we want to be able to get a little further down after we make the trade thing, and see what happens on that."

AGNEW [talking over Nixon]: "Well, it's unfortunate. I thought it would be advantageous for two reasons. First of all, in my other two trips I've stopped at Taiwan. The failure to stop at Taiwan is a very tough thing for them, I would think, because [Nixon tries to break in: "I know, I know"] this would be a way to overcome it, if it could just be a formal stop at both places. . . . I had an appointment with Henry tomorrow to discuss this. But this just occurred to me, this idea, and I'm sorry it took—"

NIXON [cutting him off]: "On the other hand, I must say that the difficulty is the China thing is not ready yet, for a stop."

AGNEW [deferentially]: "I understand."

NIXON: "We don't want to be too anxious. You know how those people are. Let me ask you, what other places did you have in mind that you would like to go to? "

AGNEW: "While we're there, what I wanted to do, I told Henry that—"

NIXON: "Would you like to go to Japan?"

AGNEW: "Frankly, what I read of Japan every day, it looks like it would be just a tremendous demonstration, and we don't need that right now."

NIXON: "We don't need that. Go to friendly countries only."

Agnew says he will be meeting with Kissinger for breakfast the next morning to discuss the rest of his itinerary, and Nixon suggests they both come to his office afterward.

NIXON: ". . . We're gonna have a hell of a lot to handle. We will not, incidentally, have made any decision on the UN thing [recognition for Taiwan] by that time, so you have no problem with that. That will not be made until later. . . ."

Before leaving, Agnew makes one other pitch: "One thing I'd like to do, I'd like to just make this a working trip and hit those countries I've hit. . . . On the way back, what I wanted to do, I wanted while my daughter is out of school, it's a great chance for her, I want to send Judy and Kim [his wife and daughter] over to Europe, and then maybe do Spain and Portugal on the way back, or something of that sort, if that's all right, or two European countries on the way back, pick them up and bring 'em home."

NIXON, seeming to ignore the idea, says: "Well, the other possibility that I was thinking of, I was thinking of possibly Iran. On the other hand—"

AGNEW: "Then I'd have to go to Israel."

Nixon: "Oh, not at all. Iran is the one country [in the Middle East] you can go to without going to Israel, you see, it's on the edge. . . . There's something can be said about [going there]."

But Agnew balks. "I'm not particularly eager to go," he says, as if dickering with a hard-sell travel agent.

NIXON: "Neither would I. It's a hell of a damned place to go to. I'd rather go to Egypt, but nevertheless." Agnew says so would he.

Still suggesting an alternative, Nixon says "the Greek thing" appeals to him, but there had been another problem there involving treatment of another administration member. "You can't do Romania, I've done that, or Yugoslavia," he says. What about elsewhere in the Balkans? "You're an absolute cinch for no demonstrations in any of those countries, that's for damned sure," the president says. "And if we could really go to any of them, I think it would be good. Now, one we've never been to is Bulgaria. Nobody's been to Bulgaria. They've always been enemies of Greece." It is beginning to sound now as if Nixon is pulling Spiro Agnew's leg.

Agnew laughs nervously. "That would get me into deep trouble, wouldn't it?" he observes. "The trouble is, Mr. President, with the Greek situation with my antecedents there, and the Greek-American community here, I'd be catching hell for not going to Greece anyway. [Talking over Nixon's pitch again] I just think myself, I think I ought to go to Greece. I think it's abnormal not to go to Greece for me—"

NIXON: "You mean you would do it at the end of your trip."

AGNEW: "Yes, pick my family up there, send them over and let them spend a few days over there."

NIXON: "Sure, by all means."

AGNEW: "But I couldn't let them go unless I stopped."

NIXON, not excited about the visit to Greece, suggests other countries in Europe—"Spain, Portugal" plus "one African stop."

AGNEW: "How about we've got to refuel somewhere on the way back. I wonder about Saudi Arabia, [but] then I'd have to go to Israel."

NIXON: [shaken again, more obviously now]: "Hell, no! Hell, no! Saudi Arabia's another country to go to. You only have to go to Israel if you go to UAR [Egypt, the United Arab Republic] or Jordan. No, sir. The Saudis would be great. Damn right . . . "

AGNEW: "Well, that's sort of on the way."

NIXON [sounding even more like a travel agent]: "Saudi Arabia would be good. That would be interesting too. I've never been there, but I'm sure it would be." As for Greece, Nixon squelched that too, for the time being, on grounds "you might give your detractors unnecessary ammunition."

Nixon then arranges for Agnew and Kissinger to join him for breakfast the next morning "so we can sit and talk about it in a leisurely way." When Agnew leaves, the president turns to Haldeman and comments: "Say no to him [about the Greece visit] but do it in a nice way at least." Haldeman the gatekeeper replies: "He ought to sit down and talk to Henry about something like that, instead of coming in and putting you in an awkward position."[2]

Thus was the vice president of the United States diverted from unwittingly horning in on Nixon's "opening to China," as well as from going to Greece and Israel. In the process, he was getting a first-class, around-the-world junket in the guise of heavy diplomacy that had never been contemplated.

(A White House memo from Kissinger's deputy Al Haig to his boss indicates that the Greece trip had already been discussed two weeks earlier. "With respect to Greece," Haig wrote in the Top Secret/Sensitive/Eyes Only memo later declassified, "he [Agnew] said he is rapidly getting into a bind and believes this visit is most important for him, both personally and politically, and he hopes, despite what will probably be State opposition that it is approved." Then Haig added in parenthesis: "I know he wants to go to Greece before going to Korea so that he can leave his family in Greece since he hates to travel with his bride."[3]

A few minutes later, Kissinger comes in and Nixon and Haldeman have some fun with him about where Agnew wanted to go.

"Can you guess?" Nixon asks his national security adviser.

"Greece," Kissinger says, "a trip to Greece."

NIXON: "No."

HALDEMAN, mischievously: "Think. Now think big, Henry. The vice president had to see the president this afternoon for five minutes on a very important idea that he had."

NIXON: "About the trip."

KISSINGER: "He wants to take his daughter to, er. . . ."

NIXON: "No. Christ."

HALDEMAN: "Go on. To where?"

KISSINGER: "Well, first to Greece and then. . . ."

NIXON: "No, no. . . . Where else would he want to go?"

KISSINGER: "Iran. . . Cyprus."

NIXON [sarcastically]: "Yeah, make a side stop. You're a man with a little mind, Henry, and limited—"

KISSINGER: "Was it China?"

NIXON: "China! Of course!"

HALDEMAN: "Of course. Why the hell would he come and ask to go to Iran?"

NIXON: "And I said it just wasn't quite ready yet. We couldn't fit it in."

HALDEMAN: "Yes, it went down pretty well."

NIXON: "He said couldn't he overfly Chiang, he's always been there before, he ought to do China at the same time, that it would be a good idea to go to both places."

Nixon, finished with having his little joke with Kissinger, turns to the dilemma of what to do to keep his junket-happy vice president satisfied. He tells Kissinger: "The other part is, where the hell else he goes, and I just don't know."

KISSINGER: "My worry, Mr. President, about Greece, is he is sure as hell gonna say something that is going to be in every European newspaper; they're gonna to play it to a fare-thee-well, and there isn't anything in it for us. If we could get—"

NIXON: "Well, why don't you put it to him in the morning this way, that you have considered [sending him to Greece] and it would be, it might very well be in our interest in October for him to go. Can we say that?"

Kissinger says, "Sure," but probably later. "With the summit behind us, the China announcement behind us," he says, "we can [then] afford having him around anywhere."

NIXON: "On the Greece thing, he's stubborn as hell—"

KISSINGER: "But he's raised it about twenty-five times. . . ." (Agnew eventually did go to Greece, in October.)

NIXON: "I think he ought to go to Korea, I think he ought to go to Vietnam. . . ."

KISSINGER: "Well, I'll be in there in Vietnam at the time."

NIXON: "Thailand."

KISSINGER: "He can go to Thailand. . . [but] he should be out of Asia as much as possible because we'd like to get people watching other parts of the world [while Nixon's China trip is being cemented]. He can't go to India, Pakistan. . . ."

They agree Agnew could go to Malaysia, Singapore, Indonesia if he wanted to, but not Vietnam. Kissinger suggests to Nixon that "you can also tell him there's a meeting with Thieu coming up just at that time. If you want to tell him," as if the president has to justify his own travel to his vice president and why he can't go there. Kissinger adds, incredibly, after the ping-pong fiasco at Williamsburg: "He's pretty discreet."

Nixon continues to rattle off to Kissinger other possibile destinations for Agnew, again in the mode of a tour director: "Saudi Arabia. Morocco. Portugal and Spain. How's that?" Nixon says he should skip the Far East except for the inauguration in Korea.

KISSINGER: "He shouldn't go to Taiwan either."

NIXON: "Oh, Christ, don't let him go to Taiwan."

HALDEMAN: "He says he has to go to Taiwan because he always goes. . . ."

KISSINGER: "He's also very self-willed. I mean, I've talked to him now about his trip for three weeks. He really has never asked what's good for the country. He plans this trip on what's interesting for him to see."

Nixon agrees: "They decide, well, wouldn't it be great if I could return to Greece? Or wouldn't it be great if I took a trip to China? They mustn't do it that way. God dammit, I think we've got a pretty good excuse, though [not to let Agnew pre-empt Nixon's historic opening to China]."

KISSINGER: "Oh, yeah. Well, China, he couldn't. If you told him go ahead, go to China, he wouldn't even know how to start."

NIXON: "We wouldn't know how to get him in."

KISSINGER: "With whom would we go to?"

Haldeman conjectures that Nixon's trip will have great impact, "something like Genghis Khan coming into town," and Kissinger says that's why it's important to get the Chinese "to keep their bar on other political visitors until you get there."[4]

Agnew, however, kept alive the flame of his own desire for a trip to the Chinese mainland. En route to Korea at the start of what turned out to be an around-the-world trip, he told accompanying reporters that "to have a chance to visit and to converse directly with the representatives of that country would be quite a privilege," though relations between the two countries remained "basically quite hostile."[5] Soon after, when news broke of Kissinger's trip to China to advance Nixon's visit, Frank Cormier of the *Associated Press* stirred the pot. He reported, citing a White House source, that "President Nixon gave Vice President Agnew no advance word of his plan to visit mainland China."[6] Agnew by this time was in Africa, and asked by reporters in the Congo about the plan, he at first offered no comment. But privately he seethed at the notion that he couldn't keep a secret or, worse, a fear that he might speak out against this latest Nixon initiative to China, as he had so recklessly done about the ping-pong diplomacy. Agnew aides insisted afterward that he did know, as a member of the National Security Council, of Nixon's plans to seek détente with China, and supported them, but not of the timing.[7]

Agnew himself wrote later: "I presume that my firm opposition to the policy of cozying up to Communist China was the main reason the White House froze me out of the Nixon discussions in that area." During his own overseas trip, he wrote, "some of Mr. Nixon's aides put out the word that I was sent out of the country so as not to be in Henry Kissinger's way when he made his secret journey to China—the journey which paved the way for the president's trip there the following February. Then they compounded the felony by not notifying me until after the story broke in the press. . . . The president certainly had no reason to believe that I would have leaked the story, because he well knew I never leaked anything—although I had access to much secret information through the National Security Council and CIA briefings. But some of his assistants were aware of my sentiments about courting the Chinese, so they left me out."[8] Such was the level of distrust toward the vice president, if not by the president, then by his aides. Agnew never could be sure who was the culprit, because Nixon so seldom communicated with him directly.

Even after Nixon had detoured Agnew around mainland China, he was nervous about having him free-wheeling across the globe. So he decided to assign Bryce Harlow to accompany him, but without informing Agnew directly that Harlow was being sent along to keep an eye on him, but Harlow's presence did not prevent more Agnew missteps. On what was intended as an uneventful month-long trip, he once again demonstrated political insensitivity in Africa. Aboard Air Force Two en route to Madrid later, he volunteered to accompanying reporters his impressions of the black leaders he had met in the Dark Continent. He said Jomo Kenyatta in Kenya, Haile Selassie in Ethiopa, and Joseph Mobutu in the Congo "have impressed me with their understanding of the internal problems, and their moderateness." He said the three authoritarian leaders were "dedicated, enlightened, dynamic, and extremely apt for the task that faces them." Then he added: "The quality of this leadership is in distinct contrast. . . with many of those in the United States who have abrogated unto themselves the position of black leaders; those who spend their time in querulous complaint and constant recrimination against the rest of society." He said American black leaders "could learn much by observing the work that has been done" in the three African nations.[9]

The comments, volunteered, came off as an echo of his hostile remarks to Baltimore black leaders in the wake of the 1968 riots after the assassination of Martin Luther King Jr. On learning of them, a leader of the Congressional Black Caucus, Representative William Clay of St. Louis, proclaimed on the House floor: "Our vice president is seriously ill. He has all the symptoms of an intellectual misfit. His recent tirade against black leadership is just part of a game played by him called mental masturbation. Apparently Mr. Agnew is an intellectual sadist who experiences intellectual orgasms by attacking, humiliating, and kicking the oppressed."[10]

According to Vic Gold, Agnew's airborne outburst also was intentional. He was incensed, Gold said later, that Nixon had sent his vice president on the round-the-world trip on a windowless plane, and that he was kept in the dark about Nixon's plans to go to China. "We were treated like baggage," Gold said, and Agnew not being told of the China trip was "humiliating. That pissed him off mightily." Agnew told him in the plane after the African stops, he said, that "the black leaders we have in the United States, they're not real leaders" like those he had just met. Then, telling Gold he knew the reporters traveling were unhappy that they hadn't had much access to him, instructed his press secretary: "You call them up here, call them up here right now. They want news? I'll give them news. I'm going to give them something they're going to want to jump out of the plane [to report]."[11]

In any event, the next issue of *Newsweek* carried a blistering account of Agnew's trip, including the African fiasco. It began: "He had already played golf in Singapore, Korea, and Saudi Arabia, and now he stood on the first tee of the best private club in Kenya's capital of Nairobi, swinging his driver like a machete. You guessed it, sports fans. This was no touring pro nor even a salesman of exploding golf balls, but Vice President Spiro Agnew, currrently flailing his way around the world in his newest role— as international troubleshooter, diplomat and spreader of goodwill."

The article reported that Agnew had "traveled with a party of 141 persons (not counting eleven newsmen paying their own way), flying in a caravan of four Boeing 707s—plus a cargo plane carrying two bullet-proof Cadillacs for Agnew's dash from airport to hotel to golf course. Eighty Secret Service men and countless embassy personnel were alerted around the world to aid and protect the vice presidential person, and he moved everywhere inside a cocoon of human flesh that never failed to dazzle his hosts." The story quoted Nairobi's *Daily Nation*: "No head of state arriving in Nairobi ever had such security."

The *Newsweek* account said Agnew had given short shrift to local government officials and "aside from hacking up the local golf course, his main outing was to a nearby hunting lodge, where in company with his private physician and his pretty, red-haired secretary, he watched two rhinos copulating."[12]

The story infuriated Agnew, and quickly brought a telegram from the American ambassador in Nairobi asking the vice president's permission to submit it to *Newsweek* as a letter to the editor. It said, among other things, that, rather than "hacking up" the golf course, Agnew had won "more than half the holes he played" with two important Kenyans and himself; that he had spent nearly two-and-a-half hours, not the fifteen minutes reported, with Kenyatta and his cabinet, and rode around in the ambassador's "four-year-old Chrysler," not one of the two bullet-proof Cadillacs mentioned.[13]

Even before Agnew returned to Washington, Nixon also was fuming over those reports that the vice president had spent an excessive amount of time in Africa on the golf links, with little pretense that he was on serious business. A Nixon conversation in the White House taped at the time recorded him lamenting to Ehrlichman: "I've never seen a guy [travel] in a more leisurely way. I didn't realize it, but Bob [Haldeman] told me he [Agnew] played golf every God-damned day of his trip. That's utter stupidity. . . . You've got to make it appear the trip's for work. You're not over there on a God-damned vacation. I feel that way, anyway. I don't mean a guy's gotta be a grind. . . . Spending four hours on a golf course and not have enough time to go out and shake hands with people in the street. Jesus Christ, you know, when I went on these trips with my wife we worked our butts off. And it made an impression. . . . I had nothing substantive. He had far more of substance than I had, but our trips really had a better effect because, by God, you were out there talking to the people, visiting hospitals and going through plants. . . ."

EHRLICHMAN, who had no love for Agnew, chimes in: "This trip is going to end up with enormous negatives. . . . There was a devastating piece in one the newsmagazines. . . ."

HALDEMAN: "*Newsweek.*"

EHRLICHMAN: "[The reporter] climaxed the report by saying that one of the highlights of this trip was an evening in Kenya or somewhere in Africa where he and his personal physician and a very attractive redheaded secretary came down from their hut to watch a pair of rhinoceroses copulate."

NIXON [laughing]: "Bull-shit! Really? Must be quite a sight."

EHRLICHMAN: "Look at those fuckin' rhinoceroses!"

HALDEMAN: "Rhinoceri!"

EHRLICHMAN: "It's a sort of Roman Emperor act that he's putting on, with a big entourage, and—"

NIXON: "Well, that's a mistake. We've overdone it, believe me. We've overdone it. . . But I mean, the security business, you know, because they shot Kennedy and Bobby. . . . The Secret Service. Christ, I went with two [agents]."

EHRLICHMAN: "But people will make allowances as long as there seems to be work being done. . . ."

NIXON: "Did he have quite a staff with him?" The president then goes off on another monologue on his vice presidential days, comparing himself to Lyndon Johnson and Hubert Humphrey in the same role.

HALDEMAN: "The vice president had his opportunity, for Christ's sake. He was brought in here and. . . the son of a bitch could have taken the place over if he wanted to. . . ."

EHRLICHMAN: "That's the very problem with the vice president. He's a Constitutional officer, and his job is what he makes it. . . . If he doesn't have it, he's gonna turn into a big pussycat, just sit around bitching all the time. What's he going to create? When you were vice president, it wasn't because the president told you what [to do]."

HALDEMAN: "Well, the Secret Service. They're the ones. . . . They walk all over him. He does anything they want."

EHRLICHMAN: "That's your point about fraternizing. I'm afraid his position now is that he has no leverage with the Secret Service. . . ."

NIXON: "In all the period I've been president and vice president, or eight years prior, I've never had a drink with a Secret Service agent, never. Or lunch, or anything. Not a God-damned thing. That's just the way I operate."[14]

In succeeding days, Agnew told friends he was also disappointed that his trip had been characterized as a means of keeping him out of the way during the negotiations for Nixon's visit to China. In an interview with the *Christian Science Monitor*, he said he fully supported Nixon's trip, and that his remarks on ping-pong democracy at Colonial Williamsburg had been "misunderstood and obfuscated to an extent." Then, unable to leave well enough alone, he added: "But I am distressed with the euphoria with which the initiative was received. There was an immediate assumption that this meant an end to all tensions between the United States and mainland China and a resolution of all our ideological difficulties. This, of course, is not realistic. . . . We've got a long way to go."

Agnew did not seem to grasp that his comment could be seen as raining on Nixon's parade. He did observe that "at least we've made a step toward discussing these matters," but "I don't think we should become so optimistic that people would feel that in case these discussions don't bring about an immediate resolution of all difficulties, they should be discouraged."[15] The latter remark could hardly have been received in the Oval Office as a rousing burst of optimism from the vice president himself. Nor did the words sound like those of a man who could be counted on to generate a positive outlook in a second term that Richard Nixon was now contemplating, with thoughts of excluding Spiro Agnew from it.

Chapter 13

COURTING CONNALLY

During Agnew's absence, Nixon had repeatedly counseled with Haldeman and Connally about what to do about the erratic vice president. When Harlow left the Agnew party and returned early from the trip, he reported some interesting intelligence to Nixon based on conversations with the vice president. Haldeman wrote: "Bryce says that he thinks that there's a three out of four chance that of his own volition, the VP will withdraw from the ticket, probably in January or so, and that he has some very lucrative outside offers that he'd like to take on, and wants to take on the battle of the press from outside the government; so that things look as if [they're] pretty much lined up."[1]

At this point, however, all suddenly was not rosy in Nixon's romance with Connally. In mid-July, when a new treasurer of the United States was hired (separate from the job of treasury secretary), Connally blew his stack because it had been done without consulting him. Haldeman wrote that the Texan was "furious" and "as a result of this and other things, he was going to check out. In other words, resign." Haldeman said he tried to calm him "but he didn't buy it. He said that he just wasn't going to tolerate this kind of thing; that obviously it's forecasting things to come. . . he was not a peon and was not going to function as a slave to the White House staff."[2]

When Haldeman informed Nixon, the president tried to smooth things out by inviting Connally to dinner on the *Sequoia*, with the plan, Haldeman wrote, to discuss the idea of making him vice president, and "if we can't work that out, we'll go for secretary of state," with efforts already afoot to discard Nixon's old friend, Bill Rogers.[3] Connally declined the dinner invitation, but three days later Nixon met with him for two hours during which the president, according to Haldeman, "took him on the mountaintop, by which he meant he talked to him about the vice presidency" again,[4] as well as his latest reservations about Agnew in light of his remarks in Africa.

On a White House tape Nixon can be heard saying to Connally: "Take for example what he said about the Negroes in Africa. He couldn't have been more right. He was exactly right." But Nixon despairs about how Agnew had put his criticism. All he had to say, Nixon offers, is that "American Negroes should be proud of their African heritage, that's what I would say."

Connally speculates that Agnew "feels like. . . he is protecting the conservatives, because he's the voice, he's the only only link to [what] the real conservatives in the Republican Party really ought to stand for." But, Connally cautions, "by next summer [in the reelection campaign], he'll be a liability to you unless y'all have an understanding. Very simple, unless you do start using him in such a way that you make a constructive force out of him. . . . If you've tried and you're not successful, that gives you your answer."[5] As always, Connally was playing the wise and impartial counselor, whose advice did nothing to diminish himself in Nixon's eyes as prospective Agnew replacement.

In another conversation on the same day with Ehrlichman and other aides about Agnew's reported remarks in Africa, Nixon observes that "I've met a lot of black African leaders. . . . I've always been impressed by their leaders," and again, that "black Americans can be very proud of their heritage." Then he turns to Ehrlichman and says, "Right, John?" Whereupon Ehrlichman snickers, laughs, and replies: "Among other things."

Nixon goes on to say he just cannot understand what was the purpose of Agnew's remarks in praising African autocrats by denigrating American black leaders. Ehrlichman responds that "the sad part of it is that Roy Wilkins had just come out to the NAACP [convention] and said, 'Look, we're gonna have to live with this fellow [Nixon] 'til '76, so we'd better start learning to get along with him.' And then this was said." The delegates, Ehrlichman tells him, "all blasted him [Agnew], the press exploited it quite a bit, and some of the blacks were pretty smart about it. They were more in sorrow than anger; 'Isn't it too bad that the president has this albatross around his neck,' that kind of a line, which I think probably in the long haul is more effective than if they had been strident about it."

Nixon brings the discussion down to "cold politics," saying he knows he isn't going to get much of the black vote regardless of what Agnew says, "but we simply aren't going to have as much of their strident opposition if we handle ourselves well, and that way we may get a few more white votes, maybe." But he asks: "What in the world did he gain by praising Mobutu or Kenyatta? Hell, what in the world does that do us? That's the point that I couldn't see. Christ, I mean, if you take 'em on, sure, the black leaders are irresponsible here."

EHRLICHMAN breaks in: "But it wasn't the kind of a crack that would get any redneck support."

NIXON: "That's my point. Hell, no, they howled because he was praising blacks, period. The rednecks down there think they're a bunch of bad people too; they think all blacks are terrible. They point out, properly so, that there isn't a democratic government run by blacks in the world, not one. You know that? Of all of the nations in Africa, not one is adequate at any sort of representative government. They're all dictatorships, basically. . . . And that's the way it's going to be for a long time. And we don't need to look down our noses at them. The Latin Americans have been that way for a hell of a long time, and will be, probably."

EHRLICHMAN offers a possible explanation for Agnew's praise of Mobutu, president of the Congo: "Mobutu, I'm told, sets a magnificent table in a high French continental style, with all of the delicacies and, you know, the flare, and it may be that the vice president was just kind of carried away with all that."

NIXON says of Mobutu: "Incidentally, he's quite an impressive fellow—big, strong, vigorous guy; over here would be pushing sod." Then he goes on to say of Agnew's discussing American policy toward China with the president of the Republic of Congo: "First of all, if he has doubts he should never express them to a foreign government. Second, as you know, Mobutu is, you know that, is a child! He's a child up here [apparently pointing to his brain], because he's never had a chance to grow up, up here. God, it's just unbelievable to me. . . ."

Going back to Agnew, Nixon starts to discourse on his misunderstanding of his role as vice president: "He has a compulsion to say, 'Well, I'm honest, this is what I honestly think.' Well, that's great. He may honestly think something, but anybody who is the vice president, or who is a member of the White House staff, or who is a member of a cabinet has no views of his own. None . . . He can't have any."

Nixon goes on that "they knew for eight years when I was vice president I never expressed a view that was not Eisenhower's," though he had some. "The thing about this, is that having done that for eight years, they think that I as President am smart enough to know that a vice president is supposed to simply be the echo of the president, and that Agnew wouldn't be doing this without my knowledge and/or approval. And I think that's the real problem. Don't you think so, John?"

Ehrlichman seizes the opportunity. "I think this all the time," he vigorously agrees.

NIXON: "A lot of people think, 'Well, God almighty, if the president always supports the vice president,' which I do, and they say, 'Well, Christ, doesn't he know you need to say that he didn't know about this? Or he's trying to speak with both sides of his mouth?"

EHRLICHMAN: "All the time. . . Yep. You see, that's the thing. It goes to your credibility, and that's what makes it so terrifically difficult. Well, at the right time, I'd like to get into this with you. I feel that with so much going for you right now, you can't afford to have the sort of debilitating negative or detraction that's involved in the process under the existing arrangement. And I think he just has to be either brought aboard or, ah, or something."

Perhaps recognizing that he is being too conspicuous in his desire to move Agnew aside, Ehrlichman then says: "And in all candor I don't think we've done enough to get him aboard. I think we've all sort of sealed him off and just sort of, and just sort of, er, assumed that nothing could be done there."

Ehrlichman is having a field day at Agnew's expense when Nixon decides to jump in with his favorite comparison. "You know, I must say one thing, though. You've got to hand it, in another context, to Connally. He's got a lot of guts, as he goes out there and sticks his chin out and gets the hell kicked out of him." In sum, Ted Agnew was getting it with both barrels—in Ehrlichman's all-out assault on him, and in Nixon's conspicuous comparison with and preference for Connally.[6]

The following day, Nixon called in Haldeman and Ehrlichman to brainstorm the Agnew problem again, and the Connally solution to it. Nixon told them, according to the Haldeman diaries, that with the approaching opening to China, he had foreign policy in hand as a political issue in the 1972 campaign, and the Democrats therefore would "zero in on the economy as the substantive issue, and the VP is the way of cutting us. Also he [Nixon] got into quite a long talk about the question of succession, making the point that he may not live through even this term, let alone a second term, because of the possibility of accident or ill health.

"That raises the question of whether Agnew's somebody that we're willing to see become P. He enumerated some of his problems, that he's dogmatic, his hidebound prejudices, totally inflexible and that he sees things in minuscule terms. We then talked about what to do to get him out, and we concluded that it's impossible for him to announce—such as in January, as he apparently is willing to do according to Harlow—that he will not run, because that would open a horrible battle for the nomination. Also, Agnew himself would be immediately dead once he does that."[7]

The actual tape of the discussion, badly garbled, includes arguments that could be made for an Agnew resignation. Haldeman says, "Agnew's position is infinitely better than his personal position, outside, if he resigns." In a second term, he suggests, "he'd have a miserable life" and would be "utterly useless. . . . But as a former vice president, he'd be a real [attraction]." Nixon offers, concerning Agnew's financial needs, that "the real thing that would help would be if he resigned and [could] do something for a network, become the president of one," which might be his only alternative because "no corporation pays that kind of money" a former vice president would want. Nixon mentions the "Bob Hope connection," and Haldeman suggests "it could be a combination of television, writing and speaking" without the strictures of the vice presidency."

NIXON: "Speak out."

HALDEMAN: "Tell it like it is."

NIXON: "He could be quite a celebrity too, couldn't he?"

HALDEMAN: "Damn right."

Nixon: "Have a hell of an audience. Say what he feels about blacks."[8]

In all this, Nixon and his inner circle sidestepped the obvious reason Agnew would want to continue as vice president: to position himself for the Republican presidential nomination in 1976.

According to Haldeman's notes, "The P then got around to raising the Connally question... and made the point that only one we could put on the ticket is Connally. We couldn't afford a battle, because out of that Reagan would clearly come up with the nomination, which would be disastrous. Conclusion then is, if Agnew is not going to be on the ticket, he must get off by resignation. Given that, the sooner he resigns, the better.... The P wants to stay one step away from it, but I should call Connally, ask him for a couple hours of free time for John [Ehrlichman] and me, and then we should just sit down and talk the problem through, see if he's got any ideas on how to approach it...."[9]

According to Haldeman's personal notes of the meeting, Nixon also instructed his aides to check on the history of Andrew Johnson, a pro–Civil War Democrat who was vice president as part of the National Union fusion under Republican Abraham Lincoln at the time of the assassination. Nixon wanted to know whether Johnson had remained a Democrat, and whether under the rules of the Republican National Committee he could nominate a Democrat, Connally, to replace Agnew.[10] Nixon obviously was not just speculating on what he liked to call "the big play."

AFTER A LONG MEETING on labor issues the next day, Nixon asked Connally and Haldeman to stay behind, and told Haldeman to repeat the conversation Bryce Harlow had had with Agnew in Korea about resigning. The vice president told Harlow, Haldeman relates, that "he has decided in his own mind that he should not try to wait until the first of next year... and in that time he's got to make up his mind whether he should step down or not." But, Haldeman adds, "Bryce doesn't think that the vice president is aware of the opportunity that exists for him to resign and for the president to appoint a vice president, and Bryce wasn't aware of it.... He looked up the law because he didn't believe me. He came back this morning and said, 'You know, it's not quite as simple as you outlined it.... The president doesn't appoint the vice president. The president *nominates* the vice president and the Senate confirms. So you gotta keep that in mind in thinking about what you're going to do, the two of you [Nixon and Connally]. The vice president has a burning passion—[The phone suddenly rings, drowning out Haldeman's next words.]—and feels he can't do it as vice president."

After taking the call on another matter, Nixon starts talking about the matter of presidential succession, recalling from his own experience how in 1955, when he and Eisenhower were approaching their reelection campaign, that the president had suffered a heart attack. "The whole attack from the left was on vice president Nixon, that son of a bitch," Nixon says. "So they tried to run against Nixon; didn't work. . . . But Agnew would be a whole lot more vulnerable than I was [seeking reelection as vice president]. I at least had some credibility. . . ." For this reason, Nixon goes on, "I feel we have to think in very bold terms, in total control terms, of what we do here." His surprise announcement that he was going to China, he says, was an example that "in the great game of politics and leadership, it is important to think in very, very bold terms, and step right up to it. So that's [the] reason, you see, I've come around to this plan I discussed with you yesterday. . . ."

Connally knows where Nixon is going. "Mr. President," he says, "may I say, I don't want [this] discussion however brief to go by without me saying again that you understand I have no ambition whatever in this direction. And even further, I'm not sure this applies from your standpoint, we'll have time, I assume, to talk about it, [from a] strictly political standpoint. The third thing, I'm not at all sure that, I suppose from a very selfish standpoint, it seems to me a vice president has less to do, has less freedom of action than the least of your cabinet [advisers], just by the nature of the job, and that's understandable. It might well be, assuming of course that I was in that position, I might be the most miserable fellow in the world, because—"

Nixon interrupts, taking Connally to that mountaintop. "You see, the point is, the point is, that you in this job, that's what it really needed and we have not had with Agnew, you in the job would be basically, you in the job would be, the, er, the president's, er, stand-in. And basically everybody would know it. Everybody. And when it came down to [protocol or] good will, the hell with that. If there was something important to do, you'd do it. But in the whole economic field, you would be, you would have a prestige and a backing that's just unbelievable, because, you see, the relationship that you and I have, I can tell, and we would have then, is really totally different than any president and vice president has had."

Comparing his own relationship with Eisenhower and Hubert Humphrey's with Johnson, Nixon piles it on. While Eisenhower treated him "extremely well," he says, he wasn't in on major decisions, and "Johnson had no respect for Humphrey, not really. . . . Johnson never told him a God-damn thing." But his own view of the vice presidency, he tells Connally, is "I frankly was hoping it would work out this way with Agnew, but he just isn't the kind of man it could work out with. My view of the vice president is basically the president's alter ego. He is there. The vice president has got to be there. We had Agnew in an office down here, you know, down in the corner office. And God-damn it, I don't say it was a great idea, but it just didn't work, but we tried, we tried. But his problem is that he just didn't understand the big play. . . . He wouldn't take, we tried every opportunity. I'd call him and all that sort of thing, but he didn't grasp the foreign thing and these dramatic things and all these places where we tried to give him a chance to lead. It simply wasn't there."

Continuing the hard sell, Nixon says: "The important thing is this, that you gotta look at it from two standpoints, three standpoints. One, from the standpoint of the election, as a political judgment. It is my view that it would be enormously helpful. Two, from the standpoint of after we get into office, I think it would be a superb combination, because then we could do things that ought to be done even now."

He tells Connally how, as Eisenhower's vice president, he often chaired the cabinet and National Security Council meetings in Ike's absence. "I can't do that today," he says. "Agnew doesn't tend to understand. . . . I try. But in terms of this thing, I have ideas about how the vice president can be used and work with the president that are very far reaching. And that brings me to the other point. There is now not only the possibility of the presidential survival, but also there's the idea of the presidential succession. In my view, whoever is going to be vice president in the next term has got to be the next president. And that's fine. That's what I would work for. I would set the thing up so that I could do it. Now, we've looked through this whole thing. . . . As you know, the whole damn cabinet, there's nobody in that cabinet that can do this job, not a damn one."

CONNALLY [humbly]: "No."

NIXON: "There's nobody in that Congress. The only one I can think of at the moment that just might be able to do it would be Ford. Ford just might. But he's the only one, and Ford's got other fish to fry. Ford doesn't have the, he's a good, regular, solid guy and there's. . . very little to say about that. . . . Let's face it. Rockefeller, well, first of all, the country, the party would not take it, and I just don't think he's the guy for it. And Reagan, that just can't be. I know Reagan, I know his strengths but I also know all of the weaknesses there. You can't have a simplicity man in this position. It's got to be somebody who has broad gauge, who has the fire of leadership, who has the, er, foreign and domestic understanding and the like, and also who's able to work with the Congress as president. But anyway, it's just something to think about."

CONNALLY: "As I said, I do think if the vice president's thinking about making a move now, I don't know how you precipate the thing, but regardless of what happens, I really think you ought to [decide] very soon in the course of this year, because I think every day that goes by, because he is a sensitive man—

HALDEMAN: "That's another thing. You've got him under [your] thumb."

CONNALLY: "It builds on him so much that—

HALDEMAN: "It eats him."

CONNALLY: "That's right. And then he'll get started, and decide he's got to stay. . . . It should be done."

NIXON: "Well, anyway, good talking to you."[11]

Haldeman wrote later that Nixon, in buttering up Connally with a glowing account about how he would be his assistant president with an option on the real thing in 1976, "didn't try to push Connally into any kind of decision, in fact very carefully avoided pushing him at all, but he obviously is giving him a pretty good shove in the right direction. It was, in its way, quite an historic meeting. . . . It's clear that Connally feels strongly that Agnew does have to go, and that he's basically decided that he'll take it, but he's obviously not going to ask for it because [he] doesn't want to be in that position. He'll have a pretty strong hand to deal from now, and it may be very difficult to work with him, but it will be interesting to see."[12] The big man from Texas, playing the reluctant dragon, seemed to be sitting pretty.

Chapter 14

WELCOME HOME, TED

IN LIGHT OF THE PLAY GIVEN AT HOME TO SOME OF AGNEW'S comments abroad, especially in Africa, and the speculation that he had been sent into temporary exile while Kissinger was on his sensitive mission to Peking, the vice president's return to Washington in late July drew more than routine interest.

Had Nixon wanted to dampen down the talk that his vice president was in hot water again, he could have motored over to nearby Andrews Air Force Base in Maryland to welcome him home. Instead, he decided to leave the chore to Secretary of State Rogers. On deplaning, Agnew shook hands with Rogers but said nothing. Both climbed into a limousine and sped off to the White House. When they arrived, Nixon greeted Agnew publicly, saying only he had done "a fine job," and escorted him into the Oval Office.

But prior to that cordial greeting, Nixon had conferred with Haldeman about how to put some distance between himself and Agnew in the wake of the controversial trip that Nixon insisted to his insiders was an inconsequential one. At the same time, however, Haldeman had advised him to make the tour sound important and successful, presumably to help deflect outside criticism and buck up Agnew. Doing so might also avoid further speculation that his vice-presidential tenure was in jeopardy—which indeed it seemed to be, as witnessed by Nixon's own taped comments.

In this effort, Nixon already had in hand a memorandum from Kissinger that said in part: "Reporting has indicated that the vice president's trip as been a great success." It quoted a comment from Nairobi that it was "an outstanding success from every point of view," and that "a number of top officials have gone out of their way to tell the [American] ambassador how pleased they were." Another from Kinshasa called Agnew's trip "a very special gesture reaffirming the unusual close friendship between these two nations," and that "President Mobutu expressed great satisfaction with the long and frank discussion he had with the vice president."[1]

But Haldeman, concerned that the press might get an indication that Nixon was dissatisfied with Agnew's performance on the trip, worried about letting press photographers into the Oval Office for pictures of the two men together. The following White House tape illustrates the degree to which Haldeman orchestrated presidential events in the Nixon years, and the uncomfortable hot potato Nixon had on his hands in dealing with, and possibly trying to get rid of, his vice president:

HALDEMAN: "Let 'em do a photo opportunity in the beginning and then kick 'em out."

NIXON: "I'm not going to be there all by myself."

HALDEMAN: "I guess the problem is, as long as it takes them to do [the photo], what do you do [with Agnew] while you're kicking them out?"

NIXON has the answer: "On Agnew's arrival, I thought of a nice compromise. Rather than having the usual picture in here, why don't they have them drive up here and I'll walk out and meet the car, and get all the press to come out, see what I mean? They're gonna drive in from Andrews, right? They can swing in. . . get all the press to be out there getting their picture, then they don't get one inside. . . . They've had a hell of a lot of pictures inside [rather than] one of us just sitting here talking. . . . It's much better to get—"

HALDEMAN: "That shows you in effect greeting him like you—I don't think people expect you to [go to] the airport. . . ."

NIXON: "I don't want to overreact to the damn thing. I mean, I think Ehrlichman reacts too much the other way, to say ignore him, because you can't do that, Bob. Put yourself in his position. . . ."

Haldeman agrees that Nixon should not do anything to unduly upset the vice president. He asks: "Do you want him to get off the ticket? Naah.

Have him quit, and kick us in the ass?" Instead, he suggests, Nixon needs to have the relationship "seen on a positive basis with the reporters, right? After all, he's got it in his hands [to stay or leave]."

NIXON agrees: "The relationship's got to be God-damn good."

HALDEMAN: "That's right. He's elected in his own right. There's nothing to be done. . . . He can still screw [us]."

NIXON: "You're God-damn right. . . . He can disagree and I can tell him not to run, I mean—"

HALDEMAN: "You can keep him from running, and you can in effect strip him of all his duties, but you can't get him out of office. It's just ridiculous."

NIXON: "What's John [Erhlichman]'s argument, that he's unpopular and I should have nothing to do with him, is that basically it?"

HALDEMAN: "John, it's kind of funny. John's usually very balanced on this. He's not making any sense."

NIXON: "Well, he thinks Agnew is a liability."

HALDEMAN: "He just thinks you should clear your hands of him completely."

NIXON: "It's not the time to do it, though."

HALDEMAN: "Don't let him rub off on you."

NIXON: "No way. No way."

HALDEMAN: "And what that would do is say his trip was a failure, and then that hurts you. What you've got to do is say that, you've got to play the good parts of his trip, and there were good parts. Even the worst press stories make the point that he's done an outstanding job in his diplomatic contacts, that there probably was a reason for him to be moving around the right, you know, fascist nations, the dictator-type nations, while you were making your move to the communist state. People see [your] intent. Sure he [Agnew] said some stupid things. You can't dissociate from those by not meeting him, by washing your hands of him."

NIXON: "It's just not the right way to treat things. There was a lot bad to write about. Curious that Henry, [who] probably got more violent enemies than Agnew on this tour than anybody, feels strongly, though, about how they gave him a bad press for all the wrong reasons. I asked him, 'Give me an honest report on it. . . . How'd he do?' He said, 'He did a hell of a good job. . . better than anybody, he made a hell of a plus out of something, which is sort of a minor negative.'"

HALDEMAN: "And the other thing he's done, he gave them a beaut of a cheap shot at the end. What he did yesterday in Portugal, was go out and play golf with Frank Sinatra. So what was the press story? Agnew ends his trip as he began, with a game of golf today with Frank Sinatra."

NIXON [chagrined]: "He played with Sinatra."

HALDEMAN: "Yeah. [pause] That's not all bad either. I mean, that's gotten a bad twist as well as a good one. . . . But he should have ended—he had a luncheon with the American community or something and then went out and played golf yesterday afternoon. And what he's done, I'm sure, is he's seen this bad press about the golf and said, 'Screw the bastards,' and gone out and played every day after that. Screw the mickey that way, so he did. He could have overcome that with just a little [skill]. You can't just blame his people, though. He won't listen to them. He won't listen to advance men, or he doesn't let people schedule him. When we were talking about scheduling, he wouldn't listen to me on scheduling. And he wouldn't listen to Bryce. He has very firm ideas on what he will and won't do. If he decides he's going to play golf, he plays golf. . . ."

NIXON: "I'm not sure, Bob, everybody watches these things as we do, though."

HALDEMAN: "I don't think they do. I think they watch what he does [and take a] shot at him that he doesn't have to take."

NIXON: "It's the whole story [of] my career . . . "

HALDEMAN: "He pays too high a price for it. . . . He could have played golf, he could have played damned near as much golf as he did. . . by [also] doing something else to give them a story. That's the other thing. He has not seen the press at all on this trip, which I find important, and he won't tell them anything. Nobody tells them anything. He's got eleven press people who have paid probably ten thousand dollars apiece to make this God-damned tour. . . he doesn't see them, and he doesn't do anything to make news. His meetings are all private meetings and they don't give them any briefing apparently afterwards, so they don't know, I was told. . . . They're flying around the world, their editors are probably just steaming—'For Christ's sake, we spent all that money to send you and you haven't filed a line of copy yet.' So what are they gonna file? Well, we can file [what happened], which is, that he went out and played golf or [sat] in his hotel room and played gin rummy with his Secret Service agents. If I were the press, after about four or five days or two weeks, I'd do the same thing, I think.

"And it's so easy, you know. Hell, on the way to the golf course, he could stop at an orphanage and pat a couple of kids on the head and the press gets a picture and a little quote about how he says it's too bad these kids are orphans, and he could go on and play golf. And nobody cares, it's so easy. . . . [Or] you'd give them so much that they couldn't cover it, and you drive them out of their minds physically 'cause they couldn't keep up."[2]

When Agnew and Rogers finally arrived from the trip at Andrews Air Force Base, Nixon met them outside the White House. Inside, they held a long post-mortem on Agnew's trip, also attended by Kissinger and John Scali, a former newsman who was then a special consultant to the president. Nixon, after having privately complained at length to his associates about the vice president's golf-playing "vacation," proceeds to insist in front of them—and Agnew—that it really had been an important and substantive undertaking! "The difficulty, of course, is in any kind of a mission like this," the taping system has him saying, "it's very hard for people, the public, to know what the hell is done. But what really matters is what really happens. . . . It's worth doing."

Agnew unsurprisingly picks up on Nixon's drift. "I enjoyed doing that. It was beneficial," he insists. "The problem of course was, the public impression of the trip was pretty bad, because what the press really wanted was for me to talk to poor people in the streets. . . . I tried to explain [it] was a useful trip." He complains of the coverage, saying at one point a reporter had pointed out "there were starving women with diseased babies along the streets. . . and that I went into towns and talked to teenagers."

Nixon [heatedly]: "Oh, for Christ's sakes, isn't that too bad! What in the name of God could you do? About the starving babies?"

Nixon segues into yet another monologue about his own trips as vice president, then turns to Rogers and says: "But God-damn, Bill, it makes you wonder about having somebody go abroad." Such observations cast Nixon as being sympathetic to Agnew in the the treatment he got from the press—not surprising in itself from a man who never tired of whining about how he himself was treated by reporters.

Agnew, resuming his lament about the press: "I want to give you a couple of reactions, Mr. President. First of all, there wasn't a single media did anything on his initiative, didn't raise a single question that had to do with [the substance of the trip]."

Nixon himself brings up the story, so aggravating to Agnew, about his not having been informed of the China initiative. The president describes the story as "crap" and "unfair," although Nixon had gone to great pains to keep the plans from all but his inner circle, including Agnew.

Nixon tells him now: "He [Rogers] brought it up this morning. . . . I didn't read the article. That was the one you were so mad about. . . . We can say with regard to the China mission, you remember our breakfast, it was just the three of us [Nixon, Kissinger, and Agnew]. If anybody in the administration had any hint about it, you had, before you left. Remember, you talked about the possibility, and I said, 'Well, there's some things going on here we can't talk about [which was not exactly what Nixon had said].' And the reason we couldn't talk about it is that we didn't know until Henry got to the God-damn place whether it would wash. . . . And we were scared to death that if anything [happened]—as a matter of fact we didn't know until Henry got to Pakistan, I didn't know, he didn't know, whether the Chinese were going to come across [to meet him]."

Agnew, taking this all in, decides to tell Nixon then and there that the culprit in leaking the negative story against him, which was technically true in saying he hadn't been informed of the plans, was somebody in the president's own entourage.

AGNEW: "I think the story got started and caused all the press furor and speculation about my not being informed, that got started because it came out of the White House, and that was the problem."

ROGERS: "Who? By God, that's something."

AGNEW: "It came out of the White House, a White House source. It came through the same source that we've [had] trouble with before."

ROGERS: "Do you know who it is?"

AGNEW: "I have a feeling I know who it is, but I'm not going to say because I don't trust—"

NIXON: "You think it did, out of the White House?"

AGNEW: "Because it came through the same bunch."

NIXON: "Well, it didn't come from the NSC? Is that what you mean?"

AGNEW: "No, it didn't come from the NSC."

NIXON: "All right, I've got to know if it did."

KISSINGER: "It didn't come from the NSC."

NIXON: "Well, I'll tell you this. That it didn't come from the Department. . . . Bill and I were out there. It didn't come from State. . . ."

The meeting then breaks into a confusing cacophony of denials from Rogers, Kissinger, and others in the Oval Office, until Nixon says to Agnew: "I'd just like to know who you think it is, that created an impression that was false." Nixon tells Scali, the old wire-service reporter: "I want you to take the responsibility through your sources and so forth, and make a big play out of this without being too obvious. But you know, there's so much crap written about the vice president's trip, that he was sent abroad without any knowledge of what was going on [about Nixon's China trip], it was just a junket. You can speak with authority with the wire services' thoughtful guys, that we have all been outraged by the coverage of this thing. . . . The trip came at a very important time, it was very important in regard to the Mideast, going to those areas, important to go to those African countries. . . . You know how to do it. But I just don't want the impression left, which is unfair, that after you go clear around the world, and had all these talks with people, which he's done at the express request of the president and the secretary of state."

Rogers, picking up on his boss's lead, reports that he has talked that morning with foreign service officers and asked what they thought of Agnew's trip. One of them, Rogers says, told him he "was disappointed with the newspaper coverage and the trip was a great success." He says "all the people in the foreign service in contact with the vice president were very impressed" by his performance and "how important it was to have this kind of quiet reasssurance" from him. "We didn't need anything on television."

Nixon then drives home the point to Scali: "I think we should emphasize this. The vice president's trip was a substantive trip and not the usual kind of goodwill trip; that we hope good will comes out of the substance, but the purpose was to have hard, substantive talks about areas on a bilateral basis. . . . You're the man to do it. . . . You can just say [of the press reports], this is a bad rap."

Scali pipes up: "Mr. President, I've already checked into that in the department because, Mr. President, I was enormously concerned, and the explanation I get was that everyone was so absorbed with China that [the

Agnew trip went] through the magazine without the usual editing, second and third double-check. . . ."

Nixon tells Scali: "What I'd like to do is get the facts and figures and just beat them [the press] over the head with them." Scali, turning to Agnew, replies: "I think this is beginning to percolate a realization that they have been unfair, Mr. Vice President, and I think I can hold the lead on that." Nixon finally dismisses Scali, telling him that Agnew "doesn't deserve to travel all around the world and get kicked in the ass about something that's not true." The president finally concludes the debriefing of his vice president by saying, "Well, glad to have you back."[3]

Here was Nixon at his most benignly two-faced. After arranging for Agnew to go off on what Nixon recognized was only an elaborate vacation, and rapping him for playing so much golf, he was justifying the junket for Agnew's sake before Rogers and Kissinger, who knew the facts, on grounds it really was substantive. He was even drawing from his own experience as a seasoned junketeer as vice president.

(Much later, Agnew's press secretary, Gold, said in an interview that Agnew believed the mysterious leaker of the damning story was Scali himself, no fan of Agnew, who had been assigned by Nixon to deny that the vice president had been in the dark about his secret mission to Peking!)[4]

The next day, when Nixon asks Colson, a staunch Agnew defender, what he thought of Agnew's trip, he says it had been "disastrously reported." Nixon, again in his sympathetic mode, confides that Agnew "was really, really very hurt. He feels he's been done in and he's hurt as the devil." And when Colson speculates that part of the problem was that Agnew was traveling to what people thought were insignificant countries, Nixon, the man who had suggested the itinerary, breaks in: "Well, as a matter of fact, it wasn't our fault. He wanted to go, you know. It was his plan. He wanted to take a vacation, and that was it."

Nixon, piling on the empathy, tells Colson: "Well, it will all work out. . . . He really got a bad deal and we all gotta make it clear to him that we think he did, and play that goal right down the line"—even as he's thinking of ditching him.

Colson: "We'll be looking for some places we can get him into where we can start rebuilding."

NIXON: "Gotta get a place where he gets a good reception. I just think we ought to do that. Where people cheer him. They will, you know. It isn't all that bad. Let's try to figure a place like that. The main thing is that if we do it, we get him to go. He's so tender about it at the moment."

Colson says he will find a place. Nixon tells him: "And let him know personally that we're all backing him up, because that's very important."[5]

On the very next day in a conversation with Haldeman captured by the taping system, however, Nixon is knocking his vice president again. When Haldeman complains that Agnew tried to put off a White House request for several days, Nixon says: "That shows a chicken-shit attitude. . . . For Christ's sakes, you know, when I was vice president, anybody from the White House, I wouldn't fool around. I knew it was important business. But you know, Bob, you've got to face it. This fellow lacks a basic, he's got a streak of smallness in him, that's his problem. I hate to agree with the press on anything, but I'm afraid they see that. Don't you? They see that he's got a lot of class. . . . He's articulate, classy, aloof, and all the rest, but by God he's got this personal streak of smallness that's unbelievable."[6]

Agnew had reason to be upset by now. The next week's issue of *Newsweek* had an item headlined: "Dump Agnew?" It said the Kenya incident "underscored the shaky place that Agnew now occupies in the hearts and minds of many Republican leaders, especially on Capitol Hill. Spirologers particularly noted how energetically the White House next dissociated itself from the Veep's observations about the blacks."

This, taken together with the transparent fact that Agnew wasn't told in advance of the president's plans to visit China [angrily disputed by Agnew], was read as a sign of deepening disaffection at the top. The article quoted an unidentified Republican senator: "There's hardly anyone left among Republicans up here who thinks he'll be on the ticket in 1972."[7]

It was speculation, in fact, that was spreading well outside the cloakroom of the U.S. Senate. After two-and-a-half years of Spiro Agnew's vice presidency, his name, which, as he had predicted, had become a household word, was not always being uttered in the laudatory sense he had hoped it would be.

Chapter 15

PLOTTING
THE BIG SWITCH

FOR FOR ALL OF NIXON'S EXPRESSED CONCERN AND ALLEGED EM-
pathy for Agnew's faux pas on his global vacation and African fiasco, the
president was getting fed up with his vice president. In true Nixonian
style, he was thinking more and more of how to unload him while making it sound like what Agnew himself wanted.

Nixon recounted later, benignly, in his memoir: "One of the first things
I had to decide about the 1972 campaign was whether to change the ticket
by choosing a new running mate. By the middle of 1971 Ted Agnew had
become increasingly disenchanted with his role as vice president. He felt,
as does almost every vice president to some degree, that the White House
staff did not treat him with proper respect, and that I had not given him
major substantive responsibilities. . . . During the first term Agnew had
become an articulate and effective spokesman for conservative positions
and issues. In this role he was wrongly underrated by the press as well as
by his partisan critics. But as I began preparing for the 1972 election, I
also had to look ahead to 1976."

Nixon then confessed his thoughts about the new object of his political affections. "I believed that John Connally was the only man in either
party who clearly had the potential to be a great president," he wrote.
"He had the necessary 'fire in the belly,' the energy to win, and the vision
to lead. I even talked with Haldeman about the possibility of Agnew's

resigning before the convention and my nominating Connally to replace him, although I knew such a move was a remote possibility at best. The only serious option would be to replace Agnew with Connally as the nominee for vice president at the convention."

Nixon wrote that he had discussed the matter with Connally but his reaction was "mixed to negative" because too many Republicans might see him as a "Johnny-come-lately" to the party. Mitchell too, he wrote, was cool to the idea.[1] Haldeman, as noted, also had held such a discussion with Connally, in which the wily Texan had professed not to have "any ideas offhand" about an Agnew replacement.

Ehrlichman, meanwhile, continued to be a sympathetic sounding board for Nixon's laments about his vice president. He wrote later: "The president told me of Spiro Agnew's gaffes of the previous week during the vice president's trip to Africa. . . The president had recently announced that he would be making his historic trip to China. Now Agnew, in Africa on a tour, had told the leader of one nation that he disagreed with the president's China policy. Agnew said he didn't think the forthcoming trip was a good idea.

"The president was very agitated. 'It is beyond my understanding,' he said. 'Twice Agnew has proposed that *he* go to China! Now he tells the world it's a bad idea for me to go! What am I going to do about him?'" "I think you ought to drop him next year," I replied. Nixon nodded. 'I've had Bob arrange for Bryce to let Agnew know I'm thinking about someone else. . . .' Nixon asked me my opinion of Agnew, and I told him it was my hope that the vice president would resign soon. He obviously was not happy in the job, did not get on well with the president or the rest of us, and was not suited to what he was expected to do . . ."

Nixon told him, Ehrlichman went on, that "I talked to John Connally for three hours yesterday. I offered him the vice presidency or, if that's not possible, then secretary of state. I want to position him as my logical successor." Ehrlichman further wrote: "Nixon said Connally had told Bob Haldeman that he was leaving; he had decided to resign from the cabinet because of the failure of some of the White House staff 'to clear personnel appointments' with him, and so on. But Nixon talked him out of resigning. 'Connally told me,' Nixon said, 'that he had no complaints about you or Bob [Haldeman]. But I want you to meet often with Connally and Bryce Harlow to figure out how the hell we can get Agnew to resign early.'" Ehrlichman then reported a contrary position on the vice president: "John Mitchell took another view of all this. He saw Spiro Agnew as a loyal defender of Richard Nixon's right flank, and he saw John Connally as a turncoat Democrat who probably couldn't be confirmed by the Democrat-controlled Senate. Before long, Mitchell had talked with Nixon, and soon most of the Connally-for-Agnew stars had gone out of the president's eyes."[2] But not quite yet.

Nixon, of course, had plans for Connally that went beyond the 1972 ticket if they could be arranged. Erlichman recalled much later: "One day the president, Connally, and I were discussing our legislative problems. Nixon remarked that over the years we had created a working coalition of Congressional conservatives and moderates which had in it as many Democrats as Republicans. Nixon and Connally speculated that Nixon had the support of millions of conservative Democratic voters too. Looking ahead... Nixon and Connally began daydreaming about forming a new political party which might attract voters all across the middle and right of the political spectrum. They could realign Congress too.... What could they call such a coalition of conservatives and moderates? We tossed out some names, borrowed from other countries. We talked about the true meaning of the labels 'liberal' and 'conservative.'

"Nixon speculated that he could get the new party started by calling a convention of the political leaders of the center and right. The Nixon people in each state could be formed into nuclei to create state parties. Nixon and Connally would be elected president and vice president in 1972 by the new coalition party and could bring in with them a majority in both houses of Congress. Both Nixon and Connally had been in politics long enough to realize the near-impossibility of quickly creating such a re-alignment, but they were sufficiently intrigued with the notion that they wanted to have more thought given to it.... I learned later that there had been a conversation between Nixon and Connally at which they agreed to wait until after the 1972 election to consider the new party further. But as far as they were concerned, it remained a possibility. I wonder if 1974 might have seen the birth of a coalition party of everyone-but-the-damn-liberals had Watergate not intervened."[3]

According to a neutral observer, Robert Sam Anson, in his book about Nixon in exile, Nixon finally concluded that Connally could reach the presidency by running for it himself in 1976 as a Republican, after which "the Republican Party would be abolished four years later." In its place, Anson wrote, a "new party would be formed along British political lines. . . . Though Connally, as president, would be the party's titular head, Nixon planned a major role for himself in its shaping and running. From his operatives in every state would come the party nucleus; from him personally would come its guiding principles. He also would direct the process of the party's creation, the assembly of its first convention, the mode and manner of its operation, and, he was certain, its eventual domination of the American political scene."[4] But the notion that John Connally would play second fiddle to Nixon did not account for the dominant will and personality of the Texan, in whose presence Nixon was reduced to schoolboy adoration.

Nixon's anxiety over Agnew, meanwhile, was increased even more by an urgent request for an audience from his old political mentor, Murray Chotiner, who delivered more depressing news about the vice president. As Haldeman recorded it: "Apparently Chotiner had been in Spain at the same time the VP was, and Agnew had pulled him aside and unloaded his troubles on him. He had launched into a tirade on the Domestic Council and E, and complained that they didn't give him anything to do, and no responsibility, they don't ask for his advice, and pay no attention to him. Said he was annoyed by low-level people calling him. The clerks call him and tell him to do things. Murray said the VP was really uptight, that creates a problem for us because we can't have him get into a huff and go off on that basis, so P wants me to talk to Mitchell and see if we can't work out some way of handling it. Also he thinks Mitchell and I should talk to Chotiner. The P asked Murray why he hadn't brought this up with Mitchell to begin with, and Murray said Mitchell cut him off, and so I'm supposed to get that straightened out. So the problems never end."[5]

Indeed they didn't. The very next day Nixon asked Haldeman, he said, to go see Agnew "to explore the conspiracy of the White House staff that he feels is out to get him. . . . The VP gave me a document from Vic Gold, which purported to conclude that John Scali [the former wire-service reporter now a foreign-policy aide] was the one who was leading a high-level White House effort to try to make the case that the VP didn't know about China, and that his attitude on China and the China question was going to result in his being dropped from the ticket. I tried to smooth the thing over a little, and didn't succeed very well, so left it that I would look into it and see what we could develop on the actual facts. I talked to the P about it later and he got all cranked up."[6]

Three days later, Haldeman wrote that Ehrlichman had taken a crack at calming down Agnew, who "thinks that in his particular circumstances [presuming his great public popularity], he should be handled differently than other VPs have been, and he made a plea for the P to cut him in on the decisions. The VP apparently continually came back to the point of China, and raised the question of how you'd feel if the P winked at his national security adviser when the subject of China came up, and then says he can't get into a discussion about that, that we had some things going on, but he couldn't talk about them. He feels that the P should have confided in him."[7] Ehrlichman also told Haldeman that Agnew "really let his hair down, that he said he has no ambitions, that it's way too early to decide on a running mate, that it's embarrassing to be confronted by the press on things he knows nothing about."[8]

Agnew's continued gripes only reaffirmed Nixon's desire to replace him with Connally. "As everyone knows," Ehrlichman wrote later, "John B. Connally was Nixon's darling boy. Of all his cabinet and staff, Nixon saw only Connally as his potential successor. Nixon was the third president whom John Connally had known well; years in the service of Lyndon Johnson had made Connally an old Washington hand. From the standpoint of experience and temperament, Connally could have been a good president from the first day he sat in the big chair. He would have been an inspirational leader, a strong executive and an able representative of the nation in world affairs. . . . As secretary of the treasury, however, Connally was more difficult to deal with. [He] expected to deal with no underlings. If the president had words for him, he wanted to be called directly, not by Bob Haldeman or me. . . . With anyone else, I would have worked around all that formality and Nixon would have backed me. But with Connally, our orders were to do it the way he wanted it done."[9]

Bill Timmons, Nixon's congressional liaison chief, later recalled the occasion when Nixon told him: "Call Connally and tell him I want him to come to the [congressional] leadership meeting, to brief the leadership on some economic issue." Timmons said: "Connally told me, 'Bill, I really appreciate that, and this has nothing to do with you. But if the president wants me to come over there, he should call me.' And he hung up. I told

Nixon. He smiled and laughed. I guess he did call him, because Connally did come over."[10] The incident said it all about the relative positions of Connally and Agnew in the Nixon pecking order.

Before Connally moved in on economic as well as fiscal matters, the administration had a babel of voices on the subject, including heavy-weights George Shultz and Arthur Burns. By the summer of 1971, the big Texan had put a stop to that. When Nixon complained of the confusion, Ehrlichman wrote later, Connally told him: "Well, if you want me to be the spokesman, Mr. President, you are going to have to order those other fellows to shut up. As of now, no one knows who to believe.'" So Nixon assembled his top economists and told them Connally would be setting the administration's economic line from then on, and if they didn't like it "you can quit."[11] Connally's conspicuously dominant role, coupled with Agnew's widely circulated falling out, produced a *News-week* cover with a picture of the tough Texan over the caption "Nixon's No. 2 Man?"[12]

Through all this, Agnew outwardly acted unfazed. A week earlier at a private meeting of officials of the Republican National Committee, Nixon had urged them: "Support the vice president. Do what you can to help the vice president. He's got a tough job and he's doing it well. He's been attacked and maligned unfairly." And the day after Nixon announced his new economic policy with Connally in charge, Agnew was on hand as the president briefed state department officials on its diplomatic aspects. Without warning, he suddenly grabbed Agnew's arm and raised it with his own over his head.[13]

Asked a few days later on a television talk show whether he was worried that he would be replaced on the 1972 ticket by Connally, Agnew said: "Not a bit. . . . There is no competition between Secretary Connally and me in the sense that we are trying to elbow each other for the vice presidential nomination in 1972. Realistically, I think many things would have to happen before I would become concerned about the possibility of a person of the other party receiving the nomination for vice president in my party. . . . I don't believe that if Secretary Connally became a candidate for vice president he would remain a Democrat." As for running himself for reelection, he said Nixon "must select the most potent and powerful vice president that he can find," and he didn't expect him to decide before the start of the election year, so "until he decides it would be fruitless for me to make any decision."[14] That didn't sound, though, like he was giving up on keeping the job.

In the Oval Office, however, Nixon continued to play with the idea of somehow getting Agnew out of the vice presidency and the line of presidential succession. In mid-September, he demonstrated in his musings with his inner circle not only his low regard of Agnew as presidential material but also his minimal regard for another key government position. With the recent embarrassing rejections of two Nixon nominees for the Supreme Court from the South, Clement Haynsworth and G. Harrold Carswell, the president was shopping around for a replacement who could be confirmed. Why not ask Agnew to resign—and take a seat on the Supreme Court! Fearing the country would be in poor hands with the potential of a President Agnew, he would simply shift him over to the highest court in the land, where he would have a critical say on the nation's bedrock of laws for the rest of his lifetime.

In a conversation with Haldeman and Ehrlichman captured by the White House taping system, Ehrlichman broaches the subject: "On my list there's two names that appeal to me, one of them probably not confirmable. That's Weinberger and Spiro T. Agnew. . . . I don't know. It's a strong question in my mind. But it's a hell of an intriguing possibility."

NIXON: "Agnew once told me he wanted to be on the Court."

Haldeman: "God, that would really rip things up. Talk about your blockbusters. They'll all say, 'What's the shoe Nixon's gonna drop next?'" (He laughs).

NIXON: "He'd be a damned good judge."

EHRLICHMAN: "He would be a good judge. I think he'd do an excellent job. He'd be articulate, he'd be highly principled."

HALDEMAN: "I'm not sure he wants it now, either."

Nixon: "I'm sure—you think he wants to stay vice president?"

HALDEMAN: "No. . . . Well maybe, or he's wiped out [as vice president]. I think—or does he want to get out and fight the battle?"

NIXON: "You know, you know, he loves this social stuff. . . . I'm so surprised by it, the movie star business.

HALDEMAN: "And he likes the movie stars. . . ."

NIXON: "He could do that, though, from the court."

EHRLICHMAN: "A justice can lead the social life. He's got a good social thing."

HALDEMAN: "He's got all the summer to do it. He can go to California and spend the summer."

EHRLICHMAN: "Oh, sure, May to October."

HALDEMAN: "Two or three months in Palm Springs and two or three at Newport."

EHRLICHMAN: "You know—"

NIXON: "Wouldn't it lead to a violent debate?"

EHRLICHMAN: "Sure it would. You'd be accused of putting him adrift in a lifeboat and using the Court as a shelf. . . ."

NIXON: "He's gotta do something else."

EHRLICHMAN: "And there are enormous negatives to it. At the same time, he is now enjoying a sort of a climate of acceptance that is probably temporary before the storm."

NIXON: "And then they'll be after us."

EHRLICHMAN: "And at that time he'd get so cut up that probably he could never pull this off. Of course, the Senate would have a golden opportunity to do you in, by refusing to confirm your vice president."

NIXON: "Yeah. Oh, Christ, it'd be awful. We couldn't give them that chance."[15]

They moved on to talk briefly about Weinberger, without result. A day later, the matter came up again, this time with only Agnew mentioned and his ally Colson also present. Nixon began with a discussion of handling Agnew, about his troubles with American youth, and what might be done about them, without mentioning the previous day's talk of the Supreme Court. Colson did his best to shore up his boss's flagging views of the vice president.

NIXON: "You always have the constant problem, is praise him, praise him, praise him. Then he'll do it. He will not do it unless he thinks it's helping him. Naturally, he wants to help us, too. He's very, very sensitive to praise. He's also very sensitive if he thinks he's not popular with what he's doing, so you've got to [reassure him]. . . . The big question is Agnew. We've talked a little about that. John [Erlichman], I just really think with Agnew that the best way at this point is to have him go all out. . . on pretty narrow, partisan talk."

COLSON [defending Agnew]: "He's very impressed, Mr. President, with his last two speeches and with the fact that he got a lot of praise at the governors' conference [!!]. . . by a national call for unity. . . . We've written this stuff, Buchanan has, in which he calls for unity but at the same time he says no more of this petty bickering. . . ."

NIXON: "The thing with Agnew is that he's just got to avoid any rash rhetoric. His tone should be the same. It should be more in sorrow than in anger, and no, no, no sort of Buchananisms, you know, no, no terribly mean, cruel things. Stay the hell off of that."

The conversation turns to Nixon's own standing in the polls relative to Agnew's. Haldeman cites a poll in which "Agnew does not come out nearly as strongly as you would think he would in Alabama. He's substantially behind you. And it doesn't show increased strength."

NIXON: "I think Agnew's constituency is extremely narrow. . . ."

EHRLICHMAN: "I don't think it could be solved going in the regular way. I think you'd have to try something fairly radical to try and solve it and see if it works."

NIXON: "What do you mean by that?"

EHLRICHMAN: "Well, I mean a grandstand play for the youth and that element. Make a college campus tour. . . ."

COLSON: "It'd be a hell of a long gamble."

EHRLICHMAN: "It's a gamble, it's a gamble, but you're not playing with very much in the way of savings. . . . In the sense that your base is so low that you haven't got much to lose. . . . My far-out idea is, for him to go in residence on campus and have colloquies and so forth."

NIXON: "Rap sessions."

EHRLICHMAN: "Yeah."

COLSON: "It'd be interesting."

HALDEMAN: "It's a long shot."

COLSON: "Better than being a disc jockey. Remember, he was going to do that?"

NIXON: "Who was going to make him a disc jockey?"

EHRLICHMAN: "Remember, he was going to go on and do someone's newscast for a week while he was on vacation, or some radio commentator or something."

NIXON: "Oh, Paul Harvey."

HALDEMAN: "Was it Paul Harvey?"

EHRLICHMAN: "Well, that is not exactly a disc jockey. . . ."

NIXON: "But I think Agnew is now the beneficiary of. . . an aura of good feeling. Don't you think so?"

EHRLICHMAN: "Yeah. Right now it's, uh, he's in very fat with the governors."

NIXON: "Nobody's kicking him around particularly."

COLSON: "No, he's come back in the last months. He's made, the low point was after the trip [to Africa]."

EHRLICHMAN: "[He's a] target of opportunity, I just have a feeling that he's going to be a major victim of this primary campaign, when things start to heat up."

As the group continues to muse over what to do with, and about, the vice president, Nixon finally introduces the idea again of making him one of the nation's nine judicial wise men. "Agnew's a red-hot lawyer," he says. "One of his great desires that he expressed, oh, a year or two years ago, was to be on the Court. I say why not put him on the Court?"

EHRLICHMAN: "It'd require a confirmation hearing, wouldn't it?"

NIXON: "What would happen?"

COLSON: "What would happen? It would [go] through like greased lightning—

NIXON: "Agnew?"

COLSON: "—through the Senate."

NIXON: "You think so?"

COLSON: "Oh, Absolutely."

NIXON AND HALDEMAN: "Why?"

COLSON: "He'd be confirmed to the Supreme Court. I don't think the Senate would turn down the vice president."

HALDEMAN: "Oh, God. Look at who the Senate is, and the opportunity they'd have to point out how stupid Richard Nixon was to accept this clod as his vice president."

COLSON: "Make themselves look very bad in the process."

HALDEMAN: "Why? He'd look great. Most of the country doesn't like Agnew."

COLSON: "How would you argue that he wouldn't have the qualifications to sit on the court?"

HALDEMAN: "Never practiced law."

NIXON: "Oh, yes."

EHRLICHMAN: "Oh, yeah."

COLSON: "Not only that—"

HALDEMAN: "Never been on the bench."

COLSON: "He's been vice president of the United States."

NIXON: "As a matter of fact, that's his strong suit. He was a damn good lawyer. A labor lawyer as a matter of fact, among other things."

EHRLICHMAN: "[Senator James] Eastland would be, of course, as very courtly and very generous with him, but you have [Democrats Birch] Bayh, you have who, [Walter] Mondale, and you have, who else? [Ted] Kennedy's on Judiciary. . . ."

COLSON: "But my point is that with Haynsworth and Carswell, they had reasons for their attack. With Agnew, it would be solely political. And it would look like they were trying to embarrass you. I mean if he wanted the appointment, and the president sent his name up, anyone who would oppose it would simply be [engaging in] crass politics."

In the end, Nixon dropped the idea, in part apparently because of concern over the fuss the press would stir up. In closing off the discussion, he argued that while he shared Agnew's hostility toward the press, the vice president needed to learn a lesson from him about dealing with it. He seemed to suggest that getting Agnew past the Senate Democrats would be too difficult "mainly because they have this alliance with the press. . . . I'm a little faster on my feet than Agnew, but that doesn't make any difference. I mean its not that he's so God-damned good. The trouble is, if you can only get across to him that he mustn't look as if he enjoys fighting the press. You know, God, how I handle the bastards. I know they're all bastards. I dislike them much more than Agnew could [have] ever dreamed of disliking them, because of their philosphy. But I stand here and take that bullshit at any time and nobody ever knows it. Correct? . . . I [took it] for eight years as vice president and two years in the House, four years in the Senate I never let them know. The only time I ever kicked 'em was after the governor's [campaign in California in 1962]. And I'm gonna kick 'em again some day. . . ."

COLSON [now massaging Nixon]: "I remember in the fifties, Mr. President. I was on the Hill in those days. You handled the antagonism much different than Agnew. Agnew's has major confrontations. . . . He's extreme the way he handles the reporters. You didn't. You were very clever in the way you [dealt with them]."[16] Colson may have disagreed with Nixon on Agnew, but he was politician enough to know how to pull the president's strings on which of them had the right approach in dealing with the common enemy of the press.

At Camp David soon after, Nixon suddenly appeared to have a change of heart about Agnew's immediate future. Haldeman wrote: "He told me to talk to the attorney general [Mitchell] about the Agnew situation again. . . . Instead of dodging it. . . it would be good to indicate his confidence in Agnew and say that if Agnew so desires, he intends to keep him on the ticket. He recalled the damage that was done to Eisenhower in '56 by his hesitation on keeping Nixon. It raised hell with the Nixon friends and the conservatives, made Eisenhower look bad, as these people pounded on it. The P's view is that Agnew is a liability, although we can't prove it, and the only way we could check this is to run a tandem trial heat process, but he still thinks he should indicate his support, whether or not he intends to drop him later, and he thinks also, it's a good way to get the P out of the black VP question, which is sure to arise. The advantages of backing Agnew now would be that it totally mutes the press on the question and it pulls the rug out from under the extreme right."[17]

Notably, in saying this, Nixon told Haldeman only that he ought to "indicate his confidence" in his vice president and that "if Agnew so desires, he intends to keep him on the ticket," adding "whether or not he intends to drop him later." Nixon laid it all out as a tactical move to take the heat off himself from pressure groups for the time being, rather than definitely deciding on Agnew and publicly saying so.

Two days later, Nixon spoke to Mitchell himself and told Haldeman that "both of them agree that the only possible replacement would be Connally, but that we can't do that if he doesn't switch parties. And Mitchell, particularly, doesn't believe Connally would take the job anyway. Mitchell feels we need Agnew as our handle to the right, and it would be a mistake to move him now. A resignation would be too big a blow to absorb. We should instead program a scenario leading to his decision at the convention not to run. Then go for the Connally move, building it up ahead of time so that we're ready for it, rathern than dumping it as a surprise. Harlow feels that the VP is in complete limbo himself about a decision as to whether or not to run again. Both of them [Mitchell and Harlow] felt very strongly that the P should talk with the VP with a complete open mind. Not decide it, but just discuss it. The idea would be to get his views and then start building towards a decision with him involved. They do feel that we should decide soon, however."[18]

Ehrlichman wrote later that "Nixon was toying with the idea of nominating Vice President Agnew to the Court. . . so that John Connally could be appointed vice president. He found 'the Agnew thing intriguing,' he told me. 'The Senate would clobber him,' I said. "Nixon nodded. 'They would attack me by rejecting him, and then Agnew would be useless; with a Senate rejection he becomes used goods,' Nixon said. Nothing more was said about Agnew." Ehrlichman added later that Agnew had persuaded Attorney General Mitchell to intervene on his behalf.[19]

Buchanan observed later: "By then, Nixon realized, 'Look, if you tear this ticket up, you're gonna antagonize and alienate the whole conservative movement, for whom Agnew was a tremendous hero.' He had a tremendous following in Middle America, he was the white knight, and he had a tremendous independent following. He was the guy who carried the banner of the Republican Party. If you had dropped him, first, it would have been a statement that you had made a mistake putting him on the ticket. And secondly, you would have damaged your own base, and why would you do that when it looked like you were playing with a pat hand?"[20]

Whatever happened, Nixon was not quite ready to make his vice president "used goods," not as long as he continued to be an effective battering ram against his critics on the hustings. With the identity of the 1972 Democratic presidential nominee still undetermined, Agnew was dispatched to attack four of the most prominent prospects—Kennedy, Muskie, Humphrey, and McGovern—on grounds of "reckless and appalling" talk about cutting defense spending with the Vietnam War still going on.

He had harsh words too for fellow-Republican Representative Pete McCloskey, a Korean War veteran and one of their party's most vociferous critics of the Vietnam policy, who had announced he would challenge Nixon in the New Hampshire primary. Mocking his shoestring effort, Agnew said McCloskey "is in such a money bind, he's been forced to auction off his personal art collection. Yesterday he sold his favorite painting—'Benedict Arnold Crossing the Delaware.'" He defended his rhetoric as "the politics of positive division" and said he welcomed "the hydrophobic hostility" of a "pompous, unelected liberal elite."[21]

Nearly every day now, however, a new reminder occurred of how the vice president could be an irritant, or a distraction on the most trivial of matters. One night over the long Thanksgiving weekend at Palm Springs, Haldeman got a phone call from Agnew at 11 o'clock, telling him about a dispute between his friends Frank Sinatra and Bob Hope over which of them was to ride with Nixon in the golf cart for their game the next day. Hope had been told, Haldeman recorded in his diary, "that the P wanted Sinatra to ride with him and that this apparently had Hope's nose out of joint [no pun apparently intended]. In any event, I told the VP that I had nothing to do with setting it up. Rose Woods had handled it all for the P and that he should call Rose, which he agreed he would do in the middle of the night."

Haldeman didn't indicate later how it had all turned out, except to note that on the flight back to Washington Nixon complained about the "sticky thing" that the Sinatra–Hope flap caused in spite of Agnew's post-midnight intervention.[22]

The care and feeding of Frank Sinatra was of particular concern to Agnew at this juncture, because the singer was strongly in his corner in the matter of his place on the 1972 Republican ticket. Agnew had fastidiously cultivated Sinatra on trips to Palm Springs, on one occasion even taking Sinatra's elderly mother to witness a space shot. The stroking worked, in that Sinatra became a major contributor to the Nixon–Agnew campaign fund. According to Agnew aide John Damgard, when speculation grew in 1971 that the vice president might be dropped from the ticket, Sinatra passed the word that there would be no more money from him if that happened. Also, a group of prominent New York conservatives headed by William F. Buckley and calling themselves the Manhattan 12 warned Nixon that heavy contributions from them would be denied if Agnew were jettisoned.[23]

When Agnew dutifully attended the annual National Governors' Conference in San Juan, Puerto Rico, he made light of all the talk about Connally replacing him. He told his old colleagues that a few days earlier he had picked up his phone in his office and heard a recorded message that said: "Your four years are up. Please signal when through." Later, at another Republican governors' meeting, in French Lick, Indiana, he reported that he had just come from Chicago, where he had stayed in the hotel's vice-presidential suite. "Secretary Connally was out of town," he said, "I asked about checkout time, and they said, 'Election Day.'"[24]

Agnew could joke about it, but the Connally talk was getting under his skin, as was the conspicuous admiration Nixon continued to display toward his new favorite, sometimes in Agnew's presence. "At a state dinner," aide Vic Gold recalled, "Nixon would talk about Connally with the vice president sitting there. Agnew had a remarkable gift of restraint and self-control. He never said a word, but he seethed."[25]

In all this he took pains to swear his fealty to Nixon, especially before conservative crowds that might be wavering. When the ultraconservative Young Americans for Freedom at a mock convention nominated Agnew for president instead of Nixon, he wrote to them: "I feel it reasonable to point out that if my efforts as vice president are indeed deserving of such support, it is only because I, as a member of the Nixon administration, have been working since January, 1969, to help carry out the president's program for our nation."[26]

Agnew continued as well to play goodwill ambassador abroad, attending a two-thousand-five-hundredth anniversary celebration in Iran and making a long-delayed sentimental journey to Greece, his ancestral home, before year's end. Privately, Nixon criticized him to Haldeman for "farting around there for a week," but on Agnew's return he had a cordial conversation of more than an hour with him in the Oval Office.[27] A post-trip memo from Rogers to Nixon reported: "The vice president's trip was a solid success and significantly furthered our foreign policy objectives in Greece, Turkey and Iran." The secretary of state, again going along with Nixon's policy of boosting Agnew's foreign gallivanting as more than vacationing, credited Agnew in Iran with taking "advantage of a major ceremonial event to achieve important substantive gains,"[28] and with demonstrating "tact and finesse of the highest order" in Greece, skillfully parrying the issue of Cyprus in Turkey.

However, Nixon's decision to send Connally to attend the inauguration of President Nguyen Van Thieu in Saigon, a customary vice-presidential task, only stimulated more speculation that Nixon was boosting Connally's foreign-policy credentials preparatory to replacing Agnew on the 1972 ticket.

Other pressures in that direction included a call on Nixon from the liberal Ripon Society to dump Agnew. In the vice president's favor, however, was a poll of delegates to the 1968 Republican convention; 76.5

percent favored his retention and 71 percent said unloading him would hurt the ticket's chances of winning in 1972. Some party conservatives formed "Americans for Agnew," and a rallying cry for him came from Lee Edwards, a prominent Washington publicist with ties to the Goldwater wing of the GOP: "In an era of ideologicial eunuchs, he stands almost alone as a man of principle."[29]

Further indications that Nixon needed Agnew to shore up his right-wing support came with the decision of a conservative Ohio congress-man, John Ashbrook, to challenge Nixon in the New Hampshire primary. Ashbrook pointedly observed that his opposition was to Nixon, not Agnew. To mollify the right wing and the South, Harry Dent, the White House political adviser from South Carolina, finally wrote to a conservative organization: "Despite what you read in the press, there is no plan to drop Mr. Agnew from the ticket in 1972."[30] But the vice president was a politician with a one-man constituency, and that one man was not Dent; he was Nixon, who continued to stop short of that statement. But Nixon also continued the subterfuge that he was happy with Agnew. When he made a passing complimentary remark about the vice president in a speech in Chicago, the grateful recipient sent him a handwritten thank-you note vowing that "you can always depend on my loyalty and my total support of your final decisions." Then he addded: "However, I won't promise not to play the advocate while you are undecided."[31] That was one promise that Nixon could have done without, and one that ran-kled those closest to the president. Agnew obviously meant "devil's advo-cate," in referring to the strain of independence in him.

Around the same time, in an interview in the *Wall Steet Journal*, the vice president indicated that private life had some appeal to him as a man of limited financial means. "Many people at my stage of life want to con-sider the welfare of their family," he said. "Despite the very substantial pay increases recently [to $62,500 salary and $10,000 expenses], the pay here still is not what you could get in outside life for equal responsibility. Nor is the tax structure very helpful; a good part of that pay is on a rubber band, and it snaps right back into the Treasury."[32]

That sort of thinking, in the end, the Nixon strategists realized, might be their best hope of getting rid of Agnew—that he would take himself out of the game. He could hardly be fired for letting his side down. He had admirably performed the central task assigned him—of being Nixon's Nixon on the fund-raising and campaign trails in castigating his critics. What had made him persona non grata with the Nixon inner circle was his interminable carping and restlessness over being inadequately used in policy matters.

But Agnew in truth was not as indifferent toward remaining on the ticket as some of his public observations and private gripes suggested. With his knowledge and approval, associates raised money to generate support for him in a poll in New Hampshire that reinforced the case for his renomination and reelection. Polling figures contradicted any notion that keeping Agnew on the Republican ticket would be damaging to its chances for four more years in power. Just as important from his own point of view, Agnew knew he was now the most popular Republican in the nation, rivalled only by Nixon. Not surprisingly, he was looking ahead, to possible or even probable nomination for the presidency in 1976, after Nixon had filled the two-term limit. He well knew the recent history of the vice presidency as the most reliable stepping-stone to presidential nomination and gateway to the Oval Office. Indeed, aide John Damgard later reported, "Agnew was fond of saying the only reason he wanted to be vice president was to be lady-in-waiting to be president. Otherwise the job wasn't challenging."[33]

As the new year began, and with the speculation continuing, Nixon agreed to a one-hour television interview with his old journalistic nemesis, CBS News White House correspondent Dan Rather. Right off, Rather asked him whether he could say "categorically and unequivocally" that he wanted Agnew on the ticket with him again. Nixon said the decision would be made the next summer at the Republican convention by the delegates. But then, startlingly to the audience, he added: "if I am a candidate I obviously will have something to say about it. My view is that one should not break up a winning combination. I believe that the vice president has handled his difficult assignments with dignity, with courage; he's at times been a man of controversy, but when a man has done a good job in a position, when he has been part of a winning team, I believe that he should stay on the team. That is my thinking at this time."[34]

That, at last, was it, or so it seemed. For all the behind-the-scenes presidential expressions of frustration and exasperation about Spiro

Agnew, and Nixon's repeated cajoling of John Connally to replace him on the ticket, he apparently had finally surrendered to what he had been convinced was political reality. It was going to be Nixon and Agnew again, under the slogan "Four More Years"; there seemed little reason to expect otherwise as the 1972 campaign began.

Chapter 16

SEPARATION ANXIETY

On the second day of the new year, what seemed to be good news for Vice President Agnew came in a report by veteran CBS newscaster Daniel Schorr. He told of a supposed falling-out between Nixon and Connally, which, if it could be believed, suggested even more reason for Agnew to expect he would remain on the Republican national ticket for 1972.

Hearing of Schorr's report from Buchanan, Nixon instructed Haldeman to call Connally and invite him to dinner in San Clemente, where the president had been spending the holidays. Connally told Haldeman all was well, but as the chief of staff subsequently wrote in his diary, Nixon later confided "that he had a very difficult time with Connally in California. That the night they had dinner at the P's house, Connally told him he had spent his time in Texas going off on a horse, thinking through his future, and he concluded that he had completed what he had come here [to Washington] for, the job that was needed, and he would be, therefore, leaving at the end of January. This he had talked over with Nellie [Connally's wife] and there was a firm decision. P really had to go to work on him, apparently, to make the point that this was not in the best interests at this time. . . . P's feeling is that we can't afford to let him go now, that we've got to pay the price that's necessary to keep him, so he [Nixon] really is, in a sense, a hostage to him. . . ."[1]

If that indeed was the case, Connally remained the driving force in the Nixon cabinet and in the president's heart. And who knew what price

Connally might exact to stay at Treasury, and close to Nixon, who seemed more dependent on him than ever? Later in January, with Connally at home with the flu, Nixon hovered over him like a mother hen. According to Haldeman in his diary, "P wants to be sure that we don't let the White House staff throw their weight on him. . . getting him to Camp David and all the other perks, have him use the Eagle [the small presidential plane] any time he goes. We should take the initiative during this time to give him the highest priority over cabinet and staff." Haldeman wrote that Nixon had instructed him to tell Mitchell, Kissinger, and Ehrlichman personally to keep Connally informed on everything and "if Connally's not for it, then the P won't do it. Wants me to make the point that the P's concerned about how hard he's working. That he knows that every performance has to be grade A, that he's relied on for so much, so he should have all the best available and we don't want any little things bothering him."[2]

That certainly did sound like a hostage situation. And again two days later, Nixon told Haldeman "to call Nellie and see if Connally would like to go to Florida and stay at the P's house for a while to recover from his cold and all. Also, he wants me to sit down and talk to Connally and say that the P says, because he's carrying such a burden and the P considers him the indispensible man, that I'm to see that his path is as easy as possible within the White House staff." But Haldeman complained in the diary that "our staff say they can't reach him," an indication of how little Connally wanted to be bothered or stroked on Nixon's orders.[3]

Ted Agnew may have felt, going into the presidential election year of 1972, that President Nixon, relying so much on Connally, was unwisely wasting a valuable policy resource in cutting his vice president out of key internal decisions. This was especially so, Agnew could tell himself, regarding domestic matters in which he had experience as a former governor. But Nixon, and his palace guard of Haldeman and Erlichman, saw the vice president's value only as an effective messenger, not as a conceptualizer. And with reelection now at the top of the administration agenda, the only role they wanted played by the vice president was the traditional one that Nixon himself had filled in Eisenhower's bid for a second term in 1956. As Nixon had been against Adlai Stevenson then, they wanted Agnew to be their attack dog against the eventual Democratic presidential nominee.

Nevertheless, Agnew continued to seek a larger policy voice. In early January, in the wake of the leaked disclosure of the Pentagon Papers on the conduct of the Vietnam War, he asked for and got a rare meeting with Nixon. In the Oval Office, he offered an idea that, in an effort to bolster Nixon's power to classify government documents without prior court authorization, could have been taken as rekindling the Agnew feud with the press.

The vice president in the taped conversation calls for "tightening it up, to make certain that only those directly authorized by the president could make a document secret," and that it would not be "a matter for the courts to decide whether or not the president properly classified the document as secret. . . . The only thing the government would have to establish," Agnew explains, "was that the president properly classified the document and that it was improperly used by the violator." It would be stipulated that the content of any such document would never have to be revealed. Agnew tells Nixon that "one piece of information revealed by Jack Anderson, seemingly innocuous to . . . 99 percent of the population, might provide to a foreign intelligence agent that one piece of a puzzle to blow the cover of an important operative or to reveal a plan that we're trying to conceal."

Nixon takes the high road with Agnew, lecturing him that while he likes the idea, "I don't like to classify things for political purposes. You see, classification could be used for political security of the administration or for the national security of this country. The latter is legitimate, the former is totally indefensible." He also says he doesn't want to pick a fight with the press on the sensitive matter. "I don't want you, although you're perfectly willing to do so, just frankly [to] be the guy that's kicking the ass off the press," he says, adding: "They should have their ass kicked off. What I meant is they will take. . . anything that touches them as being attacked by Agnew."

Nixon suggests that he talk to newly installed Supreme Court Justice William Rehnquist, who had been considering the same matter as a Justice Department official, and with White House counsel John Dean and Ehrlichman before attempting to move forward—and to make sure to say "you're exploring it on your own. . . We can't be in the business of prosecuting the press."[4]

Agnew had the satisfaction of having been heard out on his idea, but nothing came of it. After three years in the vice presidency, he had no greater policy role than when he first took the job.

As the election year began, the consensus remained that the Democrats through the primary election process would settle on Senator Ed Muskie of Maine. His level-headed performance as Hubert Humphrey's running mate in 1968, and his homey 1970 election-eve television talk to the nation, contrasted so favorably by the news media with the televised fiasco of Nixon's full-throated assault on "the rock throwers and the obscenity shouters" in Phoenix, seemed to point to Muskie as the choice. Polls of the time reflected that sentiment, establishing the senator from Maine as the Democratic front-runner.

Among activists within his party, however, who would have an inordinate influence in the process of selecting convention delegates mainly in state primaries, Muskie had one major problem. He was having difficulty making up his mind and articulating his position on the Vietnam War. By this time, opposition to the war had become a centerpiece of the party's internal debate, and although Muskie in 1971 had talked about withdrawing American troops, he often sounded an uncertain trumpet.

Another likely Democratic candidate for the 1972 nomination, Senator George McGovern of South Dakota, who had served as a sort of rallying point in 1968 for the forces of the slain Senator Robert Kennedy at the party's disastrous Chicago convention, had by now emerged as the Democrats' most forceful critic of the war. But he was not yet regarded as a serious challenger to Muskie. So it was Muskie on whom Nixon and his political strategists had focused as their likely opponent.

As early as April of 1970, Nixon had been pushing his chief operative, Haldeman, to look into Muskie's record and personal life for political vulnerabilities, along with those of Ted Kennedy and other possible 1972 Democratic candidates. Haldeman wrote in his diary then that Nixon "wants to step up political attack. Investigators on Kennedy and Muskie plus [Senators Birch] Bayh and [William] Proxmire. Also get dope on all the key senatorial candidates." Haldeman identified the investigators as two Ehrlichman agents, former New York policemen, "used to handle investigations that were outside the normal scope of the federal investigative agencies." The men he named, Jack Caulfield and Tony Ulasewicz, later received notoriety in the Watergate affair.[5]

In September 1970, Haldeman had written: "Big day for political discussions as P tries to get the line set and some action underway before we
leave [on a foreign trip]. Mainly concerned with not letting Democrats,
especially presidential candidates like Ted Kennedy, Muskie, HHH, etc.
get away with their obvious present attempt to move away from the left
and into middle of road. He's right, our people are letting them do it and
press is not nailing them."[6] And in November, Haldeman wrote: "P
wants me to launch plan for 'lib' mailings supporting Muskie to all
Democratic leaders and editors in South." The diaries helpfully explained
parenthetically: "An example of the 'dirty tricks'concept—in this case,
mailings supporting Muskie that would appear to be from a strong liberal
source and thus offensive to the conservative South."[7]

In February of 1971, in the wake of Nixon's ordered incursion into
Laos amid Democratic criticism, Haldeman wrote: "The P is very anxious that we not let the Democratic candidates look good on this issue.
Muskie has moved out in opposition and he [Nixon] wants to be sure we
keep him out on that limb and push hard to make an asset out of this."[8] In
a clear indication that the Nixon White House had Muskie in its sights
early, a later February diary entry told of "long chats with E. . . and then
with Colson on [how] his Project Muskie is coming along and some ideas
on ways to carry that further ahead."[9]

By mid-January of 1972, Nixon clearly was focusing on Muskie as his
likely fall opponent. Haldeman wrote of the president's concern about a
poll that raised a question of "Muskie's image of a strong, thoughtful man
versus Nixon as pure cosmetics. He said he might want to consider the
possibility of a joint appearance with Muskie; I don't know why in the
world he would do so." It would be better, Haldeman wrote, to turn
Agnew loose on him. "We need some action on the bomb-Muskie crew,
especially Agnew," he wrote, "he's got nothing to gain in fighting the
press anymore, but he should brutally attack Muskie, leaving Hubert and
Teddy alone for now, since Muskie's way out in front."[10]

Agnew apparently was willing, but continued to concern himself with
non-campaign matters. In early February, he called Haldeman complaining about the Legal Services branch of the anti-poverty program inherited from LBJ. "He's sort of engaged with a running brawl with the legal
services people at OEO [Office of Economic Opportunity]" who Agnew
said were attempting "to drive a wedge between him and the P. . . . It's

obvious to him that the entire establishment in Washington, D.C., has ground to a halt because of the wild-eyed kids in legal services," and that "the P, too, is pretty much disgusted with all this but doesn't realize how bad it is."[11] Haldeman tried to slough Agnew off on Ehrlichman, but he refused to work with anyone but Nixon's chief aide. "I had a meeting with the VP to work out campaign relationships," Haldeman wrote. "He says he trusts only me at the White House and wants to deal directly with me on any orders he gets from the P."[12]

While Agnew was under Nixon's directive to stick to campaigning and go after Muskie publicly, others in the campaign operation were targeting the Maine senator covertly and indirectly. As early as the previous summer, Pat Buchanan had written a memo that said: "Senator Muskie is target A as of midsummer for our operation. Our specific goals are (a) to produce political problems for him, right now, (b) to hopefully help defeat him in one or more of the [1972] primaries (Florida looks now to be the best early bet, California, the best later), and (c) finally, to visit upon him some political wounds that would not only reduce his chances for nomination—but damage him as a candidate, should he be nominated."[13]

ONCE AGAIN, IN MARCH, the silly matter of who would go to the Gridiron dinner raised its head. Nixon didn't want to, neither did Rogers, and Agnew once again was balking.

NIXON, captured on tape, asks Haldeman: "Agnew won't go?"

HALDEMAN: "I don't know. Dick Wilson [of the Cowles Newspapers, the Gridiron president] makes the argument you should go, or at the very least if you don't, that the vice president must, for a different reason, which is that the Gridiron is being kicked around by the left wing, the young reporters, the libs and all that."

NIXON: "Well, that appeals to me. The women's lib feels very, very strongly I shouldn't go. You know the women's lib, don't you? [The Gridiron at the time was an all-male club]. . . . Well, what about Agnew?"

HALDEMAN: "I don't know yet."

NIXON: "Still working on that?"

HALDEMAN: "Dick Wilson thinks if you don't go you should be out of town, and the vice president should go. In other words, if you were in town and you just gratuitously insulted them by not going, that he feels would be harmful to the old line of the press corps who are not the target."

Nixon, weighing what he will do, tells Haldeman that "of all of the Gridiron, about half of them are decent . . . [but] they always shit on me."[14]

Later that day, Haldeman wrote in his diary: "P got into the Gridiron question today. Wanting to be sure that Agnew is set to do it, so that he doesn't have to go. Also, he had told Bebe [Rebozo, Nixon's closest friend] not to go, and now he thinks he should go, and told me to call him, because they're going to rib Bebe and P thinks he ought to be there for it."[15] The next day, Nixon told Haldeman "he would go if the VP [stuck in California at a state Republican Assembly meeting] couldn't go, but he heard that [muckraking columnist] Jack Anderson was going to be there, and if he were, the P definitely wouldn't go."[16]

When Nixon next said he would go to the dinner only and not attend the mix-and-mingle beforehand, his wife and daughter Julie got into the act. Haldeman recounted that "both hit him on the fact that he should not go, would be a very bad thing for him to do [because women were excluded from Gridiron membership]. Nixon now decided he "should try to get the VP to do it. . . and that we'll play into the hands of the radicals if we're not represented. . . . Tried that on the VP, [but] the P had told him in writing he didn't have to do it this year, and he argued that neither of them should do it." So Nixon had Haldeman call Secretary of State Rogers, who said "he felt the VP should definitely not go, and he really thinks the P should, but if neither of them goes, then either Connally or Rogers should, and it ought to be Connally." In the end, Haldeman wrote, Nixon "made the decision he won't go, he won't make the VP go. . . and that's where it was left. It was interesting how everybody I discussed it with copped out and passed the buck to someone else."[17] Such were the heavy concerns that weighed on the leader of the free world.

Connally, meanwhile, was getting more fed up at Treasury. Haldeman wrote in mid-April that "he's obviously determined that he's got to go. He admitted that a lot of the problem he has with the White House staff is his fault and the way he works. He wants to control everything that affects him, he will not allow staff people whose judgment isn't as good as his to do so." Rather than "blow up and walk out mad," he said, he would leave quietly and perhaps head up a Democrats-for-Nixon organization after the primaries.[18]

Connally's decision revived Nixon's discussion with Haldeman and Ehrlichman "on the restructuring of the two-party system," Haldeman wrote, "the feeling being that the P and Connally, after the election, could move to build a new party, the Independent Conservative Party, or something of that sort, that would bring in a coalition of southern Democrats and other conservative Democrats, along with the middle-road to conservative Republicans. Problem would be to work it out so that we included Rockefeller and Reagan on the Republican spectrum, and picked up as many of the Democrats as we could.

"By structuring it right, we could develop a new majority party. Under a new name. Get control of the Congress without an election, simply by the realignment, and make a truly historic change in the entire American political structure. This intrigues the P and Connally, and it's obviously the only way Connally has any future, since he's never going to be nominated by the Democratic Party, and by Republican Party. If we formed a coalition, with the two of them being the strong men and doing it, he clearly would emerge as the candidate for the new party in '76, and the P would strongly back him in that."[19]

☙ ❧

IN LATE MAY, seven months before the start of the presidential election year, Nixon got more specific in what he wanted done, as recorded by Haldeman: "The P got into a discussion of the general political situation the first thing this morning. He wanted to track down whoever had done the attack on Julie's new teaching job to see whether there was a partisan source to it. That led him to think that we should put permanent tails and coverage on Teddy and Muskie and Hubert on all the personal stuff to cover the kinds of things that they hit us on in '62 [when Nixon lost his bid for governor of California]; personal finances, family and so forth."[20] Notably, there was no mention or evidence of the hand of Agnew, who was the out-front assailant, in any of this.

Dwight Chapin, a young former Haldeman business associate now working as Nixon's personal aide, recalling political pranks at the University of Southern California, contacted a fellow prankster named Donald Segretti. Together they set in motion a series of anti-Muskie capers that later became part of the Watergate scandal lore. They included late-night phone calls to voters during the New Hampshire primary from a phony "Harlem for Muskie Committee" and the so-called "Canuck letter" accusing Muskie of slurring Franco-Americans who made up a significant voting bloc in the New England state.

William Loeb, the publisher of the fiercely conservative *Manchester Union Leader*, wrote a front-page editorial blasting Muskie, and reprinted a *Newsweek* article that cast his wife Jane in an uncomplimentary light. Muskie as an irate husband went to the paper on a snowy morning and castigated Loeb so vigorously that he lost his temper. Muskie seemed momentarily to break down and, some wrote, cry. Others said there were no tears, only melted snow running down his cheeks, and Muskie himself denied he had cried. But the upshot was a flood of stories about the candidate's unpresidential loss of control, and his fortunes plummeted. He won the New Hampshire primary over McGovern, but so unimpressively in his neighboring New England state that he never recovered.[21]

Other similar encounters were reported and later attributed not only to Segretti and his team but also to Colson and Chotiner. With Muskie no longer a serious factor for the Democratic nomination, the efforts were transferred to McGovern, but without such notable result. Agnew was never associated with any of these "dirty tricks," but he was directed to take up overt political criticisms of McGovern on the campaign trail.

With no serious challenge on the Republican side from either McCloskey or Ashbrook, and with Nixon's statement to Dan Rather that Agnew would again be his running mate if the Republican convention in the summer so "decided," it appeared that the Nixon–Agnew team was locked in. Connally had said he didn't want to be vice president and planned soon to resign as Nixon's treasury secretary, which he did in May.

All this while, Agnew was fortifying his standing with Nixon by giving him unreserved support to take stronger military action against North Vietnam. At a National Security Council meeting in mid-May, the mining of Haiphong harbor and the bombing of Hanoi were approaching decision point. Agnew—and Connally—took pointed issue with Mel Laird's opposing argument that most of the arms traffic was being shipped south by rail, and that it would be cheaper to beef up military equipment for the Saigon regime.

Kissinger later wrote: "Agnew was unequivocal that we simply could not afford to let South Vietnam collapse; it would have disastrous international consequences, especially in the Middle East and around the Indian Ocean. We were 'handcuffing ourselves' by being 'compulsive talkers'; the president really didn't have an option."[22] With such comments, the vice president not only demonstrated his continuing commitment to Nixon; he also offered a glimpse of what an Agnew presidency might hold in the realm of foreign policy—one that would be just as aggressive as it would be in domestic matters.

Shortly afterward, on May 19, when Agnew returned from another trip to the Far East, he triggered a Nixon explosion in the Oval Office by reporting that in South Vietnam he had been told by U.S. military leaders of restrictions on bombing North Vietnam. Kissinger, clearly upset, said the U.S. Air Force had been told there were only two minor restrictions in the Hanoi area. Admiral Thomas H. Moorer, the chairman of the Joint Chiefs of Staff, was waiting at the time in Kissinger's office. Nixon summoned him and, conveying what Agnew had said, read Moorer the riot act, warning he might clean house in the military, with his particular target Air Force Chief of Staff General John G. Ryan.

Before Moorer comes in, Nixon, as heard on tape, says to Kissinger: "I've never been given [the reason] why the air force has dropped the ball [on the North Vietnam bombing]. God-damn, I really got mad. I don't care. I want that head of the air force named Ryan, he's out today—Out! Out! Out!" When Moorer appears, he gets an earful.

NIXON: "I want to tell you something, and I've said this before and I'll say it again, Ryan better get off his God-damned ass. . . . You know and I know I've ordered that God-damned air force time and time again. . . . You know and I know they do not have a restriction about [the bombing] . . . and the air force didn't do a God-damn thing for the last three days, not one good God-damn thing in North Vietnam. . . . Because the little bastards were afraid they might not make it through . . . Bullshit. . . . They're telling the vice president this. . . . Never have they had the backing they've got today and I want to know the reason for it, or there's going to be a new chief of staff all up and down the line. Right now. Is that clear?"

MOORER: "Yes, sir."

NIXON: "Now get off your ass. . . . I want you to get that son of a bitch Ryan on the phone. I want you to get [Admiral John] McCain [the commander-in-Chief of Naval Operations in the Pacific, or CINCPAC] on the phone."[23]

Agnew, having ignited the outburst, just listened. The president, for all his reservations about him, apparently still took some of his fact-finding missions seriously.

❧ ❧

MEANWHILE, THE GALLUP POLL continued to show Agnew the clear preference of Republicans to remain as Nixon's running mate. The only ripple in that consensus came in Iowa when a resolution was offered at a meeting of the state party to leave Agnew's name off a resolution endorsing Nixon's reelection. It was rejected. In New York, liberal Republican Senator Jacob Javits, charging that Agnew's "name-calling adds nothing to the substance of the debate," urged that he be replaced on the ticket by either Rockefeller or Senator Ed Brooke of Massachusetts, to no avail.[24]

Shortly before Connally quit the cabinet, he and his wife Nellie hosted the Nixons at a big barbecue party at their Texas ranch, and talk of a Nixon–Connally ticket revived in that atmosphere. But the only result was the organizing by Connally of Democrats-for-Nixon, a major fund-raising effort that also helped deliver Texas to Nixon in the fall.[25]

Several weeks later, however, the subject of replacing Agnew with Connally cropped up again in a conversation in the Oval Office, when John Mitchell told Nixon he had asked the Texan whether he wanted to be president "when he finally got around to it." Connally replied, Mitchell reported, that "he wasn't seeking it, but he always liked to be where the power was, but he knew what a hard road it was to get to be president, that you've just got to drop out of sight and then come back. But he said very flatly that in his opinion that he would not want to be the vice president for four years under any circumstances. He doesn't want it, not the vice presidency. That's what he... and he did say he wanted it, but he didn't deny the fact that he would like to be president, and that he's—"

NIXON [breaking in]: "a realist, and has enough ego to serve, to realize that of the various people on the American political scene, he's probably the best qualified."

MITCHELL: "We discussed that thought..."

NIXON: "It's true."

MITCHELL: "And it *is* true."

Nixon: "And if you were to pick, John, out of our whole cabinet, out of the whole Congress and all governors, considering age and everything else, a man of ability and of the right age to be president, Connally is the best man, in my opinion."

MITCHELL: "I agree, I agree with that."

MITCHELL went on to tell Nixon that Connally had said "what he would be interested in, and he said that while he wasn't anxious to do it, but the only thing he would ever be interested in was the secretary of state's job. So [it would be] a clear indication that somewhere along the line after your second term even starts, there'll be a hell of a lot of people jockeying in the party for the position to succeed you. And I couldn't agree with this character[ization], this be thought of now and structured to the point where you want to pursue it. I don't know what you would think about John Connally as secretary of state, other than the fact that you know he'd clean that God-damned place out as fast [as to] make your head spin."

NIXON: "It would pose, you can imagine, an enormous problem with Henry, because John Connally, if he was secretary of state, *would be* secretary of state."

MITCHELL: "He would be secretary of state to the point where Henry wouldn't be. I'm not sure whether he wouldn't interfere with *your* activities."

NIXON: "No, I don't think it would. I found that with Connally at treasury, that [while] he has God-damned strong views, but if he ever gets the program he does it, he carries it out. That's something that we can take good care of, I think, and also we have to reconsider the interest in the situation in Henry's case. It may be that you first never of course discuss this. . . that his staying on in this kind of position [as national security adviser] is not the best solution."

MITCHELL: "That may very well be."

NIXON: "He's gone so far down this road, and he's been indispensable up to this point. Something we'd never discuss with him until we're ready to do it, Henry has this enormous political strength, but he has some problems in dealing with people."

MITCHELL: "He has that. He's developing a Kissinger cult and egotism and all the rest of it."

NIXON: "Connally, of course, the very natural move to the presidency would be from secretary of state. The only other at all possibility is defense, and that's also a possibility. . . ."

But Nixon had to know that Connally was too smart, especially given his long-range political ambitions, to take on running the Pentagon in the midst of a bogged-down war in Vietnam. Inevitably, the conversation turned to Agnew, and what to do about him.

NIXON: "He has an impression, you know, that the vice president really should have the role to come in and advise the president as to what to do about bombing Haiphong. He does, he participates in the NSC, but you cannot have a situation where the vice president can come in independently for the purpose of affecting the policy. That's a very difficult [notion] to understand. I had to go through it for eight years, it's damn hard, but it's the only way a man can serve in that job" [as Nixon did under Eisenhower].

MITCHELL: "I think Ted got off on the wrong foot with all the statements about what he was going to do in intergovernmental relations and domestic affairs, and so forth. He believed that channel, you know, so when we—"

NIXON (breaking in): "He [can do] as much as he wants to."

MITCHELL: "Well, when you're in these welfare programs . . . and so forth, sent over to him and they're foregone conclusions, you know, without any of his input, this is the thing that's really riling him more than anything else."

MITCHELL clearly was sympathetic to Agnew's plight—not surprising, in that he shared the vice president's tough law-and-order posture. And his own dour personality dovetailed with the now-gloomy attitude of Agnew, aware that he remained on the outside looking in, in terms of administration policy. Perhaps to assuage Mitchell's protective feelings toward the vice president, Nixon now struck a more sympathetic note of his own.

NIXON: "As far as he's concerned, of course, [he thinks of] the future. Of course he does have the hell of a problem that I had. Financially it [the vice presidency] is a loser. I mean, of all the jobs that I've had, the vice presidency is a God-damn [job for] losers. The one thing that I do think that we might be able to do for him . . . is that I intend to bite the bullet for a residence for the vice president, and I think we can do it. I can't do it before the election but I think immediately afterwards we could simply say, now it's time for the vice president to have a residence. Don't you think so? So that will take care of a hell of a lot of economic problems. Give him a residence, and some sort of a—"

MITCHELL: "Does that cost more, or less? Keeping it up?"

NIXON: "It'd be kept up by the government . . . so he can entertain. He lives in an attic apartment. . . . Well, that's something to just work out. It would be my intention immediately after the election just to bite the bullet and go right after it and force it through the damn Congress early. And I'd say in view of the enormous responsibilities of the vice president, particularly with the need to entertain [foreign visitors] and press, it's important to have a residence. . . ."

MITCHELL: "I think that would appeal to him, financially and otherwise, because he has very frequently mentioned the problems he has."[26]

Nixon never followed through on the idea, but it eventually came to pass—inadvertently, as a partial outcome of troubles of his own not foreseen at this time, but very soon to crash down on him. His later resignation brought about, among other things, the nomination and confirmation as vice president of Nelson Rockefeller, an enormously wealthy man who had a spacious mansion in the diplomatic neighborhood of Washington. He gave it to the government as the official vice-presidential residence. Meanwhile, Agnew as vice president continued to live in his apartment—and regularly receive free groceries delivered there by a Baltimore food store whose owner had been supplying him since his days as Baltimore county executive and governor of Maryland.

Nixon, in concluding his long chat with Mitchell, pondered Agnew's future after the vice presidency: "He once told me when I saw him in New York before he came out for me that his main interest was going on the court. I don't know why the hell anybody would want to go on the court, but you know he's a—, but I don't know what Agnew would do after the vice presidency. But that's his problem to some extent."

Mitchell responded: "You don't have to worry about Ted Agnew. He's enough of a public figure where he has an enormous capacity to make money, and that's one of the things, of course, he's never had during his life. "[27]

Haldeman, who had joined the Nixon–Mitchell conversation in its later stages, recounted the conversation in his diary, adding something that the White House tape did not include. He said Mitchell reported that Connally had commited "to changing parties but asked Mitchell when he ought to do it, and Mitchell said after the election, which Connally agreed to. Mitchell feels we should go on our basis that we have to, therefore, assume that Agnew is the candidate. But we should work on a deal with him and make sure we've got things split up right without letting him develop a high price for taking the job."[28]

The language hinted that Nixon had not abandoned the idea of getting rid of Agnew, only of postponing the notion until after the reelection of the Nixon–Agnew ticket, when Agnew could be persuaded to go on his own. At any rate, according to Nixon's later memoir, "on June 12 I asked Mitchell to tell Agnew I had made the decision definitely to have him on the ticket again as my running mate. I said that we would not announce it until after the Democratic convention. This would generate interest by creating suspense; it might also lead the Democrats to soft-pedal their attacks on him at their convention just in case I decided to choose someone else."[29] This last remark indicated that as far as Nixon was concerned, Agnew was still a pawn on the chess board to be moved around at will.

New concerns, however, were about to push aside the matter of what to do about this restless and, in the mind and preoccupation of the president, increasingly unsatisfactory vice president.

Chapter 17

FROM WATERGATE
TO RE-ELECTION

Sʜᴏʀᴛʟʏ ᴀꜰᴛᴇʀ ᴍɪᴅɴɪɢʜᴛ ꜰɪᴠᴇ ᴅᴀʏꜱ ᴀꜰᴛᴇʀ Hᴀʟᴅᴇᴍᴀɴ ʜᴀᴅ ʜɪꜱ conversation with Mitchell about Agnew, five men working in one capacity or another for the Committee to Re-elect the President (CREEP) broke into the Democratic National Committee headquarters at the Watergate hotel and office complex adjacent to the Kennedy Center.

The vice president was in his Washington apartment at what then was the Wardman Park Hotel on the night of the break-in. At that time, the top operatives of the Nixon campaign, including Mitchell and his chief lieutenant at CREEP, Jeb Magruder, were in Los Angeles for meetings with leading California Republicans, and a major "Celebrities for Nixon" party the following day. On learning the news, they caught an early flight back to Washington.

Later the next day, a Sunday, Agnew, now also aware of the break-in as reported in *The Washington Post*, became restless. Looking for a tennis match, he phoned his aide and frequent partner, John Damgard, who had just returned weary from a weekend party on Maryland's Eastern Shore. Damgard, preferring in his hung-over state to play doubles, readily found a third player and, searching for a fourth, tracked down Magruder, who by this time was at Mitchell's Watergate apartment.

Unknown to Agnew, a desperate strategy meeting was going on. According to Magruder later, the "bitter, despondent" tone of it made him glad to get the tennis invitation as an excuse to get away. As Damgard remembered, Magruder said into the phone within earshot of Mitchell: "Of course I haven't forgotten. No, no. Me disappoint the vice president? Certainly not. I'll be leaving here momentarily."[1] He soon showed up at the Linden Hall indoor court off the Capital Beltway bearing his tennis racquet and a briefcase stuffed with papers.

A curious Agnew took Magruder aside between games and asked him: "Jeb, what the hell is going on?" Magruder replied: "It was our operation. It got screwed up. We're trying to take care of it." That was all Agnew wanted to hear. He told his young associate: "I don't think we ought to discuss it again, in that case."[2]

After the tennis match, as Damgard was giving Magruder a lift home, the young CREEP official suddenly asked to be driven back to the court. He had forgotten the briefcase he had left at courtside, and Damgard could tell from his manner that it must have contained something very important. Damgard complied and Magruder fetched the briefcase sitting where he had left it. Upon being dropped off at about midnight, he went to his kitchen for a glass of milk. Then Magruder took a light-gray folder from the briefcase and examined its contents. They comprised charts and descriptions of the grandiose political espionage schemes of G. Gordon Liddy, a former FBI agent, and E. Howard Hunt, a CIA retiree, working covertly under Mitchell at CREEP to undermine the Democratic campaign.

The proposed capers ran from kidnappings of anti-war demonstrators at the approaching Republican convention to bugging the rival nominees' campaign plane and buses; from luring Democratic politicians to a floating brothel at the Democratic National Convention in Miami Beach to sabotaging the air-conditioning at the convention hall. The project bore an original price tag of a million dollars, later whittled down to a fourth of that.[3] Hunt had labeled the whole bizarre operation "Gemstone," and Magruder had eventually become the custodian of the files dealing with covert operations in his office at CREEP. The Watergate break-in was among them.

Before departing Los Angeles, Magruder had phoned his administrative assistant, Robert Reisner, telling him to go into the office and take all the files to his home. Bob Odle, the campaign's director of adminstration, was already there, showing a panicked Liddy how to use a paper shredder. When Reisner couldn't get all the papers into his briefcase, he asked Odle to take the rest, which consisted of the Gemstone file. On arrival home he put the file in a closet. Later he gave it to Magruder, who had it with him when he went to play tennis with Agnew. Examining the file in his kitchen that night, Magruder recalled having asked Mitchell before leaving the apartment for the tennis court what he should do with the Gemstone papers. Mitchell, Magruder recalled, told him: "Maybe you ought to have a little fire at your house tonight."[4]

So before going to bed, Magruder took out the papers, walked into his living room, and built a fire in the fireplace. Then, examining each sheet in turn, he fed the file into the flame. The stir apparently woke his wife, Gail, who came to the doorway. She asked him: "What in the world are you doing? You're going to burn the house down." Her husband replied: "It's all right. It's just some papers I have to get rid of." When he finished, they turned in.[5]

The Gemstone file sitting at the tennis court as Agnew, Magruder, and their partners played doubles that night apparently was the closest involvement the vice president ever came to the whole Watergate scandal. He did phone Haldeman later but essentially was told to stay out of the whole business and focus on criticism of George McGovern, who by now seemed well on his way to the Democratic nomination. So Agnew did just that. For once, his isolation from the Nixon inner circle, which so irritated him, was proving to be a political blessing. According to Gold, when a reporter asked Nixon whether he had talked to Agnew about the Watergate fiasco, Nixon replied: "Of course not."[6]

Around this time, Agnew did not need to say or do much to undermine McGovern, who was having problems enough within his own party and campaign. After defeating Humphrey in the last significant primary, in California, in early June, McGovern had to overcome a convention fight over the allocation of California's delegates before finally nailing down his nomination. Then, after torturous discussion with his campaign staff, his choice of Senator Thomas Eagleton of Missouri to be his running mate backfired badly on him. Disclosure that Eagleton had had a history of mental illness, including resort to electrical shock therapy, eventually forced Eagleton's withdrawal and produced a drawn-out search for a replacement. Several prominent Democrats, seeing McGovern already as a lost cause, declined until Sargent Shriver, the

Kennedy in-law and former Peace Corps and anti-poverty chief under Johnson, accepted. The McGovern candidacy was in a shambles well before the fall campaign had begun.

On the night McGovern made his acceptance speech, Nixon had Connally in for a small dinner, with only Haldeman also present. The primary purpose was to discuss Connally's direction of Democrats-for-Nixon, but the Agnew question dominated the talk again. As Haldeman recorded later: "Connally made it clear that he felt the P could not do anything but keep Agnew on, although he thinks it's a bad choice. But he and the P agree that there's no qualification there for the presidency and he's not who we want for P, so that poses a problem of having him for VP. But I don't think Connally was making any real pitch for the job himself. . . . The P made the point that the VP can resign during the second term and that there are other possibilities for the man the P wants to set up as his successor."[7]

A week later, Nixon told Haldeman to advise Connally that he, Nixon, had no choice but to go ahead with Agnew on the ticket, but that "the P is absolutely convinced that he [Agnew] should not be the candidate [in 1976] and that there's no question about that, but the P has worked out a way to move him out after the election" and again that "the P has made up his mind who it has to be to succeed him, which Connally knows, and he has a way to work that out."[8]

During this period, Agnew was more occupied staying in Nixon's good graces than in adding to McGovern's woes. Shortly after the Democratic convention, Haldeman made this diary entry that suggested Nixon's determination to keep his ambitious vice president in his place: "He [Nixon] got into a discussion on how to handle Agnew. He feels we must not build him up in terms of where he goes and so forth. That we should put him in the South, the small states. No important duties. He feels he shouldn't have played tennis Saturday morning. He should have prepared for his press conference instead."[9]

But Agnew still did not seem to get it. As he was about to go out campaigning in Oregon in late July, Nixon decided it was time to make a firm announcement that Agnew would be on the ticket again. "The P, Mitchell and I met with the VP and the P hit him hard on the way he wants him to handle his campaign," Haldeman wrote. "Emphasizing no attacks on the press, to attack McGovern only on the issues, not personally. To ignore Eagleton, not let himself become the issue, stay non-controversial, no discussion or comment on '76. . . . The VP, incredibly, raised the point that he was going to hit the press again in Oregon. Mitchell and the P told him he must not do that."[10]

The contrasting way in which Nixon dealt with Agnew and Connally was instructive of the president's attitude toward each. When Connally in early August announced his formation of Democrats-for-Nixon, Haldeman wrote regretfully that it "was done via press conference because he [Connally] refused to take advantage of the equal time opportunity we had, so didn't get on TV, which is a real tragedy, but that's the way he wanted it, so that's the way it was done. Unfortunately, we have to handle him that way to survive."[11]

Connally by this time not only was overseeing the formation of Democrats-for-Nixon but also serving as key adviser in the Nixon campaign on strategy. He also was holding the hand of George Wallace, who was strongly anti-McGovern, to make sure he didn't succumb to pressure to run as a third-party candidate again, despite his crippling physical condition.[12] A few days later, Nixon phoned Wallace and told him Connally was his man whenever Wallace wanted anything.[13]

Instead of being able to rely on Agnew as another former governor to handle that task, Nixon had to endure more irritations from his vice president. Around this time, Haldeman wrote, "The VP called concerned about a problem with Sinatra and the Democrats. Sinatra was miffed that the VP didn't call him, instead of Connally, but he's aboard now and is giving some money."[14] Haldeman simply brushed off the lament.

Nixon, frustrated by such diversions from Agnew, wished he would stick to the one task he did best—doing an imitation of the Old Nixon against the political opposition. In 1952 and 1956 as Eisenhower's running mate, Nixon had single-mindedly zeroed in on Democratic presidential nominee Adlai Stevenson, paying little attention to his running mates. By this time, Shriver had replaced Eagleton on the Democratic ticket, and Nixon told Haldeman he "wanted to be sure that Agnew stays on an attack on McGovern, not on Shriver, that he should ignore Shriver totally."[15]

That seemed to be Agnew's intent, but as the Republican convention in Miami Beach approached, he did something, perhaps inadvertently, that rattled Nixon, or at least Haldeman, once again. As Haldeman described it: "We had a 90-minute flap with the VP regarding his seconding speeches, because he decided yesterday to have Dr. Joyce Brothers, the psychologist, be one of the seconders, and they went ahead and asked her. This obviously would be a disaster, in that it would look like he got his own psychiatrist to prove he isn't nuts like Eagleton is. After going around on it, I called him back, told him he couldn't do it, he said he wanted to check with P." So Haldeman did so. "The P agreed, [so I] called him back again, said that is the decision, he agreed to go along with it, although it would be very difficult for him, since he has now to turn her off."[16]

Once again, Agnew had been rebuffed by Nixon, via Haldeman. Had Connally made such a proposal, it was highly unlikely that it would have been rejected in that abrupt fashion. But the different personal chemistry that existed between Nixon and Agnew and Nixon and Connally explained why.

A few days before the convention opened, Nixon gave Haldeman further instructions that he did not want in any way to indicate he looked upon Agnew as the person he wanted to replace him in the White House in 1977.

Haldeman wrote: "He [Nixon] wants to be in the hall before the VP is introduced, he went through the details on how he wants the onstage procedure, that is, the VP to come up and then Mrs. Nixon up and then the family. He doesn't want anything with the two families together, and he wants to be sure the VP understands no hands-over-head type shots."[17] The latter pose, known as "the armpit shot" in the political trade, might have connoted to viewers an endorsement that Nixon did not want to convey. For all that, Nixon in his acceptance speech left the impression that all was rosy between him and his vice president. Congratulating the convention for renominating Agnew, he told the delegates: "I thought he was the best man for the job four years ago. I think he's the best man for the job today." He added, a bit prematurely as matters turned out: "And I'm not going to change my mind tomorrow."[18]

The Republican convention concluded with hardly a hitch, as Democratic efforts to fan the embers of the Watergate break-in into a full-blown campaign issue got nowhere. For all of Agnew's growing reputation as a negative campaigner, none of the stories about Nixon administration corruption and dirty tricks touched him. He was neither plugged in enough to be involved in them nor trusted enough among the policy makers and political strategists at CREEP or the White House to be told much of what was going on.

෨෦ ෨෦

As THE FALL CAMPAIGN ran its course, McGovern was unable to gain a foothold, either on the Watergate story or with his outspoken opposition to the Vietnam War. Agnew meanwhile reworked the themes that had carried the day in the 1968 campaign—law and order and the demonization of McGovern as a soft-on-communism, soft-on-protesters liberal who wanted to coddle welfare cheats with wild giveaway schemes. Once again, Agnew did not campaign with Nixon, but he aggressively defended him on Watergate.

Insisting in mid-September that he would "adopt a new style. . . that will not place a misconstruction upon my intent," Agnew nevertheless continued to accentuate the negative. In a speech in Minneapolis, he suggested that the Watergate break-in had been instigated to embarrass the president and his party. He accused Democratic National Chairman Lawrence O'Brien of trying to smear the Nixon administration with a "patently political suit" linking Republican officials to the break-in.[19]

In London, Kentucky, a few nights later, Agnew charged McGovern with "agonizing over the continuation" of the Vietnam War and condemned him for advocating amnesty for draft evaders. And in Rapid City, South Dakota, McGovern's home state, the vice president accused him of waging a campaign of "smear and innuendo"—while doing just that himself.

Neither the style nor the rhetoric of the self-proclaimed New Agnew seemed much different from those of the Old, all in the service of the man who had made him vice president.[20] Nixon repeatedly cautioned Agnew not to engage in personal attacks, and on several occasions he called on Connally to make speeches previously assigned to the vice president. Even in Agnew's supposed area of political strength, Connally was being moved in as having more credibility.[21]

Agnew nevertheless continued to relish his old role as attack dog, and any efforts to rein him in, even for legitimate reasons that had nothing to do with dissatisfaction with his style, irritated him. Of one such instance in late September, Haldeman wrote: "We had a flap tonight on the possibility of a tie vote on the Anti-War Amendment in the Senate tomorrow.

The VP was supposed to be speaking in Texas tomorrow morning. [Legislative liaison chief Bill] Timmons wanted him brought back up. He was balking. So after an entire evening of back and forth phone calls, I finally called the P who said he should come back. That he shouldn't run the risk of being caught out campaigning on a tie vote, and that even though there wasn't much chance, it wasn't worth taking any risk on it, so I called the VP and he's on his way back first thing in the morning."[22]

Throughout this time, while playing the role of loyal team player, Agnew did not fail to consider his own future, and his own prospects to succeed Nixon in the 1976 election—or before. Gold recalled later that at one point Agnew asked him about the protocol if something were to happen to Nixon before the November election or, assuming the Nixon–Agnew team was reelected, before their inaugural for a second term. Nixon's death or other departure from office in advance of the election would make Agnew president for the rest of the first term, presumably with the Republican National Committee deciding whether Agnew or someone else would become the presidential nominee in the November election. If a reelected Nixon were out somehow before his inauguration for a second term, the presidency would be vacant and the first-term vice president simply would be elevated to the position for the remaining days of the first term. But the Twenty-fifth Amendment dealing with presidential succession in the event of death, resignation, or other incapacitation did not specify who, in that event, would be inaugurated for the new term.

Beyond such hypotheticals, Agnew clearly had his eye on 1976, and how he could best position himself to be the Republican presidential nominee four years hence. Nixon likewise was already looking past the November election, but to ways of trimming Agnew's wings. Three weeks before the balloting, according to Haldeman, Nixon said he was "concerned about how we're going to cut Agnew's staff" as part of a basic second-term reorganization. It would soon become clear that Nixon intended to go beyond that in discouraging Agnew's prospects to be his eventual successor.[23]

In 1972, Agnew was not kept on such a tight leash as he had been in the 1968 campaign, with the benign Bryce Harlow on his plane. Near the end of the campaign, McGovern in a nationally televised speech accused Nixon of "cruel, political deception" on the Vietnam peace talks, charging that a claim of a "major breakthrough" was no more than a campaign tactic. A panicked Nixon ordered Agnew to put out a statement that came close to accusing McGovern of treason. But Haldeman, according to Gold later, had earlier instructed Agnew to tone down his rhetoric, so the excitable Gold, seeing a possible voter backlash, persuaded Agnew to appeal the decision. He phoned Haldeman, who checked with Nixon, and then told Agnew to "forget about it."[24] Agnew settled for saying of McGovern that "never before has desperation and thwarted ambition reduced a nominee to this level of fabricated distortion," and "never before has selfish naiveté provided such a plus for enemy propaganda."[25]

On the final weekend, the Agnew party was in Los Angeles when Haldeman called and instructed the vice president to scrap his scheduled events and return to Washington at once, to appear on one of the Sunday morning talk shows because McGovern was going to be on it. Again Gold complained to Agnew, pointing out that the Republican ticket was more than thirty percentage points ahead. But Agnew said he was following orders, so the party flew back east. On arrival, Agnew learned there was a labor strike against the television station and neither candidate appeared.[26] It was clear that Agnew was not completely on his own after all.

On election night, a resounding landslide victory for the Nixon–Agnew team appeared to assure the "Four More Years" of its campaign slogan and, regardless of what Nixon wanted, for Agnew a firm stepping-stone to a presidential candidacy in 1976. The vice president joined a noisy victory party at a Washington hotel, looking ahead to a bright political future.

☙ ❧

BUT A WEEK AFTER the Nixon–Agnew landslide victory, Nixon at Camp David called in Haldeman and Ehrlichman and addressed what now was generally called by them "the Agnew problem" and how he intended to deal with it in the second term. He was planning a sweeping reorganization that would include downsizing Agnew's staff, often a source of inner-circle criticism and ridicule in the first term. Nixon also made clear that he had no intention of assisting the vice president in using his office to advance his 1976 presidential aspirations.

Haldeman wrote afterward that "he [Nixon] wanted me to talk to him [Agnew] and explain that we have a tough thing to do here, that he must cut, that we cut all the way across including his staff. He feels that we need to keep our leverage over him, so we shouldn't break off with him now, but we do not further his interests politically in '76. We don't want him to have the appearance of being the heir apparent, [but] we also don't want to appear to push him down."[27]

This last remark seemed a Nixon recognition of the popularity and stature that Agnew had achieved in the party and with the public as a result of his high-profile speech-making in the first term. He may have gotten too big for his boots as far as the Nixon inner circle was concerned, but at the same time he had become a political force who could not be handled cavalierly either.

With the two hundredth anniversary of the Declaration of Independence coming up in 1976, Nixon told his aides it offered an ideal way to sidetrack Agnew in the second term. "We should pitch the Bicentennial for him as a great opportunity," he said, according to Haldeman later. "Agnew is not the ideal choice, but he may be the best of a bad lot."[28]

The next day, still at Camp David, Nixon called Agnew in. Haldeman and Ehrlichman, the White House "Berlin Wall," were again present, in keeping with Nixon's disinclination toward solo confrontations. "We started out by reviewing the campaign," Haldeman wrote, but they didn't get very far before "the VP started talking about the problems that he has in his role, particularly in intergovernmental relations [as liaison with state and local officials]. That they're not in the flow of policy formulation. The P interrupted and said, well, under our reorganization plans, this whole intergovernmental relations thing should be in OMB [Office of Management and Budget] or HUD [Housing and Urban Development], and our reorganization gets into this."[29]

In other words, Nixon was going to take away from Agnew the prime assignment he had given him in the first term, amid much malarkey about how the former Maryland governor was so ideally suited for it. It was a judgment severely challenged by, among other things, Agnew's fiasco of a meeting with the Republican governors on the occasion of the 1970 appointment of Democrat John Connally to be Nixon's secretary of the treasury, when so many GOP governors had just lost their seats and were job-hunting.

Nixon now told Agnew he would have Haldeman and Ehrlichman—the latter particularly not trusted by the vice president, as a rival in the domestic-affairs arena—discuss the change with him after this meeting. Nixon went on, according to Haldeman: "He said the VP should be dealing with important matters instead, that he and the P shouldn't have to take the heat on these intergovernmental matters. That they should stay out of solving their [the governors'] troubles, that he should stay on the highest level. We should set up effective machinery to handle these matters, keep the P and VP out of the crossfire and stay out of the nuts and bolts. He said what he should do, [the VP] is to continue his participation in the foreign field. Deal off a lot of the clerical stuff, get into new things, not just [be] the P's errand boy to the mayors and governors."

Then Nixon made his best snake-oil-salesman pitch: "The best big new thing would be the Bicentennial, a major public event of the administration, involving all 50 states and all foreign countries. Jimmy Roosevelt is going to be our ambassador abroad on this, and the VP could pick that up. This he should take on as a major responsibility, get it on track. It's an opportunity to get high-powered people, rather than just a mediocre staff. And he talked about enlisting our New American Majority as the focal point for the Bicentennial. . . . He should not move fast, he should get a really high power group of PR people, writers, not partisan, bring in the Democrats who have supported us."

But Agnew was not going to be an easy sell: "The VP raised the question of Indian Affairs, said he's very interested in that, [but] the P said that he thinks it's a loser and the VP should not be tied to a loser. The VP then said he had reservations about the Bicentennial, and that he wants a chance to do selected tasks in the foreign field, K [Kissinger]-type missions in the foreign area. [Agnew didn't have to point out that he wanted the sort of assignments Nixon had used under Eisenhower to boost his stature as a prospective presidential candidate.] The P agreed that he [Agnew] should not just do goodwill trips and funerals, but that he shouldn't worry about this. We'll handle it, setting him up for some single-shot negotiations, and foreign economic things. The P makes the point that what makes the VP important is what he does on the big play, not the number of jobs he has."

Haldeman concluded the entry by saying: "John and I then met with him. . . and went through the reorganization thing, which he was in basic agreement with. He [Agnew] got again into the staff and made the point that he was scared of the Bicentennial, because he thinks it could be disastrous, you can't satisfy people, and it would lead only to trouble."[30]

Agnew was not swallowing the unsubtle sidetrack. As he wrote later, "after the 1972 election, there was a lot of tough talk going around about cleaning house. In the upper echelons everybody's resignation was requested, and the word went forth that people who didn't do what the president wanted were going to have their resignations accepted." Agnew wasn't worried. "I thought," he wrote, "as a vice president who worked hard and contributed to our election by a huge majority, I will receive some praise this time. I will get a very big, important assignment. But my actual assignment made me shudder. . . . The president sat silently as John Ehrlichman said: 'We think you ought to spend most of your time working on the Bicentennial.' The Bicentennial? I could hardly believe my ears."

Agnew went on: "Gentlemen," I said, "I look upon the Bicentennial as a loser, because everybody has his own ideas about it and nobody can be the head of it without making a million enemies." So I said, 'No,' and I made it stick."[31]

Later, however, Agnew soon came up with a bright idea on the Bicentennial that he passed on to Ehrlichman. "He'd had an inspiration," Ehrlichman wrote later. "The chairmanship was vacant, and he had just the man. How about a nationally renowned—no, world-renowned—figure; an ethnic—an Italian—an able executive? How about Frank Sinatra? Agnew by now had become quite chummy with the singer and was a frequent guest at his home in Palm Springs. He apparently saw himself as Sinatra's emissary to the president."

Ehrlichman went on: "I gulped. 'I'll refer your idea to the president,' I promised. But I'd seen Sinatra's thick FBI package, full of innuendos about connections with organized crime. I couldn't imagine trying to get him through a Senate confirmation. When I told the president about Agnew's idea, he just laughed. I called Spiro Agnew back to tell him Sinatra was not acceptable, and I could tell the vice president was very disappointed. He told me how well he and Sinatra would work together. I'm sure at the time, Agnew still hoped to be vice president on July 4,

1976. And I fully expected him to be. But he didn't press hard for Sinatra's appointment. Perhaps Agnew was husbanding his strength for a battle he could foresee. Or perhaps he already sensed he was beaten."[32]

According to his press secretary, Vic Gold, a confidante at the time, Agnew was particularly crushed by having his role as intergovernmental relations liaison taken from him, and having his staff severely slashed. "He came back from that meeting [with Nixon at Camp David], he came into the office and nobody heard from him for two weeks," Gold recalled. "Then he was calling people in one by one [to tell them they were being let go]. This was not something Agnew wanted to do. As rebellious as he seemed, he said, 'Victor, there's a lot of power there and I can't fight it.'" Agnew, his press secretary recalled, interpreted Nixon's attitude toward him as signalling that "you are not going to be my successor if I can help it."[33]

❦ ❦

MEANWHILE, as part of Nixon's reorganization discussions, he had Connally in at Camp David for a long talk that again underscored that it was he, and not Agnew, that the reelected and hence lame-duck president had in mind as the next president. Unlike Agnew, Connally—back in his Texas law firm—met with the president alone and Nixon filled in his chief of staff later.

"He says that Connally has concluded," Haldeman subsequently wrote, "that there's no hope for him in the Democratic Party. He feels that if he could get the Democratic nomination he could run and beat Agnew, as a Democrat, but that he could also run as a Republican and beat [Ted] Kennedy, and he thinks that it's inevitable that Kennedy would get the [Democratic] nomination. He also, in effect, therefore decided to change parties and become a Republican. The question is a matter of timing, and what he does beyond that.

"The P discussed the possibility of an administration role with him, and the two apparently agreed it would not be wise for Connally to come [back] in. He doesn't want secretary of defense in any event, feels he couldn't take state as long as K is there. He doesn't want to do that anyway because he has a lot of opportunity to make money this year, and wants to spend his time doing that. Figures he can make $10-to-$15 million on some land deals and that sort of thing, and after that he can come back into the public sector. The P encouraged him to change parties quickly, which would send up a lot of signals and establish him clearly as a candidate for '76 and get some of the people rolling that might be able to be helpful to him. Apparently a satisfactory meeting for both people, at least the P thought so."[34]

Agnew, meanwhile, was all too cognizant of Nixon's ardor for Connally. "At first," he wrote later, "I didn't believe the reports that the president was thinking of dumping me. He would often volunteer for my benefit in the presence of others, 'That's just a lot of political talk. The biggest game in Washington is to create a fight between the president and the vice president.' However, I noticed that he became more remote towards me as his attachment to Connally grew. In a crisis, or simply when he wanted to expand on some subject to someone with whom he felt comfortable, Connally would be called to the Oval Office. . . . The press noticed immediately that Connally was being brought into the inner circle while I was being kept out."

Agnew denied any hostility toward Connally "but naturally a rivalry grew up between us," he wrote, "as the media tried to goad me into saying something against him. I remember that once, when I arrived late at a luncheon, I told this joke: 'I'm sorry to be late. I did my best to hurry, but John Connally had me down at his ranch for a barbecue, and it took me an hour and a half to cut myself down from the spit.'"[35] The audience laughed, but it wasn't funny to the increasingly rejected Agnew.

Had the vice president known the extent to which Nixon was thinking this early about positioning Connally for the presidency in 1976, he certainly wouldn't have laughed, either. Haldeman on the first day of December wrote of how a Connally-for-President discussion with Nixon and Ehrlichman led to more talk "of forming a new party. . . that you use the Republican Party as a base, but add to it the New Majority. Use Connally as the focal-point candidate, but that the P has to take the lead. The P was intrigued with this as a possibility, recognizing that you can never really go with the P's party into a majority and into a viable ongoing party." It was, as later events showed, an unduly pessimistic outlook about the GOP alone achieving majority status. Haldeman went on: "The question is whether it can be done and whether we really want to make the effort."[36]

Connally a few days later weighed in with his own view. He told Nixon, according to Haldeman, "that the third-party route just isn't workable, and there's no point in trying it. He does feel that we could do something in the way of reestablishing the Republican Party in a different way, with a new name such as the Republican Independent Party. It would clearly put a new cast on it, but not lose the base that we have now, which Connally feels is indispensable. . . . Connally's feeling, however, is that he [Nixon] shouldn't change things when they are going well, and that we're in a pretty good position now, we ought to leave it that way. . . . It was left that Connally would explore, and nothing really was settled."[37]

In early December, the vice president was saved from another demonstration of Nixon's lack of confidence in him, and a consequent boost for Connally. Agnew was poised to fly to Saigon to brief President Thieu on the peace agreement Kissinger was negotiating in Paris and was expected to consummate shortly. As complications arose, Kissinger wrote later, Nixon "developed second thoughts about Agnew's going to Saigon, fearing that once there he might side with Thieu against his own administration; he now wanted to send Connally. Haig argued him out of that because no private emissary could possibly carry the clout of the holder of a constitutional office, and because Agnew's known proclivities to the right would give added weight to his support of the agreement."[38] In the end, a breakdown in the talks led to cancellation of the trip.

In mid-December, amid much consternation among members of the cabinet, Nixon gave them all a dinner at the White House. All had been asked to submit pro forma resignations to free the president's hand for the second term and some had already been given their walking papers. Nixon made a little rambling talk about the importance of the cabinet and then, notably, had Haldeman give a toast to Agnew, rather than doing it himself.[39] Nixon and Agnew thus approached what each expected to be another four years of their political marriage, which in the first four had turned from ardent to distinctly cool at best.

In fact, the new year had barely begun when Nixon was agitating again about his grand scheme of shunting Agnew aside for the 1976 presidential nomination and, if at all possible, positioning Connally—as a Republican convert—for it. On January 8, Haldeman recorded in his diary that Nixon "told me to talk to Connally to get him to tell us when he's going to move—that if he doesn't decide on a party thing, we're going to have a problem, because we have to have another horse than Agnew. We got into the general political discussion that we can't allow Agnew to get the nomination, but there is no other real possibility except Connally."[40]

Meanwhile, Agnew had another brainstorm to bolster his own resumé in the second term.

Chapter 18

BAD NEWS
FROM BALTIMORE

Less than two weeks into the new year of 1973, Ted Agnew displayed another example of his restlessness, as critical talks on peace in Vietnam were going on in Paris and the Watergate scandal continued to simmer amid more newspaper disclosures, principally in *The Washington Post*.

As Haldeman's diary recorded: "The VP requested a meeting with the P today, [and] came in with an incredible proposal. He thought that something ought to be done to divert public attention from Vietnam and the attacks we're getting into on it. He suggested that he take a trip to Egypt to visit [President Anwar] Sadat, and see if he could try to untangle something on the Middle East. The P was obviously so astonished he didn't know quite how to answer the thing at first, but then made the point that the likelihood of anything good coming out of such a trip was almost zero, and that it would be very unwise for the VP to take the risk of being rebuffed at that high level, which was a nice way of getting him out of it.

"It was obvious that the VP kept pushing it, and saying, well, you know I could do it because of Sadat's threats, and all that sort of thing. And we finally got through to him that the P had no intention of letting him go, so he backed off that. Then admitted, really, that what he was after was a way to rebuild his own image, and that he's being attacked

because of the one substantive thing that he had was the intergovernmental relations and that had been taken away from him, so he had nothing
really of importance to do. . . . The meeting really wasn't very productive
because of the total ludicrousness of the VP's reason for coming in."[1]

Foreign travel was traditionally a way for a presidential aspirant to
boost his resumé as a man adequately backgrounded to assume "the leadership of the free world," or at least hold his own with other world leaders.
In terms of purely domestic politics, White House hopefuls often toured
what was known in the political community as "the 3-I League"—
Ireland, Italy, and Israel—to demonstrate their interest and concern to the
large Irish, Italian, and Jewish constituencies at home. Agnew's choice of
Egypt certainly did not fit into this stereotype tour of would-be presidents,
but such a trip at this point doubtless would have earned him news media
coverage, though not necessarily of the sort he was after.

Instead, Nixon gave him a more politically advantageous overseas assignment in February—a trip to South Vietnam, about which a few
weeks earlier a peace agreement had been struck in Paris. Agnew went to
Saigon to tell President Thieu on behalf of Nixon that the United States
would continue to recognize his regime as the legitimate government
there. The vice president continued on to eight other Asian nations and
had a fine time.

But the trip didn't seem to placate the frustrated Agnew for long. A
few days later Haldeman got a call from him asking "why he had been
excluded" from a breakfast meeting of the bipartisan congressional leadership. "He was distressed and more or less hung up on me," Haldeman
noted in his diary. "The reason being of course that it was a breakfast
meeting, which the P has frequently and has never included the VP, so
there was nothing unusual about it at all."[2] That was precisely what ag-
gravated Agnew—that there was nothing unusual about his always being
on the outside looking in.

The same, apparently, was the case for his wife Judy. On February 7,
close personal Nixon aide David Parker had sent a memo to Haldeman
marked "Eyes Only" and "High Priority" recommending some ideas
upon Agnew's return from the Far East, "in an effort to increase exposure
for the vice president to the president and in an effort to better build the
relationship." He listed them in bullet form, with a place below each for
Haldeman to mark his decision:

"1. Mrs. Agnew is planning on meeting the vice president when he returns to California either Friday evening or early Saturday morning. It would be a nice gesture on the part of the president and Mrs. Nixon to invite Mrs. Agnew to ride out to California with them tomorrow. Mrs. Agnew's agents would not have to accompany her on the aircraft and would be directed to meet her on arrival at El Toro and they in turn would escort her off to her hotel."

APPROVE_____ DISAPPROVE_____

"2. Earlier you had asked if it would be necessary to have the president and Mrs. Nixon host a small dinner for the Agnews, if Mrs. Agnew accompanied the vice president on his trip. Since she did not accompany him, there will be no compelling reason to host such a luncheon or dinner; however, you might want to reconsider and extend such an invitation."

APPROVE_____ DISAPPROVE_____

Lunch on Saturday _____ Dinner on Saturday _____

"3. After the president receives the vice president's report on his Southeast Asian trip, I would recommend that consideration be given to the president suggesting to the vice president that . . . (A) he take a short rest and offer him the use of his Key Biscayne home for three or four days after his Lincoln Day Address on the 12th in L.A."

APPROVE_____ DISAPPROVE___

After each of the three recommendations for a gesture of friendship and cordiality to the Agnews, the initial "H" [for Haldeman] appeared on the DISAPPROVE line.[3]

In the face of such untogetherness, the vice president could console himself, however, with the thought that Nixon was now a lame duck, and his own high standing among Republicans in the polls led to musings of a brighter political future. Agnew professed to see that "political power began to make a subtle shift, away from the president and towards me," he wrote later. Nixon, he acknowledged, "still retained a lot of power," but Agnew held that "the politicians began instinctively turning away from the president" and toward him as the frontrunner, looking to 1976.[4]

If so, there was one other circumstance that more obviously benefited the vice president; not being a Nixon insider, he continued to be kept in the dark about details of the Watergate affair. By now the scandal was swirling around the heads of the president and his chief White House aides, with several of them facing grand jury appearances. In January, the Watergate burglars and their chief accomplices had been tried before a no-nonsense federal judge, John Sirica. Five had pleaded guilty and two CREEP operatives who had pleaded not guilty, Liddy and James M. McCord Jr., were convicted of conspiracy, burglary, and wiretapping. In early February, the Senate voted unanimously to create a Select Committee to investigate Watergate, chaired by Democratic Senator Sam Ervin of North Carolina. All this threw the White House into a panic, from which Agnew as a result of his isolation was exempt.

At this time, I had just joined *The Washington Post* from the *Los Angeles Times* and was assigned to cover the Watergate hearings, writing daily color and analysis. Being at the *Post* at this precise moment put me on the fringes of a cauldron of journalistic excitement, shortly before the paper received the Pulitzer Prize for its leading role in uncovering the Nixon administration misconduct. Agnew may have been a hot item in Republican circles, but he was no more than a blip on the screen of the news business as attention and tension mounted in Washington over the developing Watergate story.

On March 19, Nixon and friends had even more reason to sweat about it. McCord took it upon himself to write a letter to Sirica telling him the other defendants had committed perjury, that others not identified had been involved. McCord's letter hinted at White House obstruction of justice and a cover-up that soon imperiled even the president's highest aides, Haldeman and Ehrlichman.

Two days later, on March 21, Nixon had a conversation with Haldeman and John Dean, the young White House counsel who had been assigned to monitor the unraveling Watergate scandal and make recommendations to Haldeman on how to cope with it. Dean is heard on a White House tape saying an old Nixon hand, Fred LaRue, was working to raise as much as a million dollars to buy the silence of the arrested Watergate burglars. "Apparently he talked to Tom Pappas [a wealthy Greek-American businessman and investor from Boston]. . . and Pappas has, uh, agreed to come up with a sizeable amount, I gather. . . from

Mitchell." A few minutes later, Dean tells Nixon that the burglars were "going to stonewall it, as it now stands. Except for [E. Howard] Hunt [one of the break-in organizers on the CREEP payroll]. That's why, that's the leverage in his threat [of talking unless he got hush money]." Haldeman interjects: "This is Hunt's opportunity," and Dean agrees.

Nixon joins in: "That's why your... immediate thing, you've got no choice with Hunt but the hundred or twenty or whatever it is, right?... Would you agree... you better damn well get that done, but fast?"

Dean: "I think he ought to be given some signal anyway...."

Dean goes on to say he had called Mitchell the previous night "and I said, 'Have you talked to, to Pappas?' He was at home and Martha [Mitchell's erratic wife] picked up the phone so it was all in, in code. 'Did you talk to the Greek?' And he said, uh, 'Yes I have,' and I said, 'Is the Greek bearing gifts?' He said, 'Well, I want to call you tomorrow on that.'"

Nixon, saying, "I am, uh, unfamiliar with the money situation," asks Dean "if you had it, where would you, how would you get it to somebody?" Dean tells him that "I gather [Fred] LaRue just leaves it in mail boxes and things like that, and tells Hunt to go pick it up.... As I say, we're a bunch of amateurs in that business." Dean goes on to say, "You got to wash money and all that sort, you know, if you get a hundred thousand out of a bank, and it all comes in serialized bills... and that means you have to go to Vegas with it or a bookmaker in New York City." Dean, with Nixon listening intently and saying, "Oh, I understand," concludes: "I've learned these things after the fact," and, laughing, "it's great shape for the next time around."[5]

In all this, the fact that Pappas was a prominent Greek-American hinted at the possibility that Agnew might have been involved in urging him to provide the hush money. But Pappas in fact was a Nixon friend and no link was established between the vice president and any approach to Pappas for this purpose. Pappas later denied providing any hush money through anybody, and Dean in an interview years afterward said he had never heard of any Agnew involvement.[6] Again Agnew's being an outsider from the Nixon inner circle was a blessing in disguise for him in the whole matter. [One Watergate investigator later produced a Chapin diary entry of an October 2, 1972, meeting with Pappas, noting that "after the entry of Pappas's name is the notation '7.' We have no explanation of the meaning of this notation, although it has been suggested that there were 7 Watergate defendants."][7] Such was one of the more slender reeds on which a hush-money tie-in was suspected.

On March 29, according to Haldeman, Senator Howard Baker of Tennessee, the senior Republican on the Ervin committee, did call the vice president on a Watergate matter, urging him to tell Nixon that "he had a firm conviction, Howard does now, that our stand on executive privilege"—prohibiting testimony by White House aides on grounds they provided private advice to him—"is very unwise in a public-relations sense, that it's hurting us and that time is of the essence on it. The president should waive the privilege and let some of the people come up." At this early point, Baker clearly sounded like a Nixon ally in a case in which he was cast as one of the investigators.

Haldeman further wrote: "The VP is concerned that this is going to put us in a bad position all the way around. He thinks that the P should say that if the grand jury wants Dean, we'll waive privilege. . . that this will disarm the Senate and that the P doesn't have to do anything with the Senate. He does want to see the P take some action to take the ball away and do something forthcoming."[8]

In Dean's report of April 5, he suggested that the vice president "take the lead" in trying, according to Haldeman later, to have "the Ervin committee cut Watergate out of their inquiry, let the U.S. Attorneys summarize that later. . . . Then Ervin could go ahead on all but the Watergate, because really the rest of it's all 'BS' anyway. The point is, we have nothing to hide, but we can't handle Watergate properly with the committee without jeopardizing the defendants' rights, and so on in a legal action."[9]

But apparently Agnew balked at even this involvement without direct orders from Nixon. Nixon wrote in his memoirs later: "I received a rather astonishing message through Harlow from Agnew [always necessarily through an intermediary] to the effect that he would speak up on Watergate, but only at a price, and that was that he would have to see the president. I told Ehrlichman to pass the message to Harlow that I didn't want under any circumstances to ask Agnew to do something that he was not convinced he ought to do on his own, that under the circumstances he should just chart his own course and of course I would chart my own course. I only hope that Bryce delivered this message in the rather meaningful way that I tried to convey it."[10] Agnew's recalcitrance led Haldeman to record that "the P's very disturbed because of the VP's unwillingness to step up on the executive privilege matter unless the P will talk to him."[11]

But Connally's advice, according to Haldeman's handwritten notes of a phone conversation on the night of April 5, was the same as Agnew's: "He says the Watergate thing has gone too far to back off of. . . . He thinks the P should waive executive privilege on the grounds that the Senate is so partisan and demagogic they've impaired the government's function. That as many of us as can should go up there, they should get it away from Haldeman and away from the White House. . . . He thinks we could say that at any cost the P has to sacrifice anybody in order to clear presidency."[12]

❧ ❧

In this atmosphere of tense maneuvering over Watergate, Haldeman got another phone call from Agnew on April 10, asking him to come to his office. "The VP called me over today," Haldeman wrote in his diary, "and said he had a real problem, because Jerome Wolff, who used to work for him back in Maryland, was about to be called by the United States attorney who was busting open campaign contribution cases and kickbacks to contractors. It seems that Wolff kept verbatim records of meetings with the VP and others, back over the years, concerning fundraising, and has a lot of quotes about how much we ought to get from a certain contractor, and so on, who has had good [state government] jobs. It wasn't shakedown stuff, it was merely going back to get support from those who had benefited from the administration, but the way it's worded, the VP feels it would sound bad.

"He made the point that [Baltimore prosecutor] George Beall is [Senator] Glenn Beall's brother, and if Glenn Beall would talk to him he could straighten him out. The VPs tried to get him to, but apparently not successfully, so he wanted me to talk to Glenn Beall, which, of course, I won't do, in order to verify a White House awareness and concern. He feels the publication of this stuff would finish the VP, because Wolff was with him for so long and is very much concerned. He agreed he'd probably get Colson into it, and that would be the best way to handle it."[13]

Haldeman immediately went to Nixon and told him of the startling development. The president later recorded his reaction in his memoirs: "I was very concerned at the prospect of Agnew's being dragged through the mud unfairly, but in view of all the other problems and our strained relations with Capitol Hill, I did not see how we could do anything to help him. In fact, the climate was such that anything we did to try to help might boomerang and be made to appear that we were trying to cover up for him."[14]

By the merest of coincidences, Agnew's troubles had begun in Baltimore on the very same day in January the Watergate burglars were sentenced in Washington. An old Agnew friend and business associate, Lester Matz, presented his lawyer a federal grand jury subpoena demanding records of his engineering firm in connection with George Beall's investigation into alleged contract kickbacks in Baltimore County. The ostensible target at the time was Dale Anderson, the Democratic county executive, but such investigations had ways of developing in other directions. Matz told the lawyer, Joseph Kaplan, that the records sought would show that his firm had been generating cash to make kickbacks of 5 percent of county public-works projects to various politicians. Kaplan, concluding that Beall was after higher-ups, advised a nervous Matz to tell all he knew, and if he did he could expect a grant of immunity. Matz said he couldn't do that, and when Kaplan asked why, he blurted out: "Because I have been paying off the vice president."[15]

Matz spent the rest of the morning telling the lawyer the whole story. Since 1962, when Agnew had become Baltimore county executive, through his tenure as governor of Maryland, and even up to the present as vice president, Matz had been paying him off for lucrative state government work contracts still generating income for the Matz firm. Once, he told a startled Kaplan, he had called on Agnew in an office he had in the basement of the White House and handed him an envelope containing about ten thousand dollars in cash.[16] Upon leaving Kaplan's office, Matz tried to phone two Agnew associates in the hope that somehow the vice president could stop the investigation, but he couldn't get through.

Beall, indeed a brother of Republican Senator J. Glenn Beall Jr., had been casting a wide net of subpeonas around Baltimore to gather clues and evidence of political corruption. But he had not been fishing for the vice president of the United States, especially one who had campaigned for his brother's election in 1970. Kaplan told Matz it was not likely Beall would prosecute Agnew, and in any event, with the information he had he could likely count on getting immunity for himself if the government really came after him.

Still nervous, Matz shortly afterward also called another lawyer, George White, who happened to be Agnew's legal counsel and friend. White went to see Beall ostensibly to inform him he would be representing Matz and to ask whether doing so might constitute a conflict of interest. It was a veiled way of inquiring whether Agnew was under investigation, and Beall assured him he was not; his target was Dale Anderson, and besides, Agnew had left office as Baltimore county executive in 1966, and the statute of limitations had run out concerning possible action against his conduct in that job.

In early February, Agnew had just returned from his Southeast Asian tour and was in Newport Beach, California, waiting to give Nixon a report on it, when White phoned him from Maryland. "He was extremely agitated," Agnew later recalled in his book on his loss of the vice presidency, *Go Quietly. . . Or Else*. "His voice was strained and he sounded like a man under tremendous pressure. He said he had to speak to me immediately about a matter that was too dangerous to discuss over the telephone. I agreed that he should fly out at once and tell me the whole story."[17]

Matz had been subpoenaed as a result of information culled from Baltimore County corporate records, specifically of an architectural firm headed by one Paul Gaudreau, that indicated that roughly 5 percent of county projects were being kicked back to Anderson's top aide, William E. Fornoff. Some prosecutorial squeezing soon yielded the names of two other engineers paying off county officials—Lester Matz and Agnew's old friend Jerome Wolff, who had been chairman of the State Roads Commission when Agnew was governor and was later on his vice-presidential staff.

"White told me," Agnew continued in his book, "that Matz and Wolff had come in to see him while I was in Asia; that they were frantic with worry; and that they had made some very transparent threats against me, alleging they were in terrible trouble and they expected me to bail them out of it. They wanted me to use my influence as vice president to make the federal government stop investigating them. If I refused, they may have to say things that would be very embarrassing to me." When Agnew asked what things, he wrote, White said: "They will say they made kickback payments to you." Agnew wrote that he told White: "That's certainly not true. In the past, they have made campaign contributions, but those certainly weren't kickbacks; the money didn't go to me personally."[18]

After White visited him, Beall dutifully notified his boss, Attorney General Richard Kleindienst, of that fact. When Agnew surprisingly called the head of the Justice Department himself expressing his concern, Kleindienst reassured the vice president that he had nothing to worry about. But on learning of Agnew's call to Kleindienst, one of Beall's young assistant prosecutors, Russell "Tim" Baker, began to think there might be something there after all.

When Wolff also received a subpoena, he naturally contacted the vice president. According to Agnew later, both Matz and Wolff called J. Walter Jones, a Maryland banker and onetime chief fund-raiser for Agnew, in a panic. Wolff, Agnew wrote, "pleaded with him for help. Wolff said, 'The prosecutors are not interested in me. They want the vice president.'. . . I felt as though I had been stabbed in the back by a trusted friend. . . . I firmly resolved that despite their threats and pleas, I would never allow Matz and Wolff to blackmail me."[19]

In Agnew's conversation with Nixon about his latest Asian trip, he apparently made no mention of this to the president. Instead, on his return to Washington he met Kleindienst over breakfast and "expressed my concern that the investigation could smear me, although I was innocent," citing "politically active left-wing Democrats" on Beall's staff who "might have targeted me as their ultimate target." Agnew also talked to Senator Beall, the prosecutor's brother, and Nixon. "Some prosecutors in Baltimore are trying to hook me up to some serious violations," he told the president. "I think they are trying to embarrass me." Nixon replied, Agnew wrote later, "They're always trying to do that. Don't worry about it. There's not going to be any problem." The president, Agnew wrote, "brushed it off. I don't think he took it seriously."[20]

By this time, however, Agnew was taking it very seriously. At Haldeman's recommendation, he went to Colson, who had just left the White House to start his own law practice, and asked him to represent him. Colson, busy with preparing his own defense against charges in the Watergate affair, had his hands full. He asked another partner in his firm,

Judah Best, to defend the vice president and Best agreed, setting up an appointment with Beall.

AGNEW'S PROBLEMS were far from any major concern at the White House at this time. "The president and his top people," Agnew wrote later, "were totally absorbed in their own problems arising from the Watergate scandal, which—although I was blissfully unaware of it—was about to blow up in their faces. . . . Having never been accepted in the White House inner circle, I took no part of what was going on in mid-April."[21]

WITH MCCORD'S LETTER to Sirica stirring the pot, and the Ervin committee pushing for testimony from White House aides, the fallout from the break-in and cover-up was now engulfing the president and his top political associates. John Dean, who had been the point man in the White House to monitor all Watergate developments and write the definitive report for Nixon on where matters stood, saw as he reviewed the situation that he himself was trapped. He decided to tell all and try to save his own skin, and went to the prosecutors. He called Haldeman the same day and told him. Haldeman's response was: "I think you ought to think about it, because once the toothpaste is out of the tube, it's hard to get it back in."[22] But Dean forged ahead, declaring he had no intention of being a "scapegoat" for all the Watergate crimes. By this time, Magruder also was talking to the prosecutors.

When Nixon got word that Dean was singing, he called in the young White House counsel and tried to persuade him to tell the prosecutors that the president, far from being involved in the Watergate plot, had been moving to unravel it. He suggested that Dean say "as a result of the president's action the thing has been broken." It was essential, he went on, that "the president should stay one step ahead of this thing" and not "let the Justice Department break this case and say, 'Look, we dragged the White House in here.' I've got to step out and do it."[23]

But Dean was having none of it. When Nixon met with Dean again two days later, and he pressed Dean either to take a leave of absence or resign outright, Dean refused. He countered by presenting Nixon with a draft letter saying essentially that he would go if Haldeman and Ehrlichman went with him.

Nixon finally faced reporters in the White House press room and sought to establish that he was in front of the parade to learn the truth about Watergate. Nearly a month earlier, he said, "as a result of serious charges which came to my attention, some of which were publicly reported, I began intensive new inquiries into this whole matter." He said he had met with the attorney general and his chief assistant to review the facts and "the progress of the Justice Department investigation," and "I can report today that there have been major developments in the case concerning which it would be improper to be more specific now, except to say that real progress has been made in finding the truth."[24]

Anyone in his administration who was indicted would be suspended, he said, and anyone convicted would be fired, and he opposed granting immunity to anyone—a not very subtle attempt to keep the canaries quiet, or at least guarded in the songs that they warbled to the prosecutors. Ron Ziegler famously or infamously declared that in light of the president's statement, all previous comments on Watergate were "inoperative." Agnew, meanwhile, had plenty to worry about over his own chirping canaries in the contracting business in Maryland.

With the whole fiasco unravelling, Nixon, in a midnight phone conversation with Kissinger, sounded desperate, beaten down, and self-pitying about the hard day he had just endured.

NIXON: "The problem I have is I can't look at it in the detached way I really should, [that] these people, God-damn it, they're guilty, throw them out and go on. But, just the personal things, God-damn—I think of these good men —"

KISSINGER [finishing the thought]: "—who wanted to do the right thing."

NIXON: "Well, it's gonna splash on a lot of 'em. . . . The real culprit, of course is, is Mitchell. He's in charge of the whole God-damn thing, and John Mitchell should step up like a man and say, 'Look, I was in charge, I take the responsibility, period.'"

KISSINGER: "I think to fire Haldeman would make him the villain."

NIXON: "Well, in the end he probably would have to go, Henry. They're gonna, you know, rip him up good."

Kissinger switches to the matter of preserving Nixon's presidency. NIXON, sighing, replies: "Well, if we can, if we can, we will, and if we don't, what the hell. . . . I've even considered the possibility of, frankly, just throwing myself on the sword, and letting Agnew take it. What the hell."

KISSINGER answers: "That is out of the question, with all due respect, Mr. President. That cannot be considered. The personality, what it would do to the presidency, and to the historical injustice of it. Why should you do it, and what good would it do? Whom would it help? It wouldn't help the country. It wouldn't help any individual involved. With all respect, I don't think the president has the right to sacrifice himself for an individual. And it would, of course, be personally unjust."[25]

Around this time, press secretary Ronald Ziegler got a phone call from Bob Woodward, the young *Washington Post* sleuth on Watergate, seeking confirmation of a report that there were new developments in the matter, and also that Agnew was about to resign. A similar call came from the *New York Times*'s Watergate bird-dog, Seymour Hersh. Ziegler passed on the report to Nixon and the Justice Department's Henry Petersen as the two were discussing the state of the case.

The Oval Office taping system on April 19 captures Nixon telling Petersen: "If there's one thing you have got to do, you have got to maintain the presidency out of this. I have got things to do for this country. I'm not going to have—this is personal—I sometimes feel like I'd like to resign, let Agnew be president for a while. He'd love it."

Petersen, a bureaucrat not a politician, replies: "I don't even know why you want the job."

Turning to Ziegler, Nixon asks: "You were talking about this story—that Agnew is getting ready to resign? That's the *Post* also?"

ZIEGLER: "Well, that's the *Post* and *Times*."

Nixon asks him what Agnew has said, and Ziegler, quoting the vice president, says, "'That's ridiculous,'" and that Agnew's new press secretary, Marsh Thomson, is "going to turn it off." Ziegler then suggests to Nixon that he have White House aide David Gergen, a friend of Woodward, call him back and say, "'Let me tell you what is going on here, Bob, is the president is going to get to the bottom of this'. . . . And then have Gergen say, 'I have checked this out at a very high level and you'd better, absolutely, not even go into. . . running a story like this. You had better just wipe it out of your mind, because there's nothing to it.'" Ziegler then assures Nixon that "this is not, as I sense it, about to break in the papers. This is rumor. . . ." Nixon replies: "Well, kill it. Kill it hard."[26]

This exchange took place nine days after Agnew had advised Haldeman that he had "a real problem," and Haldeman had already informed Nixon. In that light, it was surprising, unless Nixon was speaking just for effect, that he would have made the suggestion of stepping aside for Agnew to assume the presidency. It was a lament Nixon was to repeat at least half a dozen times in the next few weeks. Six days later, in fact, in a conversation with Kleindienst taped on April 25, he concludes by laughingly observing: "What the hell, you know, people say, 'Impeach the president.' Well, then they get Agnew, what the hell."[27]

Through all this, Agnew mostly kept his head down. The president chose now to have his loose-cannon vice president far-removed from any aspect of Watergate, even in damage control. On one occasion, when the *Los Angeles Times* reported that Agnew had commented that he was "appalled" at the Watergate saga, the vice president quickly called Haldeman and denied he had said it. Haldeman informed the president that Agnew had offered to make a statement to the press "to clear it up," and wanted Nixon to know that "the one thing I pride myself in is loyalty to the president and I would never say anything like this or do anything like this."

Nixon, upset at first, calmed down and mused about the possibility of later recruiting Agnew to defend him. According to Haldeman, Nixon said he was weighing "whether if the time comes to escalate it or not, to have Agnew go in and attack the press, basically attack the inaccuracies."[28]

Some days later, Nixon learned that the vice president had poked his nose in anyway, mentioning to Haldeman that it might be better to have the Watergate case go to a grand jury than to have it aired in "the circus" of the Senate. In a hot Oval Office exchange caught on tape on May 1, a livid Nixon let Agnew have it with both barrels for interfering.

NIXON: "A call [was] made apparently, or one of your people made for you, about a grand jury. A call or a discussion."

AGNEW: "I talked to Haldeman."

NIXON [sharply]: "Let me say, I told him [Haldeman] to forget it! It's very important that that be forgotten, you know, because, hell, the thing is only something where you're tangentially involved."

AGNEW: "I'm not involved, but it could be political—"

NIXON [briskly interrupting and dragging out the word]: "No! You understand what I mean. You're not involved at all, good God, no. But my point is, Ted, that you've got to be very sure. I don't want anybody ever to think there ever was any discussion between the vice president and members of the White House staff with regard to a grand jury. So if you'll just forget you ever talked to Haldeman. I told Haldeman when he told me about it, I said, 'For God's sake, you forget the vice president ever talked to you about it. You understand? In the present atmosphere— [Agnew tries to break in]—in the present atmosphere, they'll think, well, for God's sake, we were trying to get Glenn Beall's son [the Baltimore prosecutor; Agnew says, "Brother"]. Now, we have done something about it, but I mean, something I think we have. . . in a discreet way, maybe something has been done."

Nixon here seems to be giving Agnew some assurance that he is taking some action to alleviate or eliminate his troubles with the Justice Department, while doing nothing of the sort. He continues with his instructions to stay out of Watergate—for his own sake: "But I wanted you to know by all means, Ted, keep yourself free from all this. You've got to be free, free and independent. In other words, take your own line and the like, and you don't need to get involved in this whole business on the Watergate thing. . . . [Say that] you just have confidence. . . and stay back. You just say all the facts will come out, period. I wouldn't get into a personal position, however."

AGNEW: "Mr. President, can I say just a few things? I don't know whether you misconstrued what I did yesterday or not when I called that press conference, but I hope you didn't."

NIXON: "No, I thought it was fine."

AGNEW: "The *Times* tried to indicate that I was —"

NIXON: "No, I got your [indication]. What I meant is, they're gonna be asking you now to say something. Don't say anything. I'm just telling you, you don't need to, you see what I mean? You don't need to say a damn word."

AGNEW [painfully]: "Well, I just wanted you to know. I want to—Mr. President, I'm part of this team."

NIXON [softening somewhat]: "I know, but look, Ted, you've got to keep yourself free for—look, as you well know, there's you, there's

Reagan, who did call me last night [Agnew chuckles]. . . . You've got your constituency and I just want you to know as a friend and I want you to be [Agnew interjects, "I appreciate it"] as free as the driven snow here and by golly I understand totally. I think it's very important that you never be in a position where you appear to be at odds with the president, which I always fully supported with Eisenhower. But on the other hand you've got to appear that you are your own man, you see? They will know, because it's gonna come out, I think, it's gonna come out. But hell, you don't have anything like with Haldeman and Ehrlichman and those people. God-damn it, if something happens to them, Mitchell, it's gonna happen, hell, there's all there is to it. No reason for you to get involved at all. You didn't know any more about Watergate than I did. Thank God. Thank God we both didn't know it was going to hurt. If we had known, too bad we didn't. We'd have stopped it, we aren't that dumb."

AGNEW [plaintively]: "I'd like to take this opportunity to express the hope that I might be of more use. I don't care about—"

NIXON, after saying he has been "thinking about ways" in the reorganization and beginning to sound like a Dutch uncle to Agnew: "Give it some thought, maybe we can find some ways. But I want you to know very much . . . that I don't expect any favors from you. I don't want you to get involved. You know what I mean? Don't get out there. Look, let's face it. Those bastards in the press, you know what they are, and don't give them any opportunity to say you're against the president. Don't give them any opportunity to say you're pimping for the president, see my point? Because all they will do then will be to tear you down. Keep yourself up there. You can speak on the issues, that's the best thing, make the big plays, that's what I want you to do, and I think it will work out. In a few months, they'll find something else, because, you know, you're a fighter [alluding again in an optimistic way to Agnew's troubles]. Like you were after November third [election day], you were out there, you stuck your neck out, and I understand that, took the press on, and I appreciate that. But don't do it now. You've got just three years before this next election, and by golly if you're, you know, if you should decide to be a candidate, and God knows who's going to be it then. But gee whiz, I want you to be in a position where they cannot, in any event and in any way, have anything wrong [on you] that they can tear you down, of something you had nothing to do with." [Nixon sounds as if he wants Agnew to be his successor, while increasingly saying otherwise among his insiders.]

AGNEW [with obvious exasperation]: "I understand what you mean, Mr. President, and I certainly will be guided by that, but [laughing uneasily] I'm more interested in serving these three years, properly."

NIXON: "Well, if you can think of some things, we will do them.... [Then, laughing nervously] There's lotsa room, now!"

AGNEW [changing the subject]: "Well, I think the confrontation that was, has now come about is a good one. It's over, it's done."

NIXON: "No. It's over for now, but now they'll zero in on the president."[29]

That judgment, however, was a bit premature. Even as Nixon saw himself as the prime target of the Watergate investigation, his vice president was drawing plenty of worrisome attention back in Maryland. There, federal prosecutors were listening with increasing interest to his old friends in the contracting business.

Chapter 19

LAPSING
INSURANCE POLICY

Indeed, Ted Agnew's old Maryland friend Lester Matz and his partner John Childs, and some of their Matz employees, were already busy trying to save their own skins. The workers, under limited immunity, told the grand jury they had received bonuses that they were required to give back to their employers, who in turn would use the funds for campaign contributions or to pay off politicians.

Around this time, Judah Best, Agnew's attorney, called on Beall in Baltimore and told him, according to a Beall memo to the files, "that his client had heard cocktail-party conversation" about Agnew and that "there was deep concern about possible newspaper publicity on the investigation, which his client would be seriously hurt by, and which could not possibly be answered appropriately." Beall wrote that he had "told Best that the investigation did not involve his client and that we were very sensitive to the problems of prejudicial publicity." But Agnew feared otherwise. With Matz facing prosecution himself, the vice president wrote later, "the only thing for Matz to do was, in prosecutorial parlance, to 'trade up' and say the money had gone to me."[1] And the same was true of Jerry Wolff, also now talking to the prosecutors, and eventually of another extremely close friend, I. Harold "Bud" Hammerman, who was a key Agnew fund-raiser. Hammerman at this stage was pressing the vice president—hard, but unsuccessfully—to intervene in the Baltimore investigations of his old pals, without revealing to Agnew that Hammerman also might be a target.

The vice president's developing woes were not yet public, and in any event almost certainly would have taken a back seat to those of the president. The Watergate "horrors," as John Mitchell called them, were now coming to a decisive point. A brief question from Nixon to Haldeman late on the night of April 26 reflected the panic that had descended on the White House as a result of more evidence of the problems, and the president's desperate hope that his favorite Texan might somehow bail them all out. "What about Connally for attorney general?" Nixon asked. "Would he be approved by the Senate? It would be part of bold move." Haldeman, according to his diary, told him "I didn't think Connally would take it. He says Connally says he'll do anything he has to do, so we'll see."[2] But nothing came of Connally as Nixon's savior of last resort.

Through it all, Nixon clung to the notion of Agnew as his insurance policy against being forced out of the presidency. In one conversation around this time with Ziegler, his press secretary, the tape system catches him saying of his critics: "They can't want, frankly, to see Agnew be president. No, really, I don't see impeachment. . . . Good God, the point is, they've got to want to see this country to succeed. The whole hopes of [voice rising] the whole God-damn world for peace, Ron, you know where they rest. They rest right here in this damn chair. They can't allow, they know it, any pricky little shithouse thing, they know God-damn well, these guys, maybe the public doesn't know, but these guys know I didn't know that. Good God, except the most vicious gossips. Does Mollenhoff think I knew all about this? Maybe he does." [Clark Mollenhoff, a former *Des Moines Register* reporter, had joined the Nixon White House early in the first term as a counsel and supposedly an internal investigator.]

ZIEGLER: "He believes this."

NIXON [incredulous]: "He thinks I knew? The president knew? Shit, he knows people never tell me anything!"[3]

Around noon on Sunday, April 29, Nixon at Camp David phoned Haldeman and asked that he and Ehrlichman take a White House helicopter up there that afternoon. Prior to their leaving, Ziegler phoned Haldeman and told him Nixon was going to ask him and Ehrlichman to resign, and then fire Dean. On arrival, Ziegler took Haldeman for a walk and told him, Haldeman wrote later, that "the P has made another firm decision that he communicated to Ron this morning, which is that he, too, is going to resign. Ron said he's deadly serious and absolutely firm on it. I told him that I was sure that was not the case, that it was part of steeling himself for meeting with us, that he's creating a big crisis that he knew he couldn't meet, in order to be able to meet the lesser crisis that he has to meet."[4]

Haldeman wrote that when he got to Aspen, the presidential cottage, "the P was in terrible shape. Shook hands with me, which is the first time he's ever done that. Told me to come look at the view out the window, then stepped to the door and said let's go outside and look at the flowers and all. So we were looking at the tulips from the Aspen porch, talking about the beauty and all, and as we started back in, he said, 'Well, I have to enjoy it, because I may not be alive much longer.' We go inside and he went through a discourse, saying that while nobody knows it, and he's not publicly a religious man, that it's a fact that he has prayed on his knees every night that he's been in the presidential office. He's prayed hard over this decision, and it's the toughest decision he's ever made. He made the points on why he had to do it, but he's come to the conclusion that he has to have our resignations."

Then astonishingly, Haldeman went on, "he wants us to stay on to handle the transition. Then he went through his whole pitch about how he's really the guilty one. He said he's thought it all through, and that he was the one that started Colson on his projects, he was the one who told Dean to cover up, he was the one who made Mitchell attorney general, and later his campaign manager, and so on. And that he now has to face that and live with it, and that for that reason, after he gets his other things completed, that he too will probably have to resign. He never said that, but implied it." Haldeman wrote that he replied that Nixon couldn't resign, after which the president told him he was going to appoint Elliot Richardson, then secretary of defense, to be attorney general.[5]

On the next day, Haldeman's last in office, he called Agnew to inform him, and the vice president told him he "had almost called me yesterday, wanted to let me know about the charges that came out then, that they were terribly unfair, and that they were nothing but smoke. Said he'd like to see me before I actually left. That he would like to be as helpful as he can, and thinks this is probably the right move."[6]

Meanwhile, Nixon continued to invoke the specter of Agnew in the Oval Office to persuade himself to hang on. In a phone conversation with speechwriter Ray Price on the same day, April 30, he talked about the problem of taking all the blame on himself, wherein people would say, "Well, Christ, this poor damned dumb president, why doesn't he resign? [Then, brightening] Which may not be a bad idea. The only problem is, I mean, you get Agnew. You want Agnew?"[7] Instead Nixon settled for announcing that he was tearing down his "Berlin Wall" with the resignations of Haldeman and Ehrlichman, and also Kleindienst, and firing Dean, generating explosive newspaper headlines and dominating that night's television news reports.

With Haldeman gone, Nixon named Alexander Haig as his new chief of staff, and, as Dean's testimony threatened to blow the top off the Watergate coverup, Nixon discussed with Haig the possibility of recruiting Agnew, or Connally, to launch an attack on the singing former counsel. He is heard on tape in his EOB hideaway telling Haig that Dean's "legs have to be cut off on national television like nobody's business, but not by me. I cannot take on the little asshole. Agnew? Connally? Connally won't? I don't know. I don't know. Agnew may." Haig answered: "I think Agnew would want to and he'll do it. I think Connally will do it if it's necessary. . . ."

Even in this Agnew field of specialty, Nixon preferred the strong man from Texas. He told Haig: "We've just got to say, 'John, we have a problem we want your advice on.' Connally is a mean, tough, son of a bitch. He's got tremendous judgment and all the rest. . . . There's nothing more important to this country that he could do than this, mash this son of a bitch Dean. . . . I think maybe when he [Connally] comes in you ought to brief him on the whole God-damn thing. You know it isn't all that complicated. I explained a little of it to him. But say, for Christ's sakes, here it is, this God-damn Dean out here attacking the presidency, and we can't allow it. The president, he should have known, but he was very busy with other things." And shortly afterward: "What the hell's Agnew doing? He's never spoken up once on this God-damn thing."[8]

But Agnew was thinking more now about his own concerns. To him, the most significant development was the appointment of Richardson to replace Kleindienst, which, Agnew wrote later, "turned out to be bad news for me. Nixon would soon grow to detest Richardson. As Watergate diminished the president's power, Richardson changed from a transparent toady to a sanctimonious lecturer on morals. I don't know why Mr. Nixon put him in charge of the Justice Department, except that he may have considered this a gesture towards his enemies in the eastern establishment. Nixon had a compulsion to people who were doctrinally opposed to him. After the didactic Richardson had chosen Archibald Cox as the special Watergate prosecutor and delivered Mr. Nixon into the clutches of his own worst enemies, the president realized his mistake. But his realization came too late."[9]

Agnew no doubt would have been startled to know that in November of 1971, Nixon had told Haldeman that if anything were to happen to Warren Burger, the chief justice of the Supreme Court, Elliot Richardson "would be an outstanding chief justice" and that "he wants to keep Richardson in mind, because he thinks he would be a towering, historic chief justice."[10]

But Richardson was not Agnew's problem right now. He continued to worry about Beall and his team of three other young lawyers—Tim Baker, Ron Liebman, and especially Barney Skolnik, a Democrat who had briefly worked in the 1972 presidential campaign of Senator Muskie. Skolnik was a bird dog who was focusing on Bill Fornoff, chief aide of Baltimore County Executive Dale Anderson, to whom Matz and others were suspected of making payoffs. In mid-May, with rumors still flying, Jud Best, Agnew's lawyer and Colson's partner, decided to call on Beall again. That day, the first story about the Dale Anderson inquiry appeared in *The Washington Post*. It said that the Baltimore county executive had been notified that he was under investigation as were several persons who had worked in Agnew's previous county administration. The story said, however, that "despite this fact, sources in Baltimore, Washington, and Towson, the seat of Baltimore County, have stated categorically that the vice president himself is in no way involved in the investigation, and that widespread rumors to the contrary are without foundation."[11] Beall repeated the same assurance to Best.

But the *Post* at that time had more to go on than rumors. Bob Woodward, the young reporter who with Carl Bernstein had broken most of the significant revelations in the Watergate case, passed on to Richard Cohen, the *Post*'s enterprising correspondent in Annapolis, something his secret source called "Deep Throat" had told him: FBI files contained apparently unverified allegations that Agnew had accepted bribes while he was vice president! As Cohen and I wrote later in our book about the scandal, Woodward was told that "Agnew had taken the money in cash and placed it in a desk drawer. The amount was $2,500. The Baltimore grand jury, the source added, was heading Agnew's way and the vice president was in fact its target."[12]

The *Post*'s story, and others in the *Wall Street Journal*, shook up all the principals on the receiving end of the investigation, including Matz's lawyer, Joe Kaplan, who had been carrying around in his head the revelation that his client had dumped in his lap back in January. On Friday, May 18, he called Baker just to sound him out about the state of the inquiry on Matz. The prosecutor reminded him that his client was certain to be indicted and that time was running out on his chance to help himself. Kaplan casually replied that Matz and Childs had always been ready to cooperate but they had nothing the government would consider of value. Besides, what they did have the government wouldn't be willing to hear.

Baker's ears perked up. Matz and Childs had been offered immunity long before and Kaplan had turned it down. But now he told Baker that his clients had information with which to incriminate Fornoff, Dale Anderson's chief lieutenant, but that from what he'd heard, the prosecutors already had all they needed on him. So the only one on whom they were in a position to provide incriminating information was—Agnew! Kaplan said no doubt the government wouldn't be interested—implying that it wouldn't want to take on such a high-profile target in its own administration.[13]

Baker was indignant at the assumption. Heatedly, he told Kaplan the U.S. attorney's office was in the business of investigating and prosecuting whatever crimes it learned of, by anybody, regardless of party or position. But Agnew had been out of office as county executive since the end of 1966, he reminded Kaplan, and the applicable statute of limitations had run out. Kaplan then dropped the bomb on him. What his clients had to say involved dealings after Agnew had left Towson—when he was governor and vice president!

Rather than jumping on the opportunity, Baker outwardly kept his composure. Kaplan said he would discuss the matter with his clients, obviously with immunity in mind, and said he would get back to the prosecutor after the weekend. Baker said okay, but reminded Kaplan again of the impending indictments and hung up the phone. When he excitedly told his partners, they couldn't believe what had dropped into their hands. Earlier, Baker had half-jokingly told them they were going to get Agnew in the end. In their focus on Baltimore County, they hadn't considered that there might be illegal and indictable culpability by Agnew after he had left Towson and gone to Annapolis and then Washington.

On Monday, Baker called Kaplan, told him he had discussed the matter with Beall, and was authorized to say what he had said the previous Friday on his own—that the U.S. attorney's office was prepared to proceed. He said he knew it was a difficult decision for his clients to make but warned Kaplan again that the indictments were imminent. If they had something to say, now was the time. Kaplan told Baker they were concerned about the national implications of bringing the vice president down, what with the Watergate scandal already jeopardizing the president. Baker squeezed harder. If they didn't cooperate, they would be indicted and forced anyway to go before a grand jury on what they knew about Agnew. After more weeks of jockeying, during which Fornoff admitted taking bribes and got off without jail time, Matz, Childs, and Wolff all crumbled.[14]

MEANWHILE, important developments were occurring affecting both Agnew's situation and the Watergate case. On the same day Kaplan had told Baker that his clients had incriminating information against the vice president, Nixon under pressure had appointed as special Watergate prosecutor Archibald Cox, the eminent Harvard lawyer and former U.S. solicitor general under Democratic presidents Kennedy and Johnson. Cox promised a no-holds-barred investigation that would pursue the Watergate scandal wherever the facts took him, even into "the Oval Office."[15] Also, the Senate Watergate Committee hearings, chaired by Sam Ervin of North Carolina, were at last getting under way, assuring even more public scrutiny of the administration's huge scandal.

A week later, Richardson moved in as attorney general. The departing Kleindienst gave him only the barest hint of the Baltimore investigation into political corruption, and he had no idea at all of what was going on with Agnew. Even without that knowledge, Richardson already had a full plate in tackling a demoralized Justice Department whose flawed investigation of Watergate had contributed to bringing Cox in.

When Nixon in March had instructed the department to make a thorough inquiry, Kleindienst, who had taken over when John Mitchell left to run CREEP, basically turned the job over to Henry Petersen, the assistant attorney general in charge of the criminal division. Petersen had overseen the prosecution and conviction of the Watergate burglars, but when McCord informed Judge Sirica that others had escaped the net, Petersen was sharply criticized. The appointment of Cox was a clear rebuke to him. So Richardson had both a department morale problem and a built-in threat to maintaining his strong bureaucratic reputation—as well as an opportunity to advance his considerable political ambitions. He brought in his own team, and having now occupied four presidential cabinet posts, it was only natural that while he kept a sharp eye on the Watergate investigation, he would also continue to have an eye on the presidency itself.

On May 25, the day Richardson was sworn in as attorney general, Nixon was still talking about how the pressures of Watergate on him were making him consider resignation, if it weren't for the consequences of an Agnew presidency. He told Alexander Haig in a long phone talk: "You see, the real problem, though, is me, because the God-damn thing has gotten to me, you see, you know, because of the personal factors. And you get to the point, you know that, well, if you can't do the God-damn job you better put somebody in there that can."

HAIG, laughing: "There's no one who can. You're the one to do it."

NIXON: "Well, Agnew's just panting to get at it."

HAIG: "He might be, but that's out of the question. There's just no alternative. There couldn't be."[16]

Nixon at this time was well aware that Agnew was not much of an option. When Ehrlichman weeks after his resignation paid his last visit to the president who had forced him out, they discussed the vice president and, Ehrlichman wrote later, "by then there were rumors that Agnew was in trouble, and Haldeman had told me a few of the details in deep confidence. 'I'm going to have to get rid of him,' Nixon told me. 'They've got the evidence. Agnew has been on the take all the time he's been here!' The president was distressed for several reasons. Aside from the obvious ways that Agnew's conduct complicated the Watergate crisis, Nixon genuinely believed that as long as Spiro Agnew was vice president, most members of the House would think twice before voting articles of impeachment against Richard Nixon.[17]

Haig went on to tell Nixon that there were too many important matters coming up, including a Soviet summit. "This other thing is going to slip out of most people's consciousness," he said. "Hell, they've dug up all they can dig."[18]

A few days later, meeting with Rogers in the Oval Office, Nixon started again: ". . . we have some just ridiculous suggestion the president ought to resign and all this filthy—you couldn't resign, for Christ sakes, if you'd stole the whole God-damn White House. . . . What the hell are you going to do? Turn the reins over to Agnew? Huh?"[19]

Through this period, the relationship between Nixon and Agnew remained outwardly cordial but inwardly guarded. It reached the point that when Nixon was scheduled to have a rare face-to-face meeting with his vice president, White House aide Ken Cole sent him a couple of pages of "talking points" of the sort usually provided for meeting foreign heads of state and the like. One of them said: "The vice president will probably ask you to further clarify your promise of an expanded substantive role for him during the coming 3½ years. You should avoid any commitment of specific responsibility for the vice president at this time; however, you should recommend that he and his staff become more involved in domestic affairs by working closely with Mel Laird and Bryce Harlow, who will be joining our staff in the next few weeks."

Another "talking point" alerted Nixon to another likely Agnew pressure. "The vice president may specifically ask you for a role as the admininstration's new energy 'czar,' or he may want to regain full liaison responsibility for intergovernmental relations with governors and mayors, which is now the responsibility of the Domestic Council staff. He will also wish to become more involved in economic affairs. You should again avoid any commitment for specific responsibility and again emphasize that it is difficult to fully detail the vice president's new role until he has had an opportunity to meet with Mel Laird and Bryce Harlow. However, the vice president should know that a new energy 'czar' has already been chosen."[20] In other words, Agnew was continuing to get the same dodges that had marked his promised "expanded substantive role" almost from the start.

At the same time, Nixon was determined to keep Agnew out of the loop on his own Watergate problems. Complaining to the deposed Haldeman about what he saw as a failure of Republicans to defend him, Nixon said he had told Haig he lacked "people to fight. We just don't have anybody. You don't want to use Agnew,"[21] whose own troubles were rapidly coming to a head.

But through it all, Agnew professed his belief in Nixon's innocence and his loyalty to him, while acknowledging that the vice presidency under him was not all he had hoped it would be. In an interview with *Washington Post* reporter Lou Cannon, he confessed more than four years into the job that "quite candidly, the president hasn't defined my role yet. I don't know exactly what I'll be doing [for the rest of the second term] and it's up to the president to define it." Agnew went on: "It's an intellectual frustration for a man who's spent his time in executive government making decisions to suddenly find that he cannot make decisions anymore, that he can only recommend that they be made. It's not a debilitating frustration or a frustration that makes me want to abandon the vice presidency. . . . It's simply a frustration from a line responsibility to an advisory responsibility and it's hard to take, it really is."[22]

At the same time, Agnew continued to entertain presidential ambitions for 1976 even as the cloud of scandal darkened over him, unknown to the public. "I can assure you of this," he said in the same interview, "that if I go after the nomination it will be because I think I can get it and once having achieved it that I think I can be elected."[23]

One who thought along the same lines was 1964 Republican nominee Barry Goldwater. He told Dan Rather in a CBS interview that he expected Agnew to be the next Republican nominee and that if Watergate brought Nixon down, the "quickest way" out for the country would be for him to resign "and put Agnew in and get going." Goldwater noted, David Broder of *The Washington Post* wrote subsequently, "that Agnew is clearly free of the taint of Watergate because no one with the slightest acquaintance with his status in the administration believes he is enough of an 'insider' to have been part of the cabal."

Broder continued: "The degree of innocence is as alarming as it is genuine, for it bespeaks an isolation far more complete than that which landed Mr. Nixon in so much trouble. The fact is that Spiro Agnew, the man who sits a heartbeat or a forced resignation away from the presidency, lives today in a no-man's-land that is unhealthy for him and for the country. The vice president's office is an uncomfortable anteroom off the corridors of power, no matter who the occupant ... Agnew in Washington appears a stranger in a world he never made—alone except for a small staff and a small circle of Maryland friends."[24]

ONLY DAYS AFTER Richardson had moved into the attorney general's office, George Beall came down from Baltimore, walked in without an appointment, and asked to see him. Richardson's top assistant, J. T. Smith, a Yale Law graduate, had only been on the job a short time himself and asked a carryover secretary what the procedure was. She said simply walking in to see the big boss just wasn't done, even for a U.S. attorney, of whom there were ninety-four. So Beall was turned away with a later appointment, and left word that he had an important matter to discuss that Richardson's predecesssor, Kliendienst would, he thought, have mentioned. Beall had asked Kleindienst before he left whether he, Beall, should inform Richardson of the Maryland investigation and that there had been no involvement of Agnew at that point. Kleindienst said he would mention it, but he did so only in passing, saying Richardson ought to talk to his man in Baltimore.

It was not until about two weeks later, on June 12, that Beall came back for his appointment. By that time Fornoff had pleaded guilty and Matz and Wolff had indicated they had a lot to say about Agnew, but that was as far as it went then. As Beall filled Richardson in about the Anderson investigation, the attorney general sat smoking his pipe and idly doodling—until his visitor mentioned Agnew. Then he started taking notes. Beall told him his team was still negotiating with the prospective witnesses, and Richardson asked to be kept posted.[25]

A week later, on June 21, the lawyers for Matz and Wolff came in and told the Baltimore prosecutors they were ready to sing—to say how their clients had indeed paid off Agnew not only when he was county executive but also as governor and vice president. Contracts that Agnew had steered their way in Towson and later in Annapolis continued to yield fat rewards for the engineers, and they figured he was entitled to his continued share.

Matz and Childs had formed a firm in 1955, when Baltimore County real estate was booming, requiring the extensive construction of new roads and sewers, and the engineering expertise they entailed. Bud Hammerman, a developer, teamed up with the Matz firm and Wolff, and by 1960 Matz had begun cultivating the chairman of the county zoning board of appeals, Spiro Agnew. When Agnew ran for county executive, Matz and Childs contributed to his campaign, and thereafter, according to the prosecutors' case, a deal was arranged whereby county contracts would flow to the engineers under a five-percent kickback scheme for engineering work and half that for surveying. Part of the scam was the payment of bonuses to key Matz employees, who were required to turn over a share to Matz for distribution to cooperative politicians like Agnew. Later, when Agnew became governor, the prosecutors said, his appointment of Wolff as chairman of the Maryland Roads Commission facilitated the arrangement. The payments from Matz graduated from the use of an intermediary to Agnew directly, and continued when he became governor and then vice president.

In 1969, with Agnew no longer in a position to steer state contracts to cooperative businessmen, Matz calculated that he still owed the new vice president a cut of his largesse from contracts Agnew had generated in his previous government posts. It was in this context, the prosecutors said, that Matz had dropped by the vice president's new office in the basement of the White House and handed him an envelope containing ten thousand dollars in cash. In time, however, with Agnew no longer able to provide Matz with new contracts, the payments diminished.[26]

Agnew, in his own later account of what had happened, insisted that he had never taken any kickbacks. The whole story, he wrote, was no more than an initial effort by his Maryland accusers to pressure him to have the investigation stopped, and then the work of political enemies to sandbag him out of office. He denied that he and Matz ever really were friends, and he argued that "suspicions" of his own involvement in kickbacks were never corroborated. "What is clear from the records of the case," he wrote, "is that Wolff, Matz, and others engaged for a long time in illegal undertakings that did not concern me, and that they were in fact co-conspirators of long experience. Yet, the prosecutors were willing to believe them as long as the vice president's hide was nailed to the wall."[27]

With the testimony of the Maryland engineers in hand, Beall and company decided it was time to tell Richardson all they knew. But the new attorney general was a very busy man, and their appointment with him kept being postponed, through the rest of June. In the meantime, Richardson got a phone call from J. Fred Buzhardt, Nixon's chief legal troubleshooter at the White House. He said he had gotten a complaint—he didn't identify the source—about tactics being used by the Beall team regarding allegations against the vice president. Richardson told him if anyone had any complaints, to bring them to him.

Richardson may not have realized it at the time, but Buzhardt, who also was intricately involved in trying to keep the Watergate scandal from landing squarely at Nixon's feet, would in a short time also be a contact point in the legal and political nightmares engulfing the Nixon–Agnew administration.

On July 3, Beall, Skolnik, Baker, and Liebman finally headed down the Baltimore–Washington Parkway to deliver to the attorney general of the United States what they now considered an indictable case against the vice president of the United States. The charges ranged from accepting bribes to income-tax evasion. If they could make them stick, Richardson would be confronted with a dilemma unprecedented in the nation's history: what to do about a crooked vice president who, unless removed, would remain in the line of presidential succession to a president who himself was under a gathering cloud of corruption that could also drive him from office.

❧ ❧

Nixon, meanwhile, focusing on his own troubles, was once again turning to his personal adviser, John Connally, for how to handle increasing Republican pressures to be more responsive to questions about Watergate. The Texas wise man, in an excess of optimism, told him that in his opinion the matter had "topped out, and frankly you ought not to say anything more about Watergate at all under any circumstances." He could justify his silence on grounds the matter was before the Ervin committee.

Connally: "If you have a press conference, I would just say, 'I'm not gonna answer any questions about Watergate. I've issued my statement . . . This matter is now at hearings before the Ervin committee. I will not respond to those questions. If that's the only interest, please let someone who's interested in this country calmly ask questions.' . . . For two reasons. First, I don't know that you have anything to add to the body of information. But be that as it may. Secondly, I don't care what happens. If they really say you knew about it, either about breaking in or the cover-up, I don't think at this point it's important or critical. Don't even respond to it. Strangely enough, most of the people think you do know about it, and so... there's no way that you can prove you didn't know about it, no way."

The only thing he can do now, Connally advises, is to "go about your other business, you create as much activity in the government" as possible. The press and the Watergate committee, he says, are "gonna carry this thing to where a reaction is going to set in, and you're gonna benefit" as the public gets fed up, provided the president demonstrates he is still try-ing to do his job. "You have to be in this posture at a time when these guys are trying to persecute you. If you are, you'll come out of this in very, very good shape."

"Survive it?" Nixon says, somewhat incredulously.

"More than survive it," Connally assures him. "You're gonna come out ahead of the game... with sufficient strength to carry on any program you want to carry on." He further advises him to demonstrate real leader-ship by taking on some unpopular cause! Nixon, as usual, sounds as if he were listening spellbound at the foot of an oracle. Whether Connally re-ally believed this rosy scenario or was simply trying to buck up his fading ally in shaping his own political future, only the big man from Texas him-self knew.[28]

Meanwhile, the long shadow of Connally continued to hover over Agnew. Despite his own gathering storm, not publicly known yet, the Maryland Press Club, with whom he had often feuded, had surprisingly voted him (at a low membership turnout) its Man of the Year. The dinner honoring him occurred on the day Connally announced he was switching to the Republican Party, prompting the guest of honor to quip: "I am deeply grateful that you did not play me on with 'The Eyes of Texas Are Upon You.'" He said it in jest, but the wisecrack reflected a public percep-tion that Connally had changed parties in anticipation of seeking the GOP presidential nomination in 1976—in opposition to Agnew.[29]

As summer approached, Nixon called Agnew in and, in Haig's pres-ence, urged him, after all he had said about not getting involved for his own protection, to lead a charge against the Democratic members of the Senate Watergate investigating committee. The taping system records the vice president telling him, "I don't watch very much," but Nixon orders him—right out of the Connally playbook—to "get the word to every one of our witnesses they should take on the committee. They should show outrage. They should say you're being unfair, you're being partisan." He pointedly tells Agnew to refute all allegations as "persecution."

NIXON: "Let me just give you one assurance so you just put your mind at rest. I don't care [what they say]. In these last couple of months, three months, you know, I've been accused of everything and [that] I've covered it up. All these things aren't true . . . In my office and in yours, it cannot be done. . . . But on the other hand, one squib, they can do it and just hard line and true, and just say it is persecution, political partisan and persecution crap. What do you think, Al? . . . I'm just tired of all the charges all the time, my goodness, all the charges, I put a million dollars of campaign funds in my San Clemente house. . . ."

AGNEW [alluding to the accusations against him]: "That's just the same thing with—"

NIXON: "Yeah. You don't have any comeback like me and they all know it. We haven't stolen a thing."

In the course of encouraging Agnew to attack the Ervin committee, Nixon repeatedly rants against the injustice of the Watergate allegations against himself and, by inference at least, those against his vice president as a co-victim of partisan persecution. He tells Agnew he should point out that wiretapping was widespread in previous Democratic administrations. Agnew asks him: "That's safe to say, that newsmen were bugged, politicians were bugged?" Nixon replies: "That's right. And civil rights leaders were bugged."

AGNEW: "During the Kennedy years?"

NIXON: "Exactly. Sure they were. And you can say, 'I can say with absolute assurance, gentlemen, based on the facts in the files of the FBI.' . . . This administration, the only thing we bugged was for the national security."[30]

But the enlisting of the vice president in his Watergate defense right now was ill-timed. Nixon was right. The resignations of Haldeman, Ehrlichman, and Kliendienst, and the firing of Dean, were only the beginnings of the disintegration of the Nixon presidency, with the future of the Agnew vice presidency now also in peril.

Chapter 20

CONTESTED DIVORCE

THE SIMULTANEOUS CRISES OF THE NIXON–AGNEW ADMINISTRA-tion were rapidly intersecting now. Just as U.S. Attorney George Beall and his three young lieutenants were beginning to lay out the case against vice president Agnew to Elliot Richardson, the attorney general got an urgent White House call. He went into his private office and closed the door behind him. It was Alexander Haig, telling him that Nixon was livid over a *Los Angeles Times* story that special Watergate prosecutor Cox had started an investigation into the president's real estate dealings at San Clemente.

That was all Nixon—and Richardson—needed at this point. The paper quoted a source saying the investigation was looking into whether the president's $1.5-million home there may have been bought with cam-paign contributions or corporate and union money. Nixon was already on the ropes as a result of John Dean's June 23 testimony before the Senate Watergate Committee, which said he had warned the president that the Watergate affair was "a cancer on the presidency" that had to be cut out, but that Nixon had continued a cover up. Haig told Richardson that Nixon wanted him to find out what exactly Cox was doing regarding San Clemente.[1]

With this new burden on his shoulders, Richardson returned to his conference room to hear what Beall had to say. When the U.S. attorney got past the preliminaries and got to Agnew, Richardson perked up and started taking notes again. Beall turned to Baker to fill in the attorney

general on the latest from the lawyers for Matz and Wolff. But intermit-
tently Richardson would have to break off to take more White House
calls. On another from Haig, Nixon himself broke in to tell Richardson
that he wanted a categorical public denial from Cox that any San
Clemente inquiry was going on.

Richardson must have wondered what he had gotten himself into in
agreeing to move over to the Justice Department. Aides said later that he
was so irritated by Nixon's explosive behavior that he considered resigning then and there. But one of the factors that dissuaded him, they said,
was the realization that the Agnew situation that had just been laid out to
him could pose a monumental crisis in terms of presidential succession.[2]
He saw at once the prospective link between Agnew's dilemma and
Nixon's Watergate woes, but he never questioned that Beall and company
had developed a solid case.

"I had a kind of instinctive confidence in what appeared to me both the
decency and the professionalism of the way in which this whole thing was
being handled by Beall and his staff," Richardson said later. He recognized as a lawyer, he said, that they "were already in possession of what
on its face was more complete and convincing testimony than I had ever
been able to assemble" in similar kickback cases he had prosecuted as
U.S. attorney in his home state of Massachusetts.[3] In any event, the political imperative that had to be dealt with, Richardson realized, was to handle the Agnew charges with dispatch, and to take whatever steps
necessary to remove him from the line of succession. If the Watergate
scandal were to drive Nixon from the presidency, the country could not
tolerate having a bribe-taker ascend to its highest office.

Richardson openly discussed with the Beall team the best way to pro-
ceed. Was it constitutional to require a vice president of the United States
to testify before a grand jury? Beall said he had already discussed with
Jud Best, Agnew's lawyer, taking a deposition from the vice president.
Richardson said that in a case of such huge significance, the evidence
against Agnew had to be overwhelming, and that it had to be proved that
he took cash, as a means of establishing a strong "net worth" indictment
against him. That meant a minute accounting of everything Agnew
owned and bought during the period of alleged bribe-taking, to establish
that his legitimate income could not have covered it all—the basis for an
allegation of income-tax evasion.

Finally, on the heels of the tirade from Nixon he had just experienced regarding Cox's reported investigation into the San Clemente property, Richardson asked the prosecutors whether he should inform Nixon then of the Agnew case. They told him they were against it; they didn't want to give the vice president a heads-up on where they were in going after him. Richardson agreed not to brief Nixon yet. "I did not want to disturb him prematurely," he said later, "in the event that it should turn out that those people were not telling the truth [about Agnew's role] or that the evidence might otherwise just not add up."[4]

In all, the Baltimore Four and the attorney general had hit it off. Beall and the others, if fearful beforehand that Richardson would throttle their investigation or even try to cool it down, came away with a sense that he was engaged with them in a controlled and careful way to see that justice was done. At home in suburban McLean, Virginia, that night, Richardson told his wife, Ann, he said later, "that a bad scene was developing, and that it involved the vice president. I expected some worries about the fact that I might be perceived to have some personal animus" in seeing Agnew removed from office, in that Richardson himself was being mentioned as a prospective candidate for the Republican presidential nomination in 1976. And recent history had shown there was no better stepping-stone to that honor than the vice presidency. "It was a deeply disturbing picture," he said later. "I felt sick, almost. It was as bleak a day as I'd ever had."[5]

Agnew's own take on that day's events, as recorded later in his book, was that "Richardson proposed to confront me with the allegations of the witnesses, who had made their deals with the prosecutors, and to demand that I resign. By a not-so-strange coincidence, this rush for my resignation occurred just as Richardson was beginning to believe that the president himself was cracking under the strain of the Watergate scandal and must soon leave the presidency." The Beall team went to Washington, Agnew wrote, "to tell Richardson that two men in deep trouble themselves would implicate the vice president of the United States—if it would help them escape their own difficulties." As for the notion that Richardson himself considered resigning, Agnew wrote, "one reason he did not quit was that he believed the president was losing control, emotionally and mentally, and might soon have to hand the presidency over to me. That was a horrible prospect to the attorney general, who seems to have been determined I should never reside in the White House."[6]

As for informing Nixon, Agnew wrote that "the prosecutors emphatically objected. They were afraid that the word would get back to me and I would break the news of my being a target. They had not yet nailed down either Matz or Wolff, and they were afraid a public statement from me would change their minds—scare them off. Their plan was to sneak up behind me without warning. They were also cool to Richardson's idea of confronting me with the evidence and giving me a chance to assert my innocence. They knew their evidence would be tainted—bought from a dubious character in exchange for total immunity—and they knew I would fight."[7]

The noose was closing on the vice president. On July 9 and 10 his lawyer called Beall and was told first to call back and on the second day that, according to Agnew, "it was not appropriate for them to talk any more."[8] On the next day the Beall team had another meeting with Richardson to discuss among other things whether to inform Nixon. The attorney general asked the Baltimoreans, to their dismay, whether special Watergate prosecutor Cox should be clued in. He said he doubted it because of a partisan cast that was attributed to the staff Cox was assembling.

Beall immediately argued that the Agnew case gave the regular Justice Department a great opportunity to demonstrate its ability, in the wake of criticism that it had done an inadequate job as evidenced by McCord's letter to Judge Sirica. Richardson, to the relief of the Beall team, said it would be best to proceed without Cox. The attorney general then raised his concern that the president might learn from the press or elsewhere about the Agnew developments, putting the department in a bad light. But the prosecutors again prevailed on him to hold off rather than risk premature disclosure, and tipping their hand to Agnew.[9]

The Beall team at this point started casting its net for the remaining principal targets to come in and tell all on the record. The lawyers for Agnew's old friend and fund-raiser, Bud Hammerman, and another Maryland engineer, Allen Green, were called in for talks about what they could offer in negotiations to mitigate their own troubles. Green's lawyer and then Green himself presented details of fifty thousand dollars in cash payoffs made in plain envelopes while Agnew was governor and vice president. According to Green, when Agnew reached Washington, he said he hoped Green could continue the payments and he hoped to steer some federal contracts Green's way, though being vice president did not offer the opportunities Agnew had had as governor in Annapolis.[10]

❧ ❧

ON JULY 10, Haig in an early afternoon conversation in the Oval Office related to Nixon that the case against Agnew was about to blow wide open.[11]

HAIG: "I've got one piece of bad news that I think you should be aware of. I don't have the details, but the vice president's in some trouble."

NIXON: "It's gonna break?"

HAIG: "He thinks so. It still may not, but the fella who can hurt him has just been given full immunity and is going to testify."

NIXON: "Who is the fellow? Is he [someone] on the staff?"

HAIG: "A fellow the name of Wolff. Was on his staff, with him for nine years."

NIXON: "And on that [Capitol] Hill staff."

HAIG: "No, he's been over here in the vice president's staff here, after the vice president came to the White House."

NIXON [incredulously]: "He took him with him here? And he's going over to testify against the vice president?"

HAIG: "Well, we don't know what he's going to say but he could be very damaging."

NIXON: "[They've got] something?"

HAIG: "I wouldn't be surprised. I hate to say that. He handled contracts for the state of Maryland when [Agnew] was governor. And I think he stayed with [Democratic Governor Marvin] Mandel [Agnew's successor] for a period, and he was brought over to the vice president's staff."

NIXON: "So he was getting involved in—"

HAIG: "It involves some bad stuff."

NIXON: "Like what? Not over. . . not as vice president."

HAIG: "No, no. Nothing . . . ."

NIXON: "When he was governor."

HAIG: "Way back in his governor period. Payoffs for contracts."

NIXON: "Payoffs for campaign funds but not for the vice president's personal use."

HAIG: "Not for his personal use but for this guy's personal use and for fund raisers. There were two men involved, Wolff and another."

NIXON: "They don't have anything to do with our campaign. . . ."

HAIG: "Nobody's made any money."

NIXON: ". . . .Nobody made a stinking single cent. You know what I mean? There were no payoffs. I'll bet you the McGovern campaign was full of it. Well, let's not worry about that. And he [Agnew] may even ride it through. He may."

HAIG: "But I don't think he will."

Nixon: "Right now, the fact it happened many years ago. . . . You think he can survive?"

HAIG: "Well, he did before now."

On July 12, the urgency of resolving Agnew's fate was driven home when Nixon woke with a high temperature and chest pains. He went to work but later in the day at his White House doctor's insistence was checked in at the Bethesda Naval Hospital with viral pneumonia. According to Agnew, a White House staffer called him while Nixon was en route and told him it wasn't serious and he should play down the event if asked by reporters.

"The next morning General Haig informed me the president was doing fine," Agnew wrote later, "and wanted me to carry on my regular schedule which, of course, included whatever cabinet, leadership or National Security Council meetings had been previously set up." At such meetings, he wrote, he made it a point to conduct them from his own chair, not the president's. "The empty presidential chair—its back slightly higher than the rest—made me more aware than I had ever been," he wrote, "of the awesome responsibilities that were always only a step away. I was conscious that others in the room were also aware of that fact."[12]

Nixon was still in the hospital on July 16 when another bombshell burst. Haig informed him that Alexander Butterfield of the White House staff had just told the Senate Watergate Committee of the existence of the taping system in the president's office. (By now, similar systems were also operating in Nixon's office in the Executive Office Building and at Camp David.)

Agnew was not authorized to visit the president for several more days, and when he did call on Nixon at the hospital, Agnew wrote later, "we talked for about half an hour, mainly about Butterfield's revelation of the tapes and the Watergate situation generally. There was no mention of my impending problem, and I didn't feel that it was the proper time to discuss it. I doubt the president was even thinking about it because, at this point, nothing had come out in the press. The prosecutors and Richardson had not yet confided their intentions to General Haig."[13]

Agnew had to be uncommonly naïve to have believed that, with rumors flying around, Nixon had not heard. Haig in his own memoir later wrote that a month earlier Richardson had "told me that Vice President Agnew's name had come up in an investigation of kickbacks connected to public construction in Baltimore" that may have continued into his vice presidency. After passing on what he had just learned to Fred Buzhardt, Nixon's White House lawyer, Haig wrote: "I walked down the hall to the Oval Office and told Nixon what Richardson had just told me about Agnew. The president received the news with remarkable composure. Although I did not know this at the time, and Nixon, in typical fashion, did not bother to tell me, the president had known about the situation since April 10, when Agnew had told Haldeman about the investigation."[14] Agnew had always emphasized that he was not a member of the Nixon inner circle, but he knew enough of how it operated to know that when someone told Haldeman something, it was the same as telling Nixon.

Haig also wrote that Richardson's call had set his imagination running: "In my own mind, two words formed: *double impeachment*. I am not subject to visions, but as Richardson left my office a vivid picture grew in my mind of the president and vice president of the United States, both charged with high crimes and misdemeanors, side by side, on trial together before the Senate." Haig's "vision," however, clashed with probability, because in the worst of scenarios Nixon and Agnew would hardly have been tried together.

Haig wrote that even before informing Nixon, he had told what he had heard to Buzhardt, who accommodatingly agreed, saying: "You could have a coup d'etat with the legislative branch taking over the executive branch under the cover of the Constitution. The speaker of the House would become president." Haig protested: "But he's a Democrat [then Carl Albert of Oklahoma]. That would reverse the results of the election. We've got to find a way to decouple these two situations and deal with them one at a time. Otherwise, they'll go down together and the country will go with them."[15]

In an interview years later, Haig said: "Buzhardt concluded that this was a great risk to the president and a home run for the opposition party if they were smart enough to do it, and you could reverse a landslide election in thirty seconds. So he felt we had to separate Watergate from the Agnew case. That was the heart and soul of the White House strategy. It was costly to Nixon because he spent months solving the Agnew problem [just as] the Soviets were beginning to smell that Nixon was in real trouble, and we were seeing some manifestations of that in the Middle East [in the outbreak of the Yom Kippur War, fueled by Soviet arms to Egypt and Syria]."[16]

During Agnew's visit to Nixon at the hospital, the vice president wrote later, "abruptly, Mr. Nixon asked me what I thought he should do about the tapes." The question was a sharp departure from the previous practice of keeping the vice president out of Watergate except to encourage his public statements of support and belief in the president's innocence. Nixon told him, Agnew said, "he knew there would be demands to let the tapes tell the truth about what had transpired in the secrecy of the Oval Office since the break-in. He was terribly concerned about matters on the tapes that might affect the national security; also, he was uncomfortable about discussions he had had with individuals that they thought were entirely private. He added that much of the time he wasn't even conscious the machine was there, and really didn't know what was on the tapes."

Agnew had no hesitation in responding to Nixon's question: "I advised him to destroy the tapes. I thought then, and believe today, that the tapes should have been burned. For a man not to protect himself against hostile interpretation and dissemination of what amounts to his own private, unguarded remarks just doesn't make good sense."[17]

THE WATERGATE SCANDAL continued to unravel, with devastating consequences for Nixon. Testimony not only of Dean but also of Mitchell, Haldeman, Ehrlichman and other principals before the Senate committee, along with the relentless digging of Cox, were imperiling the president. And as Haig put it later: "The Agnew case made it even harder. All month long [through July], Buzhardt and I had been devoting the major part of our efforts to devising a strategy to quarantine the presidency from the scandal that was about to doom the vice president. The question of Agnew's future had to be decided as quickly as possible. For any number of reasons, including Nixon's waning influence in his own administration, we could not count on the president for effective help."[18]

Although Agnew did not have access to what was going on within the inner circle of the White House, he was taking the same reading—that Nixon in his physical and mental state was losing control. Indeed, Agnew wrote later, Haig as chief of staff had become "the de facto president," bent on orchestrating Agnew's departure from the vice presidency.[19]

During this sensitive period, Agnew and staff were particularly careful not to give offense to that inner circle. In an interview with the columnist Joseph Alsop, Agnew was asked whether he thought the presidential election process "has changed to a point where anyone who wants to be president has to go into the primaries." He agreed, and when Alsop asked, "Even with the loyal backing of the incumbent," Agnew replied, "I don't think that has anything to do with it. . . . I really don't think that means a great deal."

Apparently out of fear afterward that the answer might be seen as a putdown of Nixon, Agnew through Bryce Harlow sent a copy of the interview transcript to Haig. Harlow wrote: "The VP was greatly concerned over an Alsop column in *Newsweek*. He sends the enclosed record of interview to demonstrate that he was not trying to denigrate RN."[20]

But that was the least of the vice president's problems now. On July 27, the Baltimore Four made a third trip to see Richardson in Washington. They told the attorney general that with all the lines out to various principals, the press was bound to break the story and it was time to tell Nixon what was going on. Richardson grilled them again on the thoroughness of their case and said he was reluctant to give immunity to the targets and thus give Agnew the chance to argue that they were singing to save themselves. The Beall team told him no immunity had yet been granted but it was under consideration. Richardson then said he agreed it was time to inform the president, and instructed Beall to compose a formal letter to Agnew's lawyer specifying the charges against him and asking for personal records and tax returns.[21] The latter request was essential to establish income-tax evasion through a net-worth investigation.

As Richardson feared, Agnew later did allege that the witnesses against him had cooperated to save their own skins. He wrote: "Of the four witnesses relied on by the prosecutors, only one—Hammerman—was prosecuted in connection with the Agnew case, and his case was thrown out on appeal because he had been made improper promises in exchange for his testimony."[22] Actually, the other three referred to—Matz, Wolff, and Green—all were convicted but only Green, who pleaded guilty, served a short term. The others were given no jail term as part of the deal, the prosecutors reasoning that since Agnew got off, they shouldn't have to serve time. In sending a letter listing the allegations against him, Agnew later wrote indignantly, they were treating him "as if I were a common criminal—not the vice president of the United States."[23]

For all of Agnew's suspicions and hostility toward the White House, he still looked to it for assistance in his travail. For one thing, his lawyer, Jud Best, came to him through former White House political operative Chuck Colson, who had recommended Best to take Agnew's case when Colson himself, facing indictment in the Watergate affair, couldn't or wouldn't take it. Colson had continued to interest himself in Agnew's troubles, looking over Best's shoulder and sometimes joining him in meetings in Agnew's office, to the puzzlement of uninformed aides.

One of them, C. D. Ward, recalled later that up to this point he and other members of the Agnew staff had little inkling that their boss might be in big trouble. But then the vice president at a staff meeting told them that if they had any ideas on what he should do to defend himself, "I'd like to hear them," adding, "Things are going to get worse." Ward remembered thinking, "Why should he even be worried about this" if there wasn't something to the matter?[24]

After Richardson's latest briefing from the Maryland prosecutors, he sent Haig an update saying that "they have enough evidence to charge the vice president with forty felony counts for violations of federal statutes on bribery, tax evasion and corruption." Haig asked Richardson how long Agnew had before facing a grand jury and indictment. "A month, six weeks," was the attorney general's reply.[25]

Shortly after, Richardson contacted Haig and told him he wanted to see Nixon. Haig said he would get back to him, and that weekend the attorney general went to his summer place on Cape Cod to await the summons. He expected that the president, briefed in a general way by Haig on this explosive development, would want to see him on Monday morning. But the weekend passed with no word from Haig, and then two more days. Richardson returned to Washington, authorized release of the letter to Agnew, and waited some more. Finally, on Friday, August 3, about a week after Richardson had first asked to see the president, he was back at the Cape when Haig called and told him to come to the White House—but not until the following Monday!

The next day, Saturday, Haig called again and suggested that the attorney general meet on Sunday with two White House lawyers, Fred Buzhardt and Leonard Garment, to brief them so they could in turn brief Nixon before the meeting. Supposedly the president was still in the dark, but all parties had to know that if Haldeman and Haig were told something so important, it was the same as telling Nixon. But it served his own interests as well as his personal style to play dumb.

When Richardson briefed Buzhardt and Garment, the two lawyers raised questions about the motives of the Baltimore prosecutors, especially Skolnik, the one-time Muskie campaign aide. When they suggested the witnesses against Agnew were trying to save themselves, Richardson told them no immunity had yet been granted. Finally, they wondered about whether a vice president, or a president, for that matter, could be indicted before impeachment. Richardson stood solidly behind the prosecutors and their case and said he would look into the indictment question.

The issue was important to the White House lawyers, because it could be contended that the Constitution provided only one means for removing presidents and vice presidents, and that was impeachment by the legislature, not indictment in the judicial system. If Agnew were thus able to avoid indictment, it could be argued that so would Nixon, if it came to that in the Watergate mess. That night Richardson ordered quick research into the question, and an aide produced the opinion the next morning, shortly before the attorney general was to meet with Nixon and his lawyers. It held that a president as head of the executive branch could not be indicted and could even pardon himself of an offense; a vice president, with no executive power at all, could do neither, and hence could be indicted.

In the Oval Office, with Buzhardt listening, Richardson laid out the case against Agnew to the man who had selected him for the vice presidency amid effusive praise five years earlier. "The president appeared ready to believe it," Richardson said later. "His reaction was remarkably objective and deliberate. . . . He was disturbed and concerned with the correctness of any action or anything he did or did not do. At first he thought he ought to have an independent assessment of the evidence from Henry Petersen [head of the criminal division at Justice] and me, on the basis of which he could then decide whether or not the situation called for Agnew's resignation. He later concluded that he ought not to try to be fully informed about the state of the evidence, and that his position ought to be more insulated."[26] With skepticism among Agnew supporters about the motives of the Baltimore prosecutors, especially Skolnik, and Richardson as well, it was decided that the highly regarded and trusted Petersen would conduct the review and report back to Richardson and Nixon.

Nixon himself wrote later: "I knew that we were dealing with political dynamite and that I had to be scrupulously careful about the information I was receiving and how it was assessed. After their meeting with Richardson, Buzhardt and Garment sent back gloomy evaluations; they agreed with Richardson that this was one of the most solid cases they had ever seen. John Mitchell had already sent word to me that Agnew felt that Richardson was out to get him. Agnew remembered that Richardson had opposed his nomination in 1968, and he pointed out that they had disagreed repeatedly on policy matters during meetings of the Domestic Council. Agnew was also convinced that Richardson saw himself as a potential presidential candidate. . . . Objectively, I recognized the weight of Richardson's evidence, but emotionally I was still on Agnew's side. I wanted to believe him. I told Richardson that I expected him to assume full responsibility for seeing to it that Agnew was not railroaded by biased U.S attorneys and a predatory press corps."[27]

Haig said much later that while Richardson clearly wanted to be president, he saw no evidence that he manipulated the case to his own political ends. At first, he recalled, "Elliot was pretty hard on Agnew. He wanted Agnew to go to jail. He felt, in Massachusetts, a governor would go to jail for this. Who is to say a vice president shouldn't go to jail?"[28] But if so, he soon saw the situation in another light and changed his mind.

For a considerable period of time, as the Watergate scandal was unraveling, Nixon was able to take some comfort in one prospect: many if not most of the Democrats who controlled Congress, and therefore would be in charge of any impeachment trial against him, probably would think twice about removing him if doing so would elevate Agnew to the presidency. The aggressive and controversial vice president therefore might indeed be an insurance policy for Nixon against expulsion from office.

At the same time, however, it could be reasoned that if the vice president were to be impeached, taking the same step against the president might seem less drastic. But Agnew, according to Damgard later, believed the opposite: "He believed that Nixon had concluded that one of the ways he could avoid impeachment was to serve up his vice president." At first, Damgard argued, Nixon "believed an impeachment proceding would tie up the Congress for months, and neither the Congress nor the nation would have the stomach [after impeaching Agnew] to go back after the president."[29]

BUT WITH THE INDICTMENT of Agnew looming ever larger, for all of Nixon's supposed even-handedness in dealing with the matter, it was now clear that he wanted Agnew out, and the sooner the better. The president had enough on his hands already with Watergate, and who knew what conclusions would be drawn from the disposition of the case against the vice president that could be applied to Nixon's own fate? Agnew as an insurance policy against Nixon's own impeachment no longer seemed worth anything.

Agnew also entertained the notion, Damgard said, that Nixon had gone to Richardson and told him he would be the ideal Republican presidential nominee in 1976 "but that Agnew was in the way," thus giving him a particular incentive to pursue the vice president's expulsion. And Agnew believed as well, his old aide said, that the Maryland contractors and businessmen who had squealed on him had done so because they had been caught dipping into a campaign fund they had helped raise for Agnew as governor. He couldn't touch it as vice president, Damgard reasoned, and they hoped to escape jail time themselves by testifying against him.[30]

Beyond all this, Nixon had not given up on his personal desire to put John Connally, the man he so intensely admired, on the surest path to be his successor, either through ascendancy from the vice presidency or election in his own right in 1976. "That was the reason for Connally's change of parties," Haig wrote later. "As soon as Agnew's resignation became a possibility, Nixon spoke of replacing him with Connally in a matter of days. My task, as the president's crisis manager, was to do what I could to arrange matters so that Agnew's departure did the least possible damage to the president and to the presidency, and to do what I could to make sure the vacancy was filled as soon as possible by Nixon, who alone in the nation had been voted the authority to appoint a new vice president."[31]

With all this in mind, Haig wrote later, "I called on Agnew to ask him what he thought his options were. Agnew was his usual collected self. If he felt any anxiety, it did not show. Like Nixon, he blamed the situation on Maryland politics. A bunch of eager young prosecutors, he conjectured, were hoping to make a name for themselves by dragging his name into an investigation of small-time crooks. . . . Crazy slander of this kind was a cross all politicians had to bear. Agnew wasn't worried nor should I be."[32]

But the vice president in fact was very worried. "Agnew could never have been in any doubt that his resignation was wanted," Haig wrote. "He played on the fact. The president's desire for him to go was his only real bargaining chip, and he used it with great skill and dogged self-interest. He said he needed time—four or five days at least—to talk to his lawyers and plan his strategy. Maybe, he said, he would think it best to go on leave of absence as vice president while he defended himself. This situation was a strange mixture of the grand and the petty. . . . He continued to worry about smaller issues, including his pension. He was concerned about whether his years of federal service in the armed forces and government were sufficient to qualify him for benefits, and at one point he suggested to Nixon that he might be given government employment abroad after his resignation as a means of maximizing his benefits."[33]

After Richardson's briefing of Nixon, Haig called the attorney general and suggested he go see Agnew directly. Maybe he could talk him into resigning then and there. Richardson assumed that Haig's "suggestion" really came from the president, so he made an appointment to see Agnew that afternoon. When he got to Agnew's office, the vice president was there with Best and two trial lawyers from New York he had taken on— Jay Topkis and Martin London. At this time, the *Wall Street Journal* was about to break the story of Beall's letter formally notifying Agnew of the investigation, and they were considering what to say about it.

As Agnew wrote later, Richardson told him: "I am here because the president asked me to come. I would not have been here otherwise."[34] The attorney general proceeded to lay out to Agnew the case against him in grisly detail, including the Maryland engineers' accounts of paying him off for contracts received. Agnew interrupted repeatedly, declaring the reports were lies, and attacked the objectivity and motives of the Baltimore prosecutors. "He said he didn't trust the U.S. attorney's office," Richardson said later, "but if Henry Petersen were supporting these allegations, that would be different, because Henry was an experienced professional with an established reputation for fairness and courage."[35] Richardson again defended the Baltimoreans but said Petersen was indeed going to make an independent review of the evidence.

Agnew's lawyers squawked that the prosecutors were disrespectful toward the vice president of the United States, referring to him as "Agnew" rather than "Mr. Agnew." Agnew wrote later that "this may seem like a trivial thing, but it was not; it clearly reflected their arrogance and bias."[36] [He no doubt would have felt even worse had he known that the Baltimore Four among themselves had made up a nickname for him: "Spiggy."] To Richardson, Agnew repeated his poverty pitch; that he had little money and few assets, most of them tied up in a new house he had just bought. It was an unwitting invitation to a net-worth investigation.

Through all this, Nixon was dodging a personal confrontation with Agnew, who wrote later: "Immediately after Richardson left my office, I renewed my demands for an appointment to meet with the president and tell him my side of the story. I was shocked and incensed because Nixon didn't even call me. I was held off by his staff until word came in the afternoon that the president had flown to Camp David. Art Sohmer, my chief of staff, and I stayed in my office waiting for a telephone call, expecting me to be asked to join the president at his Maryland mountain retreat. We waited until nearly nine o'clock that night, when finally Sohmer came in from his office and said: 'We have just learned that the *Wall Street Journal* will break the story for tomorrow's edition. They have Beall's letter.'" Agnew replied: "It had to come from Beall's office or someone at Justice. We've got to see the president right now." But Sohmer told him: "There's something else. We're not going to Camp David. The president is sending Bryce Harlow here to see you—tonight."[37]

Shortly after, Agnew recalled, Harlow and Haig came into his office. "Well, when am I going to see the president?" he asked. In reply, he wrote later, "they went through a long recital about how hard it was for the president, beset with enemies from every quarter, to govern; what terrible complications I was causing for him; that my problem was another straw on an overloaded camel's back. I do not recall that either Haig or Harlow ever asked me, 'Are you guilty of these charges?' They just beat around the bush, talking about how bad the situation was."

Finally, Agnew wrote, Harlow told him: "This is a national crisis. Congress will act. You will be impeached." Agnew asked: "What are you here to tell me? What do you want?" Haig said: "We think you should resign." Agnew shot back: "Resign? Without even having a chance to talk to the president?" Haig replied: "Yes, resign immediately. This case is so serious there is no other way it can be resolved." Agnew asked him: "Did the president send you down here to say that?" Haig told him: "We are not here on our own." After talking all evening with Nixon at Camp David, he said, "we came here to tell you that you should resign."

Agnew wrote: "I became incensed. I stood up and began pacing the floor. 'This is ridiculous, to receive such a message secondhand,' I said. 'I'm not going to resign. I'm not going to do anything until I see the president. I want to see him just as soon as I can." It was, he commented later, as if Haig and Harlow "had brought the traditional suicide pistol into my office and laid it on my desk."

Reflecting on the confrontation later, Agnew added: "Looking back, I can see now that the White House strategists must have told each other, in so many words, Agnew has got to go, but we have to be careful not to anger his constituency in Middle America. Send Richardson in to paint the blackest possible picture. Afterward, let Agnew stew all day. Then send Harlow and Haig to see him. He likes Harlow and trusts him. See if we can't get the resignation now. Haig and Harlow left me with the bitter conclusion that I was definitely not part of the team. They were not concerned about me. They were only worried about the president. I was just a pawn on the chess board to be played in whatever way would help Nixon to survive. The White House had ruled, 'The vice president is expendable.'"[38]

Around this same time, the *Wall Street Journal* story hit the street, followed quickly by a similar one in *The Washington Post* telling of the

Justice Department's notification to Agnew that he was under investigation on charges of bribery and tax evasion in a kickback scheme. Agnew's brief statement said only "that I am innocent of any wrongdoing, that I have confidence in the criminal justice system of the United States, and that I am equally confident my innocence will be affirmed."[39]

Word of the bombshell quickly spread around the capital and beyond. Two Agnew friends telephoned one of the vice president's chief aides, Peter Malatesta, a nephew of Bob Hope, in Palm Springs, who immediately passed the news on to his neighbor and Agnew friend, Frank Sinatra. Malatesta and the singer, along with Sinatra's high-powered lawyer, Mickey Rudin, took a plane at once to Washington to help.

Agnew now saw a deep incestuous conspiracy against him, with Nixon involved but hiding behind Richardson and Haig. He wrote later: "I was locked in battle with high officials at the Department of Justice and the White House—officials of the same administration I served. These brothers were determined to force me out of office without even bothering to question the quality of the evidence against me developed by a hostile prosecuting team in Baltimore. . . . The president wanted to maintain the fiction that he was supporting me, and I presume Richardson was passed a quiet signal to do the dirty work on his own. In this way, Mr. Nixon could avoid alienating my supporters."[40]

For all that, Ted Agnew still pressed for the face-to-face appointment with his onetime political benefactor at which he could plead his case. He hoped somehow, in spite of what had just happened, for some manner of presidential intervention that could preserve what only weeks earlier he had envisioned as his own eventual course to the presidency.

Chapter 21

TERMS OF
DISENGAGEMENT

THE MEN AROUND AGNEW — HIS STAFF AND FRIENDS NOT IMPLI-
cated in the allegations of contract kickback—were distressed, and puz-
zled, about the vice president's failure to say more in his own defense. Vic
Gold, having left the job of press secretary to Agnew but still supportive
of him and believing him to be innocent, told him he needed to hold a
news conference, giving a full accounting of his behavior. But Agnew's
lawyers held that his best policy was to say no more, and let them carry
the ball.

Frustrated, the vice president still entertained the notion that the man
who could extricate him from his legal woes was the president of the
United States, and he continued to insist on an audience with him.
"Although Haig and Harlow claimed to speak for Richard Nixon in demanding that I resign at once," Agnew wrote later, "I clung to the belief
that the president himself would help me when he heard my side of the
story in reply to the version peddled to him so persuasively by Elliot
Richardson. Furthermore, I felt that Mr. Nixon at least owed me an objective view of the evidence out of loyalty, since I had never run out on
him. I had been totally faithful to him through five stormy years of our
adversaries' attacks on issues ranging from the Vietnam War to domestic
violence, so he should be equally loyal to me." The same, he said, was
true about Watergate; he believed at that time that Nixon had been

"unjustly maligned" and "victimized" by ambitious people in his presidential campaign.[1]

Agnew saw himself as an integral factor in a nefarious plot by "left-wingers determined to reverse the election results by forcing Nixon out of the presidency by a process which amounted to a coup d'etat." However, he wrote, "they would have gained nothing by kicking out Nixon only to have me come into power as his successor. They knew that I was more of a conservative than he was on major domestic and foreign policy issues. They had reason to think I would have slowed down the drift toward accommodation-at-any-cost with the Soviet Union and the People's Republic of China. To quote an old colloquial expression, replacing Nixon with me would have been 'swapping the devil for the witch.' I believed that once Nixon realized the ultimate purpose of the attack on me, he would see we were in this fight together; and that if our enemies killed off one of us politically, they would then concentrate on destroying the other. The president, being commander in chief and head of the executive establishment, still had great power and he could help me, if he would."[2]

How Agnew could have believed in such a scheme, if indeed he ever did, was mind-boggling. While he was not part of the president's inner circle, he had heard and observed enough to know by Nixon's distance from him, and his obvious preference for Connally, that the president had long before cooled toward him. And Nixon was too engaged trying to save himself from the dragon of Watergate to get involved in any rescue mission for the man he now regretted he had ever chosen to be his running mate.

Nevertheless, Agnew finally got his face-to-face meeting with Nixon on the afternoon his scandal broke in the press. They met in the president's hideaway, a suite of rooms in the Old Executive Office Building across a closed-off street next to the White House. "He greeted me warmly at the door and led me to an easy chair," Agnew wrote later, "talking all the while about inconsequentials so as not to allow the gaps in conversation he found so uncomfortable." Nixon reviewed in a monologue what Richardson had told him about Agnew's troubles, the vice president recalled, and "he seemed sympathetic and solicitous—indignant about the investigation in Baltimore. He said he understood the pressures on a governor to raise money for the ticket, and he understood where and how that money had to be raised. During all this, I had no opportunity to do other than briefly interject a word of agreement or a nod of understanding. When he finally subsided, it no longer seemed appropriate to talk about the abrupt resignation request conveyed by Haig and Harlow the night before."

Nixon continued the masquerade of concern over Agnew's plight. Finally, Agnew recalled, Nixon asked him: "Can you function effectively as vice president?" Agnew replied that he could. He then reviewed his own version of the case against him; of old business associates who, he told Nixon, "were caught in a tax evasion problem and they saw a hell of a good way to extricate themselves from it by dragging me in." The Baltimore prosecutors had the goods on them, he said, and told them "if you will just deliver Agnew to us, things will be a lot easier for you."[3]

Nixon, according to Agnew, could not have been more sympathetic. He told his vice president that he had had his own troubles with Richardson and so was going to appoint Henry Petersen to do an independent review and report back to him. "Because Richardson had mentioned Petersen at the meeting in my office the day before," Agnew wrote, "I was a little surprised that Nixon acted as if the thought had just struck him. However, I desperately wanted to believe the president had been persuaded I was not being treated fairly and that he wanted to rectify that. If Mr. Nixon, with all his Watergate troubles, believed Petersen was unprejudiced and objective, then I wanted to believe that, also. 'Well,' I said, 'if you think he's a fair man—fine.'"

Agnew apparently thought from this he had received a reprieve, though not a pardon. He told Nixon he was going ahead with a press conference the next day. "He was less than enthusiastic about that, probably because he was being excoriated for dodging the press," he wrote, "but he contented himself with cautioning me against making any statement that might hurt me later. During the whole time I was in the hideaway, not once was there the slightest suggestion that I should consider resignation. In spite of the Haig–Harlow visit the night before, I felt there was no need for me to bring up the subject. After an hour and a half with the president, I went out of his office feeling a surge of hope."[4] What had happened, obviously, was that Agnew had received the customary Nixon treatment of delivering bad news—delivering encouraging words in person and letting others administer the poison.

Sure enough, about fifteen minutes after Agnew had returned to his office, Haig and Harlow arrived again with another message. Haig told him that if he were indicted, his abilities to carry out the duties of the vice presidency would be severely impaired and that he ought to think about the practical ramifications. In other words, he was being invited again to fall on his sword. "The president believes that you have to decide what to do," Haig wrote later that he told Agnew. "He's confident that you will make a statesmanlike decision." Agnew was not buying. "I'll fight it out until the end," he told Haig.[5] The vice president had been reelected in his own right and the president did not have the power to fire him.

Haig reported Agnew's determination to dig in, to Nixon's exasperation. "Everyone thinks he has to leave," Nixon said. "Does he think he won't be indicted? Does he think he can fight it out as vice president?" Haig replied: "He thinks he can. He says, 'I'll fight it out over the next two or three years.'"[6]

The next morning, according to Haig, Nixon "instructed me to call Connally and tell him to hold himself in readiness for a meeting with the president. 'He wants to be sure,' I told Connally, 'that you aren't going to be traveling, or away, or something, especially around the fourteenth, fifteenth and sixteenth'"—when Nixon expected to get the results of Petersen's review, which might trigger Agnew's resignation. "Connally replied that he understood and would be on hand if needed."[7] The reply suggested that Connally, for all his disavowals of interest in the vice presidency, was not all that turned off by the idea after all.

That night, Nixon phoned Henry Petersen at his home. In a memo to his boss, Richardson, the next morning, Petersen wrote that the president "began to discuss the Agnew matter and said that he was certain I would do a very careful job on it, that all he wanted was the truth, but that I knew his views on immunity, and he was very concerned that persons who were receiving or making payments would be immunized in order to make a case against the vice president. He stated, of course, that I understood the decision was mine but he hoped I would be especially solicitous and careful about the type of persons to be immunized. The president added, 'Of course, when you are dealing with the vice president you are not dealing with a Boston politician.'"[8] The comments on immunization of the witnesses against Agnew, designed to loosen their tongues, seemed a strange way for Nixon to be standing aside from the matter, almost as if he were weighing in to help the vice president whose departure he hoped for.

On the afternoon of August 8, Agnew held his news conference in a studio-auditorium of the Old Executive Office Building. Television cameramen jammed the room along with more than 200 reporters, and the scene had a distinct movie-set quality about it. Agnew, tall and self-assured as ever, came out tense with indignation and did not hold back. He said the usual secrecy afforded subjects of a federal investigation was being denied him and he had to speak out. He said he had "no intention of being skewered in this fashion," and so was meeting the press and television "to label as false and scurrilous and malicious these rumors, these assertions and accusations that are being circulated."[9] One by one, he turned away with flat denials about alleged illegalities. Disingenuously, he denied knowing who was making the allegations against him.

At the same time, Agnew went out of his way to express his support of Nixon, the man he still saw as his possible life preserver in spite of all indications to the contrary. He wrote later: "Mr. Nixon did not seem to realize that I was his insurance policy against his own ouster. The left-wingers who despised us both would never push him out of the White House until they were certain I would not be around to take his place. What would be the point of exchanging a weakened Nixon for a president whose ideas seldom meshed with theirs, and who could be stubborn? Therefore, logic dictated that I must be moved aside first, by fair means or foul."[10] In Baltimore, the prosecutors watched the news conference on television and, knowing the evidence they had assembled, were convinced that Agnew was helping them hang him.

That night, Haig spoke to Richardson and told him Nixon wanted Petersen's report by August 16, eight days later. In the course of the conversation, the attorney general said he and Petersen might talk to Agnew if he so desired. According to Haig, when he informed Nixon of the suggestion, the president exploded: "I don't want Elliot to talk to him! Agnew's view is that he's trying his damnedest to get the vice president. Do *you* believe that Elliot feels that Agnew's guilty? What the hell did Agnew do what he did today for? By coming out so flatly and telling the president and the country that he's not guilty, my view is that in his own mind he has crossed the bridge and. . . under no circumstances will he resign. If he really is innocent, then he ought to find a way to resign

gracefully and fight it. We want to keep him away from the constitutional route [impeachment]. We'll just say that's out of the question."[11]

The reason was obvious why Nixon was so explicit about discouraging
Agnew from seeking escape from indictment by pursuing the impeachment process by the House of Representatives: if a vice president were to
be impeached, it might then seem all the easier to impeach a president.

As PETERSEN began his review of the allegations against Agnew, he ac-
ceded to a meeting with Agnew's new lawyers, Topkis and London. They
tried to smoke him out on more details and at the same time to question
the reliability and credibility of the young Baltimore prosecutors. They
told him that Agnew was perfectly willing to cooperate and to be interviewed by him. But Petersen, saying he intended to interview the witnesses himself, defended the Baltimoreans. He politely denied the defense
lawyers' requests for more information and turned down the offer to interview the vice president. If Agnew had anything to say, Petersen said,
he could say it to the prosecutors. They left empty-handed.[12]

Meanwhile Agnew—and Nixon—waited for Petersen's assessment.
The day after the vice president's news conference, he decided to fly out
to Palm Springs to spend a few days with his friend Frank Sinatra, staying out of public view except for playing golf. As Petersen pressed on,
major news organizations like the *Wall Street Journal* and *The Washington
Post* dribbled out new details of the investigation. And the prosecutors
continued to tighten the noose, finally gathering enough information on
the kickbacks and involvement of Agnew's close friend Hammerman in
the schemes and reeling him in. At Richardson's prodding, they intensi-
fied the net-worth investigation against the vice president. On return to
Washington, Agnew made a speech in nearby Centerville, Maryland, declaring his, and Nixon's, innocence and blaming his old nemesis, the
press, for their mutual grief. As he spoke, unknown to him, his old buddy
Hammerman was singing to the prosecutors in Glen Burnie, across the
Chesapeake Bay.[13]

On August 15, as Petersen was winding up his inquiry, Agnew released some minor personal financial statements to Beall as a holding action. But his seeming cooperation was overtaken by more news stories of
what the Maryland witnesses were saying against him. Four days later, a

story in *Time* magazine, citing unnamed Justice Department officials in Washington, sent Agnew through the roof. On August 21, he called another news conference and attacked the Department for "a clear and outrageous effort to influence the outcome of possible grand jury deliberations." He said he was writing Richardson asking for an investigation into the leaks, making clear that for once he was not going after the press; he wanted the leakers nailed.

Richardson hastened to denounce the leaks and called on the press to show "restraint in what they report." But privately he seethed at Agnew's attempt to give his already beleaguered department a black eye. Leaks happened all over Washington, but these seemed to point to the White House as the leaker as a way to raise the temperature under Agnew to resign.

The president, however, in a televised news conference on the lawn of his summer White House in San Clemente, expressed shock and said he had ordered Richardson to conduct an investigation. Any Justice employee found to have leaked would, he promised, be "summarily dismissed from government service."

Of the man whose sins in Maryland he now knew from Haig and Richardson, and whose departure he now so transparently desired, Nixon incredibly said: "My confidence in his integrity has not been shaken, and in fact has been strengthened by his courageous conduct and his ability even though he's controversial at times, as I am, over the past four and a half years." He made a point of limiting his confidence to "the performance of the duties he has had as vice president, and as candidate for vice president"—the period of Agnew's public service for which Nixon had been responsible. He said it would be "improper" for him to comment about the charges of misconduct when Agnew was a county executive and governor, and "the talk about resignation even now. . . would be inappropriate."[14] Agnew gratefully called Nixon and thanked him.

At the same time, the White House told the *New York Times* that attempts by Agnew's lawyers to cook up a joint legal strategy for the president and vice president, based on executive privilege and non-indictability, had been flatly spurned. Nixon's lawyers distinctly did not see the president and Agnew as being in the same boat. For one thing, they believed executive privilege and immunity from indictment extended only to the president; his old sidekick Ted was on his own.

On September 1, with Nixon back in Washington, Agnew met with him for two hours at the White House. He wrote later: "I told Nixon I despaired of finding any court in the Washington area or in Maryland that could possibly treat me fairly, since the minds of most people had been poisoned against me by the outrageous propaganda emanating from the Justice Department and being featured in such sensational fashion in the Washington area and by the national news media. Therefore, I said, I felt obliged to take my case to the House of Representatives. I believed that if a congressional committee would hear the witnesses on both sides, their sessions would be televised across the country. I would make my defense not to the congressmen alone but to the American people, who would be watching the drama on television, just as they had been staring at their TV sets during the Watergate hearings that summer."[15]

The scheme of "going to the House" was transparent. Agnew wrote later that television would show up the Maryland witnesses as "free-wheeling, experienced wheeler-dealers in trouble with the law" who were bent on saving themselves. More pointed, though, was his rationale that "the House members, all of whom had experienced the problems of raising campaign funds, would understand the situation much better than a Baltimore jury, which would be heavily influenced by the zealous prosecutors determined to ruin me."[16]

Unmentioned by him was the possibility that other House members might have had similar problems then or in the past. He began to cozy up to leading House Republicans, including the party's leader, Gerald Ford, inviting him out of the blue several times to play golf at the Burning Tree club. On the course, Ford wrote later, "I sensed that he had something else on his mind."[17]

Basic arithmetic encouraged going to the House, because even if he were impeached in that majority Democratic body, the action would only be the equivalent of a grand-jury indictment. The case would then go to trial in the Senate, where a two-thirds vote of the whole, or sixty-seven senators, would be required for conviction. With forty-three Republicans in the Senate, party loyalty could save Agnew. Beyond that, there might be a number of Democrats who would prefer to see him stay in office as an additional albatross around the necks of Nixon and his party. And if, as some speculated, Nixon might after all select former Democrat John

Connally to fill a vacancy caused by Agnew's removal, senators of Connally's old party might balk at the switch.

"My plan to take my case to the House," Agnew wrote later, "touched off a commotion in the Nixon inner circle." Nixon, he said, told Haig who told Buzhardt and Richardson, and together "they set out immediately to short-circuit my move." They knew, he said, going to the House "would close the door on any possibility" of his resigning quickly because "I would carry on the battle on Capitol Hill for many weeks." Also, he wrote, "if the vice president could be impeached by the House and tried by the Senate, there would be plenty of people around who would want to make it a doubleheader." Beyond that, impeachment hearings "would expose not only the concentrated efforts of the prosecutors to wreck me, but also the pressure from the White House to make me resign. The doors of a lot of closets would swing open and the skeletons come marching out!"[18]

Around this time, according to Mel Laird, then serving as Nixon's domestic counselor at the White House, he and Bryce Harlow got a visit from Richardson, who briefed them on the seriousness of the allegations against Agnew. As a result, Laird said, he spoke to several leading Republicans in Congress, including Representative John Anderson of Illinois, "reminding them to be a little careful about getting into a real defensive thing" in behalf of the beleaguered vice president.[19]

Indeed, the White House wanted urgently to detour Agnew's taking what was being called "the impeachment track." An issue for Nixon as well as for Agnew was whether the Constitution required that impeachment be the first or only means of removing a president or vice president, or he could be indicted first in a court of law. Richardson now had in hand an opinion that a vice president could be indicted but a president could not.

THROUGH EARLY SEPTEMBER, Agnew was left in the dark about what the White House and the prosecutors were up to. He complained to Haig: "This is the most bizarre thing I've ever seen. All we have is what we see in the newspapers. Why can't we be leveled with?" Haig wrote later that "Agnew developed the belief that Richardson was going to refer his case to the House of Representatives for possible impeachment. He [Agnew] wanted to preempt the attorney general by asking Congress to decide his case, and he asked whether the president would support him in this maneuver by writing a letter to the House of Representatives." But that was not about to happen.

"This bit of bravado agitated Nixon but produced no result—at least for the moment," Haig reported. "The president, frustrated by Agnew's refusal to resolve the situation by resigning, asked me to call John Connally and tell him he still regarded him as the next vice president of the United States, and as his own successor in due course. 'The president just wanted to be sure,' I told him, 'that you just held tight... to reassure you that everything is precisely the same in his view.' Connally, ever cool-headed, responded, 'Okay, Al. I'll be talking to you.'"[20]

On September 8, the White House asked Richardson to hold off taking Agnew's case to the grand jury, to give Nixon aides Haig and Buzhardt more time to persuade the vice president to resign. The wary Baltimore Four objected to any further delay, and Richardson's worry mounted about leaving Agnew in the line of presidential succession. No one could tell what Nixon's fate in the Watergate fiasco would be, or, in fact, his state of health. The attorney general wanted the vice president out, and if he could be persuaded to jump before he was pushed, so much the better.

Two days later, Nixon sent Haig and Buzhardt to Agnew to give him a still stronger push over the side. Beforehand, he told Haig, again employing his usual circumvention: "I want Agnew to know, without Buzhardt telling him I know, what a very strong case there is, so that my rather limited support will be understood ... He has not told me everything he should.... He has never once mentioned what I mentioned to Eisenhower, that I would get off [the Republican ticket in 1952] if Eisenhower requested that." Haig told Nixon: "He has said, 'I am fighting for my life.'" To which Nixon replied: "He has never said, 'I want to do what's best for the country.'"[21] This recollection did not, however, square entirely with the way Nixon had maneuvered to remain Eisenhower's running mate.

As Agnew later recalled the visit of Haig and Buzhardt, the president's lawyer "began with a cold, clinical, pessimistic analysis of the case against me. He said the Justice Department's top officials considered it strong enough so that I could be indicted, convicted and sent to prison. Then

Haig moved in, saying, 'Richardson has a hard case. He wants to throw it to the grand jury, with witnesses testifying under oath. If you dump this on the House, the prosecutors will send the grand jury record to the [impeachment] committee and you'll be playing high-risk ball.'" Haig added, Agnew wrote, that "all the key witnesses will be indicted—will plead and testify."[22]

Agnew said he pressed again for taking the impeachment track, asking Haig: "Why do you think the congressional process is bad?" Haig replied that Nixon was against it and "the president may not back you." Agnew asked whether Nixon wouldn't "wait until all the evidence is in?'" Haig said he would, "but you could face both impeachment and indictment, the worst of both worlds. If Elliot Richardson comes up with sworn testimony, he will send it to the grand jury." Agnew pleaded: "Can't the president tell Richardson to send it to the House instead?" Haig replied: "Not until they finish taking testimony under oath." Agnew concluded later: "I was to be a living demonstration that the president spurned cover-ups, let the chips fall where they might—this was the whole idea behind the White House move to make me quit. Haig kept insisting I must resign at once. I stubbornly refused. So the general and Buzhardt left my office empty-handed, without my resignation."[23]

Notwithstanding the vice president's resolute stand, his lawyers were starting to see the handwriting on the wall against him. The next day they called Richardson and told him they wanted to discuss the "procedural options" open to their client. The term plea bargaining was not mentioned, but Richardson, Petersen, and the Baltimore Four saw the lawyers' initiative as a possible first step to negotiating a deal. In preparation, Richardson met with the others and laid out the objectives that would have to be achieved: Agnew's resignation, a just outcome that would be publicly perceived as such, and full disclosure of the case against him that would assure that perception. The emphasis on justice would preclude simply letting the vice president resign at no price to him beyond loss of his high office.[24]

The following morning, September 12, Richardson, Petersen, and Beall met with the Agnew lawyers, Best, Topkis, and London, for what turned out to be only preliminary sparring. Topkis said they were about to advise Agnew that under the Constitution he could not be indicted and therefore his recourse was going to the House. Richardson said that did not square with his own legal advice. Topkis argued that going to a grand jury would lead to leaks and "a circus in Baltimore," to which Richardson, knowing Congress's reputation as a sieve, incredulously replied: "How could you possibly consider even a leaky grand jury more of a circus than a proceeding on the Hill?" Topkis replied: "Because we will get our licks in on the Hill, and we cannot do so in a grand jury, which is one-sided." Richardson warned him that with the Justice Department's case against Agnew so strong, he would pay a high price for their getting their licks in. He cut off the jockeying by telling the lawyers he would press for an indictment.[25]

That night, Haig and Buzhardt squeezed Agnew some more. According to Agnew later, they told him that his good friend Bud Hammerman's testimony of taking kickbacks from the engineers had been corroborated by them, and that Haig said: "It's a hell of a situation. If we go along with the move to the House, Elliot will move concurrently and ask Speaker [Carl] Albert to hold it up. Albert will want to wait. . . . The president has made some feelers. . . . You won't be supported. . . . The president has lost his ability to exercise any power. The House action will take six months. There will be a clamor for a trial."

Agnew wrote that Haig, continuing to press for resignation, "became so rough with me" that Best asked the vice president to leave so he could talk alone with Nixon's emissaries. When he had gone, Best told them: "I'll not have my client lacerated by you any longer. What's the deal? How do you plan to handle it? What will you give me if he resigns? Let's cut out the bullshit and work something out."[26]

Later, after Haig and Buzhardt had departed, Agnew wrote, "Best sat down with me and suggested that we at least sound out the administration about arrangements for me to resign, but only with positive guarantees that I would not be prosecuted. I was so worn out and frustrated after seven months in this pressure cooker, and so fearful about the harm which the controversy was causing my wife and family, that I said wearily, 'Well, let's explore what terms we can get.'"[27]

The same night, Best called on Richardson and told him he was ready to talk about a deal. The attorney general called in Petersen and a meeting was set for the next morning, September 13. Just before it started, Richardson called Beall and instructed him to start presenting the evidence against Agnew to the grand jury in Baltimore, setting in motion one flank of the maneuver to force the vice president's hand. Then he turned to his own personal role—the plea bargaining that he was determined, at a minimum, would get Spiro T. Agnew out of the line of presidential succession.

Through all these machinations, a flood of telegrams to Agnew imploring him not to resign, and castigating Nixon for not helping him, was engulfing his office. A "registered Republican" woman from Belleville, New Jersey, wired: "I have supported the president all through the Watergate affair but no longer care if they can allow this sort of thing to happen to you." Another woman, from Sundance, Wyoming, wrote that she was "disgusted with Nixon. He seems to be hoping that your implied troubles will take the pressure off him and that you can be the public scapegoat. . . I do think he is entitled to finish out his term, but not at your expense. Why can't he be loyal? He thinks only of Nixon, apparently." A man from Chicago urged Agnew to "allow me to continue to believe in you and the H— with Nixon and the demented crooks around him. Do not resign." A woman from Peoria: "Richard Nixon is a power-mad person who will hurt anyone who gets in his way." And a couple from Lexington, South Carolina, said of Nixon: "If he had used and trusted you more and others less, there would have been no Watergate."[28]

None of these pleas, however, would weigh on the scales of Agnew's fate now, about to be placed in the hands of his defense lawyers and Attorney General Richardson, a Republican never identified with the Silent Majority that was now clamoring for the vindication or at least the survival of their champion.

Chapter 22

PARTING OF THE WAYS

Fᴿᴏᴍ ᴛʜᴇ sᴛᴀʀᴛ ᴏꜰ ᴛʜᴇ ɴᴇɢᴏᴛɪᴀᴛɪᴏɴs ᴡɪᴛʜ Rɪᴄʜᴀʀᴅsᴏɴ, ɪᴛ was clear to Judah Best, Agnew's lawyer, that the vice president was not going to walk away from the allegations against him merely by surrendering his high office. The attorney general quickly dismissed the possibility, so Best put his cards on the table. Agnew was willing to plead *nolo contendere* to a single count. It would mean he was not contesting the charges against him and was accepting the penalty assigned as if he had admitted guilt. In exchange for resigning the vice presidency, he also wanted the government's recommendation to the judge that he not be sent to prison.

The plea would enable Agnew to continue insisting, as a private citizen, that he had not committed any crime. Richardson would not agree without discussing the matter with the Baltimore prosecutors. After Best left, he summoned the Beall team to Washington for a long discussion of options. Richardson knew that staying out of jail was Agnew's prime concern. The Baltimoreans wanted him to serve some sentence, but Richardson now saw jail time mainly as a threat to force him to resign. As far as he would go, he said, was to call for no jail time only if the judge insisted on his making a recommendation. Tim Baker argued against letting Agnew go free because it could be seen as favoritism to a high political figure.[1]

As the Justice lawyers weighed the plea possibilities, Haig informed Nixon in general terms what was on the table. "If that doesn't satisfy him

323

[Agnew]," the president told Haig, "I may have to play tough."[2] As for Agnew, he reached out to friends on Capitol Hill for support. He invited Barry Goldwater to his home in suburban Maryland, where, Agnew said, the fiesty Arizona senator told him: "Hang in there and fight. They're just trying to ride you out. Go to the House, but don't tell the White House—just go on your own."[3] Goldwater called Harlow at the White House and complained, prompting Harlow and Buzhardt to fly to Arizona to show him some of the evidence of Agnew's sins. "I don't give a damn if Agnew is as guilty as John Dillinger," he told them; Agnew was entitled to the presumption of innocence and the prosecutors should take what they had to a grand jury.[4]

On September 15, Richardson instructed that a letter be drafted for Best laying out the terms demanded. Beyond resignation, the Justice Department wanted a plea from Agnew "supporting conviction of a criminal charge" arising from the investigation, full disclosure by the department of the facts on which allegations were based, and acknowledgment by him "in open court" that he had taken bribes as a public official in Maryland. The letter informed Best that the investigation was continuing, and evidence was continuing to go to the grand jury.

Meanwhile, Agnew stewed over his treatment, especially by the White House. "For a while, I seriously considered closing my suite in the Old Executive Office Building next door to the White House," he wrote later, "and moving lock, stock and barrel to my small suite in the Senate Office Building, thus symbolically cutting loose from Nixon and drawing into a tight shell to fight by myself. But I didn't see how I could win that way, in the long run. And I still clung to the hope that somehow the president would see what was happening and come to my defense. So I listened to my lawyers and considered the terms we might get in return for my resignation."[5]

Two days later, Agnew told Best that "I would contemplate one concession to the prosecutors: I would discuss pleading *nolo contendere* to a single minor charge of underpaying my income taxes. I would do so even though I did not really believe I owed the government an extra cent. We had to do something to break the deadlock. But this was not nearly enough to appease the voracious appetites of Richardson and his men. They were out for blood. They wanted me to crawl in surrender, plead guilty to a felony such as bribery or extortion, and admit having received money knowing it had come from engineers for the purpose of influencing state contracts. They prepared a letter to that effect for me to approve. Of course I had not the remotest idea of ever groveling like that."[6]

Yet, as Topkis countered with an offer to plead *nolo* to a misdemeanor without admission from Agnew of knowingly taking a bribe, the vice president had Topkis hand Richardson an incredibly groveling statement obviously intended to soften up the prosecution. He reneged on his own previous claim that the investigation was "politically inspired," said he knew Richardson "to be a straight-shooting and devoted public servant," and said he had endorsed Beall's appointment as U.S. attorney in Maryland. They were "only doing their jobs," he wrote. "I have no reason to complain of anything they have done." As for Nixon, he said, "[n]or do I believe that the president had any role in his matter. I have been honored to serve in this administration. I have always held him in the highest regard as my President and my friend. I hold him in that regard today."[7] (Later, Agnew explained away the letter: "In order to allay Petersen's fear that I might attack the Justice Department, my lawyers had drafted an obsequious statement for me to make. . . . I gagged when the statement was presented to me, but I was told it was the only way that Richardson might abandon his insistence on the letter admitting my guilt of bribery and extortion. . . .")[8]

More negotiations did not cause Richardson to budge from his insistence that there be full disclosure of the facts against Agnew. As far as he would go on no jail time for him was to make a recommendation to the judge, not as a stipulation of the deal. The only matter left was what Agnew would be allowed to say in court in reply to the charges. In another meeting on September 18 with Agnew's lawyers, described in a memo by Beall, Richardson argued that Nixon "should not be perceived as railroading the vice president out of his job. It is essential that the vice president not be able to walk out of the courtroom, hold a press conference and suggest that, while denying all guilt, he was forced to step down. The only way to avoid that contingency is for him to acknowledge in open court the substance of the government's case."[9]

Agnew's kind words for Nixon in the fawning letter about Richardson and Beall may have been a nudge for what the vice president hoped even at this late date would be an intervention by the president. But Haig wrote later that on the next day, he "told Agnew what was happening and warned him that the president would expect him to resign for the good of the country if the grand jury returned an indictment. This statement shattered his composure. 'Resign?' Agnew said, with what seemed to be genuine astonishment. 'Don't I get a presumption of innocence? I didn't suggest *he* [Nixon] ought to resign over Watergate. I want to see the president and I want to see him now!'"[10]

Haig's report, Agnew wrote later, "was a threat to strike terror in any man's heart. Although I knew Mr. Nixon would prefer that I resign as a convenience to him, I had been counting on him at least to stand by me publicly or to stay neutral—not to join my enemies openly. . . . In the back of my mind was the question, How much of Nixon's policy toward me was really his own, and how much was dictated by Haig? The president insulated himself so well it was impossible to find out which orders came from him and which from the people around him."[11]

It seemed incredible that Agnew could continue to entertain the idea that Nixon was no more than a hand puppet in all this, manipulated by Haig, Richardson, and the prosecutors in Baltimore. But whatever he really thought, the next day he got another face-to-face meeting with Nixon, the sort from which the president usually cringed. As Agnew recalled it, he asked Nixon "to support me in my fight for my life," telling him, 'I have not misused the public trust." Nixon said he believed him, after which Agnew asked directly: "Will you support me? It is impossible for me do anything else but fight." But Nixon hedged, telling him: "You must do what is best for you and for your family." Agnew told Nixon that he "would be willing to resign and plead *nolo contendere* to a tax misdemeanor to end this whole miserable business. But I emphatically added I would not step down unless absolutely guaranteed that I would not be prosecuted on any felony charges such as bribery or extortion. . . . I would take my chances on a trial in court, rather than crawl."

Nixon said nothing to give his vice president reason to think he would throw him a life preserver. Still, Agnew wrote, "It was hard for me to believe that this president would become my enemy. I was not his enemy. I was just one of the worst complications he could have had. He was trying to consolidate his problems into as small a ball as possible and deal with them head on, and anything on the periphery added trouble. As I left his office, I felt sure I had convinced him that I would fight all the way if Richardson did not come around to my terms for resignation."[12]

If Agnew had trouble believing Nixon might be working against him, voters supportive of the vice president did not. Telegrams streamed in to him from around the country. One from Waterboro, Maine, said: "We are behind Nixon 25 percent. We are behind Agnew 100 percent. Don't back down." Another, from Paramus, New Jersey, told him: "Do not resign. The people are with you. Let Nixon resign. Fight on."[13]

Directly or indirectly, Agnew's talk with Nixon served the purpose of getting the president, urgently desirous of getting rid of his vice president, more involved in pressuring Richardson to soften his terms for resignation. The attorney general was summoned to the White House that night for tough talks with Haig and Buzhardt, in which he reiterated his nonnegotiable terms and they pressed him on Nixon's behalf to find a way to meet Agnew's most rigid points of resistance. The stumbling block continued to be, Richardson said, his insistence that Agnew explicitly acknowledge "guilt not only of the specific one count of a felony" but, in open court, of "complicity in acts that amounted to bribery and extortion."[14]

After sleeping on whether he was being "unduly formalistic," Richardson wrote later, he decided to hold firm. The next morning he called Buzhardt and told him. To the attorney general's surprise, Haig called him back and said Nixon felt the same way! Apparently he was concerned about a clash with Richardson at a time when his lawyers were in negotiation with Watergate prosecutor Cox over release of the White House tapes. Nevertheless, it remained in Nixon's interest that means be found to achieve Agnew's resignation short of an indictment that could challenge the Justice Department's view that a president could not similarly be indicted. Petersen drafted language that talked of "a long-standing practice" in Maryland of payments by contractors to the governor and saying Agnew, in "the national interest," was pleading "nolo" to the charge of taking such payments, which he had failed to report. This was a far cry from the full case built by the prosecutors in Baltimore, and they loudly complained to Richardson, but the draft went to Best, who said he would show it to Agnew over the weekend.

That Friday night, however, *The Washington Post* broke the story of the plea bargaining—the first strong public indication that the vice president might be willing to deal away his office. He was furious, concluding that the story had been leaked by the Justice Department to damage him and weaken his bargaining position. The weekend came and went with no reply from Agnew. Ziegler meanwhile got hold of a new Gallup Poll for *Newsweek* and sent it to Nixon. On the question of whether Agnew should resign, only 16 percent said yes, to 66 percent no. If Agnew were indicted, however, 58 percent said yes, to 30 no. Among those polled, when asked who should replace Agnew if he did resign, Connally led the list with 24 percent, to 19 for Barry Goldwater, 15 for Howard Baker and 14 for Nelson Rockefeller.[15]

On Monday morning, September 25, concerned that the plea bargaining might have collapsed, Richardson and Petersen went to see Nixon, who had directed that Petersen review the case. Nixon wrote later: "Petersen went over the principal allegations and gave me his conclusion that it was an 'open-and-shut case.' He said that Agnew would be found guilty and would have to serve a prison term. Richardson said he was now ready to send the evidence to the grand jury." That news did not sit well with the president, whose own lawyers were arguing that he could not similarly be indicted over the Watergate case. He asked Richardson to have the Justice Department prepare an opinion on whether the Constitution would allow the indictment of a sitting vice president.

In his later memoir, Nixon raised the question in a way that suggested he simply had wanted to help Agnew. "The Constitution specifically provides that a president can be removed from office only by being impeached and convicted," he wrote; "only then can he be indicted in criminal proceedings and brought to trial for his offenses. Although the vice president is not specifically mentioned in this clause of the Constitution, I argued that a case could be made that he would be in the same position."[16] But Richardson said later that "we had arrived at the conclusion that irrespective of the political overtones of the situation the president is not subject to indictment, but all other officers are."[17]

Richardson told Nixon that in taking Agnew before a grand jury he would argue that the vice president could be indicted and tried before any impeachment process. But, he said, after such an indictment he would be prepared to turn the matter over to the House of Representatives if it chose to start impeachment against Agnew before a criminal trial began. The White House, the attorney general wrote later, liked that idea in preference to such a trial.[18]

For all of Nixon's feigned solicitude for Agnew, all his actions regarding Agnew's fate were based on saving his own skin in Watergate. At the very time, Nixon was wrestling with what to do about the White House tapes, which special prosecutor Cox was seeking. According to one of Richardson's aides, the president told his attorney general that he was "looking forward to getting the Agnew thing over with, at which point he would fire Cox." Richardson did not seem at that point to take the comment seriously.[19]

Soon after Richardson and Petersen had left the Oval Office, Agnew was ushered in for another pitch to Nixon for his help, and told him that he "had decided to wait no longer to take my case to the House of Representatives. I would seek a hearing there in hopes of winning vindication." He said he was going to Capitol Hill to see Speaker Albert. Nixon asked him to wait until that afternoon, Agnew wrote later, then "telephoned the Justice Department and made sure the prosecutors had not yet gone to the grand jury. Mr. Nixon wanted to keep the way clear for me to resign. . . . I suggested the president go on television and tell the people that I could not have a fair trial in view of the countless leaks against me."[20]

Instead, Nixon issued a statement after their meeting saying nothing of Agnew's reiterated insistence of innocence, merely commending his past service in a way that could sustain his own good standing with the vice president's Silent Majority constituency: "He has won the respect of millions of millions of Americans for the candor and courage with which he has addressed the controversial issues of our time. As he moves through this difficult period, I urge all Americans to accord the vice president the basic, decent consideration and presumption of innocence that are both his right and his due."[21]

Nixon wrote later that Agnew had told him "he would reconsider resigning only if he were granted complete immunity from prosecution," which clearly was not going to happen. "Then, for a moment, his manner changed," Nixon wrote, "and in a sad and gentle voice he asked for my assurance that I would not turn my back on him if he were out of office." The president did not record any reply.[22]

Agnew later insisted there was no question that the White House had played an active role in removing him from the vice presidency, with added incentives only in the president's power to grant. Buzhardt, on Nixon's behalf, Agnew wrote, "offered a few carrots," including a promise "to place every member of my vice-presidential staff in another federal position of comparable salary. . . . They agreed that I could have a small transition staff and office so that my vice-presidential papers could be catalogued. . . . They promised that my Secret Service protection would be continued for six months after I resigned."[23]

(Agnew wrote later that all the promises were kept, except that he was given the protection for only four months. The agents, Agnew said, were "withdrawn without warning while I was visiting Frank Sinatra to attend the late Jack Benny's eightieth birthday party in mid-February 1974. . . . Suddenly one evening, the Secret Service with me [twelve agents whom Agnew jokingly referred to as the 'dirty dozen'] received orders to cease my protection at midnight. The White House communications people came in that same evening and pulled out the White House phones, and the agents left at midnight. I had not been notified by anyone until the head of my detail informed me. It was an eerie occasion and a sad one. . . . It was like losing part of my family when they left.")[24]

One reason the White House was in a hurry to remove him, Agnew said he learned later, "was that the president was desperately eager to get Archibald Cox out of the job of special Watergate prosecutor to stop him from pressing for the secret White House tapes. Nixon could not risk the upheaval at Justice that inevitably would follow the discharging of Cox until he pacified Richardson with my scalp. So again I was treated like a pawn in the game—the game of Watergate cover-up."[25]

That afternoon, Speaker Albert agreed to see Agnew, at Ford's request. The vice president formally requested that the House open an impeachment investigation of the charges against him, "in the dual interests of preserving the Constitutional stature of my office and accomplishing my personal vindication." He argued that the Constitution barred any other kind of criminal proceeding against a sitting vice president. He cited a precedent in the House investigation of profiteering against Vice President John C. Calhoun in 1826, which after six weeks exonerated him. Albert heard Agnew out, then called in the other House leaders of both parties. The controlling Democrats made clear that they saw no reason to give Agnew a possible escape route. Nixon wrote subsequently that he did all he could for his embattled (in part by him) vice president:

"Though I seriously doubted that it would be granted, I had the congressional relations staff talk with leading House Republicans, urging them to support the request."[26]

The next day, Albert, who also had been informed by Richardson that grand jury proceedings were going forward, announced that Agnew's request had been turned down. It would be improper, he said, for the House to intercede when the matter was before a federal court. Agnew's lawyers indicated that they would try to block the grand jury procedure, arguing that news leaks had prejudiced a fair trial, and that the Constitution barred indictment of a vice president. But before they could do so, the Baltimore prosecutors had already begun calling witnesses against Agnew. The motion to block indictment was filed anyway but in the end got nowhere.

As if the intersection of the Agnew and Nixon travails were not enough, Agnew conjured up a scenario whereby he would resign, Nixon would nominate a replacement but Congress would balk at confirmation, Nixon would die or resign, and the presidency would fall to—Carl Albert! But Agnew later intoned in his book: "The Speaker, a man of small stature but great integrity, refused even to think of attaining the presidency by partisan trickery."[27]

Agnew figured he had one other recourse with which to save himself. He had risen in the previous five years from "Spiro Who?" to the household name, as he had promised when he was nominated as Nixon's running mate. He still had his Silent Majority constituency around the country, and if he could raise its voice as one in his defense, and create an uproar within the Republican Party in the process, Nixon might persuade Richardson to relent on the most disagreeable of his terms for Agnew's resignation. Amidst all his woes, the vice president had been invited to speak to the National Federation of Republican Women, a bulwark of his support, in Los Angeles. He had accepted, stopping on the way in Palm Springs to visit his still-loyal friend Sinatra.

At dinner the night before his speech, after a round of golf, Sinatra began to prod his guest not to take what was happening to him lying down. "Frank was outspoken in favor of my going on the offensive," Agnew wrote later, "and thought I should make it clear to the public that I was being destroyed by the systematic ignoring of my constitutional rights. Everyone [at the dinner] wanted me to take off the gloves and fight back, and most thought the Los Angeles rally would be a perfect forum. However, I was depressed about the failure of our attempt to obtain a hearing in the House of Representatives and the duplicitous actions of the president, who, it was now clear to see, was not being candid with me. Nevertheless, I feared totally alienating a man who held so much power and who was being driven to the wall by the Watergate prosecutor and the news media."

The next morning on the flight to Los Angeles aboard the vice-presidential jet, Agnew wrote, "looking over the prepared speech that I would be delivering in less than two hours, it suddenly struck me that it just wouldn't do. These women, and all my supporters out there, were entitled to know how I felt—what was happening. I began to make some notes on the back of an envelope I found in my pocket. My mind was clear, logical. The ideas flowed. It felt right, very right. I decided to cut down on the prepared speech and 'wing' the thoughts I was noting at the end. I didn't say anything to anyone, but suddenly the depression was gone. I felt confident, ready for battle."[28]

This scenario made it sound as if Agnew's decision to go on the public offensive was spontaneous. Actually, he had signaled the tactic two days earlier in an interview on background with columnist James Reston in the *New York Times*. Reston wrote that Agnew "has made up his mind about the next phase of what he calls his 'nightmare.' He does not intend to resign, even if he is indicted by the Baltimore grand jury, but to fight for exoneration through the courts, and keep appealing to the House of Representatives for a full and open hearing, no matter how long it takes."

Reston went on to identify Agnew's principal target in his offensive: "Mr. Agnew is obviously angry at Mr. Petersen and the criminal division of the Justice Department. He feels they are on the defensive because, as he suspects, they did not turn up much evidence in the Watergate case that came out later in the Senate hearings, that they mishandled an important case about organized crime, that they resented the appointment of Archibald Cox as special prosecutor. . . and were trying to make up for their losses at his expense."

Reston noted that Agnew wasn't criticizing Nixon "but is less sure about members of the president's staff," and that Nixon "has never pressed him to resign or even take a single step he did not want to take." The *Times* interview concluded that Agnew "guesses that despite many doubts, he really would have tried for the presidency in 1976 but this is obviously 'all over' now," but that he had just begun to fight to clear his name.[29]

At the Republican women's convention, Agnew strode into the hall and up to the rostrum as Sinatra and others in his party quietly slipped into the rear. Amid cheers and signs of "Spiro My Hero," he proceeded quickly through the prepared portion of his speech and then turned to his defense. "In the past several months I have been living in purgatory," he announced, only glancing at his jotted-down notes. Reviewing what he called "undefined, unclear and unattributed accusations" against him, he declared to an erupting roar of support: "I am innocent of the charges against me." Insisting, in a blatant falsehood, that he had "no idea that I was the target of an investigation" until he had received Beall's letter laying out the charges, Agnew took dead aim at Petersen. He charged that "conduct of high individuals in the Department of Justice, particularly the conduct of the chief of the criminal investigation division of that department, is unprofessional and malicious and outrageous." This was the same Henry Petersen in whom, when Nixon said he was asking him to review the evidence, Agnew had expressed confidence.

The vice president told the crowd that if he could question the officials under oath, as his lawyers were seeking [with little prospect of success], and were to find that they "have abused their sacred trust and forsaken their professional standards, then I will ask the president of the United States to summarily discharge those individuals." The reason he was attacking his own Justice Department, he said, was that he suspected they were turning on him because the "upper echelons" had been so "severely stung by their ineptness in the prosecution of the Watergate case. . . that the president and the attorney general have found it necessary to appoint a special prosecutor and they are trying to recoup their reputation at my expense. I'm a big trophy."

Without referring to Petersen by name, Agnew said "one of those individuals has made some very serious mistakes. In handling his job he considers himself a career professional, in a class by himself, but a recent examination of his record will show not only that he failed to get any of the information about the true dimensions of the Watergate matter but that he also through ineptness and blunder prevented the successful prosecution of high crime figures because of wiretapping error. Those are the reasons why he needs me to reinstate his reputation as a tough and courageous and hard-nosed prosecutor. Well, I'm not going to fall down and be his victim, I assure you."

Taking on the Justice Department of Agnew's own administration was politically risky enough; singling out Henry Petersen, the man Nixon had personally chosen to get the facts in the case for him, was an even greater gamble. And linking what he saw as the conspiracy against him to Petersen's alleged failures in the early Watergate investigation was nothing if not daring, and it was skating on thin ice regarding the president's patience. Furthermore, Petersen had not initiated the investigation against Agnew, nor was he prosecuting it. If the vice president was so incensed, he should have taken his ire out on George Beall and his three associates in Baltimore, and on Richardson, who was overseeing the effort to remove him from office.

Agnew concluded his attack on Petersen by telling the audience that far from seeking to suppress the facts, he had tried to take his case to the House of Representatives and that no matter what, "I will not resign if indicted!" The crowd erupted again in cheers and applause. "Our Constitution says that every man is entitled to a fair trial and a presumption of innocence [which was what he would get if he did not resign, and what he had tried to avoid by going to the House]. I intend to rely on the spirit as well as the letter of those guarantees. I would forsake the principles of the Founding Fathers if I abandoned this fight. And I do not intend to abandon it."[30]

On leaving the platform to more acclaim, the vice president went to a private room, where he told California Republican leaders that it wasn't realistic for him now to entertain thoughts of being a presidential prospect in 1976. But he urged them all to work for a party victory in the congressional elections of 1974. Then, with Sinatra and the rest of the party, he returned to Palm Springs for a couple of relaxed days of golf and tennis. One of the party said later Agnew was a relieved man now that he had gotten the message off his chest.

In Washington, Petersen heard the first, formal part of the speech on his car radio as he was driving home for lunch. He was eating in another room with the television set on in the adjacent living room when Agnew got to the bitter references to him. He ran to the set, telling his wife that the vice president had "just made a terrible mistake." He explained later: "That's so commonplace in this business—for the prosecutor to be attacked when he's got a very, very strong case." But he told her: "I'm not going to be able to say anything. This is going to be a tough week, and we're just going to have to grin and bear it, and it will all resolve itself when the evidence comes out." Petersen reached for a phone and told Richardson: "If you haven't heard this, you had better get a transcript of it because not only has he attacked me, but the rest of the department looks like a dumb ass." He told his boss he was leaving town for southern Maryland to escape the avalanche of calls certain to come his way.[31]

Nixon was at Camp David when Haig phoned him about Agnew's outburst against Petersen in Los Angeles. The president wrote later: "I had just finished talking with Rose Woods [his secretary], who had come up earlier in the day to start typing the conversation from the tapes subpoenaed by the special prosecutor." Nixon's invoking of executive privilege on them had been challenged, he said, and "I wanted to break the paralysis caused by the court battles. Rather than take the case to the Supreme Court I had begun to consider a compromise; submitting written summaries of the tapes. . . after national security discussions and other matters irrelevant to Watergate had been deleted." That matter seemed at first to be much more on Nixon's mind right then than Agnew's fate.

But when it sank in to the president that his vice president was declaring open war on the man he personally had designated to find out the truth about Agnew, he recognized that Agnew in effect was making war on Nixon himself. The president had said in his press conference nearly two weeks earlier that anyone who had leaked about the Agnew case would be "summarily dismissed," and the attack on Petersen amounted to calling Nixon's bluff. Nixon contacted Richardson, was assured that Petersen had not leaked to the press, and expressed his confidence in the actions of his Justice Department.

Agnew continued to look for devils other than Nixon. He wrote later that he was convinced Haig had cooked up a story that the vice president's plan was to attack Petersen first, then Beall, then Richardson and the president himself. Haig had done so, Agnew wrote, to get Nixon to go after him. Haig must have told Nixon, Agnew wrote, "Agnew has gone wild—attacking Petersen, saying he will not resign. You may be next. We've got to lower the boom on him *now*."[32]

But Nixon continued to be distracted by Watergate. Back in Washington on Monday, October 1, he recalled later, Rose Mary Woods came into his office "visibly agitated. She said she thought she might have caused a small gap" in the tape of a conversation he had had with Haldeman on June 20, 1972. Nixon wrote that this was his first knowledge of the infamous eighteen-and-a-half-minute missing segment, which remained one of the most tantalizing mysteries of the Watergate saga. Afterward, he wrote, "It had been a busy morning, so Haig and I went for a long drive around Washington in order to talk about the problem that was foremost in my mind: what to do about Agnew. Compared to this, a few minutes missing from a non-subpoenaed tape hardly seemed worth a second thought."[33]

Agnew, however, was making it impossible for Nixon to shunt his situation to the back burner. In a few days, he was to be in Chicago for a scheduled dinner speech for the United Republican Fund. The new Agnew press secretary, Marsh Thomson, decided it would be a good idea to entice the press by saying " the vice president's in a fighting mood." The remarks, which Agnew later characterized as "a blunder of horrific dimensions," ran on the front page of *The Washington Post*. Haig immediately telephoned Art Sohmer, Agnew's chief of staff, and told him straight out: Nixon wanted no more attacks on his Justice Department or on Petersen. If there was another one, there would be no deal on resignation, and that meant an indictment, jury trial, conviction, and a jail sentence for the vice president.

Then Nixon held a rare informal news conference in the Oval Office. While saying he considered Agnew's decision not to resign even if he were indicted "altogether proper," he made a point of observing that the allegations against him were "serious and not frivolous" and of defending Petersen. On the same day, the judge who was to preside over the case in Baltimore, Walter E. Hoffman, assembled the members of the grand jury in open court. He instructed them to judge the matter of indictment of the vice president only on the facts presented, not on what had appeared in the news media.

AFTER NIXON'S NEWS CONFERENCE, he flew to Florida for the weekend. He was accompanied by Buzhardt, who that afternoon had received a call from Best saying, according to Nixon, "that Agnew was ready to resume discussions about a plea." Best flew to Miami and spent much of the night conferring with Nixon's lawyer.

As Nixon wrote later, "earlier Best had pointed out to Buzhardt that Agnew was just a few months short of being eligible for retirement with a federal pension. He had wondered if there were not some way to give him a consultancy that would keep him on the government payroll and carry him over the pension deadline. I told Buzhardt we could not do it at this time. Agnew had also asked if he could keep his Secret Service protection for a while, and he was concerned about what would happen to his staff. I promised that I would see to it that his Secret Service protection was extended, and that we would do our best to find jobs for his staff members. It was agreed that on Saturday, October 6, Buzhardt would call Richardson to arrange for the talks to begin again."[34]

Nixon in his memoirs later painted himself as a sympathetic and benign observer of Agnew's travails, though he had actively prodded his lawyers to get the vice president out of the way. Agnew meanwhile, faced with the monumental humiliation of being driven from the nation's second-highest office and out of earlier strong prospects of being the next Republican presidential nominee, focused on his evaporating perks.

His lawyers were still pressing for an inquiry into news leaks and to block Agnew's indictment on constitutional grounds, but the wheels of justice were turning now and threatening to run over him. Late efforts by some House Republicans to bring his plight to the House were getting nowhere. His Los Angeles speech hadn't generated much money for a legal defense fund undertaken by Republican financial angel W. Clement Stone for a long fight in the courts. Richardson was still dug in on his tough resignation terms. Finally, there was that or-else warning from Nixon, via Haig, to desist in his attacks.

In this pessimistic environment, Agnew made his now highly anticipated speech to a packed crowd in the Conrad Hilton ballroom in Chicago. In contrast to the aggressiveness of his Los Angeles remarks, he was so restrained that David Broder of the *The Washington Post* observed that the vice president looked as if he had just heard some awful news, or had been kicked in the groin. He began by telling the reporters: "Tonight is not going to be an X-rated political show. It's just going to be PG. So if you have to go someplace, go. A candle is only so long before it burns out." He then delivered a pedestrian Republican policy speech, the only notable part of which was support of President Nixon as a man who had been enduring "most unbelievable pressures." That previous reference to a burned-out candle, gloomily delivered, sounded like nothing less than unconditional surrender. Reporters' efforts to get clarification were frustrated as the vice president went back to the Drake Hotel for dinner in a private club.[35]

But their suspicions were valid. Agnew, on returning from Chicago, instructed Best to contact the White House. "Go speak to Buzhardt," he said. "See what can be done."[36] Best also met with Richardson and quickly reached agreement on two last items on which the attorney general insisted—some acknowledgment that Agnew's offenses went beyond his years as governor, and that he would have no say over what Justice's full disclosure would include.

On Saturday, as the Agnew case at last appeared to be approaching a conclusion, a major development halfway around the world plunged Nixon into a huge foreign-policy crisis. Egypt and Syria suddenly attacked Israel, and the invasion drove home more than ever to Richardson the necessity of getting Agnew out of the line of presidential succession. Nixon already was under tremendous emotional pressure from the Watergate debacle, and there were rumors that he might be cracking under the strain. As Agnew himself melodramatically put it, "the world could conceivably be approaching the brink of a nuclear catastrophe. Richardson had been worrying about Nixon's emotional stability—or lack of it—ever since the president's illness in July; now, more than ever, the attorney general sought to kick me out and bring in a new vice president who might, at any time, have to move into the White House."[37]

On Sunday, October 7, Richardson spent several hours pacifying the Baltimore Four, who still would have preferred indicting Agnew, by convincing them that they should not be "playing Russian roulette with the United States over a few words."[38] As for sentencing, Richardson said again he would make no recommendation unless required by the judge. The stage was now set for the final inning—presenting the final settlement to Judge Hoffman for plea-bargaining approval on Monday, October 8, when the judge would be back in town after attending a wedding.

Among the Nixon aides in Florida that weekend was Pat Buchanan, the speechwriter for both Nixon and Agnew. He was busy working on a

major Nixon speech on Watergate when Haig called him in and told him
the president wanted a new tentative ending in which he would reveal
that Agnew was resigning. Haig told him he should include the name of
the man who would be nominated in Agnew's place. It was not Connally,
or Gerald Ford, or Nelson Rockeller or Ronald Reagan, Buchanan said
later, adding that he was not at liberty to say who, except that it would
have been a surprise.[39]

On Monday morning, the Justice Department team of Petersen, Beall,
and Skolnik and the Agnew lawyers—Topkis, London, and Best—met
in secret with Judge Hoffman in a room at the Olde Colony Motor Lodge
in Alexandria, Virginia, just outside Washington. Some initial sparring
by Topkis worried the Justice team that Agnew's lawyers would try to
minimize the significance of a *nolo contendere* plea. After telling Hoffman
that his client would waive indictment and plead *nolo* to one count of tax
evasion for 1967, when he was governor of Maryland, Topkis said Agnew
would exercise his "right of allocution"—giving his side of the story.
Hoffman broke in to remind Topkis that a *nolo* plea amounted to an acceptance of guilt without obliging the government to prove it. It didn't
give the defendant the right to declare his innocence.

Next, Topkis told the judge, to the astonishment and dismay of the
Justice team, that it was their "common belief" that it wouldn't be necessary to give Agnew a jail term. Petersen contradicted him, saying the
government preferred to leave the matter up to the judge. Topkis said
his client had not authorized him to make a deal without the judge giving some assurance that he wouldn't be sent to jail. Again, after much
back and forth, Hoffman said he would not commit himself one way or
the other. At the same time, the judge said he understood the special
circumstances involved and what Agnew had already endured. If he
didn't want to accept Hoffman's decision in court, he could always reject it and face indictment. At this point, Topkis asked for and received
a recess until the next day, when the group would meet again, this time
at the Justice Department. Before they broke up, however, Petersen
asked Hoffman whether he would go along if both parties agreed on
the matter of imprisonment. It was a way of inquiring whether the
judge would agree if Richardson did recommend no jail time. Hoffman
said that certainly would make it easier for him. Petersen took that as
a "yes."[40]

When Best reported the status of the negotiations to Agnew, he had his lawyer tell Haig and Buzhardt at the White House: "We will not do anything unless Richardson and the Department of Justice assure us there will be *no* incarceration." For himself, Agnew wrote later: "I was determined that unless they guaranteed me 'no jail,' there would be 'no deal.' I might just as well take my chances with White House threats and a Baltimore jury, prejudiced and biased as it might be, rather than resign the vice presidency and be railroaded to prison despite my innocence. I was deathly afraid of a double cross."[41]

In routing Agnew's insistence to the White House rather than directly to Richardson, it was clear the vice president continued to see mediation or pressure from Nixon as his best and only avenue of escape from the fate he now most desperately wanted to avoid. At the same time, Agnew outwardly remained his customary calm-and-collected self. While the lawyers were huddling with the judge, he had flown up to New York with some of his staff for talks with friends and a leisurely dinner at one of his favorite restaurants.

The next day, Richardson decided to join the final session with Hoffman, to determine for himself whether he had to recommend no jail time to push the judge across the finish line. At the outset, he told Hoffman that the government's lawyers were split on the question of sentencing, but he inferred from what the judge had said the day before that his recommendation would be helpful to him, and so was prepared to offer it. Hoffman observed that if the defendant were just another lawyer, he would be inclined to give him jail time and probation, as a deterrent to errant lawyers generally. But Agnew was the vice president, and Hoffman said he recognized that a matter of great national interest was involved, and in such circumstances he would certainly want to hear from the attorney general. Richardson said he too would normally recommend a jail sentence, but the fact that Agnew was in direct line of succession to the presidency, and could be called to assume it at any moment, had convinced him of the urgency of achieving his resignation. And so, as a condition of getting it quickly, he was recommending no jail time. Hoffman said he would give the recommendation great weight, and all sides, knowing what that meant, were at last satisfied.[42]

Richardson, however, first made a point of stating that the prosecution could have sought and achieved on the basis of the evidence gathered "an indictment charging bribery extortion," but to have done so "would have been likely to inflict upon the Nation serious and permanent scars," through either a trial or impeachment by Congress. "It is unthinkable," Richardson told the judge, "that this nation should have been required to endure the anguish and uncertainty of a prolonged period in which the man next in line of succession to the presidency was fighting the charges brought against him by his own government."[43]

Conditions were agreed upon for Agnew's arraignment before Hoffman in Baltimore, which was set for the next day. It was considered imperative that the vice president submit his resignation before the arraignment so that Agnew would appear as a private citizen. A phone line would be held open from the courtroom to the office of Secretary of State Henry Kissinger. There, in keeping with protocol, an Agnew representative would be poised to hand the vice president's letter of resignation to Kissinger the moment it was clear there would be no last-minute snag in the deal.

Agnew's lawyers notified him of the arrangement later in the afternoon. He sat down and wrote a one-sentence letter of resignation:

"Dear Mr. Secretary:

"I hereby resign the office of vice president of the United States, effective immediately.

"Sincerely, Spiro T. Agnew"

Then, in a second letter, he wrote to Nixon:

"Dear Mr. President:

"As you are aware, the accusations against me cannot be resolved without a long, divisive and debilitating struggle in the Congress and in the courts. I have concluded that, painful as it is to me and to my family, it is in the best interest of the nation that I relinquish the vice presidency.

"Accordingly, I have today resigned the office of vice president of the United States. A copy of the instrument of resignation is enclosed.

"It has been a privilege to serve with you. May I express to the American people, through you, my deep gratitude for their confidence in twice electing me to be vice president."[44]

The letter, understandably, conveyed no thanks to Nixon for his support through Agnew's greatest ordeal. The vice president rose and walked over to the Oval Office to inform the president of the outcome— to restate his alibis and make one last pitch for help as the private citizen he would become the next day. Nixon, who by now knew of the deal, described the hypocritical scene later: "We shook hands and sat down in the chairs in front of the fireplace. I spoke first, saying that I knew his decision had been very difficult for him. I knew that he was by nature a man who would almost rather have lost everything fighting, even from his disadvantaged position, than have won the assurance that he would not go to prison at the price of having to compromise with his opponents. I told him how much I had appreciated his hard campaigning in 1968, 1970 and 1972 and the dedicated way he handled all his assignments from me. I asked about his wife and family; I knew how painful it had been for them."

Nixon went on: "He was particularly embittered by what he considered the hypocrisy of the members of Congress who had formerly served as governors. He repeated his belief that most of the governors in other states had followed practices such as those common in Maryland. He emphasized that he had always awarded contracts on the basis of merit, and he felt that the amounts he had received had been so small that no reasonable critic would claim that they could have influenced him to make a decision that contravened the public interest. He said that he could not see that what he had done was unethical."

Then came the pitch: "He mentioned that after a few months he would like to have some kind of foreign assignment; he thought that he could be particularly effective in a Far Eastern country, perhaps Japan. He said that he supposed the IRS would be harassing him the rest of his life. 'You know, they were even charting up how much I paid for my neckties,' he said bitterly. Our meeting was over. I shook his hand and told him that I wished him well. I said that he could always count on me as a friend."[45]

Of this last encounter, Agnew wrote later: "I looked at the president, his face gaunt and sorrowful. It was hard to believe he was not genuinely sorry about the course of events. Within two days, this consummate actor would be celebrating his appointment of a new vice president with never a thought of me. But of course, I didn't know that. My eyes filled with his solicitous words. I was conscious of how tragic the moment was for me and my loved ones. Here I was in the Oval Office for the last time, about to leave in disgrace the office I had fought and worked for so hard. I felt

no rancor toward Mr. Nixon, only ahead, burdening sadness. I was about
to let a lot of people down."

Agnew wrote that he told Nixon that "the people's confidence in their
government must be restored," and that "I will do all I can to be helpful
to you, Mr. President." It was hard to see, though, what that might be at
this point or anytime in the future. He concluded: "As I was leaving,
Nixon put his arm around my shoulders, shook his head, and said again
how awful it all was. Incongruously, I suddenly had the feeling that he
couldn't wait to get me out of there. We shook hands and I walked
numbly out of the Oval Office—and out of the White House for what I
supposed was the last time."[46]

Shortly after two o'clock the next afternoon, vice president Spiro T.
Agnew and his lawyers, and Attorney General Elliot L. Richardson and
his team of prosecutors were assembled in the federal courtroom of Judge
Walter E. Hoffman in Baltimore. Agnew, told by Judah Best that the
plea-bargained deal was in place, authorized Best to phone Kissinger's office and have his letter of resignation delivered to the secretary of state.
From that moment, Agnew was a private citizen and would not have to
face a felony charge as the vice president. Grimly, he went through the
prescribed ritual of waiving his right of indictment, accepting the plea of
nolo contendere, and then listening to Richardson's charges and his rationale for recommending that no jail time be assigned. Then, at Hoffman's
instruction, Agnew rose and read the prepared statement of admission of
behavior as agreed to in the plea bargaining.

He started by saying his decision to enter the plea was an act of sacrifice
for the public good. It rested, he said, "on my firm belief that the public
interest requires swift disposition of the problems which are facing me"
and that "a full legal defense of the probable charges against me could
consume several years" in which "intense media interest in the case would
distract public attention from important national problems—to the country's detriment."

As to the allegations of witnesses "that I and my agents received payments from consulting engineers doing business with the state of
Maryland during the period I was governor," Agnew said, "I admit I did
receive payments during the year 1967 which were not expended for political purposes and that, therefore, these payments were income taxable

to me in that year and that I so knew." But he insisted "no contracts were awarded to contractors who were not competent to perform the work. . . and I deny that the payments in any way influenced my official actions. . . . My acceptance of contributions was part of a long-established pattern of fund-raising in my state. At no time have I tried to enrich myself at the expense of the public trust."[47] In other words, Agnew wasn't denying that he had taken payoffs, only that they hadn't influenced his actions. It was a face-saving to which the prosecutors had reluctantly agreed.

The judge thereupon accepted the plea and sentenced him to three years of unsupervised probation and a fine of ten thousand dollars. At long last, the nightmare was over.

Citizen Agnew was swiftly escorted from the courtroom and, in a bit of irony, whisked by the Secret Service to the Loring Beyer Funeral Home in suburban Randallstown, where his wife, Judy, and other family members were gathered to mourn the death on the previous day of his half brother, Roy Pollard, of a massive stroke. Later, the Agnews and their daughter Susan went for dinner at Sabatini's, the former vice president's favorite restaurant in Baltimore's Little Italy, and then home to Kenwood, a Maryland suburb just outside Washington.[48]

Nixon in his memoirs cast the Agnew resignation in terms of his own fight for political survival. He wrote that it "was necessary although a very serious blow, because while some thought that his stepping aside would take some of the presssure off the effort to get the president, all it did was open the way to put pressure on the president to resign as well. This is something we have to realize: that any accommodation with opponents in this kind of fight does not satisfy—it only brings on demands for more."[49] In so saying, Nixon seemed to be suggesting that the prosecution of Agnew was somehow part and parcel of the case against him—get Agnew first, then Nixon. Perhaps he hoped that, by casting Agnew and himself as targets of the same prosecutorial scheme, he could obscure the fact that in fact he was an active player in accomplishing Agnew's demise.

So ended the political marriage of Richard Nixon and Spiro Agnew. But the president remained embroiled in the separate scandal that ten months later would inflict on him the same fate just met by his vice president. According to Richardson later, Agnew had barely been shoved out the door when Nixon raised the matter of his own political survival, threatened as it was by Special Prosecutor Archibald Cox's bid for the White House Watergate tapes. "After we had finished our discussion about Mr. Agnew, and as we were walking to the door," Richardson wrote, "the president said in substance, 'Now that we have disposed of that matter we can go ahead and get rid of Cox.' There was nothing more said."[50]

As for Agnew, though he was now free of his deep fear of incarceration, he continued to shoulder a mountain of bitterness and resentment toward Nixon and his associates. For all of Agnew's expressions of support and trust in the president during his own ordeal, he knew he had been willfully betrayed by him.

Supporters of the now-deposed vice president showered him with more telegrams of regret, some of them heaping the blame on Nixon. A Baltimorean, on hearing the news, wired Agnew: "Your resignation is a sad day for America. We all know Nixon stabbed you." A man from Longwood, Florida, cabled: "Sorry you resigned. Would like to see you come back fighting. I think Nixon let you down. We are with you." A couple from Peru, Indiana, messaged: "We would still rather have you than Richard Nixon." From a man in Lynn, Massachusetts, came this: "You are a saint compared to that devil Nixon who has poisoned every decent human being that he has come in contact with. You should never have resigned. You should be president." And from another couple in Broomfield, Colorado: "We oppose your head being put on the sacrificial block by Mr. Nixon, who needed a more dramatic situation than his own."[51]

The legal skirmish over the Nixon–Agnew divorce was over, but in the years that were to follow, the spurned Agnew's rancor and that of many of his faithful would persist undiminished.

Chapter 23

FRIGID AFTERMATH

In the Watergate-plagued White House of Richard Nixon, Ted Agnew quickly became a nonperson, as Nixon had expected and hoped in his stealthy and hypocritical campaign to remove him from the vice presidency. The president's chief of staff, Alexander Haig, commented later that "Agnew's departure showed how right Nixon had been about the effect of his resignation. He was forgotten instantaneously by the public and the press, and I do not recall ever hearing his name mentioned in the White House again."[1]

On the same day that Agnew resigned, however, Nixon dutifully followed protocol and wrote to him, in typewritten form:

"Dear Ted:

"The most difficult decisions are often those that are the most personal, and I know your decision to resign as vice president has been as difficult as any facing a man in public life could be. Your departure from the administration leaves me with a great sense of personal loss. You have been a valued associate throughout these nearly five years that we have served together. However, I respect your decision, and I also respect the concern for the national interest that led you to conclude that a resolution of the matter in this way, rather than through an extended battled in the courts and the Congress, was advisable in order to prevent a protracted period of national division and uncertainty.

"As vice president, you have addressed the great issues of our times with courage and candor. Your strong patriotism, and your profound dedication to the welfare of the nation, have been an inspiration to all who have served with you as well as to millions of others throughout the country. I have been deeply saddened by this whole course of events, and I hope that you and your family will be sustained in the days ahead by a well-justified pride in all that you have contributed to the nation by your years of service as vice president.

"Sincerely, Richard Nixon"[2]

In his own hand, Nixon also wrote a note that sought to convey a bit more warmth and promise of friendshp:

"Dear Ted:

"On such a sad occasion our hearts go out to you and your splendid family. Take comfort from the fact that your dedicated service as vice president will in the end be more remembered than those unfortunate events which currently dominate the news. In these next few months and the years ahead you will find out who your real [underlined] friends are. Count me and the entire Nixon family among them. You have been wounded but I predict you will recover and fight again another day.

"RN"[3]

About two weeks later, still another Nixon letter came to Agnew at his home in Kenwood, Maryland, together with "the chair you occupied across from mine at the cabinet table." It is, Nixon wrote, "a symbol of the strength and wisdom you brought to that that task [as vice president] as well as to the highest councils of the government itself. Therefore, I particularly wanted to make a personal gift of that chair [which was government, not Nixon, property], which I hope you will take as a token of both friendship and esteem. I am confident that the same strength and wisdom will help you through these difficult days, and I am also sure that in the years to come the knowledge that you were right about the great issues will maintain that strength and vindicate that wisdom."[4]

Nothing was said, however, in any of these letters from Agnew's "real friend" about his forlorn pleas for some overseas governmental assignment or his other concerns about survival in the private sector. With little financial well-being or prospects, Agnew, according to his old campaign aide John Damgard, had to borrow $10,000 from his friend Frank Sinatra to pay his fine. In fact, Agnew wrote later, the singer sent him $30,000 not only for the fine but also to help with "my family expenses until I could find some way to make a living." Subsequently, Agnew wrote, when the

Internal Revenue Service slapped him with a bill for $150,000 in unpaid back taxes and threatened to lift his passport, Sinatra bailed him out again with a $200,000 transfer to his bank account. "As time went by and my business improved through my numerous trips overseas, I earned an adequate income and paid back the last of the Sinatra loans in 1978."[5]

But Ted Agnew never stopped accusing Nixon and his inner circle of doing him in. In 1980, in his book, *Go Quietly. . . Or Else*, a detailed argument of how he had been railroaded out of the vice presidency, he went so far as to suggest there may have been a White House plot to kill him to get him out of the line of presidential succession. In the book's preface, he sarcastically referred to his acrimonious political divorce by mocking one of the president's Nixon's favorite phrases: "As a man I once knew often said, let me make one thing perfectly clear."[6]

Agnew wrote that not long before he left Washington for his accusatory speech in Los Angeles days before his resignation, "I received an indirect threat from the White House that made me fear for my life." He quoted from what he said was a memorandum for the record written by his military aide, General Mike Dunn. It said Dunn a couple of hours earlier had met with Haig in Haig's office and had been told that "Justice believes that it has an ironclad case for conviction" and that it "could move successfully with what the IRS alone has produced," based only on Agnew's 1967 income tax return. Haig told him, Dunn wrote, "the clock is running—it will be too late once an indictment is obtained to do this gracefully." Haig told him that "Nixon has been completely supportive to date, [but] once 'facts' are made known to people, further support from Nixon [will be] impossible."

Dunn's memo, Agnew wrote, said Haig assured him that in return for the vice president's resignation and "an admission of guilt on the tax charge, there would be no futher trouble with the federal government and no jail sentence. . . . In any event, after indictment, we are off to the races and cannot control the situation any longer—anything may be in the offing. It can and will get nasty and dirty." The memo quoted Haig as saying: "Don't think that the game cannot be played from here."

Agnew went on: "Haig's threat made me realize, with a sickening shock, that I had finally lost the last slim thread of hope that the president would help me in my fight. On the contrary, he had turned against me and become my mortal enemy." Agnew wrote that Dunn was told that if the vice president refused to resign, he would get no help whatever from the White House, that Clement Stone would be told to drop the legal defense fund, and that "Nixon would publicly blast me, turn the prosecutors loose, and I would go to jail." Dunn also was told, Agnew wrote, that the vice president should not forget that because the Agnews had filed joint tax returns, his wife could also be found "criminally liable" in the net-worth investigation. "It was the lowest blow of all," Agnew wrote.

Finally, he wrote, Haig had reminded Dunn that "the president has a lot of power—don't forget that." The remark, Agnew said, "sent a chill through my body. I interpreted it as an innuendo that anything could happen to me; I might have a convenient 'accident.'. . . I knew that men in the White House, professing to speak for the president, could order the CIA to carry out missions that were very unhealthy for people who were considered enemies. Since the revelations have come out about the CIA's attempts to assassinate Fidel Castro and other foreign leaders, I realize even more that I might have been in great danger. Haig's words to Dunn, that after indictment 'anything may be in the offing,' could only be construed as an open-ended threat. I did not know what might happen to me. But I don't mind admitting I was frightened. This directive was aimed at me like a gun to my head. . . . I feared for my life. If a decision had been made to eliminate me—through an automobile accident, a fake suicide or whatever, the order would not have been traced back to the White House any more than the 'get Castro' orders were ever traced to their source."[7]

This then was the "indirect threat" that he had kept secret since his resignation. "Perhaps I overreacted," he wrote, "but my mental state after months of constant pressure was hardly conducive to calm and dispassionate evaluation." For good measure, Agnew fingered Haig, the "de facto president," as the villain in the piece, saying he was convinced "that Haig desired not only to move me out, but in due course, after someone had been brought into the vice presidency, to move Mr. Nixon out too. I really think that by this time, Al Haig already knew enough about the discrepancies in the tapes—and the truth about Nixon's involvement in the Watergate cover-up—to be convinced that eventually the president himself must go. And Haig did not want me in the line of succession."

Agnew insisted that he had "no idea how much hot water the president was in. I did not believe the Watergate allegations, and I defended him. If I had known the truth about his involvement and why he was withholding his tapes from the special prosecutor," he wrote later, "my actions would not have been as benign as they were. I felt I had no chance to win a fight against the president. If I had known how weak Nixon really was, I might have fought it out. I regret that I never confronted Mr. Nixon about the threatening message from Haig. I guess it was partly out of fear and partly knowing from experience he wouldn't give me a straight answer that I never asked Nixon if he personally authorized the threat to 'get nasty—and dirty.'" Agnew went on, "I did not have the hindsight, of knowing for sure how I was being railroaded, until long after I was out. . . . In the end, the president turned out to be nearly as devious as the Nixonphobes claimed."

In the end also, Agnew insisted, the one and only thing that had brought him back to plea-bargaining was "Mr. Nixon's threat, relayed by Haig, that things would 'get nasty—and dirty' unless I resigned at once. The White House told Richardson I was driven back to the table by the net-worth investigation, which was supposed to show I had received huge amounts of tainted money. But that was an absolute lie concocted by the ugly truth: that Haig had put the heat on me with his threats."[8]

Agnew's self-serving explanation for his ultimate surrender to the combined White House–Justice Department effort to remove him from the line of presidential succession was transparent and vigorously denied as ridiculous by Haig in an interview years later.[9]

Actually, according much later to sources close to Agnew, it was not this supposed "death threat" that finally persuaded him to fold his cards and resume the plea bargaining. It was that exhaustive IRS net-worth investigation that he had mentioned in his last talk with Nixon. He was correct in telling Nixon that the IRS agents did chase down how much he had paid for a couple of neckties—$6.18 for the pair at Oliver's Men's Shop in Towson in 1968, and similar purchases elsewhere.[10] But that wasn't what Agnew didn't want revealed in any fuller disclosure of the net-worth's discovery. Rather, according to these sources, corroborated in part by prosecutors, it was the purchase of an expensive watch and other quality jewelry bought for a woman other than his wife, and according to one source a new foreign sports car as a Christmas present. Agnew, they said, feared the transactions would reveal to his wife an extra-marital affair he had been carrying on for some time with a regular member of his traveling party.[11]

In his book, Agnew wrote that the IRS had calculated that he had about $17,000 in unreported income over seven or eight years on which taxes were due. He said he estimated he had received about $12,000 in gifts from friends that were not taxable and didn't have to be reported. "Part of the threat to me," he wrote, "was the reminder that my wife could be implicated in the tax charge; they could prosecute her, too, because we filed joint returns."[12] The formal charge was that Ted and Judy Agnew had jointly reported income of $26,099 for 1967 and paid taxes of $6,416 when the actual income was $55,599, on which $19,967 in taxes should have been paid.[13]

In a televised farewell talk to the public five days after his resignation, Agnew sought to correct "misconceptions" about why he had taken that step. He noted that except for the decision not to contest the *nolo contendere* charge of tax evasion, "I flatly and categorically denied the assertions of illegal acts" of the government witnesses, and "repeat and I emphasize that denial tonight." He charged that "the government's case for extortion, bribery and conspiracy" that was not pursued as part of the plea bargain "rested entirely on the testimony of individuals who had already confessed to criminal acts and who had been granted total or partial immunity in exchange for their testimony against me," and whose accusations were "not independently corroborated or tested by cross-examination" but were "published and broadcast as indisputable fact."

While saying his plea was "the equivalent of a plea of guilty" for the purpose of the bargain struck in court, he insisted "it does not represent a confession of any guilt whatever for any other purpose."[14] This rationale enabled Agnew thereafter to contend in effect that he had been railroaded out of the vice presidency, and he continued long after to do so.

❧ ☙

FOR ALL THE FOCUS on his unaccounted-for income, Agnew's resignation left him a man required to hustle on his own to sustain the standard of living to which he had become accustomed as vice president. Nixon, finally free of Agnew, replaced him with the popular House minority leader, Gerald R. Ford, and was able to throw all his energies once again into trying to save his presidency. Yet he too was accumulating huge personal debt for his legal defense in the Watergate scandal, which was moving inexorably toward the same fate Agnew had just suffered—removal from high office.

In choosing Ford to replace Agnew, Nixon finally had to abandon his cherished notion of picking John Connally and putting him on the path to the presidency. But according to Haig, as late as three weeks before Agnew's resignation Nixon had still been weighing nominating the impressive Texan. Haig recalled later that Nixon had remained "determined to fight for Connally's appointment in the face of advice from Harlow and Ziegler that it would face strong opposition in Congress." Nixon told him, Haig said, "We've crossed that bridge. We cannot back off. If John Connally is willing to go, we'll go. . . . What's the option? Ford? . . . I'm no damned healer. I want to be, but they won't let me."

Haig said he told Nixon "we won't have peace" if he tried to force Connally on an unwilling Congress of untrusting Republicans and Democrats resentful toward their defected colleague. Nixon replied: "There are worse things than fighting a battle. So they turn him down. If they do, he'll be a national hero. . . . I can't give in."[15] How Nixon had come to that rather unusual conclusion, Haig did not record.

According to Mel Laird later, Nixon called him and Bryce Harlow into his EOB office and told them he had offered the vice presidency to Connally. They were not high on the idea. "We got a group organized [of House and Senate leaders of both parties], Laird said, "and brought them in [to the Oval Office] about five o'clock in the evening and convinced Nixon. They said that under the Twenty-fifth Amendment [on filling a vice-presidential vacancy] they would have a hell of a time confirming Connally. Bryce and my point was that we would have the responsibility for [achieving] the confirmation and that it would be very difficult. . . and to a man they all stood up and agreed with Bryce and me. And Nixon backed off of Connally, not because he didn't think he was best. I had nothing against Connally, but he had just gone through a change of party and he was having some other little difficulty around town, and we felt it would be difficult getting him confirmed in a Democratic Congress, whereas we felt we could get Jerry [Ford] confirmed without much trouble. Kissinger and Haig were for Rockefeller at the time, but it was not serious."[16]

In any event, Nixon did give in, though Haig in his memoir wrote that as late as four days before Agnew's resignation, he had Haig check with

Connally again on whether he would take the position if it were offered to him. But on the morning after Agnew bowed out the president instructed Haig to call Connally and let him down easily by telling him: "You know that the fundamental consideration of the Boss is that you be the 1976 candidate for the party. . . . Secondly, that you be vice president [in the interim]. That is his personal preference."[17] But when Haig went on to say that Nixon had met with the Republican congressional leaders and others on the Hill, Connally countered: "I gather they are unenthusiastic about me or anyone else [to replace Agnew] who would be a candidate [for president in 1976]." Haig replied: "Because you are a winner."

But then Haig told him why Nixon could not risk nominating him. "We are probably going to fire Cox within a week or ten days," he said. "There is a good chance that if your name goes forward Saturday that you will be held up in any event. There could be a merger for impeachment [of both the president and the vice president]. That is the great danger." In saying this, Haig was espousing his favorite theory, but one that at this point had been invalidated by Agnew's resignation. "If [you should] lose in the Senate [on confirmation]," Haig said, "the president feels [it] would be a disaster for you in '76."

Haig then told Connally that Nixon was considering nominating Ford as the safest bet to achieve confirmation. The news, somewhat surprisingly, did not seem to sit well with Connally, who for so long had expressed a lack of interest in the vice presidency. Haig wrote that Connally now indicated "he was willing to take his chances on the nomination process with all its dangers. He thought he could prevail, and by so doing give Nixon the vice president he really wanted. It was better, he said, to lose by being strong than to win by compromising. He did not agree that defeat would hurt him as a candidate for election. If he were defeated "on a partisan basis, I don't know of any better springboard that I could have."[18]

Later that night, Haig told Connally again that more soundings on the Hill strengthened the notion that he could not be confirmed. Still Connally pressed. According to Haig, he argued: "Al, I don't want to be a hostage. I don't care what they say they will do. . . the American people will win out. This decision should not be made on whether I can be confirmed. Because I think I will be confirmed. It may be a bloody battle. . . . If [the president] is not prepared to go all out, we ought not to start it."[19]

Nixon wanted Connally, but at this point not enough to take on Congress when its Watergate inquiry was breathing down his neck. So Connally, according to Haig, finally accepted that the nomination would go to Ford, saying it would be a good choice. Haig afterward pointed out that in light of the fact that Connally later was indicted in a milk-pricing scandal, his appointment could have produced his double-impeachment nightmare after all, though Connally eventually was acquitted of the charges against him.

As far as the Nixon–Connally musings about the Texan winning the Oval Office as a Republican in 1976, after which a new party would be created with Nixon masterminding it behind the scenes, that idea may still have been alive. When Nixon settled on Ford as Agnew's successor, Ford had already promised his wife Betty that he would retire from politics at the end of 1976, he wrote later. Therefore, he told Nixon, "just because I'd be serving as vice president for the remainder of his term didn't mean I'd expect to be the presidential nominee in 1976." Nixon replied: "Well, that's good, because John Connally is my choice for 1976. He'd be excellent." Ford wrote that he answered: "That's no problem as far as I'm concerned."[20] Later, obviously, he changed his mind about running himself.

Only two days after Agnew's resignation, the Supreme Court by a 5–2 vote ordered Nixon to release the incriminating White House tapes to Watergate Special Prosecutor Cox. At first, in an ironic twist, Nixon considered using the Justice Department's efficient work in bringing about Agnew's resignation as a rationale for getting rid of Cox. In a letter to Richardson, Nixon wrote: "Both you and the Department of Justice merit commendation for your performance in the difficult matters relating to the vice president. The Department clearly demonstrated its capacity to administer justice fairly and impartially, under the most difficult and sensitive circumstances, without fear or favor, regardless of the individuals involved." The letter continued without a "therefore," but the implication was clear: "Today, I have decided that all criminal matters now under investigation should be handled within the institutional framework of the Department of Justice. Accordingly, you are directed to relieve Special Prosecutor Archibald Cox of all responsibilities. . . ."[21]

The letter was never sent. Instead, the White House dreamed up an unsatisfactory compromise whereby summaries of the tapes would be released, verified as accurate by an "independent" party—Democratic Senator John Stennis of Mississippi. Cox balked at the clearly evasive tactic and Nixon ordered Richardson to fire him. The attorney general refused and resigned himself, as did his deputy, William Ruckelshaus, leaving the onerous task to the department's solicitor general, Robert Bork. The resultant Saturday Night Massacre was a severe blow to the Nixon presidency. Cox's successor, Leon Jaworski, continued the Watergate investigation and the pursuit of the White House tapes that proved to be Nixon's undoing.

Agnew probably took little solace from the fact that soon after his own departure, Richardson also was driven from the Nixon administration, though under much more honorable circumstances. The deposed former vice president was too pre-occupied with his own fate, and its cost. He wrote later: "It is possible that I lost not only the vice presidency, but the presidency. For if I had carried on my battle for vindication through the impeachment process and the courts, I would still have been vice president at the time Nixon resigned. If he had resigned I would have become president. This was the one event... which Richardson was determined to prevent no matter what happened. Of course, Mr. Nixon could have used my refusal to resign as an argument for his staying in office. This would have been the more likely result. It is ironic that Nixon thought he was helping himself by shoving me out; the truth is that if he had kept me in office, he might have held onto the presidency. He [presumably Richardson] had to get rid of me first, then move a more malleable man into the vice presidency (Gerald Ford admirably filled the bill), then shove Nixon out and Ford in. They followed the script in one-two-three order with perfect precision. Too late President Nixon realized he had been suckered by his foes into going along with my ruination, ostensibly to save himself."[22]

❧ ☙

WHILE NIXON was struggling to survive this politically disastrous series of events, Agnew was out about the country and the globe with a struggle of his own to launch a new career in the world of business. At home, the Maryland Bar Association did not make it easier by petitioning the state supreme court to take disciplinary action against him as a lawyer, and in time he was disbarred. But he was cashing in on some of the show-business connections he had made through Frank Sinatra. Frank Jamison, the husband of actress Eva Gabor, a Sinatra neighbor, in late November took Agnew on as a consultant for a new Los Angeles firm said to be engaged in international trade. Agnew also began work on a novel about a vice president with ambitions on the presidency. At the same time, although Nixon had made no pledges to Agnew as he was out the door, the administration did find jobs in it for most of Agnew's vice-presidential staff.

With resentment still boiling within him, Agnew six months after his resignation was the subject of a newspaper column by Jack Anderson providing a few details of the pressures he said were brought against him to resign. But he saved the purported "death threat" for his 1980 book, *Go Quietly. . . Or Else.* The column reported that "suppressed statements to the prosecutors. . . dealt with allegations that a Maryland contractor had provided Agnew with a call girl in exchange for government favors," a charge he told Anderson was "laughable" and "ridiculous," coming from a "congential liar. . . a wild man."[23]

Such allegations continued to obstruct his efforts to present himself as a straight-arrow middleman for U.S. firms. When the World Book encyclopedia included an account of allegations of bribery and extortion against him in the Justice Department's long exposition of the facts it had gathered, Agnew wrote of his objections, saying the account showed a left-wing prejudice.

In his pursuit of international business, the former vice president became a globe-trotter, his interests taking him to South America, his ancestral Greek homeland, Asia, and the Middle East. In each place, his former occupation as the stand-in to the American president opened doors to foreign potentates, if not necessarily their wallets. He often traveled with assistance from U.S. embassies abroad.

While Agnew was knocking on important governmental doors in all corners of the world, Nixon back home had come to his ultimate political demise on August 8, 1974, with his own resignation to avoid House impeachment and certain Senate conviction for the Watergate crimes and cover-up. By now Nixon had accumulated huge legal debts in his failed defense. But unlike the outgoing and confident Agnew, he chose dismal seclusion back at his former presidential retreat in San Clemente, where for months he brooded over his fall from power and grace.

No communication occurred between them, which for Agnew at least was no particular burden or change, since he rarely had been able to talk to Nixon in the five years they worked close by in the White House and Executive Office Building on Pennsylvania Avenue.

About a year after Agnew's resignation, he got involved in a land development deal in Kentucky with potential investors from Kuwait, as a consultant to a man named Walter Dilbeck, whom he had met while visiting Sinatra in Palm Springs. The Associated Press reported that Agnew would be paid $100,000 a year and a share of the profits. Later, Agnew and Dilbeck were reported involved in operating a coal mine in Oklahoma and tapping into other financial resources in the Middle East and Japan, to finance their enterprises.[24]

In February 1975, however, Agnew broke off the relationship, calling Dilbeck a publicity seeker who with "exaggerations and outright misstatements" sought to promote his interest "at the expense of my integrity" and the success of their undertakings. Dilbeck responded that Agnew's apparent preoccupation with the Arab powers was distasteful and unsatisfactory in light of Dilbeck's "long-standing association with many Jewish people and interests in this country."[25]

In August 1975, with professional golfer Doug Sanders, Agnew sought a Coors beer distributorship in Texas, but he withdrew the application when, the brewery reported, he said his involvement would hurt Sanders's chances because of his own *nolo contendere* plea in 1973, and his lack of Texas residence.[26] He also entered into a mysterious relationship with Tongsun Park, the South Korean operative whose dealings with and lavish entertaining of certain congressmen on shipments of surplus American rice underwent a long investigation.

In November 1976, Agnew indicated that he had not abandoned the fights for which his vice presidency had made him famous, by announcing plans for a new "Education for Democracy" nonprofit foundation. He said that for two years he had "waited for more well-known, national spokesmen (yes, I said spokesmen, not spokespersons) to take up the fight against the apologists for the revolutionaries who are intent on destroying the strengths of our great country," and was "tired of waiting, and perhaps you are too." He said he was "not planning to use this foundation as a base for flying around the country making political speeches or anything like that. That's not what it's intended for."[27] In any event, there was not a great clamor for political speeches from either Agnew or Nixon. In the more than twenty years after their respective resignations, neither one was ever invited to attend, let alone speak, at any of their party's national conventions.

Little was heard of Agnew's foundation thereafter, except for an accusation by the Anti-Defamation League of B'Nai B'Rith that Agnew would use it "for the purpose of organizing a movement to reflect his anti-Israel, pro-Arab views." Later, much was made of the fact he was due an $80,000 fee for setting up a deal for a Maryland firm to build modular schoolrooms in Saudi Arabia.[28]

In 1976, when his novel, *The Canfield Decision*, came out, it made the *New York Times* best-seller list for six weeks in spite of, or perhaps because of, the criticism, and sold more than 70,000 copies in hard cover. The novel involves a vice president who intends to run for president, and who intentionally takes a position on a critical foreign policy issue contrary to that of the president [just as Agnew had done in opposition to Nixon's SALT I agreement]. In the book, when the president strikes a deal with the Soviet Union and China on arms control that magnifies the policy breach with his vice president, the president pointedly states that his stand-in president does not speak for the administration.

Agnew's fictional vice president is on a Far East trip at the time and acknowledges to the traveling press that the deal was made without his knowledge [similar to the real circumstances surrounding Nixon's opening to China]. As more questions are raised about his differences with the president, he refuses to resign and instead gets into another row that triggers a cabinet revolt. In a subplot, a murder is committed implicating the imaginary vice president, who also is having an extra-marital affair with a female cabinet member. Agnew wrote later: "My enemies attacked the book in two inconsistent ways. Some said it was the worst example of prose ever seen. Others said it was too well written for me to have authored it. I challenged the latter group, but they refused the confrontation."[29]

Through it all, Agnew remained a hounded man. At the end of 1976, when his three-year probation ended, a lawyer sought a pardon for him from Gerald Ford, the man Nixon had nominated to replace Agnew in 1973 and who, as president, had pardoned Nixon in 1974. Ford's press secretary, Ron Nessen, confirmed the request and referred the inquiry to the Justice Department, where nothing came of it. Agnew's secretary said Agnew had not authorized the request and did not know its source.[30] What's more, the Internal Revenue Service in early 1977 said it was auditing Agnew's past returns, and later sent him a bill for $268,482 when a civil court held that he did receive the kickbacks mentioned in the 1973 case that led to his resignation.[31]

My last personal encounter with Agnew came shortly afterward, when I spied him at a table with friends, later identified by him as some old Secret Service agents, at a restaurant in a downtown Washington hotel near the *Post*. I walked over and, admittedly somewhat mischievously, proposed that I write another book telling his side of the resignation story. In the book he subsquently wrote himself, he described his reaction: "I burst out laughing every time I think of that incident. After dipping his pen in poison to write two books about me, Witcover had the nerve to ask me to help him write another!"[32] I took that as a "No."

In 1977, the Agnews moved to Rancho Mirage, California, a few miles from Palm Springs and their friends the Sinatras, and occasionally visited their old Ocean City, Maryland, summer haunts. The Nixons, meanwhile, essentially holed up at what formerly had been known as the Summer White House at San Clemente. There, the former president warded off various legal challenges and pressed legal claims while whittling down huge legal bills by writing a series of books on foreign policy, many of which became best sellers. He was only occasionally seen in public and he and his wife later moved to the small town of Upper Saddle River in northern New Jersey, where he sometimes held small off-the-record dinners with favored and sympathetic members of the news media.

In May of 1977, Nixon finally addressed Agnew's plight and resignation in a television interview with British personality David Frost. He continued the fiction that he was little more than an uninvolved bystander as Richardson and Petersen recommended the deal whereby his vice president traded his office for escape from jail time. He told Frost that he had favored Agnew taking "the impeachment track" in the House, but he got a ruling from Bork as solicitor general that "the Constitution did not specifically include the vice president in the clause with regard to impeachment being the only recourse against a president."

Therefore, he told Frost, with Agnew facing "a kangaroo court' [in Baltimore] where he'd have no chance and serve a prison term," resignation was his only out. He told Frost that Richardson "was playing very hardball," not mentioning that through his own agents, Haig and Buzhardt, he was pushing very hard himself to achieve Agnew's removal from office.

Whether Agnew was guilty or innocent, Nixon said, "under the circumstances it became an irrelevant point" by then. "I'm not going to sit here and judge Spiro Agnew," he piously told Frost. "I know that he feels he didn't get enough support from the White House. I know that he feels some people were undercutting him. I know that he has bitter feelings, certainly about me in this respect. All I can say is that it was a no-win proposition. I felt that in my heart he was a decent man. He was a courageous man. He made mistakes; I made mistakes. Perhaps in the conduct of our dealings with the press and some political leaders and the rest. . . but I do not think for one minute that Spiro Agnew. . . consciously felt that he was violating the law, and basically that he was being bribed to do something that was wrong. . . because of a payment."

Nixon could not end the Agnew segment of the interview without getting in one of his old slaps at liberals in the news media against whom he shared Agnew's deepest animosity. "I also believe there has been a double standard, and as far as Spiro Agnew is concerned," he said, "because he was a conservative, because he was one who took on the press, he got a lot rougher treatment than would have been the case had he been one of the liberals' favorite pin-up boys. . . You know exactly the ones I mean. Those that go down the liberal line and who can see all of the wickedness among the conservatives and when it's on their side, well, 'Ha, ha, ha, isn't that just fun and games?'"[33]

The remarks in sum were an infinitely better defense of Nixon's former vice president than he had ever made when he had an opportunity to come to his aid. If the intent was to gloss over or obscure the duplicity and deviousness of his own behavior throughout Agnew's ordeal, what Nixon had said and done in private, and within the counsels of his own inner circle, was ample witness to that behavior.

In the interview, Nixon acknowledged that he had not "had any contact" with Agnew since the night the man walked out of the Oval Office after telling Nixon he would be officially resigning the next day. "I can well understand, putting myself in his place," he told Frost, "that he feels that things could have worked out differently."[34]

When, seventeen years later, Richard Nixon died and was buried near his private presidential library at his birthplace in Yorba Linda, California, hundreds of notables from his two successful campaigns for the presidency and his administration gathered at the site. Nixon's daughters, Tricia and Julie, somewhat surprisingly invited Agnew to attend. Tricia's husband, Ed Cox, phoned Agnew's former aide John Damgard with the invitation and Damgard passed it on, but Agnew firmly told him: "I'm not going." Damgard coaxed him: "You've got to go. This is the man who made you vice president, not once but twice. You'd be very conspicuous by your absence."[35]

Apparently Damgard was persuasive. David Keene recalled that Agnew "wrote me a two- or three-page letter explaining why he thought he ought to go to the funeral even though he thought Nixon was an ass-hole."[36] So Agnew went. According to Damgard, who accompanied him, the former vice president was welcomed with open arms by his former colleagues.

Before President Bill Clinton and others spoke, Agnew explained his presence to reporters. "I decided after twenty years of resentment to put it aside," he said. "I'm here to pay tribute to the man's many accomplishments and to express our sympathy to Tricia and Julie and the family we always thought highly of. The last time I talked to him was the day I resigned [actually the night before]. He tried to call me after that several times, but I didn't take the calls because, at the time, I felt totally abandoned. But that's all past."[37]

Less than a year later, Agnew made his final notable public appearance, in Washington, in a corridor outside the U.S. Senate, over which he had presided for nearly five years. He received much applause from the approximately 300 friends, old colleagues, and the curious in the Capitol, present for the dedication of a bust of him, placed with those of previous vice presidents. Senate Republican Leader Bob Dole noted that Agnew had taken on the task of presiding personally over the Senate more than had any predecessor. Republican Senator Ted Stevens of Alaska praised him for having cast the tie-breaking vote for construction of the Alaska pipeline. A Democrat, Senator Daniel Patrick Moynihan of New York, said the ceremony was proper, because "it's a prescribed rule of the Senate."

Agnew, in brief comments, was candid. "I'm not blind or deaf to the fact that some people feel that this is a ceremony that should not take place, that the Senate by commissioning this bust is giving me an honor I don't deserve. I would remind these people that, regardless of their personal view of me, this ceremony has less to do with Spiro Agnew than with the office I held, and had conferred on me by the American people, two decades ago."[38]

Eighteen months later, when Agnew died and was buried in Towson, Maryland, there was none of the fanfare that had marked the departure of the man with whom he shared glory and rejection as the only team of president and vice president to have been forced from office. In the end, Nixon's comment on Agnew in 1968, noted earlier, served as a commentary on the first man's judgment and the performance of the second in high office. "There is a mysticism about men," Richard Nixon had told reporters then. "There is a quiet confidence. You look a man in the eye and you know he's got it—brains. This guy has got it. If he doesn't, Nixon has made a bum choice."[39]

As for Spiro Agnew, his boast and objective at the time Nixon chose him, that his was not "a household name" but that he intended to make it one, had certainly been realized. Long after his resignation, his old staff man, David Keene, ran into him and Agnew said to him: "You can never escape your past." He told Keene of walking down a street in Copenhagen and being accosted by an American stranger. "All of a sudden he froze and he looked at me," Agnew said, "and he pointed at me and he said, 'You're Spiro Agnew!'" The former vice president replied, "Yes, I am." And the man offered his hand and said: "Lay some rhetoric on me, man."[40]

In that case at least, Agnew was remembered for his smoking speech. But others recalled him for the disgrace that the crimes he committed, not only in Maryland but those carrying over into his vice presidency, had brought upon him.

❧ ❧

In the purely political sphere, Nixon was guilty not only in his original choice of Agnew but also in then denying him as vice president entry into his inner circle. Nixon failed adequately to take advantage of whatever experience and talents this former governor had in domestic policy. Instead he used him primarily as a political hatchetman against his critics in the opposition party, in the streets, and on the rebellious campuses of a nation in turmoil.

Against the history of nine vice presidents ascending to the presidency by death or resignation of the president, including five of the last eighteen, the imperative for a presidential nominee to make a wise and measured choice of a running mate is all too clear. That recognition came very late to Richard Nixon, faced himself with being forced from office.

If there was any tangible benefit of the mismatched marriage of Nixon and Agnew, it could be argued that it led to a more enlightened selection of subsequent vice presidents and running mates, but hardly in all cases. Elevated vice president Gerald Ford chose a seasoned Nelson Rockefeller after Nixon's resignation in 1974 but dropped him in 1976 under conservative pressures. He then picked veteran Senator Bob Dole, whose own smoking rhetoric as a campaigner may have contributed, along with Ford's pardon of Nixon, to the incumbent's narrow defeat. In the same year, Democratic presidential nominee Jimmy Carter selected another Senate veteran of experience, Walter F. Mondale, and—albeit reluctantly—Republican presidential nominee Ronald Reagan in 1980 accepted, as his running mate, a man of many governmental roles in George H. W. Bush.

But in 1984, only three election cycles after Agnew had resigned in disgrace, Democratic presidential nominee Mondale chose as his running mate little-known Geraldine Ferraro, a congresswoman from New York of very modest accomplishment. His selection was a longshot gamble that her gender would bring him the support he lacked on his own to upset popular Republican President Ronald Reagan, and the gamble fell far short.

When it became the senior Bush's turn, he astonished fellow Republicans by choosing the hapless Senator Dan Quayle, a man youthful beyond his years and a political lightweight who became the brunt of ridicule for his public gaffes of word and deed. Bush of all recent presidents should have been aware of the need to select a person as his running mate qualified to be president if destiny were to so dictate. In the first weeks of his own vice presidency, the president under whom he served, Reagan, narrowly escaped assassination. Yet Bush as president himself did not exclude Quayle from his inner circle in quite the way the isolated and withdrawn Nixon had shunted Agnew. Despite a rocky, gaffe-laden first term, Bush stuck with Quayle for a second time in 1992.

Subsequent presidents Bill Clinton and George W. Bush broke clearly from the Nixon–Agnew pattern by selecting seasoned men as their vice presidents—Senator Al Gore in 1992 and former Congressman, White House Chief of Staff, and Secretary of Defense Dick Cheney in 2000—and bringing them into the heart of their decision-making processes. Cheney was included in Bush's inner circle to the extent that, widely perceived as much more experienced and powerful than the man who picked him, questions circulated after their election about which of them truly was in charge of the country. In a different way, that choice also underscored the critical nature of the vice-presidential selection, inasmuch as Cheney eventually became more controversial than many of his predecessors in the job.

To be sure, the selection of any running mate is always somewhat of a crapshoot. Previous experience in politics or government is no certain guarantee that the person chosen, if elevated to the presidency, will meet the demands of the office. Harry Truman, for example, was rated by many as a pedestrian senator when Franklin D. Roosevelt, under pressure from Democratic political chietains, acquiesced in his selection in 1944. Yet he was judged ultimately to have served with decisiveness and distinction.

In any event, a retelling of the Nixon–Agnew debacle can be a reminder to future presidential nominees of their need to act on what they always say in making that choice: that they are naming the person they believe is best able to assume the presidency if destiny so requires.

Furthermore, seldom has the telling of history been better if unintentionally served by an American administration than this one, which provided so much raw material for present and future narrators. Haldeman's daily memos on life in the Oval Office and their insights into the mind and machinations of the president are invaluable. Even more so are the White House tape recordings that Nixon ordered and preserved—unprecedented artifacts of one of the darkest chapters in the nation's political annals.

Richard Nixon liked to say, "Let me make one thing perfectly clear." Thanks to all these artifacts, we now know with perfect clarity how and why the strange political union of Nixon and Agnew came undone.

NOTES

INTRODUCTION

1. Interview with John Damgard, Washington, Sept. 11, 2005.
2. Spiro T. Agnew, *Go Quietly . . . Or Else*, pp. 33–34.

CHAPTER 1: SNARED ON THE REBOUND

1. Jules Witcover, *White Knight: The Rise of Spiro Agnew*, p. 123.
2. Ibid., p. 183.
3. Ibid, p. 184.
4. Ibid., pp. 184–85.
5. Ibid., p. 185.
6. Interview with Nelson Rockefeller, New York, 1967.
7. Ibid.
8. Garry Wills, *Nixon Agonistes*, p. 285.
9. Witcover, *White Knight*, p. 193.
10. Ibid., p. 199.
11. Ibid., p. 200.
12. Ibid., p. 201.
13. Interview with John Sears, Washington, Sept. 12, 2005.
14. Ibid.
15. Interview with Sears, 1968.
16. Witcover, *The Resurrection of Richard Nixon*, p. 280.
17. Interview with George Hinman, New York, 1969.

18. Witcover, *White Knight*, p. 206.

19. Ibid., p. 160.

20. Ibid., p. 162.

21. Ibid., p. 21.

22. Ibid.

23. Ibid., p.22.

24. Ibid.

25. Ibid., p. 24.

26. Ibid., p. 205.

CHAPTER 2: SPIRO WHO?

1. Witcover, *White Knight*, p. 207.

2. Ibid.

3. Ibid., p. 208.

4. Ibid.

5. Ibid., p. 209.

6. Ibid., p. 211.

7. Interview with Spiro T. Agnew, Tulsa, Okla., 1968.

8. Witcover, *White Knight*, p. 212.

9. Ibid., p. 213.

10. Ibid.

11. Ibid., pp. 218–19.

12. Interview with Sears, Sept. 12, 2005.

13. Ibid.

14. Ibid., pp. 217–18.

15. Ibid., p. 218.

16. Ibid., p. 219.

17. Witcover, *The Resurrection of Richard Nixon*, pp. 337–38.

18. Witcover, *White Knight*, p. 220.

19. Richard Nixon, *RN: The Memoirs of Richard Nixon*, p. 310.

20. Witcover, *The Resurrection of Richard Nixon*, p. 343.

21. Witcover, *White Knight*, p. 221.

22. Ibid., p. 224.

23. Witcover, *The Resurrection of Richard Nixon*, p. 353.

24. Ibid., p. 354.

25. Witcover, *Crapshoot: Rolling the Dice on the Vice Presidency*, p. 179.

26. Witcover, *The Resurrection of Richard Nixon*, p. 354.

27. Nixon, *RN*, p. 313.

28. Witcover, *White Knight*, p. 228.

29. Ibid., p. 229.

30. Ibid., pp. 228–29.

31. Ibid., pp. 229–30.

32. Nixon, *RN*, p. 312.

33. Witcover, *White Knight*, p. 230.

34. Ibid, p. 231.

35. Ibid., p. 235.

36. William Safire, *Before the Fall: An Inside View Of the Pre-Watergate White House*, p. 56.

37. Witcover, *White Knight*, p. 234.

38. Ibid., p. 36.

39. Roger Morris, *Richard Milhous Nixon: The Rise of an American Politician*, pp. 59–73.

40. Witcover, *White Knight*, pp. 40–57.

41. Ibid., pp. 62–149.

CHAPTER 3: NIXON'S NIXON

1. Witcover, *White Knight*, pp. 234–35.

2. Interview with Richard Nixon, Portland, Ore., May, 1968.

3. Witcover, *White Knight*, p. 243.

4. Interview with Patrick Buchanan, McLean, Va., Aug. 15, 2005.

5. Interview with Sears, Sept. 12, 2005.

6. Witcover, *White Knight*, p. 239.

7. Ibid., p. 240.

8. Ibid.

9. Ibid, p. 241.

10. Ibid.

11. Ibid.

12. Ibid., p. 242.

13. Ibid.

14. Ibid.

15. Ibid., p. 244.

16. Ibid., p. 245.

17. Ibid.

18. Ibid., p. 346.

19. William Safire, *Before the Fall*, p. 70.

20. Witcover, *White Knight*, p. 247.

21. Ibid.

22. Ibid., p. 248.

23. Ibid., p. 253.

24. Ibid.

25. Safire, *Before the Fall*, p. 75.

26. Witcover, *White Knight*, p. 258.

27. Ibid., p. 261.

28. Ibid. p. 263.

29. Nixon, *RN*, p. 320.

30. Interview with Buchanan, Aug. 15, 2005.

31. Witcover, *White Knight*, p. 265.

32. Ibid., pp. 265–66.

33. Witcover, *Resurrection of Richard Nixon*, p. 389.

34. Witcover, *White Knight*, p. 266.

35. Ibid., pp. 266–67.

36. Ibid., p. 267.

37. Witcover, *Resurrection of Richard Nixon*, pp. 432–33.

38. Witcover, *White Knight*, p. 277.

39. Witcover, *The Year the Dream Died*, p. 427.

40. Witcover, *White Knight*, p. 280.

41. Ibid., p. 281.

42. J. Anthony Lukas, *Nightmare: The Underside of the Nixon Years*, pp. 283–84.

43. Interview with Sears, Sept. 12, 2005.

CHAPTER 4: GREAT EXPECTATIONS

1. Witcover, *Crapshoot*, p. 231.

2. Ibid., pp. 18–19; Witcover, *White Knight*, p. 284.

3. Witcover, *Crapshoot*, p. 138.

4. Ibid., p. 232; Witcover, *White Knight*, pp. 284–85.

5. Interviews with Victor Gold, Washington, August 17, 2005, August 3, 2006.

6. Agnew, *Go Quietly . . . Or Else*, p. 36.

7. H. R. Haldeman, *The Haldeman Diaries: Inside the Nixon White House*, p. 27.

8. Interview with Victor Gold, Washington, August 3, 2006.

9. *Haldeman Diaries*, p. 27.

10. White House Special Files, Haldeman Notes, Box 40; February 5, 1969.

11. Ibid., February 6, 1969.

12. Haldeman Diaries CD, February 8, 1969.

13. Herbert G. Klein, *Making It Perfectly Clear: An Inside Account of Nixon's Love-Hate Relationahip With the Media*, pp. 165–67.

14. Witcover, *White Knight*, p. 286.

15. Ibid., p. 293.

16. Ibid., p. 288.

17. Ibid.

18. Agnew Collection, Maryland Room, Hornbake Library, University of Maryland; Series III, Subseries 7, Box 1.

19. Ibid.

20. *Haldeman Diaries*, p. 52.

21. Haldeman Notes, April 24, 1969.

22. *Haldeman Diaries*, p. 53.

23. National Security Files, Box 836, VP—1969–1970; April 24, 1969.

24. Ibid., May 7, 1969.

25. White House Special Files, President's Personal Files, Box 5 (Spiro Agnew), May 16, 1969.

26. Ibid., July 18, 1969.

27. Ibid., July 25, 1969.

28. Telephone interview with Melvin R. Laird, June 15, 2006.

29. John Ehrlichman, *Witness to Power: The Nixon Years*, p. 106.

30. Telephone interview wth Alexander Butterfield, June 8, 2006.

31. Witcover, *White Knight*, p. 288.

32. Ibid., p. 289.

33. Ibid., p. 290.

34. Ibid., p. 291.

35. Interview with Damgard, Washington, Sept. 11, 2005.

36. Interview with C. D. Ward, Washington, June 9, 2006.

37. Witcover, *White Knight*, p. 292.

38. Ehrlichman, *Witness to Power*, pp. 144–45.

39. Ibid., p. 145.

40. Ibid.

41. Ibid., p. 146.

42. Ibid.

43. Witcover, *White Knight*, p. 292.

44. Ehrlichman, *Witness to Power*, pp. 146–47.

45. Ibid., p. 147.

46. National Security Files, Box 836, VP—1969–70, September 29, 1969.

47. Ibid., October 2, 1969.

48. Ibid., December 10, 1969.

49. Witcover, *White Knight*, p. 303.

50. Ibid., pp. 302–03.

51. Ibid., p. 303.

52. *Haldeman Diaries*, p. 99.

53. Witcover, *White Knight*, p. 304.

CHAPTER 5:
AROUSING THE SILENT MAJORITY

1. Witcover, *White Knight*, pp. 304–05.

2. Ibid., p. 306.

3. Ibid., p. 307.

4. Ibid.

5. Ibid., p. 308.

6. *Haldeman Diaries* CD, October 30, 1969.

7. Witcover, *White Knight*, pp. 308–09.

8. Ibid., pp. 309–10.

9. Ibid., p. 310.

10. Ibid.

11. *Haldeman Diaries*, p. 107.

12. Nixon, *RN*, p. 411.

13. Witcover, *White Knight*, p. 311.

14. Ibid., p. 312.

15. Ibid.

16. Ibid., pp. 313–14.

17. *Haldeman Diaries*, pp. 107–09.

18. Ibid., p. 109.

19. Ibid.

20. Ibid.

21. Witcover, *White Knight*, pp. 317–18.

22. Bruce Oudes, *From the President: Richard Nixon's Secret Files*, p. 70.

23. Witcover, *White Knight*, p. 320.

24. Ibid.

25. *Haldeman Diaries* CD, December 2, 1969.

26. Ibid., December 13, 1969.

CHAPTER 6:
HOT-AND-COLD HONEYMOON

1. *Haldeman Diaries*, p. 111.
2. National Security Files, Box 836, December 4, 1969.
3. Ibid., January 20, 1970.
4. Oudes, *From the President*, p. 92.
5. Haldeman Notes, Box 41, February 20, 1970.
6. Ehrlichman, *Witness to Power*, p. 147.
7. *Haldeman Diaries*, p. 128.
8. Ehrlichman, *Witness to Power*, pp. 147–48.
9. *Haldeman Diaries* CD, March 3, 1970.
10. *Associated Press*, March 15, 1970; *Haldeman Diaries*, p. 138.
11. Oudes, *From the President*, p. 100.
12. Ehrlichman, *Witness to Power*, pp. 143–44.
13. Ibid., p. 111.
14. Witcover, *White Knight*, pp. 327–28.
15. *Haldeman Diaries*, p. 147.
16. Ibid., p. 150.
17. Memos in White House Central Files, Box 35, April 13–23, 1970.
18. Memo in White House Central Files (Nils Boe), Box 35, June 4, 1970.
19. Witcover, *White Knight*, p. 329.
20. Ibid., pp. 331–32.
21. Ibid., p. 334.
22. Henry Kissinger, *White House Years*, pp. 491–92.
23. Ibid., p. 499.

CHAPTER 7:
BIG MAN ON CAMPUS

1. Witcover, *White Knight*, p. 335.
2. Ibid, p. 336.
3. *Haldeman Diaries*, pp. 159–60.
4. Witcover, *White Knight*, p. 337.
5. *Haldeman Diaries*, p. 161.
6. Ibid, p. 162.
7. Ibid.
8. Ibid., pp. 162–63.

9. Witcover, *White Knight*, pp. 337–38.

10. Witcover, *Crapshoot*, p. 240.

11. Witcover, *White Knight*, p. 348.

12. Ibid., p. 339.

13. Ibid., p. 340.

14. Ibid., p. 342.

15. Oudes, *From the President*, pp. 136–37.

16. *Haldeman Diaries*, pp. 169–70.

17. Ehrlichman, *Witness to Power*, pp. 148–49.

18. Witcover, *White Knight*, pp. 343–44.

19. Ehrlichman, *Witness to Power*, pp. 149–50.

20. Witcover, *White Knight*, pp. 344–45.

21. Ibid., p. 345.

22. Ehrlichman, *Witness to Power*, p. 151.

23. Ibid., p. 152.

24. *Haldeman Diaries*, p. 174.

25. Ibid.

26. *Haldeman Diaries* CD, June 18, 1970.

27. Ehrlichman, *Witness to Power*, p. 152.

28. *Haldeman Diaries* CD, June 22, 1970.

29. *Haldeman Diaries*, pp. 175–76.

30. Ehrlichman, *Witness to Power*, p. 103.

31. Witcover, *White Knight*, pp. 345–46.

32. Ehrlichman, *Witness to Power*, p. 103.

33. *Haldeman Diaries*, p. 179.

34. Ehrlichman, *Witness to Power*, p. 103.

35. *Haldeman Diaries*, p. 180.

36. Haldeman Notes, Box 41, January 8, 1970.

37. Witcover, *White Knight*, p. 330.

38. *Haldeman Diaries*, p. 186.

39. Witcover, *White Knight*, pp. 346–47.

40. Oudes, *From the President*, p. 50.

41. Witcover, *White Knight*, p. 348.

CHAPTER 8:
PURGE OF THE RADIC-LIBS

1. Safire, *Before the Fall*, p. 318.

2. Witcover, *White Knight*, pp. 356–57.

3. Ibid., p. 358.

4. *Haldeman Diaries*, p. 192.

5. Safire, *Before the Fall*, pp. 318, 321–22.

6. Witcover, *White Knight*, pp. 359–60.

7. Ibid., pp. 363–65.

8. Ibid., pp. 368–69.

9. Safire, *Before the Fall*, p. 318.

10. Witcover, *White Knight*, pp. 374–75.

11. Ibid., p. 376.

12. Ibid.

13. Ibid., pp. 376–77.

14. Ibid., p. 377.

15. Ibid., p. 378.

16. Ibid.

17. Ibid., pp. 378–79.

18. Interview with Damgard, Washington, Sept. 21, 2005.

19. Witcover, *White Knight*, p. 379.

20. Ibid.

21. Ibid., p. 380.

22. Ibid., pp. 382–83.

23. Nixon, *RN*, p. 491.

24. Witcover, *White Knight*, p. 384.

25. Ibid.

26. Ibid., p. 385.

27. Ibid., p. 386.

28. Ibid.

29. Ibid., pp. 388–89.

30. Ibid., p. 390.

31. Ibid., p. 369.

32. Ehrlichman, *Witness to Power*, pp. 153–54.

33. *Haldeman Diaries*, pp. 205–06.

34. Nixon, *RN*, p.493.

35. Witcover, *White Knight*, p.391.

36. Ibid., p. 392.

37. Ibid.

38. *Haldeman Diaries*, pp. 206–07.

39. Nixon, *RN*, p. 494.

40. Witcover, *White Knight*, p. 393.

41. Oudes, *From the President*, p. 168.

42. Witcover, *White Knight*, p. 394.

43. Nixon, *RN*, p. 495.

CHAPTER 9:
MARRIAGE OF CONVENIENCE

1. Witcover, *White Knight*, pp. 396–97.
2. *Haldeman Diaries*, p. 208.
3. Witcover, *White Knight*, p. 397.
4. Ibid., p. 398.
5. Ibid., pp. 398–99.
6. Ibid., p. 400.
7. Ibid., p. 401.
8. Ibid.
9. Ibid., p. 404.
10. Interview with John Sears, September 12, 2005.
11. *Haldeman Diaries*, p. 135.
12. Ibid., p. 212.
13. *Haldeman Diaries* CD, December 4, 1970.
14. Ibid.
15. *Haldeman Diaries*, pp. 215–16.
16. *Haldeman Diaries* CD, December 5, 1970.
17. Haldeman Notes, Box 42.
18. Ibid.
19. Witcover, *White Knight*, p. 404.
20. Ibid., pp. 404–05.
21. Ibid., pp. 405–06.
22. Ibid., pp. 406–07.
23. Oudes, *From the President*, pp. 192–93.
24. *Haldeman Diaries* CD, December 29, 1970.
25. Ibid., December 30, 1970.
26. *Haldeman Diaries* CD, January 11, 1971.
27. *Haldeman Diaries*, p. 252.

CHAPTER 10:
THINKING THE UNTHINKABLE

1. *Haldeman Diaries* CD, February 11, 1971.
2. Haldeman Notes, Box February 11, 1971.

3. Nixon Tapes, OVAL 454–9, February 20, 1971.

4. Witcover, *White Knight*, p. 414.

5. White House Central Files, Subject Files, FE 38, February 2, 1971.

6. Ibid., February 10, 1971.

7. Ibid., February 24, 1971.

8. *Haldeman Diaries* CD, February 27, 1971.

9. White House Central Files, Subject Files, FG 38, February 27, 1971.

10. *Haldeman Diaries* CD, February 27, 1971.

11. Interview with Victor Gold, August 17, 2005.

12. Interview with John Damgard, September 11, 2005.

13. Interview with David Keene, Washington, August 17, 2005.

14. Interview with John Sears, September 12, 2005.

15. Nixon Tapes, OVAL 473–8, March 25, 1971.

16. Spiro T. Agnew Collection, Maryland Room, Hornbake Library, University of Maryland; Series III, Subseries 7, Box 5, March 13, 1971.

17. Nixon Tapes, EOB 246–26, April 7, 1971.

18. Interview with John Dean, Washington, July 13, 2006.

19. Nixon Tapes, EOB 246–26E, April 7, 1971.

20. *Haldeman Diaries*, p. 269.

21. Interview with John Damgard, August 3, 2006.

22. Nixon Tapes, WHT 1–15, April 7, 1971.

23. Nixon Tapes, EOB 247–4, April 7, 1971.

24. Nixon Tapes, EOB 247–9, April 13, 1971.

25. Nixon Tapes, OVAL 479–3, April 14, 1971.

26. Nixon Tapes, EOB 247–9, April 13, 1971.

27. *Haldeman Diaries*, p. 272.

CHAPTER 11:
BULL IN A CHINA SHOP

1. Interview with William Timmons, Washington, August 17, 2005.

2. Witcover, *White Knight*, p. 414.

3. Ibid., pp. 415–16.

4. Interview with Victor Gold, August 17, 2005.

5. Interview with David Keene, August 17, 2005.

6. *Haldeman Diaries* CD, April 20, 1971.

7. Nixon Tapes, OVAL 483–4, April 20, 1971.

8. *Haldeman Diaries*, p. 275.

9. Nixon, *RN*, p. 549.

10. *Haldeman Diaries*, p. 275.

11. Ibid.

12. Witcover, *White Knight*, p. 417.

13. Kissinger, *White House Years*, p. 713.

14. Spiro T. Agnew, *Go Quietly . . . Or Else*, pp. 31–32.

15. Oudes, *From the President*, p. 252.

16. Witcover, *White Knight*, p. 419.

17. *Haldeman Diaries* CD, May 22, 1971.

18. Ibid., June 6, 1971.

19. *Haldeman Diaries*, p. 307.

CHAPTER 12:
ANYWHERE BUT PEKING

1. *Haldeman Diaries* CD, June 4, 1971.

2. Nixon Tapes, OVAL 512–27, June 4, 1971.

3. National Security Council Files, Box 837 (VP 1971–72), May 20, 1971.

4. Nixon Tapes, OVAL 512–27, June 4, 1971.

5. *Detroit Free Press*, June 29, 1971.

6. *Associated Press*, July 19, 1971.

7. Witcover, *White Knight*, pp. 420–21.

8. Agnew, *Go Quietly . . . Or Else*, pp. 34–35.

9. *New York Times*, July 18, 1971; Witcover, *White Knight*, p. 421.

10. Ibid., pp. 421–22.

11. Interviews with Victor Gold, August 17, 2005, August 3, 2006.

12. *Newsweek*, July 26, 1971.

13. Agnew Collection, University of Maryland, Series III, Subseries 11, Box 8.

14. Nixon Tapes, EOB 263–9, July 21, 1971.

15. Witcover, *White Knight*, pp. 422–23.

CHAPTER 13: COURTING CONNALLY

1. *Haldeman Diaries* CD, July 9, 1971.

2. Ibid., July 15, 1971.

3. Ibid., July 16, 1971.

4. Ibid., July 19, 1971.

5. Nixon Tapes, EOB 262–5, July 20, 1971.

6. Nixon Tapes, OVAL 540–9, July 20, 1971.

7. *Haldeman Diaries* CD, July 20, 1971.

8. Nixon Tapes, EOB 264–5, July 21, 1971.

9. *Haldeman Diaries* CD, July 20, 1971.

10. Haldeman Notes, Box 43, July 21,1971.

11. Nixon Tapes, OVAL 541–2, July 21, 1971.

12. *Haldeman Diaries* CD, July 21, 1971.

CHAPTER 14:
WELCOME HOME, TED

1. Kissinger memo to Nixon, July 28, 1971.

2. Nixon Tapes, OVAL 549–4, July 28, 1971.

3. Nixon Tapes, OVAL 549–25, July 28, 1971.

4. Interview with Victor Gold, Washington, August 3, 2006.

5. Nixon Tapes, OVAL 552–5, July 30, 1971.

6. Ibid.

7. *Newsweek*, August 2, 1971.

CHAPTER 15:
PLOTTING THE BIG SWITCH

1. Nixon, *RN*, p. 674.

2. Ehrlichman, *Witness to Power*, pp. 154–55, 261.

3. Ibid., pp. 259–60.

4. Robert Sam Anson, *Exile: The Unique Oblivion of Richard M. Nixon*, p. 146.

5. *Haldeman Diaries*, pp. 332–33.

6. Ibid., p.333.

7. Ibid., p. 335.

8. *Haldeman Diaries* CD, August 2, 1971.

9. Ehrlichman, *Witness to Power*, p. 257.

10. Interview with William Timmons, August 17, 2005.

11. Ehrlichman, *Witness to Power*, p. 261.

12. Witcover, *White Knight*, p. 423.

13. Ibid., pp. 423–24.

14. Ibid., p. 424.

15. Nixon Tapes, OVAL 575–7, September 17, 1971.

16. Nixon Tapes, OVAL 576–6, September 18, 1971.

17. *Haldeman Diaries* CD, September 21, 1971.

18. Ibid.

19. Ehrlichman, *Witness to Power*, p. 136; and phone interview with Ehrlichman.

20. Interview with Patrick Buchanan, August 15, 2005.

21. Witcover, *White Knight*, p. 426.

22. *Haldeman Diaries*, p. 378.

23. Interview with John Damgard, September 11, 2005.

24. Witcover, *White Knight*, p. 424.

25. Interview with Victor Gold, August 15, 2005.

26. Witcover, *White Knight*, pp. 426–27.

27. Nixon Tapes, OVAL 601–2, October 26, 1971.

28. White House Special Files, October 27, 1971.

29. Witcover, *White Knight*, p. 428.

30. Ibid.

31. White House Special Files, President's Personal Files, Box 5 (Spiro Agnew).

32. Witcover, *White Knight*, pp. 432–33.

33. Interview with John Damgard, September 11, 2005.

34. Witcover, *White Knight*, pp. 437–38.

CHAPTER 16: SEPARATION ANXIETY

1. *Haldeman Diaries* CD, January 19, 1972.

2. Ibid., January 29, 1972.

3. Ibid, January 31, 1972.

4. Nixon Tapes, OVAL 646–2, January 12, 1972.

5. *Haldeman Diaries*, p. 148.

6. Ibid., pp. 197–98.

7. Ibid., p. 213.

8. Ibid., p. 244.

9. Ibid., p. 249.

10. Ibid., p. 395.

11. *Haldeman Diaries* CD, February 3, 1972.

12. *Haldeman Diaries*, p. 396.

13. Lukas, *Nightmare*, p. 151.

14. Nixon Tapes, OVAL 682–9, March 10, 1972.

15. *Haldeman Diaries* CD, March 10, 1972.

16. Ibid., March 11, 1972.

17. Ibid., March 20, 1972.

18. *Haldeman Diaries*, p. 441.

19. *Haldeman Diaries* CD, April 22, 1972.

20. *Haldeman Diaries*, p. 293.

21. Lukas, *Nightmare*, pp. 155–64.

22. Kissinger, *White House Years*, p. 1184.

23. Nixon Tapes, OVAL 726–1, May 19, 1972.

24. *The Washington Post*, July 8, July 19, 1972.

25. John Connally (with Mickey Hershkowitz), *In History's Shadow: An American Odyssey*, pp. 259–62.

26. Nixon Tapes, OVAL 730–13, June 12, 1972.

27. Ibid.

28. *Haldeman Diaries*, p. 470.

29. Nixon, *RN*, p. 675.

CHAPTER 17:
FROM WATERGATE TO RE-ELECTION

1. Interview with John Damgard, August 3, 2006.

2. Jeb Stuart Magruder, *An American Life: One Man's Road to Watergate*, p. 247.

3. Lukas, *Nightmare*, pp. 216, 222.

4. Magruder, *An American Life*, p. 247.

5. Ibid., p. 248.

6. Interview with Victor Gold, August 17, 2005.

7. *Haldeman Diaries* CD, July 13, 1972.

8. Ibid., July 20, 1972.

9. Ibid., July 25, 1972.

10. Ibid., July 21, 1972.

11. Ibid., August 9, 1972.

12. Ibid., July 24, 1972.

13. Ibid., July 30, 1972.

14. Ibid., August 9, 1972.

15. *Haldeman Diaries*, p. 492.

16. Ibid., p. 495.

17. Ibid., p. 498.

18. Nixon acceptance speech, August 8, 1972.

19. *The Washington Post*, September 20, 1972.

20. *The Washington Post*, September 24, 1972.

21. *Haldeman Diaries* CD, September 13, 1972.

22. Ibid., September 25, 1972.

23. *Haldeman Diaries*, p. 515.

24. Interview with Victor Gold, August 17, 2005.

25. *The Washington Post*, November 5, 1972.

26. Interview with Victor Gold, August 17, 2005.

27. *Haldeman Diaries*, p. 534.

28. Ibid.

29. *Haldeman Diaries* CD, November 14, 1972.

30. Ibid.

31. Agnew, *Go Quietly . . . Or Else*, pp. 37–38.

32. Ehrlichman, *Witness to Power*, p. 155.

33. Interview with Victor Gold, Washington, August 17, 2005.

34. *Haldeman Diaries* CD, November 16, 1972.

35. Agnew, *Go Quietly . . . Or Else*, pp. 38–39.

36. *Haldeman Diaries* CD, December 1, 1972.

37. Ibid., December 5, 1972.

38. Kissinger, *White House Years*, pp. 1428, 1432, 1438–39.

39. *Haldeman Diaries*, p. 557.

40. *Haldeman Diaries* CD, January 8, 1973.

CHAPTER 18:
BAD NEWS FROM BALTIMORE

1. *Haldeman Diaries*, p. 566; CD, January 11, 1973.

2. *Haldeman Diaries*, pp. 581–82.

3. White House Central Files, Subject Files, FG 38, February 7, 1973.

4. Agnew, *Go Quietly . . . Or Else*, p. 40.

5. Nixon Tapes, Watergate Trial Transcript, March 21, 1973, pp. 33–35, 91–92.

6. Interview with John Dean, Washington, July 13, 2006.

7. White House Central Files, Subject Files, FG 38, February 19, 1974.

8. *Haldeman Diaries* CD, March 29, 1973.

9. *Haldeman Diaries*, pp. 625–26.

10. Nixon, *RN*, p. 814.

11. *Haldeman Diaries*, p. 626.

12. Halderman Notes, Box 47, April 5, 1973.

13. *Haldeman Diaries*, pp. 629–30.

14. Nixon, *RN*, p. 816.

15. Richard M. Cohen and Witcover, *A Heartbeat Away: The Investigation and Resignation of Vice President Spiro T. Agnew*, p. 5.

16. Ibid.

17. Agnew, *Go Quietly . . . Or Else*, p. 41.

18. Ibid., p. 43.

19. Ibid., pp. 46, 49.

20. Ibid., pp. 49–51.

21. Ibid., p. 58.

22. Lukas, *Nightmare*, p. 306.

23. Ibid., p. 324.

24. Lukas, *Nightmare*, p. 327.

25. Nixon Tapes, Abuse of Governmental Power, E–255, 38–92, April 17, 1973.

26. Nixon Tapes, Abuse of Governmental Power, E–271–72, 439–22, April 19, 1973.

27. Nixon Tapes, Abuse of Governmental Power, E–257, 38–159, April 25, 1973.

28. Nixon Tapes, Abuse of Governmental Power, E–288, 895–14, April 13, 1973.

29. Nixon Tapes, Abuse of Governmental Power, E–288, 908–24, May 1, 1973.

CHAPTER 19:
LAPSING INSURANCE POLICY

1. Agnew, *Go Quietly . . . Or Else*, pp. 58–59, 55.

2. *Haldeman Diaries*, p. 666.

3. Nixon Tapes, Abuse of Governmental Power, E–276, 432–1, April 27, 1973.

4. *Haldeman Diaries*, pp. 671–72.

5. Ibid, p. 672.

6. Ibid., p. 674.

7. Nixon Tapes, Abuse of Governmental Power, E–263, 164–48, April 30, 1973.

8. Stanley I. Kutler, *Abuse of Power: The New Nixon Tapes*, pp. 419–20.

9. Agnew, *Go Quietly . . . Or Else*, pp. 59–60.

10. *Haldeman Diaries* CD, November 1, 1971.

11. Cohen and Witcover, *A Heartbeat Away*, pp. 77–78.

12. Ibid., p. 78.

13. Ibid., p. 81.

14. Ibid., pp. 84–85.

15. Ibid., p. 85.

16. Nixon Tapes, Abuse of Governmental Power, E–306, 39–16, May 25, 1973.

17. Ehrlichman, *Witness to Power*, pp. 142–43.

18. Nixon Tapes, Abuse of Governmental Power, E–306, 39–16, May 25, 1973.

19. Nixon Tapes, Nixon–Rogers conversation, May 28, 1973.

20. White House Special Files, Central Files, FG 38, 1971–74, June 14, 1973.

21. Nixon Tapes, Abuse of Governmental Power, WHT 45–66, May 5, 1973.

22. *Washington Post*, May 16, 1973.

23. Ibid.

24. Ibid., June 19, 1973.

25. Cohen and Witcover, *A Heartbeat Away*, pp. 101–03.

26. Ibid., pp. 90–96.

27. Agnew, *Go Quietly . . . Or Else*, p. 49.

28. Nixon Tapes, Abuse of Governmental Power, E–435, 932–1, June 5, 1973.

29. Agnew Collection, University of Maryland, Series III, Subseries 3, Box 11, May 3, 1973.

30. Nixon Tapes, Abuse of Governmental Power, E–445, 940–2, June 14, 1973.

CHAPTER 20: CONTESTED DIVORCE

1. Cohen and Witcover, *A Heartbeat Away*, p. 106.

2. Ibid., p. 108.

3. Ibid., p. 109.

4. Ibid., p. 111.

5. Ibid., p. 112.

6. Agnew, *Go Quietly . . . Or Else*, pp. 78–79.

7. Ibid., p. 81.

8. Ibid.

9. Cohen and Witcover, *A Heartbeat Away*, pp. 121–24.

10. Ibid., pp. 127–30.

11. Nixon Tapes, Abuse of Governmental Power, E–454, 947–15, July 10,

1973.

12. Agnew, *Go Quietly . . . Or Else*, p. 86.

13. Ibid., p. 87.

14. Alexander M. Haig, *Inner Circles: How America Changed the World*, pp. 350–51.

15. Ibid.

16. Interview with Alexander Haig, Arlington, Va., August 10, 2006.

17. Agnew, *Go Quietly . . . Or Else*, p. 87.

18. Haig, *Inner Circles*, p. 353.

19. Agnew, *Go Quietly . . . Or Else*, p. 95.

20. White House Special Files—Haig, Box 2 (Agnew).

21. Cohen and Witcover, *A Heartbeat Away*, pp. 131–32.

22. Agnew, *Go Quietly . . . Or Else*, p. 91.

23. Ibid.

24. Interview with C. D. Ward, Washington, June 8, 2006.

25. Haig, *Inner Circles*, p. 353.

26. Cohen and Witcover, *A Heartbeat Away*, p. 146.

27. Nixon, *RN*, p. 913.

28. Interview with Alexander Haig, August 10, 2006.

29. Interview with John Damgard, September 12, 2005.

30. Ibid.

31. Haig, *Inner Circles*, p. 354.

32. Ibid.

33. Ibid., p. 355.

34. Agnew, *Go Quietly . . . Or Else*, p. 98.

35. Cohen and Witcover, *A Heartbeat Away*, p. 149.

36. Agnew, *Go Quietly . . . Or Else*, p. 100.

37. Ibid., p. 102.

38. Ibid., pp. 102–04.

39. Cohen and Witcover, *A Heartbeat Away*, p. 153.

40. Agnew, *Go Quietly . . . Or Else*, pp. 95–96.

CHAPTER 21:
TERMS OF DISENGAGEMENT

1. Agnew, *Go Quietly . . . Or Else*, p. 105.

2. Ibid., pp. 106–07.

3. Ibid., pp. 107–09.

4. Ibid., pp. 109–10.

5. Haig, *Inner Circles*, p. 356.

6. Ibid., p. 357.

7. Ibid., p. 358.

8. White House Central Files, Subject Files, FG–38, August 8, 1973.

9. Cohen and Witcover, *A Heartbeat Away*, p. 161.

10. Agnew, *Go Quietly . . . Or Else*, p. 130.

11. Haig, *Inner Circles*, p.358.

12. Cohen and Witcover, *A Heartbeat Away*, pp. 171–74.

13. Ibid., pp. 171, 179–87.

14. Ibid., pp. 202–03.

15. Agnew, *Go Quietly . . . Or Else*, p. 140.

16. Ibid., pp.140–41.

17. Ford, *A Time to Heal*, p. 101.

18. Agnew, *Go Quietly . . . Or Else*, p. 141.

19. Telephone interview with Melvin R. Laird, June 15, 2006.

20. Haig, *Inner Circles*, p. 361.

21. Ibid., p. 360.

22. Agnew, *Go Quietly . . . Or Else*, p. 142.

23. Agnew, *Go Quietly . . . Or Else*, pp. 142–43.

24. Cohen and Witcover, *A Heartbeat Away*, pp. 220–21.

25. Ibid., pp. 221–22; Agnew, *Go Quietly . . . Or Else*, p. 145.

26. Agnew, *Go Quietly . . . Or Else*, p. 146.

27. Ibid.

28. Agnew Collection, University of Maryland, Series III, Subseries 3, Boxes 1, 5.

CHAPTER 22:
PARTING OF THE WAYS

1. Cohen and Witcover, *A Heartbeat Away*, pp. 228–30.

2. Haig, *Inner Circles*, p. 363.

3. Agnew, *Go Quietly . . . Or Else*, p. 151.

4. Ibid.

5. Ibid., p. 152.

6. Ibid.

7. Cohen and Witcover, *A Heartbeat Away*, pp. 242–43.

8. Agnew, *Go Quietly . . . Or Else*, p. 153.

9. Ibid., p. 154.

10. Haig, *Inner Circles*, p. 362.

11. Agnew, *Go Quietly . . . Or Else*, p. 157.

12. Ibid., pp. 157–58.

13. Agnew Collection, University of Maryland, Series III, Subseries 3, Box 1, September 18, 1973.

14. Cohen and Witcover, *A Heartbeat Away*, p. 244.

15. White House Special Files, Central Files, FG 38, l971–74, September 23, 1973.

16. Nixon, *RN*, pp. 916–17.

17. Cohen and Witcover, *A Heartbeat Away*, pp. 252–53.

18. Ibid., p. 253.

19. Ibid., p. 272.

20. Agnew, *Go Quietly . . . Or Else*, pp. 163–64.

21. Ibid., p. 164.

22. Nixon, *RN*, p. 917.

23. Agnew, *Go Quietly . . . Or Else*, p. 149.

24. Ibid., pp. 149–50.

25. Ibid., p. 150.

26. Nixon, *RN*, p. 917.

27. Agnew, *Go Quietly . . . Or Else*, p. 171.

28. Ibid., pp. 177–79.

29. Cohen and Witcover, *A Heartbeat Away*, pp. 263–64.

30. Ibid., pp. 266–68.

31. Ibid., pp. 269–70.

32. Agnew, *Go Quietly . . . Or Else*, p. 182.

33. Nixon, *RN*, pp. 919–20.

34. Ibid., p. 920.

35. Cohen and Witcover, *A Heartbeat Away*, pp. 285–88.

36. Agnew, *Go Quietly . . . Or Else*, p. 194.

37. Ibid., pp. 194–95.

38. Cohen and Witcover, *A Heartbeat Away*, p. 287.

39. Ibid., p. 293.

40. Ibid. pp. 302–12.

41. Agnew, *Go Quietly . . . Or Else*, pp. 196–97.

42. Elliot Richardson, statement to Judge Walter Hoffman, October 10, 1973.

43. Cohen and Witcover, *A Heartbeat Away*, pp. 319–23.

44. Agnew, *Go Quietly . . . Or Else*, pp. 198–99.

45. Nixon, *RN*, pp. 922–23.

46. Agnew, *Go Quietly . . . Or Else*, p. 198.

47. Cohen and Witcover, *A Heartbeat Away*, pp. 248–50.

48. Agnew, *Go Quietly . . . Or Else*, pp. 18–19.

49. Nixon, *RN*, p. 1005.

50. Theodore H. White, *Breach of Faith: The Fall of Richard Nixon*, p. 259.

51. Agnew Collection, University of Maryland, Series III, Subseries 3, Box 5, October 10, 1973.

CHAPTER 23:
FRIGID AFTERMATH

1. Haig, *Inner Circles*, p. 367.

2. Nixon, *RN*, p. 923.

3. White House Special files, President's Personal Files, Box 5, October 10, 1973.

4. Ibid., October 29, 1973.

5. Agnew, *Go Quietly . . . Or Else*, p. 204.

6. Ibid., p. 11.

7. Ibid., pp. 186–192.

8. Ibid., pp. 191–92.

9. Interview with Alexander Haig, August 10, 2006.

10. Cohen and Witcover, *A Heartbeat Away*, p. 290.

11. This information regarding the critical aspect of the net-worth investigation against Agnew was provided on the condition that names of individuals involved would not be disclosed.

12. Agnew, *Go Quietly . . . Or Else*, p. 192.

13. Cohen and Witcover, *A Heartbeat Away*, p. 349.

14. Agnew Collection, University of Maryland, Series III, Subseries 3, Box 11.

15. Haig, *Inner Circles*, p. 368.

16. Telephone interview with Melvin R. Laird, June 15, 2006.

17. Haig, *Inner Circles*, p. 368.

18. Ibid., pp. 368–69.

19. Ibid., p. 369.

20. Ford, *A Time to Heal*, p. 105.

21. Haig, *Inner Circles*, pp. 394–95.

22. Agnew, *Go Quietly . . . Or Else*, pp. 202–03.

23. *The Washington Post*, April 19, 1974.

24. Ibid., September 1, 1974; January 5, 1975.

25. Ibid., February 8, 1975.

26. Ibid., August 19, 1975.

27. Ibid., November 2, 1975.

28. Ibid., April 8, 1978.

29. Agnew, *Go Quietly . . . Or Else*, p. 220.

30. *The Washington Post*, December 10, 14, 1976.

31. Ibid., January 5, 1983.

32. Agnew, *Go Quietly . . . Or Else*, p. 213.

33. Ibid., David Frost interview, May 26, 1972.

34. Ibid.

35. Interview with John Damgard, September 11, 2005.

36. Interview with David Keene, August 17, 2005.

37. *Baltimore Sun*, April 25, 1994.

38. Ibid., March 25, 1995.

39. Witcover, *White Knight*, p. 234.

40. Gerald and Deborah Hart Strobert, *Nixon: An Oral History of His Presidency*, p. 432.

BIBLIOGRAPHY

Agnew, Spiro T. *Go Quietly . . . Or Else*. William Morrow, New York, 1980.

_____. *The Canfield Decision*. Playboy Press, Chicago, 1976.

Ambrose, Stephen E. *Nixon: The Triumph of a Politician 1962–1972*. Simon & Schuster, New York, 1989.

_____. *Nixon: Ruin and Recovery 1970–1990*. Simon & Schuster, New York, 1991.

Anson, Robert Sam. *Exile: The Unique Oblivion of Richard M. Nixon*. Simon & Schuster, New York, 1984.

Cannon, James. *Time and Chance: Gerald Ford's Appointment with History*. HarperCollins, New York, 1994.

Cohen, Richard M., and Witcover, Jules. *A Heartbeat Away: The Investigation and Resignation of Vice President Spiro T. Agnew*. The Viking Press, New York, 1974

Connally, John and Herskowitz, Mickey. *In History's Shadow: An American Odyssey*. Hyperion, New York, 1994.

Dean, John W. III. *Blind Ambition*. Simon & Schuster, New York, 1976.

_____. *Lost Honor: The Rest of the Story*. Stratford Press, Los Angeles, 1982.

Ehrlichman, John. *Witness to Power: The Nixon Years*. Simon & Schuster, New York, 1982.

Emery, Fred. *Watergate: The Corruption of Politics and the Fall of Richard Nixon*. Touchstone, New York, 1994.

Ford, Gerald R. *A Time to Heal: The Autobiography of Gerald R. Ford*. Harper & Row, New York, 1979.

Garment, Leonard. *Crazy Rhythm: From Brooklyn and Jazz to Nixon's White House, Watergate, and Beyond*. Random House, New York, 1997.

Gulley, Bill. *Breaking Cover*. Simon & Schuster, New York, 1980.

Haig, Alexander M. *Inner Circles: How America Changed the World*. Warner Books, New York, 1992.

Haldeman, H. R. *The Haldeman Diares: Inside the Nixon White House*. G. P. Putnam's Sons, New York, 1994.

Hung, Nguyen Tien and Schecter, Jerrold. *The Palace Guard*. Harper & Row, New York, 1986.

Hunt, E. Howard. *Undercover: Memoirs of an American Secret Agent*. Berkley/Putnam, New York, 1974.

Kissinger, Henry. *White House Years*. Little Brown, New York, 1979.

Klein, Herbert G. *Making It Perfectly Clear: An Inside Account of Nixon's Love-Hate Relationship with the Media*. Doubleday & Co., New York, 1980.

Kutler, Stanley I. *Abuse of Power: The New Nixon Tapes*. Touchstone, New York, 1998.

Lukas, J. Anthony. *Nightmare: The Underside of the Nixon Years*. Viking Press, New York, 1976.

Marsh, Robert. *Agnew the Unexamined Man*. M. Evans and Co., New York, 1971.

Magruder, Jeb Stuart. *An American Life: One Man's Road to Watergate*. Atheneum, New York, 1974.

Morris, Roger. *Richard Milhous Nixon: The Rise of an American Politician*. Henry Holt, New York, 1990.

Nixon, Richard M. *RN: The Memoirs of Richard Nixon*. Grosset & Dunlap, New York, 1978.

Osborn, John. *The Fifth Year of the Nixon Watch*. Liveright, New York, 1974.

Oudes, Bruce, ed. *From The President: Richard Nixon's Secret Files*. Harper & Row, New York, 1989.

Safire, William. *Before the Fall: An Inside View of the Pre-Watergate White House*. Doubleday & Co., New York, 1975.

Strober, Gerald S. and Strober, Deborah H. *Nixon: An Oral History of his Presidency*. HarperCollins, New York, 1994.

Summers, Anthony. *The Arrogance of Power: The Secret World of Richard Nixon*. Viking, New York, 2000.

White, Theodore H. *The Making of the President 1972*. Atheneum, New York, 1973.

_____. *Breach of Faith: The Fall of Richard Nixon*. Atheneum, Reader's Digest Press, New York, 1975.

Wicker, Tom. *One of Us: Richard Nixon and the American Dream*. Random House, New York, 1991.

Wills, Garry. *Nixon Agonistes: The Crisis of the Self-Made Man*. Mariner, New York, 2002.

Witcover, Jules. *White Knight: The Rise of Spiro Agnew.* Random House, New York, 1972.

_____. *Crapshoot: Rolling the Dice on the Vice Presidency.* Crown, New York, 1992.

_____. *The Resurrection of Richard Nixon.* G. P. Putnam's Sons, New York, 1970.

_____. *The Year the Dream Died: Revisiting 1968 in America.* Viking, New York, 1997.

INDEX

PublicAffairs is a publishing house founded in 1997. It is a tribute to the standards, values, and flair of three persons who have served as mentors to countless reporters, writers, editors, and book people of all kinds, including me.

I.F. STONE, proprietor of *I. F. Stone's Weekly*, combined a commitment to the First Amendment with entrepreneurial zeal and reporting skill and became one of the great independent journalists in American history. At the age of eighty, Izzy published *The Trial of Socrates*, which was a national bestseller. He wrote the book after he taught himself ancient Greek.

BENJAMIN C. BRADLEE was for nearly thirty years the charismatic editorial leader of *The Washington Post*. It was Ben who gave the *Post* the range and courage to pursue such historic issues as Watergate. He supported his reporters with a tenacity that made them fearless and it is no accident that so many became authors of influential, best-selling books.

ROBERT L. BERNSTEIN, the chief executive of Random House for more than a quarter century, guided one of the nation's premier publishing houses. Bob was personally responsible for many books of political dissent and argument that challenged tyranny around the globe. He is also the founder and longtime chair of Human Rights Watch, one of the most respected human rights organizations in the world.

For fifty years, the banner of PublicAffairs Press was carried by its owner Morris B. Schnapper, who published Gandhi, Nasser, Toynbee, Truman, and about 1,500 other authors. In 1983, Schnapper was described by *The Washington Post* as "a redoubtable gadfly." His legacy will endure in the books to come.

Peter Osnos, *Founder and Editor-at-Large*